BERNARD BURNES

Managing change

A Strategic Approach to Organisational Dynamics

SECOND EDITION

London · Hong Kong · Johannesburg · Melbourne · Singapore · Washington DC

PITMAN PUBLISHING
128 Long Acre, London WC2E 9AN

A Division of Pearson Professional Limited

First edition published in Great Britain 1992
Second edition published 1996

© Bernard Burnes, 1996

The right of Bernard Burnes to be identified as Author
of this Work has been asserted by him in accordance
with the Copyright, Designs and Patents Act 1988.

ISBN 0 273 61118 6

British Library Cataloguing in Publication Data
A CIP catalogue record of this book can be obtained from the British Library

10   9   8   7   6   5   4   3   2   1

Typeset by Avocet Typeset, Brill, Aylesbury, Bucks
Printed and Bound in Great Britain by Clays Ltd, St Ives plc

The Publishers' policy is to use paper manufactured from sustainable forests.

MANAGING CHANGE

A Strategic Approach to Organisational Dynamics

Don Gresswell Ltd., London, N.21   Cat. No. 1207   DG 02242/71

TO SUE, DUNCAN AND STUART

Contents

ACKNOWLEDGEMENTS

....

The second edition of this book, like the first edition, would not have been possible without the generous encouragement and assistance of a large number of people. Space does not permit me to name them all, but I am nevertheless extremely grateful to them, one and all. However, there are six of my colleagues, students and ex-students at the Manchester School of Management for whose assistance, ideas and comments I would like to give special thanks: Hakeem James, Adrian Nelson, Steve New, Mohammad Salauroo, Penny West and Paul Whittle. I would also like to thank Pitman Publishing for their encouragement and patience.

Finally, and most importantly, I am irredeemably indebted to my wife, Sue. As was the case with the first edition, her painstaking reading and editing of draft after draft of this book have improved it beyond recognition. It is not too much to say that she deserves as much credit as I do for what is good about this book.

Nevertheless, despite all the help and assistance I have received, any faults or shortcomings in the final product are mine and mine alone.

INTRODUCTION

> **There is nothing so practical as a good theory. (*Kurt Lewin*)**[1]
>
> **All models are wrong, some models are useful. (*George Box*)**[2]

The above two quotations could have been written especially to sum up the dilemma most people face when trying to come to terms with the literature of organisational change. What almost everyone would like is a clear and practical change theory which explains what changes organisations need to make and how they should make them. Unfortunately, what is available is a wide range of confusing and contradictory theories, approaches and recipes. Many of these are well thought-out and grounded in both theory and practice; others, unfortunately, seem disconnected from either theory or reality. Furthermore, though change theory requires an inter-disciplinary perspective, each of the major approaches tends to view organisations from the disciplinary angle of its originators – whether it be psychology, sociology, economics, or whatever – which can result in an incomplete picture. Regardless of what their proponents may claim, therefore, we do not possess at present an approach to change which is theoretically holistic, universally applicable, and can be practically applied. It follows that, to paraphrase George Box, all change theories are partial but some are useful. This means that for those wishing to understand or implement change, the prime task is not to seek out an all-embracing theory but to understand the strengths and weaknesses of each approach and the situations in which each can best be applied.

One central purpose of this book, therefore, is to aid this search for understanding by describing and discussing the key approaches to and theories of organisational change. The intention is to allow those who study and carry out organisational change to make their own judgement about the benefits, applicability and usefulness of the approaches on offer. The theme underpinning the book is that organisations and managers can exercise a wide degree of choice in the approach to change which they adopt. The appropriateness of each of the available theories is dependent upon the type of change being considered and the constraints under which the organisation operates. Constraints and objectives are not immutable. Rather than choosing the approach to change which their situation demands, organisations can instead choose to influence the constraints under which they operate, in order to fit in with their preferred approach or with the style of operation and the objectives they wish to pursue.

---

[1]Quoted in West (1995)
[2]Quoted in Norrie (1993)

There can be few who now doubt the importance to an organisation of the ability to identify where it needs to be in the future, and how it can accomplish the changes necessary to get there – although there is a great deal of dispute about how difficult or possible this is. However, though some might assume that managers do not need to understand organisation theory, strategy theory, change theory or any other theory in order to manage and change their organisations, this would be to underestimate the extent to which managers and others in organisations are influenced, assisted or potentially misled by theory. Increasingly managers are exhorted to adopt the teachings of the latest management guru. Nevertheless, as Part One will demonstrate, and as Mintzberg and Quinn (1991:xii) have observed:

> **Whether we realise it or not, our behavior is guided by the systems of ideas that we have internalized over the years. Much can be learned by bringing these out into the open, examining them more carefully, and comparing them with alternative ways to view the world – including ones based on systematic study (that is, research).**

These 'systems of ideas', or organisation theories as they are more commonly called, are crucial to change management in two respects. First, they provide models of how organisations should be structured and managed. Second, they provide guidelines for judging and prescribing the behaviour and effectiveness of individuals and groups in an organisation.

To understand why and how to change organisations, it is first necessary to understand their structures, management and behaviour. As Mintzberg and Quinn indicate, it is clear that in many organisations there is no clear understanding of these theories. It follows that choices with regard to the appropriateness of particular structures and practices, and the way they are chosen and implemented, are founded on limited knowledge and perhaps false assumptions. Change cannot hope to be fully successful under these circumstances. Consequently, a full understanding of these theories is necessary if informed choices are to be made when instigating and implementing change. For this reason, these will be examined critically in relation to each other, and also in comparison with how organisations are in reality as opposed to how theorists suppose them to be. The aim is not to provide a 'hands-on' practical guide to organisational change – though readers may find that this book is useful in that respect as well. Rather the aim is to provide an understanding of the theories and approaches to change that are on offer, to indicate their usefulness and drawbacks, and to enable the reader to choose for her- or himself which 'models are useful' and when.

The book is organised into four parts. **Part One, Organisation theory – the rise and fall of the rational organisation,** provides a comprehensive review of organisation theory. Chapter 1 deals with the emergence of modern forms of organisation in the Industrial Revolution, and the first attempts in the early years of the twentieth century to provide a theory of how organisations should operate – the Classical approach. This was an approach which portrayed organisations as machines, and people as mere cogs in those machines.

Chapter 2 reviews the two main challengers to the Classical school: the Human Relations approach and Contingency Theory. These emerged in the 1930s and 1960s respectively. The former makes the case for seeing organisations as social systems, which rely for their success on the co-operation and commitment of their personnel. The latter, Contingency Theory, argues against there being one theory or approach for all organisations and all situations. Instead, it proposes that the approach an organisation adopts should be dependent (i.e. contingent) on its particular circumstances.

Chapter 3 compares the Culture–Excellence approach developed in the West and the Japanese approach to managing organisations. These are the two main and most influential contemporary approaches to managing organisations. This chapter discusses their similarities and differences, particularly in their view of people.

The conclusion drawn from the above three chapters is that all the main organisation theories fail to accommodate and explain the importance and implications of culture and politics. These form the subject of Chapter 4. This chapter and Part One, conclude that, by accident and design, organisation theories attempt to remove choice from organisations by specifying what they need to do in order to be successful. The review of organisational culture and politics, however, together with evidence from the earlier chapters, shows that managers do have a wider scope for shaping decisions than much of the organisation literature suggests. This theme of managerial choice is continued in Part Two.

Part Two, Managing change – approaches and choices, comprises two chapters, examining the literature on strategic management and change management respectively. Both chapters effectively conclude that the particular circumstances and constraints which appear to affect organisational choice can be influenced and changed, allowing organisations, to an extent, to choose the particular approach to strategy and change which best suits them.

Part Three, Case studies in strategy development and change management, comprises three case study chapters. The ten case studies are all of real organisations, though in some cases their names and some of the details which would identify them have been changed to protect confidentiality. Nevertheless, the situations described are drawn from real life and show the opportunities, difficulties and constraints faced in developing strategy and implementing change.

Part Four, Managing choice, comprises the concluding two chapters of the book. Chapter 10 combines the insights and perspectives from the previous three sections to present a Choice Management–Change Management model (containing three interlinked elements – choice, strategy and change) to provide an understanding of how managers and organisations can and do exercise choice and manage change.

Given the importance attached to the role of managers in developing strategy and managing change, Chapter 11 reviews what managers do and how they do it. In particular, the role of leadership and management development is examined. The chapter and the book conclude that if, as argued, managers have considerable choice over what to change and how to change it, then this lays a considerable responsibility on their shoulders. How organisations change and develop has enormous consequences, not just for their employees and owners, but for society at large. In order to avoid the worst consequences of unemployment and social fragmentation, managers need to act in the broader interests of all their stakeholders – employees, shareholders, themselves and the wider community.

THE SECOND EDITION

Since the publication of the first edition of this book, I have received many helpful comments from readers and users and I have used these as a guide to writing the second edition. While retaining a similar structure and approach to the first edition, the second edition has been substantially revised and extended, incorporating the following:

- *a new chapter covering organisational culture and politics;*
- *a significant revision and extension of the work on strategy and change management which not only updates the literature review but, more importantly, reorganises the way it is presented in order to provide the reader with a clearer picture of the differences between the main approaches;*
- *eight new case studies, and two which have been retained from the earlier edition have been brought up to date with the companies' latest developments;*
- *an entirely new chapter pulling together the evidence from both theory and practice, and presenting a Choice Management–Change Management model;*
- *the concluding chapter on management revised to incorporate the literature on leadership.*

As in the first edition, unless apparent from the text, I have used the terms he and she interchangeably.

ORGANISATION THEORY: THE RISE AND FALL OF THE RATIONAL ORGANISATION

Chapter 1

FROM TRIAL AND ERROR TO THE SCIENCE OF MANAGEMENT

The rise of organisation theory

INTRODUCTION

In Britain and the rest of the industrial world today, it is almost impossible to imagine life without the plethora of organisations which comprise and make possible our everyday life. Yet organisations in their modern form – indeed, in almost any form – were virtually unknown before the Industrial Revolution, 200 years ago. In the intervening period, not only have organisations in their many shapes, sizes and manifestations come to reach into every facet of our lives, but they have also acquired an equally diverse range of theories, schemes and semi-sacrosanct beliefs about how they should be structured, managed and changed.

This chapter sets out to explore and discuss the origins of organisations, from the Industrial Revolution to the early years of the twentieth century, when the first detailed and comprehensive organisation theory emerged. The key themes of this chapter are as follows:

- *Although industrialisation was primarily concerned with the move from a subsistence economy to a money-market economy, the main enabling mechanism for this was the creation of the factory system.*

- *The pattern and purpose of industrialisation varied from country to country. While in Britain and the USA it was very much driven by individuals seeking profit maximisation, in mainland Europe a different approach can be seen. In Germany in particular, but also in France, industrialisation was more*

> *state-sponsored, and aimed more to further the economic/military objectives of the state than to increase the profit-making capacity of individuals.*
>
> ● *The development of organisation theory is synonymous with the need by managers to legitimate and enhance their authority to initiate change.*

The chapter begins by showing how the rapid expansion of national and international commercial activity created the conditions for the British Industrial Revolution, from which emerged the factory system, the precursor of all modern organisations. It is argued that the driving force behind this development was the merchant class. It will also be stressed that two key features of the early factory system were its *ad hoc*, trial-and-error nature, and the antagonistic relationship between owners and employees, or – to use the terminology of the period – masters and servants.

The chapter then goes on to show that British industrial practices, methods and technologies were 'exported' to other European countries and the USA, with similar results in terms of employer–employee relations. As the nineteenth century progressed, and organisations grew in number and size, trial and error increasingly gave way to more considered and consistent approaches to work organisation. This development was especially pronounced in the USA and continental Europe, as industrial leadership moved away from Britain and towards these areas.

What emerged, separately, were three different but complementary attempts by Frederick Taylor in the USA, Henri Fayol in France and Max Weber in Germany to replace the *ad hoc*, rule-of-thumb approach to organisations with a universally applicable blueprint or theory for how they should operate. These three approaches, each focusing on different organisational aspects, coalesced into what later became known as the Classical school of organisation theory. This approach to organisations is characterised by the horizontal and hierarchical division of labour, the minimisation of human skills and discretion, and the attempt to construe organisations as rational-scientific entities. It is argued that one of the key objectives of the Classical school, especially the Scientific Management component, was to legitimise the managerial right to plan and implement change by showing that it was the only group able to analyse the work situation scientifically and rationally, and to devise the most appropriate and efficient methods of operation.

The chapter concludes by arguing that the Classical approach, while being a significant advance on what went before, was badly flawed. In particular, its view of human nature and motivation not only was inaccurate, but also alienated workers from and made them resentful of the organisations which employed them. The precepts of the Classical school, however, were not solely aimed at constraining workers' ability to make and block change; in addition, by laying down hard and fast rules of what was and was not best practice, they constrained management's freedom of action, thus alienating many managers as well as workers.

With hindsight, the attempt by Taylor, Fayol and Weber each in their own way to formulate a system of reciprocal obligations between managers and workers appears to be less a decisive break with the past and more an attempt to recast feudalism in a more scientific, rational framework. Certainly, in the late nineteenth century, French, German and American managers of European descent did share a recent and common feudal heritage which might have made them well disposed towards a system which substituted a code of joint obligation in place of management–worker conflict. Indeed, in Germany the rise of bureaucracy which Weber described was itself a direct product of the Prussian feudal tradition. However, though many managers undoubtedly did long for and believe in an – albeit mythical – age when workers readily did as they were told, this ignored the fact that most American immigrants left Europe to escape just such a system, while French workers took pride in the belief that their Revolution had ended feudal despotism. Only in Germany was it possible to say that the feudal tradition remained strong, though not unopposed.

THE RISE OF COMMERCE AND THE BIRTH OF THE FACTORY

The pivotal event which shaped the world into the form we now see around us was the British Industrial Revolution, which began in the late eighteenth century. Before it, most societies were based on small-scale, self-sufficient agricultural production, with the vast majority of the population, some 80 to 90 per cent, living in the countryside. By the end of the nineteenth century, after the Industrial Revolution had run its course, the reverse became the case, in the leading industrialised countries at least, with most people living in urban centres and depending on industrial and commercial activities for their livelihood (Landes, 1969).

Britain was the pioneer industrial country; it was the model that other European nations and the USA sought to emulate in their attempts to transform traditional agrarian economies into urban societies based on science and technology (Kemp, 1979). The key development of the Industrial Revolution towards this process of societal transformation was the creation of the factory system. It was this that gave the impetus to, and created the model for, all that was to follow. As Weber (1928:302) pointed out, the factory's distinguishing characteristic was '… in general … not the implements of work applied but the concentration of ownership of workplace, means of work, source of power and raw materials in one and the same hand, that of the entrepreneur.' Or, to put it another way, it was the way the entrepreneur 'organised' the elements of production which distinguished it from what went before.

This tells us what changed, but it does not explain why or how in a few score years organisations came to dominate our lives. To answer this, it is necessary to appreciate the great surge of economic activity – especially the international trade in textile products – which arose in the seventeenth and eighteenth centuries. This trade gave an enormous impetus to textile production in Britain, which in turn had a knock-on effect in all other spheres of economic activity (Mathias, 1969).

Before and during the early part of the British Industrial Revolution, textile production was carried out as an agricultural by-occupation based on family units. As demand increased in the eighteenth century, however, some 'men and women [became] specialist spinners or weavers, thinking first of wool, treating work on the land as, at most, a by-occupation' (Ashton, 1948: 23). Allied to this, a new mechanism sprang up to link producer and consumer: the 'putting-out' system – whereby a large merchant would 'put out' work to a number of independent domestic producers.

The advantage to the merchant was threefold: it was cheap – there were few overheads; it was flexible – production could be easily expanded or contracted; and it avoided the difficulties involved in directly employing a workforce. However, as demand continued to increase in the late eighteenth century, this system became more complex and more costly, and eventually it became too cumbersome (Pollard, 1965). The chain of intermediaries linking producer to consumer became increasingly difficult for the large merchant to control. There were many problems with the putting-out mechanism: dishonesty (on both sides) was rife; deliveries were late; and quality often poor. Laws attempting to control producers could do nothing to rectify the fundamental weaknesses in the system. The incompatibility between the large and complex organisation of distribution and the multitude of tiny domestic workshop units, unsupervised and unsupervisable, was bound to create tensions and drive merchants to seek new ways of production – ways whereby they could establish their own managerial control over the production process (Pollard, 1965).

There was also an incompatibility between different cultures. For the merchant, the expansion of markets was a chance to maximise profits in order to live in grand style. For the rural domestic producer, involved in long hours of backbreaking work, it created the conditions for increased leisure. As Marglin commented:

> **... wages rose and workers insisted on taking out a portion of their gains in the form of greater leisure. However sensible this may have been from their own point of view, it is no way for an enterprising capitalist to get ahead. (*Marglin, 1976:35*)**

It was the merchant, therefore, who began the move towards the factory system – not because the merchant had an innate desire to run factories or exercise direct control over labour, but in order to take full advantage of expanding market opportunities to reap ever greater rewards.

Nevertheless, there was no headlong rush to create a new economic order overnight. The earliest factories, if that is not too grand a word for them, were small, unpowered weaving or spinning sheds which used existing technology and methods. A few very large factories – such as Wedgwood's Etruria Works in Stoke-on-Trent – were established, but these were the rare exceptions. Indeed, in 1780, the investment in fixed equipment and stock in the textile industry, which was the leading edge of the Industrial Revolution, was only £10 per worker, and the average factory employed no more than 10 or 12 people. By 1830, when the textile industry had grown to employ 100,000 people and the average factory size was 137, the investment in fixed equipment and stock had only increased to £15 per worker, and 50 per cent of the workforce was still home-based (Hobsbawm, 1968; Pollard, 1965; Tillett, 1970). Given this situation, it is hardly surprising that capital investment was quickly recovered and that it was running expenses, mainly wages and raw materials, which formed the bulk of manufacturing costs. It is this, and the original motive for moving to the factory system in the first place (to have greater control over labour), which explain the prevailing attitude of employers towards labour in the nineteenth century.

The relationship between employers and employees

British employers based their attitude towards employees on two basic propositions:

1 Labour is unreliable, lazy and will only work when tightly controlled and closely supervised.

2 The main controllable business cost is labour; therefore the key to increased profits is to make labour cheaper, and/or increase its productivity, by getting employees to work harder, or for longer hours, for the same, or less, money.

In this respect, as contemporary writers such as Charles Babbage (1835) and Andrew Ure (1835) observed, workers' skill was seen as at best an inconvenience and at worst a threat, because it could be scarce, costly and allow workers a strong bargaining position.

As might be expected, employers' hostility was reciprocated by labour. Workers exhibited a strong dislike for, and reluctance to become part of, the factory system. As Pollard (1965) noted, this was for three main reasons:

1 The factory system involved a wholesale change of culture and environment and the destruction of small, tightly knit communities in which the workers lived. Hard though the life of cottage industry was, it had given workers a measure of independence and some control over what they did, when they did it and how.

2 The discipline of the factory was harsh and unremitting with men, women and small children all expected to work long hours, often seven days a week, in appalling conditions.

3 Given the lack of alternative organisational forms on which to establish factory life, employers often modelled them on workhouses or prisons. Indeed, to square the circle, some workhouses and prisons turned themselves into factories and their inmates into little more than slaves. Thus factories acquired the same stigma as was attached to prisons and workhouses.

Thus, the antagonism that existed between owners and workers was based on a genuine clash of interests – one which has echoed through the industrial world ever since.

If this picture of the factory system in the nineteenth century seems bleak to us, it is nevertheless accurate, as is shown in the work of its proponents such as Charles Babbage and Andrew Ure, social reformers such as Seebohm Rowntree, political activists such as Frederick Engels and contemporary novelists such as Charles Dickens. Nor was this aspect of industrialisation restricted to Britain. Studies of other European countries and the USA have shown similar tensions, sometimes even more violent, between the old and the new methods of working, and between employers and employees (Bruland, 1989; Chapman and Chassagne, 1981; Mantoux, 1964; Pelling, 1960).

In defence of the factory owners, who must take responsibility for what emerged, it should be said that their own experience was limited and there were no textbooks to guide them. That they should 'copy' what models existed reflected both the common view of labour among the owning classes, and a lack of alternative organisational forms on which to base the emergent factory system. As other nations industrialised, noticeably Germany, France and the United States, they too adopted similar organisational forms and espoused similar attitudes towards labour. This was partly because they were seeking to emulate Britain's success by copying her approach. It was also because these societies, like Great Britain, were riven by hierarchical and horizontal divisions which were inevitably reproduced in the workplace.

Industrialisation and the organisation of work

The system of organising work which came to characterise industrial life in Britain and most of continental Europe, and even the USA, by the end of the nineteenth century was based on the hierarchical and horizontal division of labour. Though this represented a significant break with the past in terms of how work had previously been organised, it was not out of step with the social stratification of European society nor with feudal traditions of obedience. The articulation and propagation of the principle of the division of labour owed much to the work of Adam Smith. In his book, *The Wealth of Nations*, published in 1776, Smith used the now famous example of pin-making to illustrate what he saw as the advantages of the division of labour. He pointed out that a pin could be made entirely by one person doing everything, or by a number of people each specialising in one aspect of its production. For three reasons, he believed the latter was more efficient.

1 A worker who constantly performs one simple task will quickly acquire greater dexterity than one who performs a variety of tasks.
2 It avoids the loss of time necessitated by one person moving from one task to another.
3 The concentration of attention on one special task leads to the invention of machines which aid the productivity of labour and allow one person to do the work previously performed by many.

Smith's ideas were given flesh and form in Britain by pioneering factory owners such as Josiah Wedgwood, and Matthew Boulton and James Watt. At his Etruria pottery works, Wedgwood developed a production system which split the work process down into separate departments, each with its own specialist supervisor. Work was organised almost on a flow-line basis with the skill involved in each operation reduced to a minimum in order, in Wedgwood's own words, 'to make machines of men as cannot err' (quoted in Tillett, 1970:37). Matthew Boulton and James Watt developed a similar approach at their Soho Works in Birmingham in the 1770s. They also kept detailed production records, a practice virtually unknown at the time (Roll, 1930). Wedgwood, Boulton, Watt and a few others were the architects of the factory system. By their organisation of work on and off the shopfloor, they created models which later managers would copy and adapt to their own needs and circumstances.

This approach to the organisation and control of work spread outwards from Britain. As Bruland (1989:165) observed:

> **There was a fairly direct international diffusion of these changes from Britain, the originating economy: British workers, in most parts of Europe, played a significant role in spreading the new work systems, in training local workers, and in the adaptation of the work force to the new rhythms of work.**

As the nineteenth century progressed, this approach to work organisation became more developed and systematised. Charles Babbage (1835) developed a method of applying the division of labour principle to the detailed analysis of any job. He emphasised the need for and advantage of dividing tasks between and within mental and manual labour. He envisaged three 'classes' employed in the work process: the entrepreneur and his technical specialists who would design machines and plan the form of work organisation; operative engineers and managers who would be responsible for executing such plans and designs, based on only partial knowledge of the processes involved; and the mass of employees, needing only a low level of skill, who would undertake the actual work. Thus, in Babbage's (1835:vii) view:

> **... the master manufacturer, by dividing the work to be executed into different processes, each requiring different degrees of skill or force, can purchase exactly the precise quality of both which is necessary for each process ...**

Though coming from separate traditions, Smith's work was also in tune with the Prussian bureaucratic school, and undoubtedly the efficient organisation of German industry in the late nineteenth century owes much to a combination of the two approaches.

The pioneers of these developments in work organisation, whether in Britain, Germany and other European countries, tended to be strict disciplinarians who used their personal authority to impose the new working arrangements on a usually reluctant workforce (Chapman and Chassagne, 1981). Therefore, change tended to be managed by imposition and force rather than negotiation and agreement. It is not surprising that it should be so. In the main these were countries which had been, in the recent past, feudal economies dominated by warrior elites. In Germany, this was still the case. Even where there had been a decisive break with the past, as in France, this seems merely to have reinforced rather than removed patterns of social rigidity and authoritarianism.

In such situations, resistance to or questioning of change was unlikely to be met by understanding or tolerance. Predictably, there was strong resistance, both active and passive, to the introduction of new working patterns and methods (Kriedte *et al*, 1981). Though this resistance could and did take the form of physical violence against factories and equipment, a more frequent manifestation was high labour turnover. One of the largest Manchester cotton spinning firms, McConnell and Kennedy, had an average turnover in the early nineteenth century of 100 per cent per year – a high but not uncommon rate (Fitton and Wadsworth, 1958; Pollard, 1965). A similar situation existed in other European countries. In Germany, for example, employers 'were generally satisfied if they achieved partial success in creating a stable core of skilled workers ... Turnover was the most persistent labour problem confronting employers' (Lee, 1978:460). This situation clearly gave those workers whose skills were most in demand a significant bargaining position, which allowed them to raise their wages and determine the pace of work. It also acted as a spur to employers, however, to seek methods of reducing their reliance on skilled labour (Bruland, 1989). One of the main ways that entrepreneurs responded was through technological developments aimed at replacing or reducing employers' reliance on skilled labour.

A contemporary observer of the nineteenth century industrial scene, Andrew Ure (1836:viii–ix), drew special attention to the role that technology could play in this process:

> **By developing machines ... which require only unskilled instead of skilled labour, the cost of labour can be reduced [and] the bargaining position of the worker reduced.**

It becomes clear why workers not only opposed the advent of the factory system but also, even when it became established, continued to oppose strongly changes in work practices and the introduction of new equipment. Even in the present day, where change tends to be preceded by consultation and its beneficial effects are stressed, there is still a tendency for those concerned to feel apprehensive of, if not downright resistant towards, change (Smith *et al*, 1982). Therefore, it is not surprising that in a harsher and more authoritarian age, where organisational and technological change were seen as weapons in the battle for control of the workplace, that change management should be by imposition and coercion, and occasion the response, which it did.

Nevertheless, despite the increasing opposition of 'organised' labour, the work practices associated with the factory system gradually permeated every aspect of industrial and commercial life, albeit only on a piecemeal basis. Even by the end of the nineteenth century, there was no unified or accepted approach which managers could apply to organisations in their entirety, though in Germany the application of the Prussian bureaucratic model allied to the approach to industrial organisation of Adam Smith was proving influential. Yet the developing factory system could not shake off the legacy of its origins or ignore the continuing battle between labour and management over control, rewards and skill. As the following shows, this was as much the case in continental Europe and the USA as it was in Britain.

Europe

The history of Europe since 1800, at least in economic terms, is essentially the history of industrialisation, of structural change through which industrial sectors grew and non-agricultural sectors came for the first time to dominate economic life. In general, for most of the nineteenth century, continental Europe lagged behind Britain in terms of industrial development. However, just as Britain was something of a patchwork quilt in terms of the pace of development of individual industries and regions, so too was the rest of Europe (Davis, 1989). As Pollard (1981) explained, European industrialisation developed from a few core regions. In Britain, southern Lancashire, the West Riding of Yorkshire, and that part of the West Midlands called the Black Country were the engines of growth. In northern Europe, the area between the Scheldt, the Meuse and the Rhine rivers had a special role to play, while to the east, Silesia, Bohemia and Moravia became leading centres of industrial progress. In the south, it was northern Italy and Catalonia which led the way.

Nevertheless, though mainland Europe did have its pockets of progress, industrialisation did not spread from these at the same rate nor in the same manner as it had in Britain. The most outstanding feature of British industrialisation was its self-generating or autonomous nature. Nowhere else could these conditions be exactly reproduced. To use an analogy, once the wheel has been invented, others cannot reinvent it. What they can do is adopt it and adapt it to their needs and circumstances.

Therefore, Britain became a model to be consciously followed. In the same way that Japan has become a focus for study, discussion and emulation by Westerners in the last 20 years, so Britain was similarly regarded in the early nineteenth century. Regular visits were made by foreign governments and private entrepreneurs to discover and copy British methods and technologies. In some instances, British investors, entrepreneurs and inventors were encouraged by the governments of France, Germany and other European states to help develop their economies – all with the aim of reproducing and overtaking Britain's industrial lead.

For some, especially Germany and France, the process of industrialisation was less a matter of material progress by organisations and individuals pursuing profit maximisation, and more concerned with the maintenance of their position in the world. Just as they sought to challenge Britain's military might, so they sought to emulate her industrial power. They could not and would not let Britain dominate the world without a struggle. Therefore, though the advent of industrial capitalism was in all countries characterised by the rise of a class of industrialists who aggressively sought to maximise their own wealth, the context in which this occurred varied from country to country.

In Britain and the USA, the context favoured individual entrepreneurs pursuing their own self-interest. In Germany, and to a lesser extent France, industrialisation was sponsored by the state and for the state. The prime motive was to build the economic and military might of the state rather than the wealth of the individual. Where these were compatible, the state was happy to maintain a watching brief. Where free enterprise and competition were seen as counter-productive to the objectives of the state, however, it intervened to reduce competition either through the creation of cartels and monopolies, or by state ownership/funding, as was the case with much of the European railway system. In Denmark, on the other hand, the operation of the market was constrained not by the state but by the creation of co-operatives, which allowed small-scale farming and business, and the way of life they represented, to survive where in other countries such enterprises were overwhelmed by larger competitors.

Therefore, though other countries used Britain as a model and benchmark, the actual process of industrialisation in each depended upon the unique political, social and economic circumstances that prevailed there. In some cases these gave primacy to profit maximisation, in others the interests of the state held sway, while in further cases sectional interests successfully challenged the power of the market. Consequently, influential though the British example was, once the necessary technique, capital and enterprise were introduced abroad and any element of conscious emulation had worn off, the industrialisation assumed a different character (Kemp, 1979). The continental countries did not and could not simply duplicate British experience.

There were some fundamental similarities, however. All European societies, to a lesser or greater extent, were structured on a hierarchical basis, with those in positions of power strongly influenced in their view of the rest of society by feudal traditions of subservience and obedience. This was as much the case in post-revolutionary France as in Britain, and even more so in Prussia and Russia. It follows that the organisational forms and labour relations which characterised the emerging factory system in Britain found fertile ground elsewhere in Europe (Cipolla, 1973).

Despite this, other countries did not copy Britain unthinkingly or on a wholesale basis. As latecomers, they could, especially with the encouragement of the state, leapfrog some of the stages of industrialisation, which was one of their principal advantages, but they could not close the gap between themselves and Britain overnight. Ashworth (1987) commented that even as late as 1850, apart from Belgium, Europe had little mechanised industry to speak of; 50 years later, however, Britain's position as the leading industrial nation had been taken by Germany, and other nations were also rapidly closing the gap. The reasons for this are many and complex, involving social and political as well as economic factors (Mathias and Davis, 1989). A brief look at industrial development in Germany, France and Scandinavia illustrates this.

Germany

Within the space of a generation in the middle years of the nineteenth century, Germany was transformed from a collection of economically backward states forming a political patchwork in Central Europe into a unified empire, driven forward by a rapidly expanding, technologically driven industrial base (Kemp, 1979). Germany's progress was so rapid that, though it industrialised much later, by the end of the nineteenth century it had overtaken Great Britain as the world's premier industrial nation. This transformation, accompanied as it was by the deliberate resort to military force as an instrument of national policy and an atmosphere of fierce nationalism, represented an event of major historical significance (Borchardt, 1973).

The two key factors which were primarily responsible for the nature and pace of German industrial development were, first, the geographical and political conditions of the country and, second, the fact that German industrialisation was derived and not autonomous.

With regard first to geography and politics: not until the late nineteenth century did Germany possess an integrated territory with an economic and administrative centre. Up to the nineteenth century, Germany was a collection of feudal fiefdoms which often warred with each other, rather than a unified nation. In 1789, 'Germany' comprised some 314 independent territories each with their own rulers, internal markets, customs barriers, currencies and trading monopolies. This internal fragmentation, as much as anything else, was probably the key obstacle to industrial progress. This did not change until the Congress of Vienna in 1815, which reduced the number of German states to 39. Each individual state then began to remove internal customs barriers and develop better communications systems, which opened the way for greater economic co-operation with other states.

Unlike other countries, however, economic progress was neither driven nor accompanied by a democratisation of society. German society in the nineteenth century remained dominated by a feudal hierarchy. This was characterised by Prussian 'Junkerdom' with its military traditions and ambitions, and its autocratic behaviour. Unlike their counterparts in other countries, the German nobility were not diminished by industrial progress; rather they managed to seize the reins of commercial power to bolster their position. This was due, in many instances, to their retention of regional monopolies over trade, industry and the supply of labour.

This leads on to the second key feature of German industrialisation – the fact that it was state-promoted rather than free market-driven. The drive for industrialisation, especially in Prussia, which came to dominate the rest of Germany, was not primarily motivated by economic factors. Rather industrialisation was seen as the process of building a strong and powerful state in which the old nobility continued to dominate. Therefore, for Germany, the fact that industrialisation was accompanied by the development of a strong military machine and the continued dominance of the Prussian Junkers was not an unfortunate coincidence, but its major objective.

Industrial progress in Britain exerted a strong influence on Germany. This was partly because it provided a model to emulate, but mainly because Germany saw industrial power and military power as two sides of the same coin. Unless Germany could catch up with and overtake Britain's industrial lead, Germany felt that it would be relegated to the status of a second-class state.

The transformation of Germany into an industrial superpower owed much to the role played by Prussia. From the early nineteenth century onwards, Prussia used its economic and military position as the most powerful German state to subdue the other German states and exclude possible rivals, especially Austria. The prime weapon in the Prussian arsenal was the creation of an all-German customs union (the *Zollverein*). Because of its size, Prussia could determine the rules for the *Zollverein* and, whenever and wherever it was extended, could ensure it was to Prussian advantage.

The customs union, because it opened up trade, also gave a boost to the development of better transportation and communication links, especially railway building (though the latter really took off once the Prussian military came to appreciate its strategic significance for the rapid transit of troops and materials). It seems very clear that, more than the emergence of any one industry, it was the creation of a single market and the boost to consumption that this brought about which was the key factor in Germany's economic progress in the nineteenth century (Kemp, 1979).

By 1834, practically all of Germany was included within the customs union and, though it did not come about until 1871, this provided the essential precondition for political unification. The fact that both political and economic unification were driven by and dominated by Prussia gave German industrialisation its distinctive character. The new German state which was established in 1871, for all its acceptance of universal suffrage and a national parliament, remained an autocracy ruled by the Hohenzollern dynasty, which still rested on the support of the traditional landed nobility of eastern Germany. It incorporated the bureaucratic and militarist traditions of the old Prussia and remained profoundly conservative.

Indeed, it was the adoption of the Prussian bureaucratic model by both state and industry, combined with close links between both, which gave German industry its unique form. Unlike Britain, where the majority of firms remained relatively small and business operated in an *ad hoc* fashion, with each company pursuing its own interests, in Germany large, bureaucratically structured organisations became the norm. In addition, the state did not hesitate to intervene directly, for example when it nationalised the railways, if it believed the private sector could not or would not serve the national interest.

Given that the state saw German industry as almost an extension of government, it is not surprising that it sought to bolster managerial authority and restrict workers' rights. This also very much reflected the Prussian autocratic tradition of expecting and enforcing obedience from those lower down the social order. Therefore, in most – though not all – enterprises, employers took the view that they had a right to treat their workers however they pleased. A German employer regarded himself as a patriarch, as the master in his own house in pre-industrial terms, with total responsibility for the whole social organism of his enterprise and generally well beyond this. This type of self-esteem made German employers particularly un-yielding in any situation of conflict.

One consequence of this was that the industrial and political climate became increasingly radical after the political and economic unification of Germany in 1871, though to no great effect. This period also saw the rapid development of the German economy. In 1870, the leading British enterprises were much bigger than their largest German competitors; by 1900, this position had been reversed. In many cases this was the result of governmental and banking encouragement to move to vertical integration. Furthermore, cartels and monopolies, frowned upon elsewhere, received official endorsement in Germany, which encouraged more orderly growth and longer-term investment decisions than might otherwise have been the case.

By the end of the nineteenth century the German economy had outstripped its British counterpart, but had not succeeded in avoiding either the same debilitating conflict between employers and employees, or the rise of political groups and parties which challenged the nature and purpose of capitalism. The influence of the Prussian autocratic tradition, however, as well as the development of a strong bureaucratic approach within both private and public sector organisations, and the close relation-ship between industry and state, meant that industrial and political resistance was met by a unified and implacable alliance between employers and government. Though prepared to use welfare provisions, sickness benefit, old age pensions, etc., to reduce social tensions, the state was not prepared to cede one iota of industrial or political authority.

France

As in Germany, the process of industrialisation in France was driven by the desire to emulate Britain, rather than by any form of 'spontaneous combustion'. However, despite having the advantage of much earlier state encouragement than Germany, France's industrial revolution was late in starting and did not reach maturity until towards the end of the nineteenth century (Dunham, 1955; Fohlen, 1973). The slow and late development of industry in France appears to have been caused by two key factors: political change and agrarian stagnation, both of which were inextricably linked with the French Revolution of 1789.

In the eighteenth century, little separated France and Britain in industrial terms. With much encouragement from the monarchy, French industry adopted British machines and equipment. British entrepreneurs and inventors were even persuaded to establish factories in France. During the last years before the French Revolution, the king paid great attention to the economy. A twin-track approach to industrial development was instituted. On the one hand, much state aid and encouragement were poured into industry; while on the other hand, there was the suppression of every obstacle to individual entrepreneurship, whether they be the privileges of the craft guilds or the ancient rights of the aristocracy.

Though these initiatives gave a significant boost to industrialisation, progress was halted, and even reversed, by the French Revolution in 1789 (Marczewski, 1963). To an extent this is surprising, given that those who dominated the Revolutionary Assemblies were men of property and substance, though drawn from the law and professions rather than the business world. They believed in upholding property rights, abolishing hereditary privilege and vested interests, and providing a favourable climate for entrepreneurship. They also introduced laws that placed employees in an inferior legal position to their employers and which prohibited them from combining for the purpose of bargaining. Nevertheless, the benefits of these to entrepreneurs were outweighed by other consequences of the Revolution. Foremost among these was the loss of France's colonial empire, together with its isolation, by the British naval blockade, from key markets such as the United States. The result was not only that France lost crucial imports and exports, but also that it was cut off from the prime source of technical and organisational innovation – Britain.

It was not until the final defeat of Napoleon in 1815 that France was once again able to concentrate on developing its economy rather than fighting wars. As before, the state took a lead in encouraging economic development, notably through the development of roads, canals and later railways. It also sought to stimulate the domestic economy by introducing import controls. However, this seems only to have allowed industry to keep outdated methods and equipment and maintain higher prices longer than might have been the case if it had not operated in a protected market. Only after 1850, with the upsurge in economic activity across Europe and the coming to power of Napoleon III, does the French economy really seem to have taken off.

The other main factor which held back industrialisation was the backward state of agriculture. The peasantry were already developing as an important group even before the French Revolution. The price they exacted for supporting the Revolution, however, the ownership of the majority of agricultural land, made them a powerful but reactionary force to which all sections of the property-owning classes had to pay attention. The consequences of this for industrialisation were twofold. First, the agricultural sector, unlike in Britain and Germany, remained self-sufficient and inefficient for most of the nineteenth century. As such, it was incapable of generating either wealth for investing in industry or demand for manufactured goods produced by industry. Second, by depressing the rate of population growth, it prevented the mass population exodus from the countryside to the towns and thus starved industry of a ready supply of cheap labour. This situation was further exacerbated by the continuing opportunities for home work which, by supplementing agricultural incomes, extended the viability of rural life longer than might otherwise be the case.

Nevertheless, the continued existence of a large rural population, even up to the dawn of the twentieth century, was not just a product of land ownership and the presence of home work. It also owed a great deal to the presence of import barriers which allowed peasants to maintain inefficient production methods, in comparison with their British counterparts, and reduced the need either to borrow money for new equipment or to sell plots which were too small to be viable.

Import barriers also produced a strong bond of self-interest between peasants and factory owners, both of whom saw free trade as a threat to their way of life. As one observer commented, 'Competition was always possible in France, it simply did not happen to be a preferred form of conduct' (Sheahan, 1969:25).

For industrialists, the result was similar. The absence of foreign competition, allied to low levels of domestic demand, allowed the typical business to remain family-owned, and also relatively small. Finance for industrial expansion was raised from family members rather than financial institutions, which in turn restricted the size of the banking sector. Indeed, such was the shortage of domestically generated capital and risk-orientated entrepreneurs that the building of railways, so vital to the development of the French economy, could not have taken place without foreign capital and state support (Kemp, 1979).

Therefore, unlike Britain, industrialisation in France never was driven by, or resulted in, individual enterprise or profit maximisation. For the state, the object-ive was a strong France. For the peasant and small entrepreneur, the objective was to make a reasonable living in the context of the rural and urban cultures they supported and valued.

Scandinavia

Having looked at how the three largest and most advanced European countries – Britain, Germany and France – industrialised, we shall now move on to examine how three of the smaller states – Sweden, Denmark and Norway – responded to the challenge of industrialisation. In 1800, the total population of these three countries was just over four million people – Sweden 2.35 million, Denmark 0.93 million, and Norway 0.88 million. By 1910, it was still less than 11 million – Sweden 5.5 million, Denmark 2.8 million, and Norway 2.4 million. The historical links between these countries were very close, and up to the First World War they operated a monetary union. Though each had occupied a position of importance on the international stage, due to their seafaring traditions, by the mid-nineteenth century the standing of all three countries had declined. In fact, Norway and Sweden had become two of the poorest countries in Europe, which was a prime reason for the large-scale emigration from these countries to the USA in the nineteenth century (Milward and Saul, 1973).

Despite growing pockets of industrial production, in the nineteenth century their domestic economies were weak, and all three countries depended heavily on exporting the products of their agricultural, mining and forestry industries to their more industrialised neighbours, especially Great Britain. That they were able to adapt their export efforts to the changing demands of the international economy bears witness to the entrepreneurial skills of these countries.

However, political, economic and social developments in these three countries in the nineteenth century, particularly in Denmark, laid the foundations for the creation of the 'Nordic model' of industrial relations which emerged in the 1930s. This arose from the so-called 'historic compromise' between capital and labour, which extended co-operation between employers and social democratic governments over national economic policy into the industrial relations field. At a national level, it was agreed that the efforts of social democratic governments to bring about economic growth would not challenge the capitalist nature of production. Trade unions accepted this approach in exchange for basic trade union rights. This paved the way for an end to lock-outs and other such tactics by employers, and the creation of government-backed approaches to industrial democracy and further extensions of workers' rights (Dolvik and Stokland, 1992; Ferner and Hyman, 1992; Kjellberg, 1992).

These developments happened at different times and at a different pace in each country. Denmark led the way in the late nineteenth century, and Norway and Sweden followed a decade later, though the 'Nordic model' did not really establish itself fully until the 1930s and 1940s. However, the close ties between these three countries meant that political and industrial developments in one affected the other two. Hence the phrase 'Nordic model' was coined to describe similarities between the tripartite approaches adopted by government, employers and trade unions in each country, and the fact that these were distinct from practices elsewhere in Europe (or the rest of the world for that matter). For the moment, however, we are more concerned with the process of industrialisation in the nineteenth century and how this paved the way for these later developments.

Sweden

For Sweden, the nineteenth century brought a rapidly rising population, which was matched by an increasingly productive agricultural sector that not only fully met domestic needs, but also developed a strong export market in grain, especially to Britain. The productivity of agriculture reflected the growing flexibility and commercialisation of this sector, facilitated by a series of gradual and peaceful rural reforms.

The iron trade also occupied an important position in the Swedish economy for much of the nineteenth century. This was due in no small part to its ability to adopt technological innovations, mainly from Britain, and the ability of Swedish iron-masters to seek out new international markets. By the end of the century, this had led to fewer but larger units of production, and the industry began to reflect the structures and methods of the leading European producers.

Despite the growth of agriculture and iron production, the most spectacular element in the growth of the Swedish economy was the boom in timber exports (Jorberg, 1973). Up to the 1830s, Swedish exports were only a fraction of those of Norway. However, the increasing urbanisation of Britain and growing demand for timber from France and Germany transformed the pattern of demand and supply. By the 1860s, softwood accounted for 40 per cent of all Sweden's exports, a situation which lasted well into the 1880s.

With over 20 million hectares of productive forest, Sweden possessed the largest such area in Europe, after Russia. The growth in markets was matched by the introduction of new methods and techniques, especially the use of steam engines and fine-bladed saws at the mills. The transfer of land ownership from the state to the private sector in the early nineteenth century also aided the development of the timber industry by allowing entrepreneurs to obtain timber rights often at ridiculously low prices, sometimes for no more than a sack of flour. Such a situation attracted many ruthless entrepreneurs whose regard for reforestation and conservation were negligible.

This combination of high demand, cheap wood and ruthless entrepreneurs created the conditions for a very sharp boom in timber exports, at least in the short term. Though after 1875 the state reversed its policy and began to reacquire forests, the timber companies also began to buy farmland, with its attendant forest rights. Gradually, the industry came to be dominated by a few large companies, some of which were foreign-owned. However, this concentration of ownership did make it easier for the state to oblige producers to take a more responsible approach to conservation and reforestation.

Given the dominance of the forestry industry, which relied almost exclusively on waterways for transportation, it is not perhaps surprising that railways came late to Sweden – not until the 1850s. It is also not surprising, given this situation, that it was government push rather than demand pull which gave the impetus to the Swedish railway system. Remarkably, by 1914 Sweden had 25 kilometres of railway per inhabitant, twice that of any other European country. It also had a thriving industry producing rolling stock and engines for both the domestic and export markets (Jorberg, 1973).

Nevertheless, by 1870, industry and handicrafts only employed 15 per cent of the population. There were no industrial centres to rival those of Britain, Germany and France. Even the iron districts were small separate communities. After 1870, however, there was a rapid expansion of the Swedish industrial base, so much so that in the 40 years up to 1914, the Swedish economy grew faster than any other in Europe. Even so, to put this picture in perspective, it should be noted that all the workers involved in Swedish engineering exports in 1912 totalled no more than those to be found in one large German railway works.

For a small country, however, dependent on its natural resources, Sweden's progress was significant. There were a number of reasons for this. First, changes in the eighteenth century had removed barriers to social mobility and created the conditions for the emergence of entrepreneurs. Second, these entrepreneurs showed an unrivalled ability to exploit Sweden's natural resources and take advantage of developing export markets. An additional factor was the high quality of the Swedish educational system. This provided an educated workforce able to adapt to changing industries, technologies and products. Therefore, though it would be wrong to underestimate the great asset of Sweden's natural resources, neither should one forget the contribution made by human capital. The combination of a less hierarchical society than elsewhere in Europe and a well-educated and skilled workforce clearly paved the way for the advent of the social democratic approach to society which has become the hallmark of Sweden in the twentieth century.

On the other hand, it would be misleading to forget that, as elsewhere in Europe, industrialisation was a harsh process. Entrepreneurs could be very rapacious, and much of the technology and many of the methods they employed were imported from the more advanced nations, especially Britain. Consequently, though the Swedish government tended to be more keen to intervene than was the case in Britain, industrialisation was accompanied by the same sort of clashes between capital and labour, and the growing incompatibility between an agricultural economy based on self-sufficiency and a capitalist economy based on money.

By the end of the nineteenth century, Sweden had developed a small industrial base, by comparison with Britain, Germany and France, but one which was flexible and competitive. However, the organisation of labour and the technology deployed tended to be imported from the bigger industrial nations. It imported the poor labour relations which existed elsewhere as well.

Denmark

Though Sweden's industrial base was modest by international standards, it was in advance of that of Denmark and Norway (Jorberg, 1973). For Denmark, as for Sweden, it was changes to agricultural production which gave a large boost to the economy in the nineteenth century.

Traditionally, Denmark had relied on the export of two commodities, grain and cattle. Trade in the former grew rapidly in the nineteenth century. Much of the grain was produced on marginal land, however, which was no longer economically viable after the collapse of world grain prices in the 1870s. After the early 1880s, imports outstripped exports.

On the other hand, the keeping of livestock and dairy produce showed a remarkable growth throughout the century. By the end of the nineteenth century, Denmark had a thriving export trade in butter and beef. By 1913, Denmark exported 80 per cent of its butter production, mainly to Britain where it had 40 per cent of the market; in that year, only Holland and Argentina exported more live cattle than Denmark. The latter part of the nineteenth century and the early twentieth century also saw a twelvefold rise in the production and export of pork (Milward and Saul, 1973).

One hindrance to the export of pork was the incompatibility between the large scale of the export market and the numerous small producers. This was overcome in the 1880s, however, with the establishment of the first co-operative bacon factory. By 1914, 53 per cent of pig breeders were supplying to co-operatives. The idea of co-operatives buying, processing and selling produce had grown up in the dairy industry, and was later taken up by egg producers as well as pig breeders. Similar organisations were also used to purchase bulk feedstuff and fertilisers. The impetus behind the development of co-operatives was the smaller farmers' fear of being exploited by their larger colleagues, who could afford to purchase the latest technology exclusively for their own use (Jorberg, 1973).

Therefore, unlike most other European countries, Denmark found a method of making small-scale farming production compatible with large-scale international demand. Nor were these co-operatives purely economic and technical organisations. Though this was their primary purpose, they also had a social and political role, and were anti-landowner. The growth of co-operatives along with their attendant 'folk high schools' was crucial, not only in educating farmers, but also in uniting them as an effective political force. Indeed, the party of small farmers, in alliance with the social democrats, headed governments from 1909 to 1910 and from 1913 to 1920. Not only does this show the political influence and socialist leanings of the co-operative movement, but it explains the emergence of the 'Nordic model' in Denmark some 20 years earlier than in the other two Scandinavian countries. The development of co-operatives was also one of the main reasons why there was no reduction in the numbers employed in Danish agriculture in the nineteenth century.

Though in some ways Denmark had a relatively thriving economy, its industrial base was, even relative to its size, on a more modest scale than in Britain, France or Germany. As an example, by 1911, the Danish cotton industry employed only 3,282 people, no more than one big mill in Britain. In total, there were only 108,000 workers employed in factories at this time.

In contrast, there was a tremendous growth in the service sector, not just in transport and communications, but also in financial and trading services. These latter tended to be concentrated in Copenhagen, where by 1910 half the country's population lived. By 1911, service activities accounted for 36 per cent of the occupied population, as opposed to 32 per cent in Norway and 19 per cent in Sweden.

One of the remarkable features of Danish industrialisation in the nineteenth century was the degree to which it preserved rather than destroyed the peasant and craft traditions. In agriculture, this was mainly due to the rise of co-operatives for processing and selling produce. In industry, the need to cater mainly for a small and discerning home market, allied to a well-educated workforce, kept the craft tradition, and – for most of the nineteenth century – the guild system, alive. Even in 1914, 84 per cent of Danish workers were still in establishments employing five or less people. By contrast, in Sweden in 1912, only 24 per cent of workers were in establishments employing 10 or less people.

Therefore, even though Denmark was less industrially advanced than some bigger European countries, it could however claim to have avoided the clash of cultures and the rise of industrial conflict which characterised the industrial revolution elsewhere in Europe.

Norway

Just as the process of industrialisation differed considerably between Sweden and Denmark, this was also the case with Norway. Like the other two countries, Norway was dependent on exports, but these were service-based rather than product-based. Shipping was its chief earner. In 1880, shipping accounted for 45 per cent of all exports.

Its links with Sweden and Denmark tended to be political rather than economic. Up to 1814, it was part of the Kingdom of Denmark, and in that year the King of Sweden also became the King of Norway. Though Norway remained an independent state, the political and economic ties with Sweden were considerable until the union ended in 1905.

Of the three Scandinavian countries, Norway was slowest to industrialise and, unlike the other two, this was neither preceded nor accompanied by the modernisation of agriculture. Nor was the stimulus to industrialisation generated internally. Rather, when industry really began to flourish, just before the First World War, it was brought about by an influx of foreign capital wishing to take advantage of Norway's potential for cheap hydro-electricity.

Up to this point, however, Norway had made few steps towards becoming an industrial economy. In agriculture, Norway was held back by a combination of poor soils, difficult climate and extremely inefficient internal communications. Indeed, a marked feature of the Norwegian economy was the very poor contact and bad communications between various regions within the country, no doubt a consequence of the mountainous terrain, which meant that it was often easier to import goods from abroad rather than to move them from one part of Norway to another (Jorberg, 1973). This led to a dual economy: the increasingly prosperous urban areas which grew rich on the export of goods and services, and a subsistence agricultural economy in the countryside.

Accordingly, the towns prospered and the countryside stagnated with small peasant farmers tending to be the agricultural norm into the twentieth century. At the end of the nineteenth century, such was the low level of productivity of Norwegian agriculture that butter exports, worth 3.3 million Kroner, were dwarfed by imports of grain and animal feedstuff worth 83 million Kroner. Norway had no other food exports of importance, except for fish (Milward and Saul, 1973).

On the other hand, Norway was mercifully free of the social rigidity of many other European countries where the nobility stood at the top of the social pyramid. Instead, uniquely, merchants and gentlemen farmers formed the top layers of society, serfdom was rare, and there was a lack of the social injustice that seemed inevitably to accompany industrialisation in the more advanced countries. This may account for the willingness of employers and trade unions, particularly in the metal industries, to favour co-operation over conflict from the early 1900s (Dolvik and Stokland, 1992; Kjellberg, 1992).

The staple industries of the Norwegian economy in the nineteenth century were fishing, timber and shipping, along with a shipbuilding industry which was a product of all three. In the early years of the century, it also exported iron, but this trade was virtually killed by British and Swedish competition. The main employers were shipping, where some 33,000 were employed in the merchant marine in 1860, and fishing, both of which had only weak links to the rest of the economy. There was also a small, fragmented, engineering industry which in 1850 only comprised 12 factories employing a total of 200 workers. From the 1840s there was a rapid growth in the textile sector. Even so, in 1860 this still only accounted for 3,000 workers out of a total of just under 20,000 industrial workers. The biggest industrial sector was forestry, employing almost one in three workers. (Jorberg, 1973).

Therefore, because of its small population size, the lack of demand from the countryside, and the reliance of the towns on exports for their prosperity, Norway's industrial expansion was linked very closely to the export trades. When exports boomed, domestic demand increased; when exports fell, so did domestic demand. In addition, because its industrial sector was small, Norway found it difficult to generate capital domestically. As an example, in 1870, half of the mining industry was foreign-owned. However, with the development of closer economic links with Sweden in 1873, the market for Norwegian industry was expanded considerably.

Developing quite separately from the rest of the economy, the real growth industry of the nineteenth century was shipping. Shipping emerged during the eighteenth century as a subsidiary of the timber trade, but in the nineteenth century it developed entirely independently of Norway's own transport needs. Instead, it catered to the needs of other countries, especially Britain and its colonies. It owed its existence to the country's shipbuilding tradition, the availability of local timber and the ready supply of cheap labour. From 1850, the industry grew rapidly, growing fivefold in the years up to 1880, by which time it was the third largest in the world, greater even than that of France and Germany. After 1900, however, the industry declined, owing to a fall in freight rates and to the advent of steam-powered vessels. The industry was very fragmented, which meant that raising capital was difficult. Though this was not a problem with the small, wooden ships which had been the backbone of the industry, it became one with the need for larger, steam-powered vessels which were much more expensive. Furthermore, Norway lacked both the raw materials, iron and steel, and the skills to build steam ships. Indeed, in the immediate pre-war years, only 20 per cent of the industry's requirements were met from home production. Therefore, by 1914 there were clear signs that shipping was in decline.

The advent of hydro-electric power at the end of the nineteenth century, however, did make a significant difference to Norway's industrial development. Once the technology had been established, no country in Europe was better placed to exploit it than Norway, with its plentiful supply of waterfalls. To turn this into a reality, however, required both capital and a use for the resultant cheap electricity. Both of these were to come from abroad. By 1914, hydro-electric power, financed by foreign capital, was used to produce synthetic fertiliser and aluminium. The attraction for foreign investors was cheap power. Almost all of the output was sold abroad, much of it without further processing.

These developments had a significant impact in terms of increasing Norway's foreign earnings. The result was that some 14 per cent of the industrial labour force was directly employed by foreign firms by 1909, with considerable numbers being indirectly employed. These workers tended to be concentrated in the more capital-intensive industries and larger workplaces. This led to a law being passed which limited foreign ownership of Norwegian industry.

In many respects, with the stagnation of timber and shipping, the advent of modern chemical and metal industries was highly desirable. In another respect, however, they also showed the weakness of Norwegian industrialisation. Both these industries were heavily dependent on foreign capital; both were capital- as opposed to labour-intensive; and neither developed or needed a local supply or distribution network. Therefore, neither really impacted greatly, at least in the pre-war period, on the wider Norwegian economy.

Considering these three Scandinavian countries as a whole, the picture of industrialisation by the early twentieth century was very mixed. Sweden was probably the most advanced and Norway the least, with Denmark much nearer the former than the latter. Because of population size, natural resources and history, however, none had developed an industrial base capable of competing with those of the leading European countries.

As elsewhere in Europe, all three tended to import methods and technologies from the more advanced countries, especially Britain. It would appear that the process of industrialisation, where it was reliant on foreign capital and methods, tended to reproduce the British experience of poor labour relations. Particularly in Denmark, however, there were signs that different organisational forms allied to existing social structures and expectations, together with the growth of social democracy, held out the promise of avoiding the vicious employer–employee clashes experienced elsewhere.

Nevertheless, in Europe as a whole, for the most part, those who created and controlled the large business organisations which were becoming the norm still had to rely on their own experience and judgment, but with growing frustration over their inability to control and organise these bodies fully and effectively. There was also a realisation among some that, while change was inevitable, they lacked an effective and, as far as their employees were concerned, acceptable way of managing it. Therefore, by the end of the nineteenth century, there was a growing awareness of the need to develop an approach to organising work which was a more systematic and less harsh and arbitrary an approach than what had gone before. Though this was already, to an extent, taking place in Germany with the rise of bureaucracy, the country where the most conscious and consistent search for a theory of organisation was being pursued was the USA.

The USA

In the USA, for a number of reasons, the need for a workable, overall approach to organisational design and control, which legitimised the authority of managers to initiate change, was perhaps more acute than anywhere else. The USA had industrialised far more rapidly and on a larger scale than any other nation. Only in the 1860s, after the Civil War, did the USA begin to industrialise in earnest; but by 1914 it had become the premier industrial nation, with the highest per capita income in the world. In the period 1860 to 1914, employment in manufacturing rose from 1.3 million to 6.6 million, and the population as a whole rose from 31 million to 91 million (Habakkuk and Postan, 1965). The USA was still very much at this time influenced by Europe, and initially at least adopted similar approaches and methods in organising and running industry. However, the size of the typical American organisation quickly grew much larger than those in Europe. While the average British and French business was still the small, family-owned firm, in the USA it was the monopoly, which dominated an entire industry, or the conglomerate, which had substantial holdings in several industries. As an example, in 1900 Dale Carnegie sold his steel company for the enormous sum of $419 million to a group of financiers. They merged it with other steel concerns to create a monopoly steel producer employing 200,000 workers and valued at $1.3 billion. This was at a time when the British industry, which had led the world, comprised 100 blast furnaces owned by 95 separate companies.

As might be imagined, the numbers of Americans employed in factories and offices grew rapidly – almost tripling between 1880 and 1910 (Levine, 1967; Zinn, 1980). The rocketing increase in demand for labour could not be met by the indigenous population alone and was fuelled by successive waves of immigration. While solving one problem – the shortage of labour – this created others. The culture shock of industrial work, a foreign language, and problems of housing and social integration created enormous pressures in American society. Alongside this was the arbitrary and ruthless discipline of the factory system, where workers were treated as so much industrial cannon fodder. It was a time of rapid social, technological and organisational change, a time where entrepreneurs did not so much expect to manage change as to impose it, and those who could not or would not accept this situation were treated harshly. Consequently, most industries found themselves sitting on a pressure cooker which could, and frequently did, explode in unexpected and violent ways. If management-labour relations were poor in most European countries, they were far worse in the USA (Pelling, 1960).

The American approach to industrial development owed little to government aid or encouragement, and much to individual entrepreneurship. For this reason American entrepreneurs had much more in common with the free market approach to industrial expansion of their British counterparts than to the state-sponsored traditions of Germany or France. Therefore, the German approach to industrial organisation, bureaucracy, which might seem appropriate given the size of American companies, was not attractive. In any case, it tended to operate best in situations where growth and demand were stable or predictable, which in Germany the government tried to facilitate. American growth patterns were volatile and unpredictable, however.

Consequently, there was great pressure to find organisational arrangements which would allow employers to control and organise their employees in a manner that reduced conflict, was cost-effective, and was applicable to the American environment and philosophy. It was also becoming recognised that it was not sufficient just to develop a more systematic approach to the organisation of work; there was also a need to develop an approach to managing change, which would persuade workers to accept rather than reject or resist the introduction of new methods, techniques and technologies. Therefore, with the spirit of endeavour, determination and confidence which seemed so much a part of the American character at this time, managers and engineers set out to remedy this situation. Though similar developments were taking place in Europe, they lacked the intensity, commitment and scale of events in the USA. This is no doubt why one of the earliest and most enduring approaches to organisation theory emerged in the USA, and why the USA continued to dominate the development of organisation theory.

ORGANISATION THEORY: THE CLASSICAL APPROACH

As can be seen, at the end of the nineteenth century, there was a clear need to replace the rule-of-thumb approach to organisational design and management with a more consistent and organisation-wide approach. This was not because of an academic interest in the functioning of organisations, though this was present, but in order to improve their performance, enhance their competitiveness and – an increasing concern at the time – to sustain and legitimate managerial authority. This was certainly the case in the USA, where explosive growth and a workforce suffering from culture shock had created dangerous social pressures which questioned the legitimacy of managerial power, and even the capitalist system itself. This was also true in Europe. Although Europe industrialised earlier, it was not only having to come to grips with the increase in size and complexity of business life, but it was also facing considerable, and unexpected, competitive pressure from the United States.

Nevertheless, these difficulties could not quench the innate optimism of the age. It was a time, much more than now, when people dealt in certainties and universal truths. There was a feeling of confidence that any goal, whether it be taming nature or discerning the best way to run business, could be achieved by the twin power of scientific study and practical experience. All over the industrialised world, groups of managers and technical specialists were forming their own learned societies to exchange experiences, to discuss common problems, and to seek out in a scientific and rational fashion the solution to all organisational ills – to discover 'the one best way'.

Out of these endeavours emerged what was later termed *the Classical approach* to organisational design and management. It was an approach, as the name suggests, which drew heavily on what had gone before, taking from writers such as Adam Smith and practitioners such as Josiah Wedgwood and leavening their ideas with contemporary experience, views and experiments. This approach, reflecting the age in which it emerged, portrayed organisations as machines, and those in them as mere parts which respond to the correct stimulus and whose actions are based on scientific principles. The emphasis was on achieving efficiency in internal functions, seeing organisations as closed and changeless entities unaffected by the outside world. Though this approach first originated in the early part of this century, its influence on managerial practices and assumptions is still strong today, but its credibility among academics has waned (Kelly, 1982 a and b; Rose, 1988; Scott, 1987).

The Classical approach, or the scientific-rational approach as it is sometimes called, while not being homogeneous, is characterised by three common propositions.

- *Organisations are rational entities. They are collectivities of individuals focused on the achievement of relatively specific goals through their organisation into highly formalised, differentiated and efficient structures.*

- *The design of organisations is a science. Through experience, observation and experiment, it has been established that there is one best universal organisational form for all bodies. This is based on the hierarchical and horizontal division of labour and functions, whereby organisations are conceived as machines which, once set in motion, inexorably and efficiently will pursue and achieve their pre-selected goals.*

- *People are economic beings. They are solely motivated by money. This instrumental orientation means that they will try to achieve the maximum reward for the minimum work, and will use whatever bargaining power their skills or knowledge allow to this end. Therefore, jobs must be designed and structured in such a way as to minimise an individual's skill and discretion, and to maximise management control.*

The key figures in the development of the Classical approach were Frederick Taylor (1856–1915) – and his loyal lieutenants Frank and Lillian Gilbreth – in the USA, Henri Fayol (1841–1925) in France and Max Weber (1864-1920) in Germany. All were writing in the first two decades of the twentieth century, though Weber's work was not generally available in English until the 1940s. Their work is outlined in the following sections.

Frederick Taylor's Scientific Management

Taylor was a highly controversial figure during his lifetime and still remains so more than 80 years after his death. This was partly because his theory of management was a direct challenge to both workers and managers. However, a large part of the hostility he generated during his lifetime was due to his own character. Rose (1988:23) stated that 'Taylor was a notorious neurotic – many would not hesitate to write crank; and there is even a case for upgrading the diagnosis to maniac.' He was certainly a zealot when it came to promoting his own ideas and would tolerate no challenge to them, whether from workers or management. Not surprisingly, though he attracted devoted followers, he also engendered fierce dislike.

Taylor was an American engineer who, through his experience as a machinist and manager in the engineering industry, made a major contribution to the development of managerial theory and practice in the twentieth century (Locke, 1982; Rose, 1988). However, his original attempts to improve productivity (or as he put it, to stamp out 'soldiering') were less than successful. Not only was his use of sacking, blacklisting and victimisation counter-productive, but also the bitterness which this provoked haunted him for the rest of his life. It was his failure to achieve change by, as Rose (1988:37) termed it, 'managerial thuggery' which led him to seek an alternative method of change management which the workers, and management, would accept because they could see that it was rational and fair. Thereafter, his sole preoccupation became the pursuit and promotion of a scientific approach to management.

There can be little doubt that the publication of his *Principles of Scientific Management* in 1911 laid the foundation stone for the development of organisation and management theory. Taylor's primary focus was on the design and analysis of individual tasks; this process inevitably led to changes in the overall structure of organisations. Such was the impact of his work that it created a blueprint for, and legitimated, the activities of managers and their support staff. In so doing, he helped to create the plethora of functions and departments which characterise many modern organisations.

Before Taylor, the average manager tended to operate in an idiosyncratic and arbitrary manner with little or no specialist support. Taylor saw this as being at the root of much industrial unrest and workers' mistrust of management. Though criticised for his anti-labour postures, Taylor was also highly critical of management behaviour, which may account for this group's initial lack of enthusiasm for his ideas (Scott, 1987). After Taylor, managers were left with a 'scientific' blueprint for analysing work and applying his 'one best way' principle to each job in order to gain 'a fair day's work for a fair day's pay'.

These last two phrases sum up Taylor's basic beliefs:

- *It is possible and desirable to establish, through methodical study and the application of scientific principles, the one best way of carrying out any job. Once established, the way must be implemented totally and made to operate consistently.*

- *Human beings are predisposed to seek the maximum reward for the minimum effort, which Taylor referred to as 'soldiering'. To overcome this, managers must lay down in detail what each worker should do, step by step; ensure through close supervision that the instructions are adhered to; and, to give positive motivation, link pay to performance.*

Taylor incorporated those beliefs into his precepts for Scientific Management, comprising three core elements: the systematic collection of knowledge about the work process by managers; the removal or reduction of workers' discretion and control over what they do; and the laying down of standard procedures and times for carrying out each job.

The starting point is the gathering of knowledge:

The managers assume ... the burden of gathering together all the traditional knowledge which in the past has been possessed by the workman and then of classifying, tabulating and reducing this knowledge to rules, laws and formulae ... (Taylor, 1911b: 36)

This lays the groundwork for the second stage: increased management control. As long as workers possess a monopoly of knowledge about the work process, increased control is impossible. Once the knowledge is also possessed by managers, however, it becomes possible not only to establish what workers actually do with their time, but also by 'reducing this knowledge to rules, laws and formulae', to decrease the knowledge that workers need to carry out a given task. It also, importantly, paves the way for the division of labour.

The last stage is that 'All possible brain work should be removed from the shop and centred in the planning ... department ...' (Taylor, 1911a:98–9) The divorce of conception from execution removes control from the worker, who no longer has discretion as to how tasks are carried out.

> **Perhaps the most prominent single element in modern scientific management is the task idea. The work of every workman is fully planned out by management ... and each man receives in most cases complete written instructions, describing in detail the task which he is to accomplish, as well as the means to be used in doing the work. This task specifies not only what is to be done but how it is to be done and the exact time allowed for doing it. (*Taylor, 1911b:39*)**

This completes the process of gaining control over workers by managers. The workers become 'human machines', told what to do, when to do it and how long to take. More than this, however, it allows new types of work organisation to be developed, and new work processes and equipment to be introduced; thus workers move from having a monopoly of knowledge and control over their work to a position where the knowledge they have of the work process is minimal, and their control is vastly reduced. The result is not only a reduction in the skills required and the wages paid, but also the creation of jobs which are so narrow and tightly specified that the period needed to train someone to do them is greatly reduced. This removes the last bargaining counter of labour: scarcity of skill.

According to Taylor, this transforms not only workers' jobs but also managers' jobs.

> **The man at the head of the business under scientific management is governed by rules and laws ... just as the workman is, and the standards which have been developed are equitable'. (*Taylor, 1911a:189*)**

Taylor stated that the 'scientific' basis and equal applicability of his methods meant they were neutral between labour and management; therefore they legitimated managerial action to analyse and change work methods, because managers are merely applying science to determine the best method of work. He claimed that his approach benefited both the worker and the company. The worker was enabled and encouraged to work to his maximum performance and be rewarded accordingly, while the company benefited from higher output.

Though seen as something of an anti-trade unionist, which he probably was, he was also strongly critical of management. He believed that many of the problems organisations faced in implementing change were due to the arbitrary and inconsistent approach of managers. Indeed, though trade unions were very suspicious of Scientific Management in general and Taylor in particular, managers seemed even more antagonistic. In fact, after his death, Taylor's acolytes spent much time in the 1920s wooing the American unions with a considerable degree of success; they never achieved the same success with management (Rose, 1988). The main reason for this was that, though managers were anxious to find an approach which would curtail labour resistance to change and improve productivity, they were not prepared to subject themselves to a similar degree of discipline.

As Taylor's biographer, Copley (1923:146), stated in relation to managerial resistance to Scientific Management at the Bethlehem Steel Company:

> **Let us consider what Taylor was contending for. It was essentially this: that the government of the Bethlehem Steel Company cease to be capricious, arbitrary and despotic; that every man in the establishment, high and low, submit himself to law [i.e. that managers should obey the principles of Scientific Management].**

Taylor believed passionately in the need to reform managerial authority: to base it on competence rather than the power to hire and fire. It is one thing to ask one's subordinates to change their ways and accept new rules and methods, but it is another thing entirely for management to acknowledge that they too need to change, and change radically. No wonder that Taylor met managerial as well as worker resistance.

Nevertheless, even though managers resisted the full implementation of Taylorism, the new and rapidly expanding breed of industrial engineers, charged with developing and implementing new methods, techniques and technologies, found in Taylor and his contemporaries' work a blueprint for transforming the workplace and increasing their control and status. One consequence of this, brought about by the use of job cards and other forms of work recording and analysis systems, was a massive increase in the amount of paperwork that needed to be processed. Managers complained about the growth of 'industrial bureaucracy', but the benefits it brought by enabling average times and costs, etc., to be calculated easily outweighed the increase in clerical costs.

Throughout the 1920s, the adoption of Scientific Management grew in America, though rarely in the full form laid down by Taylor. On a very limited basis it was also introduced into Europe. Indeed, the leader of the Russian Revolution, Lenin, was much taken with Taylor's work, though in the main it met with hostility (Rose, 1988). It was not until after the Second World War, however, through the auspices of the Marshall Plan for rebuilding Europe's war-torn economies, that Scientific Management was promoted and adopted on any significant scale outside America. Ironically, the contribution of American trade unions, through their role in the Marshall Plan, was crucial in promoting Scientific Management in European enterprises (Carew, 1987).

Though often claiming that his system was innovative and unique, which in terms of its presentation as scientific and neutral it was, it can be seen that Taylor drew on many of the management practices and attitudes towards labour which were prevalent during the nineteenth century. He was also heavily indebted to many contemporaries and associates who helped develop the work study techniques necessary to implement Scientific Management (Kempner, 1970). His greatest debt was to Frank and Lillian Gilbreth, who were not only pioneers of work study but also Taylor's most vigorous promoters, both before and after his death in 1915.

The Gilbreths and work study

Much of modern work study (a central element of the Classical approach) owes its origins to the methods and techniques developed in the first quarter of this century by Frank and Lillian Gilbreth (*see* Gilbreth and Gilbreth, 1914). The work was initiated by Frank Gilbreth, who was a contemporary of Taylor's. In many respects their careers were similar. Taylor began his career on the shopfloor and later rose to eminence as a manager and management consultant. Frank Gilbreth rose from being a bricklayer to running his own construction company, as well as being a leading campaigner for Scientific Management. Lillian Gilbreth was a trained psychologist who collaborated closely with her husband (Thickett, 1970).

The Gilbreths developed a number of procedures for breaking work down into its constituent components. Flow process charts were used which split work into five basic elements: operations, transportation, inspection, storage and delay. Arising out of this, they developed a method of minutely analysing tasks which broke handwork into seventeen basic elements. Examples of these are:

Grasp   Begins when hand or body member touches an object. Consists of gaining control of an object.

Release Begins when hand or body member begins to relax control of object. Consists of letting go of object.

Plan   Begins when hand or body members are idle or making random movements while worker decides on course of action. Consists of determining a course of action. Ends when course of action is determined.

The purpose of this microanalysis was not only to establish what was done, but also to discover if a better method of performing the task in question could be developed. In this respect, they did much original work in establishing the distinction between necessary and unnecessary movements. The latter were to be eliminated immediately and the former further analysed in more detail to see if they could be improved, combined or replaced by special equipment.

If this sounds remarkably similar to Adam Smith's Pin Factory, mentioned earlier, this is no accident. The Classical approach is descended from Smith through the nineteenth century pioneers of work organisation. Though remarkable in the level of minute detail to which they reduced tasks, the Gilbreths were only, as they saw it, taking Smith's maxims to their logical conclusion. If in the process they give the impression of dealing more with machines than people, that too is no accident. Like others who propounded the Classical approach, they viewed organisations and workers very much as machines. The work study methods developed by the Gilbreths and their successors are still widely used today, not just in manufacturing industries, but in all areas of life from hospitals to computer programming (Grant, 1983).

The Gilbreths were also concerned that, having established the best way to carry out a task, this should not be undermined by selecting the wrong person to carry it out or by creating the wrong environment. Therefore, they set about analysing employee selection and establishing environmental criteria with the same determination they had applied to analysing work performance. In neither case, however, could they achieve the same microanalysis that characterised their work study technique; what finally emerged were effectively opinions based on their own 'experience', rather than being the product of experiment and observation.

The Gilbreths were devoted to one objective – to discover the best method of doing any job. They were firm supporters of Frederick Taylor and his work and saw their efforts as contributing to the enhancement of Scientific Management. Like Taylor, they saw themselves as creating a neutral system which benefited both labour and management. They felt that any increase in boredom or monotony brought about by their methods would be compensated for by workers' opportunities to earn more money.

While the Gilbreths and Taylor devoted their efforts to improving the productivity of individual workers, there were others who took a wider but complementary perspective.

Henri Fayol and the principles of organisation

Fayol was writing in France at the same time as Taylor was propounding his views on Scientific Management in the USA. He began his working life as a mining engineer and eventually rose to the position of Chief Executive, taking over an ailing mining company and turning it into a much admired and financially strong enterprise by the time he retired. In his 'retirement' he founded the Centre for Administrative Studies, whose role was to propagate Fayol's ideas through management education. Undoubtedly, the Centre had a profound influence on the practice and theory of management in both the public and private sectors in France.

Fayol did not draw his views on organisations solely from his own experience as a manager. His education at one of the *grandes écoles*, and his subsequent career as a chief executive of a large mining company, placed him among the élite of senior administrators in business, government and the armed forces. Therefore, though he spent his working life in the coal mining industry, his practical knowledge of business was informed by and fits within the intellectual and administrative traditions of French society.

His working life, in the late nineteenth and early twentieth centuries, coincided with a rapid period of industrialisation in France. It was a time when industrial unrest was rife, with frequent strikes by railway workers, miners and civil servants.

As with the USA, in this period of rapid growth and change, there was an unwritten consensus that French business and government needed a theory of management, no matter how basic (Cuthbert, 1970). Unlike Taylor and the Gilbreths, however, Fayol's focus was on efficiency at the organisational level rather than the task level: top down rather than bottom up (Fayol, 1949). Though this clearly reflects Fayol's own practical experience, it also shows the combined influence of the French intellectual tradition, with its preference for addressing philosophies rather than practicalities, and the administrative tradition, which sought to identify and lay down general rules and restrictions applicable to all situations.

Given his background, it is not surprising that Fayol was more concerned with general rather than departmental or supervisory management, and with overall organisational control as opposed to the details of tasks. This does not, however, place him in opposition to Taylor. Rather the combination of Taylor's work at the task level and Fayol's at the organisational level make their views complementary rather than contradictory. Furthermore, both emphasised strongly the need for professionally educated managers who would 'follow the rule' rather than act in an arbitrary or *ad hoc* fashion.

Fayol (like all the Classical school) was concerned with developing a universal approach to management which was applicable to any organisation:

> **There is no one doctrine of administration for business and another for affairs of state; administrative doctrine is universal. Principles and general rules which hold good for business hold good for the state too, and the reverse applies (*quoted in Cuthbert, 1970:111*)**

Therefore, in business, public administration, or indeed any form of organisation, the same universal principles apply. According to Fayol, these are as follows (Mullins, 1989:202–3):

1 *Division of work*. The object is to produce more and better work from the same effort, through the advantages of specialisation.

2 *Authority and responsibility*. Wherever authority is exercised, responsibility arises. The application of sanctions is needed to encourage useful actions and to discourage their opposite.

3 *Discipline*. This is essential for the efficient operation of the organisation. Discipline is in essence the outward mark of respect for agreements between the organisation and its members.

4 *Unity of command*. In any action, any employee should receive orders from one superior only; dual command is a perpetual source of conflicts.

5 *Unity of direction*. In order to co-ordinate and focus effort, there should be one leader and one plan for any group of activities with the same objective.

6 *Subordination of individual or group interests*. The interest of the organisation should take precedence over individual or group interests.

7 *Remuneration of personnel.* Methods of payment should be fair, encourage keenness by rewarding well directed effort, but not lead to over-payment.

8 *Centralisation.* The degree of centralisation is a question of proportion and will vary in particular organisations.

9 *Scalar chain.* This is the chain of superiors from the ultimate authority to the lowest ranks. Respect for line authority must be reconciled with activities which require urgent action, and with the need to provide for some measure of initiative at all levels of authority.

10 *Order.* This includes material order and social order. The object of material order is avoidance of loss. There should be an appointed place for each thing, and each thing should be in its appointed place. Social order requires good organisation and good selection.

11 *Equity.* There needs to be fairness in dealing with employees throughout all levels of the scalar chain.

12 *Stability of tenure of personnel.* Generally, prosperous organisations have a stable managerial team.

13 *Initiative.* This represents a source of strength for the organisation and should be encouraged and developed.

14 *Esprit de corps.* This should be fostered, as harmony and unity among members of the organisation are a great strength in the organisation.

According to Fayol (1949), it is the prime responsibility of management to enact these principles. Consequently, in order to achieve this, he prescribed the main duties of management as:

- **Planning** – *examining the future, deciding what needs to be done and developing a plan of action.*
- **Organising** – *bringing together the resources, human and material, and developing the structure to carry out the activities of the organisation.*
- **Command** – *ensuring that all employees perform their jobs well and in the best interests of the organisation.*
- **Co-ordination** – *verifying that the activities of the organisation work harmoniously together to achieve its goals.*
- **Control** – *establishing that plans, instructions and commands are correctly carried out.*

Fayol was a gifted and highly successful businessman who attributed his success to the application of his principles rather than personal ability. Certainly, he was one of the pioneers of management theory, and many of his principles are still taught and practised today. However, part of the success of his work lay in the fact that he was writing for a receptive audience, and at a time when management practice and ideas were becoming international currency. Just as Taylor's system arose at the time when a need for a management theory had grown among the business community in the

USA, so Fayol's was aimed at a similar demand in France, where the business community was developing rapidly but on an *ad hoc* basis.

Unlike Taylor, though, he attempted neither to denigrate trade unions openly nor to castigate managers. Nor did he share with Taylor a belief that the interests of managers and workers were necessarily the same or ultimately reconcilable. He did believe, however, that much industrial unrest could be eliminated by fairer, more consistent, and firmer management; particularly where this reduced the need for trade unions or their ability to organise. He also believed in the need to educate and train managers. His views were not seen as a direct attack on existing managers; rather, they were in harmony with the approach taken by managers in the larger private enterprises and those operating in government and the armed services. This is not surprising because, by and large, they and Fayol were educated in the *grandes écoles* and shared a common intellectual approach. In addition, Fayol did not generally try to impose his ideas directly on individual organisations. Instead, he preferred to influence managers indirectly through a process of education. In the light of the reaction in America to Taylor's attitude, many would consider this a wise move.

The USA and France were not the only countries where developments in management practice and thought were being studied and documented. In Germany, at this time, Max Weber was charting the growth and merits of bureaucracy.

Max Weber on bureaucracy

Though Weber's work on bureacracy is much clearer and more detailed, there is a considerable affinity between it and Fayol's work on the principles of management. Both were concerned with the overall structuring of organisations, and the principles which guide senior managers in this task. Though writing in the early part of the twentieth century, it is unlikely that Weber's work was known to Fayol and, as it was not translated into English until the 1940s, even more unlikely that either Taylor or the Gilbreths knew of it.

Unlike other proponents of the Classical approach, Weber was an academic – a sociologist – rather than a practitioner. His work on administrative structures was only a limited aspect of his major interest in the development of Western civilisation. From this Weber concluded that the rise of civilisation was a story of power and domination. He noted that each social epoch was characterised by a different form of political rule, and that for a ruling élite to sustain its power and dominance, it was essential for it both to gain legitimacy and to develop an administrative apparatus to enforce and support its authority (Weber, 1946).

Weber (1947: 328) identified three types of authority:

1 *Rational-legal* – resting on a belief in the 'legality' of patterns of normative rule, and the right of those elevated to authority under such rules to issue commands.

2 *Traditional* – resting on an established belief in the sanctity of immemorial traditions and the legitimacy of those exercising authority under them.

3 *Charismatic* – resting on devotion to the specific and exceptional sanctity, heroism or exemplary character of an individual person, and of the normative patterns or order revealed or ordained by them.

Weber argued that, in the context of the rational-legal authority structures which prevailed in Western societies in the twentieth century, the bureaucratic approach to organisation was the most appropriate and efficient. Under bureaucracy, laws, rules, procedures and predefined routines are dominant and not subject to the vagaries and preferences of individuals. They give form to a clearly defined system of administration – whether it be public administration, such as the Department of Social Security, or private administration, such as the Halifax Building Society – where the execution of routine, pre-programmed procedures is all important. Weber considered this approach to be both appropriate, because it was the ideal tool for a centralised administration where the legitimacy of those in power was underpinned by the rule of law, and efficient, because the bureaucratic approach mechanises the process of administration in the same way that machines automate the production process in factories.

Weber frequently asserted that the development of bureaucracy eliminates human fallibility:

> **Its [bureaucracy's] specific nature ... develops the more perfectly the more bureaucracy is 'dehumanised', the more completely its success in eliminating from official business, love, hatred, and purely personal, irrational and emotional elements which escape calculation. (*Weber, 1946:217*)**

Bureaucracy is characterised by the division of labour, a clear hierarchical authority structure, formal and unbiased selection procedures, employment decisions based on merit, career tracks for employees, detailed rules and regulations, impersonal relationships, and a distinct separation of members' organisational and personal lives. It must be borne in mind, however, that Weber's bureaucratic model (or 'ideal' organisation), though inspired by developments in Germany at the time, was a hypothetical rather than a factual description of how most organisations were structured. It was his view of the characteristics that organisations should exhibit in modern societies based on rationality and law. How Weber saw these organisational characteristics supporting and reproducing rational-legal authority is best seen by contrasting them with the traditional administrative forms based on patronage (*see* Table 1, p. 37) (Weber, 1946 and 1947).

For Weber, therefore, bureaucracy provided a rational-legal form of organisation which distinguished itself from, and eradicated the faults and unfairness of, previous administrative forms by its mechanical adherence to set rules, procedures and patterns of authority. It removed the system of patronage and eliminated human variability, replacing it by the rule of law. In Weber's view, the principles of bureaucracy were universally applicable to all organisations, big or small, public or private, industrial or commercial.

Table 1: Comparison of Weber's concept of rational-legal authority with traditional authority

Characteristics of rational-legal authority	*Characteristics of traditional authority*
Areas of jurisdiction are clearly specified: the regular activities required of personnel are allocated in a fixed way as official duties.	The allocation of labour is not defined, but depends on assignments made by the leader, which can be changed at any time.
The organisation of offices follows the principle of hierarchy: each lower office is controlled and supervised by a higher one. However, the scope of authority of superiors over subordinates is circumscribed, and lower offices enjoy a right of appeal.	Authority relations are diffuse, being based on personal loyalty, and are not ordered into clear hierarchies.
An intentionally-established system of abstract rules governs official decisions and actions. These rules are relatively stable and exhaustive, and can be learned. Decisions are recorded in permanent files.	General rules of administration either do not exist or are vaguely-stated, ill-defined, and subject to change at the whim of the leader. No attempt is made to keep permanent records of transactions.
The 'means of production or administration' – for example, tools and equipment or rights and privileges – belong to the office, not the office-holder, and may not be appropriated. Personal property is clearly separated from official property, and working space from living quarters.	There is no separation of a ruler's personal household business from the larger 'public' business under their direction.
Officials are personally free, selected on the basis of technical qualifications, appointed to office (not elected), and recompensed by salary.	Officials are often selected from among those who are personally dependent on the leader – slaves, serfs, and relatives, for example. Selection is governed by arbitrary criteria, and remuneration often takes the form of benefices – rights granted to individuals which, for instance, allow them access to the ruler's stores, or give them grants of land from which they can appropriate the fees or taxes. Benefices, like fiefs in feudalistic systems, may become hereditary and sometimes are bought and sold.
Employment by the organisation constitutes a career for officials. An official is a full-time employee and looks forward to a lifelong career in the agency. After a trial period, he or she gains tenure of position and is protected against arbitrary dismissal.	Officials serve at the pleasure of the leader, and so lack clear expectations about the future and security of tenure.

Just as the work of Taylor and Fayol can be understood as representing a combination of their backgrounds and the state of the societies in which they lived, so is this the case with Weber. The Prussian bureaucratic tradition dominated both the public, and to a large extent, the private sectors in Germany. It was seen by the ruling élite as the ideal method for ensuring that the objectives of the state and the objectives of individual enterprises were adhered to. It also fitted in with the Prussian militaristic tradition of unquestioning obedience to superiors, which was a prevalent view in both public and private organisations. It must be remembered, of course, that the state and private enterprises in Germany were not primarily obsessed with profitability or individual aggrandisement. The key objective was to build Germany as the premier military and industrial power in Europe. Competition at the level of the individual or the individual enterprise was a concept which carried much less force in Germany, and even France, than in the USA or Britain. German industry and government were more concerned with ensuring that all sections of the country pulled in the same direction. Where competition threatened this, it was eliminated by the state, either by direct intervention, such as nationalisation of the railways, or by indirect intervention, through the formation of cartels and monopolies. In carrying out this grand plan for German development, bureaucracy was found to be the ideal tool.

It follows that bureaucracy did not need a Taylor or Fayol to develop or promote it; it already existed, was accepted by management, and was prospering, in Germany and other advanced countries, especially in the public sector. What Weber did was to give it intellectual respectability by arguing that it was particularly suited to the needs of (what he saw as) the rational and secular societies which were becoming the norm in the Western world.

The appeal of bureaucracy, to governments and large organisations at least, can be seen in the way that bureaucracy is an ever-present and pervasive feature of modern life. It would be misleading, however, to give the impression that its development in Germany, or elsewhere, was uncontentious. In Germany, in the early years of this century, it tended to be the purpose and consequences rather than the principles of bureaucracy which were attacked. At an overall political level, the growth of radical parties of the left reflected growing concerns over Germany's military aims and the state's concomitant close links with business, and in particular its perceived preference for aiding capital rather than labour. At the level of the individual enterprise, the growth of militant trade unions, often linked to the parties of the left, reflected the growing frustration of workers who resented the autocratic approach of management and its resistance to collective bargaining.

CONCLUSIONS

It is not an inevitable fact of life that modern societies are characterised by organisations of all shapes and sizes; this is the product of a particular combination of circumstances. The rise of capitalism in Britain and other European countries in the seventeenth and eighteenth centuries created new opportunities and new problems which could not be accommodated under the old order. The result was a move away from self-sufficient, autonomous, individual units to collective units of production controlled by an entrepreneur. It was entrepreneurs who, in pursuit of ever-greater profits, created the factory system in Britain which became the basis of modern organisational life. The central features of the factory system were: autocratic control, division of labour, and antagonistic relations between management and labour.

Though starting at different times and moving at their own pace, most European countries, and later the USA, adopted and adapted the British approach to industrial organisation. As the nineteenth century progressed, however, the nature of industrialisation began to vary from country to country, reflecting the unique circumstances and needs of the host society. In Germany, the objectives of the state determined that large-scale public and private bureaucracies became the norm. In France, the state also played a role in shaping industrialisation, but in this case it was to perpetuate small-scale, inefficient business and agricultural operations. In both countries, individual pursuit of profit maximisation was less important than in either Britain or the USA. In Scandinavia, especially Denmark, the emergence of a more collective and less ruthless approach to industrialisation could be discerned.

Nevertheless, in the transition from a subsistence economy to a money economy, one clear image stands out above all else: the antagonism between employers and employees. The factory did not emerge because it was a more efficient means of production *per se*; it emerged because it offered entrepreneurs a more effective means of controlling labour. This meant that the factory was also a battleground, with employers seeking to impose new conditions and technologies, and workers – when they could – attempting to resist change.

As the nineteenth century progressed, managers became increasingly aware of the shortcomings of their *ad hoc* and inconsistent responses to new challenges and opportunities, and the counter-productive nature of resistance to change. A more coherent approach to structuring and running organisations was required: one which legitimated managerial authority, especially to initiate change. This crystallised into the Classical approach.

Though writing in different countries and from different perspectives, the proponents of what later came to be known as the Classical approach all adopted a similar perspective towards what they saw as one of the main issues for modern societies: how to create organisations that efficiently and effectively pursue their objectives. Taylor, supported by the work study techniques of the Gilbreths and others, concentrated very much on the operational level, arguing for his 'scientific' method of analysing, designing and managing jobs. However, his insistence on the consistent and unbiased application of scientific principles, and the emphasis he placed on all members of an organisation obeying rules and procedures, were as much a challenge to managerial beliefs and behaviour as they were to the beliefs and behaviour of shopfloor workers. Fayol, in contrast, was concerned less with operational issues and more with the overall administration and control of organisations. Therefore, to an extent, his could be called a top-down approach, while Taylor was working from the bottom up. Weber sought to put organisations in a wider historical and societal context, bringing together both the detailed tasks to be carried out in organisations and general principles governing them.

Though Taylor's approach required a radical change in managerial behaviour and a significant increase in organisational bureaucracy, the objective of his system was to improve the productivity and efficiency with which manual workers carried out the tasks ordained for them by management. Everything else was, as Taylor would have put it, the outcome of pursuing this objective to its logical conclusion. The need to provide managers with rules and systems for running the entire enterprise, and not just that part of it dealing with manual labour, was a means of achieving his objective rather than a prime aim. This is where the work of Fayol and Weber has proved so crucial: together with Taylor's work, it comprises a system for running an entire business in a coherent and consistent fashion.

Therefore, taken together, their views are, broadly, complementary, and reflect an approach to organisations and people based upon a number of basic assumptions:

- *There is a 'one best way' for all organisations to be structured and operate.*
- *This approach is founded on the rule of law and legitimate managerial authority.*
- *Organisations are rational entities – collectivities consistently and effectively pursuing rational goals.*
- *People are motivated to work solely by financial reward.*
- *Human fallibility and emotions, at all levels in the organisation, should be eliminated because they threaten the consistent application of the rule of law and the efficient pursuit of goals.*
- *For this reason, the most appropriate form of job design is achieved through the use of the hierarchical and horizontal division of labour to create narrowly focused jobs encased in tight procedures and rules, which remove discretion, dictate what job-holders do and how they do it, and which allow their work to be closely monitored and controlled by their direct superiors.*

Seen in the context of the early twentieth century, when there appeared to be a substantial questioning of – and challenge to – managerial authority by workers, the Classical approach had many merits: not least in its attempt to replace arbitrary and capricious management with rules and procedures which apply equally to everyone in the organisation.

Similarly, it is important to see this work in terms of what went before. Weber explicitly drew on history to support his views; the historical debts of Taylor and Fayol, though not openly acknowledged in their work, are clearly there. From Smith, through Wedgwood, Boulton and Watt, Babbage and Ure can be traced key elements of the Classical approach: the division of labour, the distrust of human variability, the need for written rules, procedures and records, the need for rational and consistent management and objectives. Parallel to these are key themes that run through other aspects of nineteenth century life: the search for the rational, scientific, universal principles which govern the natural world, the belief in the Protestant work ethic, the emergence of Social Darwinism, the greater democratisation of societies and the gradual reduction of laws favouring one class or group over another.

All these strands coalesced – not always neatly – in the Classical approach, creating (in retrospect) the first real and consistent attempt at a theory, a set of guidelines, for constructing, managing and changing organisations. However, given that it grew out of and was designed to meet particular circumstances, so its appropriateness began to be questioned and criticised as circumstances changed.

Taylor and his adherents have been criticised both for their lack of scientific rigour and their one-dimensional view of human motivation (Burnes, 1989; Kelly, 1982 a and b). Indeed, as Rose (1988) argued, Taylor portrayed human beings as 'greedy robots': indifferent to fatigue, loneliness and pain, driven solely by monetary incentive. For Taylor, material incentives were the only effective incentives to work. For this reason, he opposed everything else in the workplace which, in his opinion, undermined managers' attempts to introduce individual incentive systems, whether it be friendships, group loyalty, trade unions, or whatever. Taylor has also been attacked for over-emphasising the merits of the division of labour. The critics' argument is that the creation of jobs which have little intrinsic satisfaction leads to poor morale, low motivation and alienation. Indeed, such are the forces aligned against Scientific Management that it is difficult to find a facet of it that has not been attacked (Locke, 1982; Littler, 1978).

Fayol has been attacked on three fronts: first, that his principles are mere truisms; second, that they are based on questionable premises; and third, that the principles occur in pairs or clusters of contradictory statements (Massie, 1965; Simon, 1957). In addition, Fayol, like Taylor, can be construed as being against trade unions. Certainly, he believed in the pre-eminence of management and its right to make changes how and when it wanted, so long as these were based on his general principles. He also believed, unlike Taylor, that management and labour were fundamentally in conflict. Therefore, his recommendations were partly aimed at eliminating the conditions in which trade unions can flourish, in the interests of his overall aim of establishing the legitimacy of managers to manage.

Weber's arguments for bureaucracy have also received criticism. For instance, Udy (1959) questioned Weber's assertion that bureaucracies are necessarily rational, while Parsons (1947) suggested that Weber puts forward contradictory arguments for the basis of authority within bureaucracies. Robbins (1987) pointed out that bureaucracy is most frequently attacked for encouraging goal displacement:

- *Rules become ends in themselves rather than means to the ends they were designed to achieve.*

- *Specialisation and differentiation create sub-units with different goals which then become primary to the sub-unit members. Not only does this lead to conflict between sub-units, but the accomplishment of sub-unit goals becomes more important than achieving the organisation's overall goals.*

- *Rules and regulations become interpreted as setting minimum standards of performance rather than identifying unacceptable behaviour. Staff can become apathetic and merely perform the bare minimum of work.*

- *The unthinking and rigid application of standardised rules and procedures can lead to their being applied in inappropriate situations, with dysfunctional consequences.*

Robbins (1987) also pointed out that bureaucracy can alienate both employees and customers/clients. For the former, being treated as mere cogs in a machine leads to a sense of powerlessness and irrelevance. For the latter, being presented with a rigid and faceless organisation, which appears to serve its own ends rather than its customers/clients, can be frustrating and, when the provision of welfare services are involved, heartbreaking. Mullins (1993) also pointed out that bureaucracy is often associated with secrecy and attempts to prevent legitimate public access to vital information on the performance of government and large organisations. Weber's work on bureaucracy has also received criticism because of his lack of attention to informal and social processes, in particular the way that individuals and groups can and do struggle to promote their own interests and goals above those of others in the organisation (Crozier, 1964).

It should also be noted that, though broadly complementary, the approaches of Taylor, Fayol and Weber were developed separately and with different objectives in mind. There are, consequently, tensions and inconsistencies between them. Fayol stresses the importance of *esprit de corps* and individual initiative. Taylor and Weber would find the former irrelevant and the latter dangerous. Likewise, the unchanging rigidity of bureaucracy, as portrayed by Weber, leaves little scope for the continuous search for improvement in methods and productivity advocated by Taylor and Fayol. Taylor's advocacy of functional supervision, which in effect meant a worker being responsible to different supervisors for different aspects of his/her job (some four or five supervisors in total), would have been viewed as a threat to discipline and good order by both Weber and Fayol, who were fierce advocates of unity of command – each worker should receive orders from one superior only.

One of the main criticisms of the Classical approach as a whole is that its view of people is negative. Bennis (1959:263) called the Classical perspective one of 'organisations without people' because it is founded on the belief that people can be reduced to the level of cogs in a machine. It can also be argued that, in any case, it is impossible to remove the element of human variability from the running of organisations and that attempts to do so are counter-productive. Rather than making people work more efficiently in pursuit of organisational goals, it alienates them from their work and makes them resentful of it (Mayo, 1933). This is a point developed by Argyris (1964), who argued that the Classical approach restricts the psychological growth of individuals and causes feelings of failure, frustration and conflict. Instead, he believes that the organisational environment should provide a significant degree of individual responsibility and self-control, commitment to the goals of the organisation, productiveness and work, and an opportunity for individuals to apply their full abilities. These developed as central issues for the proponents of the Human Relations approach, which emerged in the 1930s as a reaction to the 'de-humanised' Classical approach. This, together with Contingency Theory – the third approach to organisations to emerge in the twentieth century – will be discussed in the next chapter.

Chapter 2

DEVELOPMENTS IN ORGANISATION THEORY

From certainty to contingency

INTRODUCTION

The current belief is that organisations need to become smaller and more focused in order to increase their competitiveness (Handy, 1989; Peters, 1994). Certainly, there are many examples where this has been the case: Zeneca splitting from ICI, Hanson Trust floating off many of its American operations, and Volvo disposing of its non-automotive business. Nevertheless, over the last ten years the trend still seems to favour expansion, mainly through acquisitions and mergers, rather than contraction (Burton *et al*, forthcoming). In the car industry, there has been the recent takeover of Rover Group by BMW, and the earlier purchase by General Motors of a substantial interest in SAAB. In the financial field, the Hong Kong & Shanghai Bank purchased Midland Bank, and the Dutch bank, ING, have recently taken over the bankrupt Baring Brothers bank, while in the food and drink sector, Nestlé's acquisition of Rowntree and Guinness' takeover of Louis Vuitton Moet Hennessy spring to mind. The most recent large-scale takeover has been in the pharmaceutical industry, where Glaxo purchased Wellcome. Therefore, those seeking to promote a trend towards smaller organisations will find little to encourage them in the private sector. The public sector appears to offer more fertile ground for their ideas, however.

In the nineteenth century, the public sector in most advanced countries probably employed no more than a few tens of thousands and accounted for only a small percentage of gross national product (GNP). In the UK, for example, the public sector only employed around 16,000 civil servants in 1854. By the early 1990s, in the UK, it employed nearly five million people and accounted for nearly 40 per cent of GNP. Indeed, such is the size of the public sector that the National Health Service in Britain is Europe's largest employer, with almost one million staff and a turnover in excess of £30 billion (HM Treasury, 1992).

As with the private sector, the reasons for the growth of the public sector are many and varied. Probably the single biggest reason is the growth of welfare provision: health, pensions, unemployment insurance, etc. In most countries, these account for the largest proportion of government expenditure, although defence, education and support for industry are also big spenders.

Nevertheless, from the early 1980s onwards, the growth in the size of the public sector began to be reversed. Beginning with the election of the first Thatcher government in the UK in 1979, there has been a general attack on the size and purpose of government. This has led to the privatisation and contracting out of many functions. This tendency took hold in many European countries in the late 1980s, and in the mid-1990s, is finding favour in the USA (Flynn, 1993; Osborne and Gaebler, 1992).

In both the private and public sectors, therefore, there is much talk and, at least in the latter, some evidence of organisations becoming smaller and more focused, though whether this is a temporary fashion or a permanent trend, only time will tell. If smallness does prove to be the shape of things to come, however, the period dealt with in this chapter – the 1920s to 1960s – may well be looked back on as the golden age of organisational growth, when those who ran both public and private sector bodies became convinced of the need for and their ability to run ever-larger organisations. This growth in the size, and spread, of firms and public bodies also saw the further take-up and development of the Classical approach. In the public sector, and also in large private sector concerns, bureaucracy was unquestionably seen as 'the one best way'. The other key element of the Classical approach, Scientific Management, was less well received. In the USA, the death of the irascible Taylor did much to overcome the early resistance to Scientific Management, especially among some trade union leaders. Despite its espousal by Lenin in Russia, however, it met with stiff resistance in Europe. In the 1930s, Scientific Management and a stream-lined version, the Bedeaux system, were rejected by both unions and management in a large number of European countries (Carew, 1987; Rose, 1988).

Therefore, although the Classical school could claim some success, especially in the USA, there was much resistance. The growth of organisation size and complexity, and the resistance to the Classical school (or at least the Tayloristic part of it) merely acted to spur both academics and practitioners to greater efforts to understand the activities of, and provide guidelines for, organisations. This could have led to the development and strengthening of the Classical approach, and clearly this did happen to an extent (see the work of Ralph Davis, 1928, on rational planning). As this chapter will show, however, in the main, what emerged were two new approaches to organisations: the Human Relations approach, which originated in the 1930s, and the Contingency approach, which was developed in the 1960s.

The first half of this chapter describes the Human Relations approach. This approach was a reaction against the mechanistic view of organisations and the pessimistic view of human nature put forward in the Classical approach. It attempted to reintroduce the human element into organisational life, and claim for itself the title of the 'one best way'. In particular, it contended that people have emotional as well as economic needs, and organisations are co-operative systems which comprise informal structures and norms as well as formal ones. This left managers with something of a dilemma – which 'one best way' should they adopt, the Classical or Human Relations one?

As the second half of this chapter will show, it was in response to this dilemma that Contingency Theory developed in the 1960s. Contingency Theory began by questioning and rejecting the idea that there is a 'one best way' for *all* organisations. Instead, it argued for a 'one best way' for *each* organisation. It did not, therefore, reject the Classical approach and the Human Relations approach; instead it maintained that the structures and practices of an organisation are dependent (i.e. contingent) on the circumstances it faces. The main contingencies it proposed were environmental uncertainty and dependence, technology and organisation size. After discussing the merits and drawbacks of the Human Relations approach and Contingency Theory, the chapter concludes that neither appear to be the solution to all known organisational ills as their proponents claim. In particular, it is argued that both fail to reflect and explain the complexities of day-to-day organisational life.

THE HUMAN RELATIONS APPROACH
....

Even while the Classical approach was still struggling to establish itself, the seeds of a new approach to organisational design were already being sown. The origins of what later became known as the Human Relations approach can be traced to studies on work fatigue carried out in Britain during World War One and work in the USA, at the same time, on employee selection, which gave new insights into employee motivation (Burnes, 1989). This work was developed and extended in the 1920s by Myers (1934) in Britain and Mayo (1933) in the USA, providing new perspectives on organisational life. These studies gave substance to a growing suspicion that the Classical view of organisations as being peopled by machines motivated by money was badly flawed. Indeed, in 1915, the United States Congress took a stand against the use of Taylor's techniques in their establishments (although Scientific Management was becoming more accepted in private industry and was beginning to cross national boundaries, not always successfully (Rose, 1988)). Similarly, though the growth of bureaucracy was gathering pace, so too was people's antagonism towards faceless, machine-like organisations where employees and customers alike lost their individuality and became numbers.

In addition, as Davis and Canter (1955) argued, it is necessary to recognise that jobs and work organisation are social inventions put together to suit the specific needs and reflect the culture, ideology and the governing concept or ethos of the time. Therefore, to understand the emergence of the Human Relations movement it is necessary to be aware of the changes taking place in Western society prior to and just after the Second World War.

In the 1930s, in many countries, there was the emergence of a more collectivist ethos than had previously been the case. In the USA, this was brought about by the reaction to the Depression of the 1920s and 1930s. The election of FD Roosevelt and the advent of his 'New Deal' introduced a new element of collective provision and concern into a previously highly individualistic nation. It also heralded the advent of 'Big Government' in the USA. In Europe, this collectivist ethos led to greater social concern; collective provision was led by the Scandinavian countries, and reflected the election of social democratic governments and a general mood of co-operation rather than conflict in industry in these countries. Similar developments also became the cornerstone of the rebuilding of Western Germany after the end of the Second World War. The legacy of the collective effort needed to win the war was also evident in the UK with the construction of the Welfare State.

It was in the USA in the 1930s and 1940s that substantial evidence first emerged in print which challenged the Classical view of organisations and allowed the Human Relations approach to stand alongside, if not quite supersede, it. The main precepts of the Human Relations approach were almost diametrically opposed to those of the Classical approach. In particular, it argued that:

- *People are emotional rather than economic-rational beings. Human needs are far more diverse and complex than the one-dimensional image that Taylor and his supporters conceded. People's emotional and social needs can have more influence on their behaviour at work than financial incentives.*

- *Organisations are co-operative, social systems rather than mechanical ones. People seek to meet their emotional needs through the formation of informal but influential workplace social groups.*

- *Organisations are composed of informal structures, rules and norms as well as formal practices and procedures. These informal rules, patterns of behaviour and communication, norms and friendships are created by people to meet their own emotional needs. Because of this, they can have more influence on individual behaviour and performance, and ultimately on overall organisational performance, than the formal structure and control mechanisms laid down by management.*

For these reasons, organisations can never be the predictable, well-oiled machines envisaged by the Classical approach. Therefore, in most respects, the Human Relations approach represents a distinct break from the ideas of the Classical school. Similarities exist in two important ways, however. The first is their shared belief in organisations as closed, changeless entities. Once organisations have structured themselves in accordance with the correct precepts, then, regardless of external or even internal developments, no further changes are necessary or desirable. This leads on to the second similarity: proponents of both believed they had discovered the 'one best way'; regardless of the type, nature or size of organisation, their precepts were the correct ones.

With that in mind, we can now begin to examine in detail the case for Human Relations. Despite the work of precursors, no one doubts that the Human Relations approach began in earnest with the famous Hawthorne Experiments.

Elton Mayo and the Hawthorne Experiments

The name of Elton Mayo is inextricably linked with the 'Hawthorne Experiments' which took place in the Western Electric Company's Hawthorne Works in Chicago during the 1920s and 1930s. Though Mayo publicised and took credit for masterminding these, the exact role played by Mayo is unclear even to the most rigorous of investigators (Smith, 1987). Did Mayo design and implement the experiments himself? What was the role of his colleagues at Harvard? How frequently did he visit the Hawthorne Works? The questions are now unanswerable; what is clear is that his writings on the Hawthorne Experiments and his later work have given Mayo the reputation, perhaps undeserved, of being the dominant figure in the Human Relations movement (Rose, 1988). Having stated the difficulty in separating out the myth from the man, we should not let that undermine the significance of Hawthorne's work or what we know of Mayo's and his colleagues' contribution, even if we cannot clearly identify who did what.

The Hawthorne programme was originally devised by Western Electric's own industrial engineers in the 1920s to examine the effects of various levels of lighting on workers' productivity. The engineers established control and experimental groups; the latter were subject to different levels of illumination as they carried out their work while the lighting of the control group was left unchanged. At the outset this looked like a standard Scientific Management experiment in the mould of Taylor and the Gilbreths. What the engineers were expecting was a set of unambiguous results which would allow them to establish the 'one best' level of illumination. This did not happen and, instead, data began to emerge which challenged the very basis of Scientific Management.

The engineers had expected the performance of the experimental group to vary with increases and decreases in illumination and for an optimum level to be established, but as the illumination was varied, so output continued to increase. Indeed, output only decreased in the experimental group when the lighting became so dim that it was difficult to see. More puzzling still, output in the control group, where no changes were made, also increased. It was in 1927 that Western Electric called in Mayo and his colleagues to investigate these apparently contradictory findings. In the years which followed, a series of experiments were carried out in which groups of workers were subjected to changes in hours, payment systems and rest periods. The subsequent changes in output, and the reasons for these, undermined many of the assumptions regarding organisations and human behaviour previously perceived as sacrosanct (Mayo 1933; Roethlisberger and Dickson, 1938).

The experiments were monitored continuously; from this work, Mayo and his colleagues concluded that it was not the changes in working conditions which affected output, but the fact that those workers involved had been singled out for special attention. This acted to increase their morale and make them want to perform better. It was the very fact that they were being studied which produced the increased performance; this later became known as the 'Hawthorne Effect'. This accounted for the improved performance by the original control group, even with no changes to the lighting in their area: they also felt 'special' because they were being studied. These findings led Mayo and his group to move the focus of their work away from the reaction of individual workers to changes in their working conditions. Instead, they began to investigate the role and behaviour of the 'informal' groups that workers themselves established, and the norms and attitudes of these groups.

As a result of this work, Mayo and his colleagues put forward two major propositions which came to form the core of the Human Relations approach. The first related to the importance of informal groups within the formal structure of organisations. The Western Electric studies demonstrated the need to see the work process as a collective, co-operative activity as opposed to an individual, isolated one. The studies showed in particular the important effect that the informal, primary work group has on performance. These groups tend to develop their own norms, values and attitudes which enable them to exert strong social, peer-group pressure on individuals within the group to conform to group norms, whether this be in relation to the pace of work or attitudes towards other groups and supervisors. Taylor had also noted the pressure that groups of workers could exert over their members to make them conform; he believed, however, that this was abnormal behaviour which could be remedied by tight managerial control. What the Western Electric studies demonstrated was that far from being abnormal, such behaviour was perfectly normal.

The second proposition put forward by Mayo and his colleagues was that humans have a deep need for recognition, security and belonging. Rather than being purely economic beings, the Hawthorne Experiments demonstrated that workers' performance and attitudes could be influenced more by their need for recognition and security and, also, by the feeling of belonging engendered by informal groups. This latter point in particular reflected, in Mayo's view, a deep-seated desire by humans as social beings for intimacy, consistency and predictability. Where these social certainties were lacking, workers would deliberately seek to manufacture them by creating their own informal work groups. Therefore, rather than seeking to eradicate or undermine the workings of these informal groups, as Taylor had advocated, the Western Electric studies showed that management needed to gain the collaboration and co-operation of such groups if they were to get the best performance from workers.

It is generally agreed (Mullins, 1989; Rose, 1988) that the Western Electric studies had a dramatic effect on management and organisation theory. The studies ushered in an era where the Economic Man of the Classical approach was supplanted by Social Man. It was no longer possible for managers to ignore the effects of organisational structures and job design on work groups, employee attitudes and management–worker relations. The crucial issue became one of social relationships – Human Relations – in the workplace. In future, the focus of good management practice would shift to the importance of leadership and communication in order to win over employees. As the 1930s and 1940s progressed, other work began to emerge which both substantiated and broadened those findings.

Chester Barnard and co-operative systems

Barnard was an executive with American Telephone and Telegraph, whose book *The Functions of the Executive* (1938) has a comparable place in the Human Relations literature to that of Fayol's work in the literature of the Classical school. In this work, Barnard put forward the idea of organisations as co-operative systems. In so doing, this gave him a double claim to fame: not only did he draw attention to the co-operative nature of organisational life, but he was also one of the first to treat organisations as systems rather than machines. He was in frequent touch with Mayo and his colleagues at Harvard, and closely followed their work at Western Electric. Therefore, although *The Functions of the Executive* was a personal and idiosyncratic work, reflecting Barnard's own distinct views and opinions, it was far from being bereft of academic substance. Indeed, his book was the first systematic attempt in English (Weber's work on bureaucracy was still not translated into English at this time) to outline a theory of organisations as a whole. In this respect, Barnard can claim both to have made a substantial contribution to the Human Relations approach and to have laid the groundwork for subsequent writers such as Selznick and Simon (Robbins, 1987; Scott, 1987).

An organisation is a co-operative system, he argued, because without the willingness of its members to make contributions to and to pursue its goals, it cannot operate effectively. Like others that espoused the Human Relations approach, he believed co-operation could not be achieved solely by monetary incentives. Instead, he advocated a mixture of monetary and non-monetary inducements. Similarly, co-operation by itself would not be effective unless an organisation also possessed a common purpose: clear and realistic goals and objectives which the organisation's members could understand, relate to and pursue. Establishing this common purpose, in Barnard's opinion, had to be the responsibility of those at the top of the organisation, but achieving it required the co-operation of those at the bottom, and all levels in between. This leads to another of Barnard's assertions: the flow of authority is not from the top down but from the bottom up. He defined authority not as a property of management but as a response by subordinates to superiors. If subordinates did not respond willingly and appropriately, then no authority existed. In this example, as in many others, he both reflected the influence of and supported the findings of the Western Electric studies, which drew attention to the ability of workers through social groupings to facilitate or frustrate the will of management.

In order to avoid a negative response from workers, Barnard advocated systematic and purposeful communication. Indeed, he portrayed the organisation as a purposeful, co-ordinated system of communications linking all participants in a manner which not only encouraged the pursuit of the organisation's common purpose, but also legitimated the premises on which it was based. However, he argued that this does not happen automatically or accidentally; it is the product of effective leadership. This is why Barnard stressed the key role of the executive in leading the organisation by facilitating communication and motivating subordinates to high levels of performance; such developments could only come from the top.

Given the emphasis placed by Barnard on the setting and pursuit of clear object-ives, and in his approach in general, there is a degree of overlap with the work of the Classical school. What significantly distinguishes him from them, however, is his insistence on the non-rational, informal, interpersonal, and indeed moral basis of organisational life.

Barnard rejected the idea of material incentives being the only incentives to make people work purposefully. Indeed, he saw them as being 'weak incentives' which needed to be supported by other psychological and sociological motivators if organi-isations were to be successful in achieving their common purpose. In so challenging the effectiveness of material incentives, he was to receive substantial support a few years later from a more academic source.

Abraham Maslow's hierarchy of needs

Abraham Maslow, an American psychologist, was one of the first to differentiate between and classify different types of human need. For Taylor and his adherents, there was only one form of need: material/monetary need. Mayo *et al* and Barnard took a different view; they drew a distinction between material and non-material needs, but made no distinction within these two categories. Maslow (1943) ident-ified five distinct forms of human need which he placed in a hierarchical order. He argued that, beginning at the lowest level, a person had to satisfy substantially the needs at one level before he or she could move up the hierarchy and concentrate on 'higher order' needs.

In ascending order, the five levels in Maslow's Hierarchy of Needs are:

● *Physiological needs – hunger, thirst, sleep, etc; only when these basic needs have been satisfied do other needs begin to emerge.*

● *Safety needs – the desire for security and protection against danger.*

● *Social needs – the need to belong, to gain love and affection; to be in the company of others, especially friends.*

● *Esteem needs – these reflect a person's desire to be respected – esteemed – for their achievements.*

● *Self-Actualisation needs – self-actualisation is the need to achieve one's full potential. According to Maslow, this will vary from person to person and, indeed, may differ over time, as a person reaches a level of potential previously considered unattainable and so goes on to strive for new heights. For these reasons, self-actualisation is a continuously evolving process throughout a person's lifetime.*

Though not designed specifically for organisational analysis, but rather in the context of life in general, it can be seen why Maslow's work was so readily accepted by proponents of the Human Relations approach. For them, it explained why in some situations Tayloristic incentives were effective, while in other situations, such as the Hawthorne Experiments, other factors proved more important.

Applying Maslow's hierarchy of needs to human behaviour in organisations, it can be seen that people will first of all be motivated by the desire to satisfy physiological needs through monetary rewards. Once those have been substantially satisfied, however, workers will seek to satisfy – be motivated by – their safety needs, such as job security and welfare benefits. In a similar fashion, once safety needs are substantially met, these will fade into the background and social needs will come to the fore; people will want to be accepted as part of a group, to share common intents and aspirations with the group, to experience the bonds of friendship and loyalty. Clearly, these social needs played an important role in the Hawthorne Experiments, as did esteem needs. After social and esteem needs are substantially met, finally self-actualisation needs come to the fore. However, as mentioned above, the need for self-actualisation never wanes but tends to act as a continuing spur to further achievements.

Clearly, Maslow's work cannot be transferred fully into the organisational setting, given that most jobs do not allow individuals to approach, let alone attain, self-actualisation. Even very basic physiological needs are beyond the reach of many millions of people in the world. Nevertheless, in distinguishing as he does between types of intrinsic (non-material) and extrinsic (material) motivators, and arguing that, at any one time, it is the unmet needs which act as positive motivators, Maslow has had an enormous impact on job design and research (*see* Child, 1984; Smith *et al* 1982). The influence of Maslow's theory of needs can be seen in the work of other exponents of Human Relations, especially Douglas McGregor.

Douglas McGregor and Theory X – Theory Y

One of the most widely cited Human Relations writers is Douglas McGregor. He developed his views from his personal experience as a manager, consultant and academic rather than from empirical research.

McGregor (1960) argued that there are basically two commonly held views of human nature: a negative view – Theory X; and a positive view – Theory Y. He believed that managers' behaviour towards their subordinates was based upon one or other of these views, both of which consist of a certain grouping of assumptions about human behaviour.

Theory X consists of the following assumptions:

- *The average person dislikes work and will avoid it wherever possible.*
- *Employees must be coerced, controlled or threatened with punishment if they are to perform as required.*
- *Most people try to avoid responsibility and will seek formal direction whenever possible.*
- *Workers place security above other factors relating to employment and will display little ambition.*

Theory Y, on the other hand, comprises a group of assumptions which gives a much more positive view of human nature:

- *Most people can view work as being as natural as rest or play.*
- *Workers are capable of exercising self-direction and self-control.*
- *The average person will accept and even seek responsibility if they are committed to the objectives being pursued.*
- *Ingenuity, imagination, creativity and the ability to make good decisions are widely dispersed throughout the population and are not peculiar to managers.*

Theory X and Theory Y are not statements about what people are actually like, but rather the general assumptions that managers, and the rest of us, hold about what people are like. The fact that such views may not have a base in reality is irrelevant if managers act as though they are true. Managers who adhere to Theory X will use a combination of stick and carrot methods to control their subordinates, and will construct organisations that restrict the individual's ability to exercise skill, discretion and control over their work. Those managers who adhere to Theory Y will adopt a more open and flexible style of management. They will create jobs that encourage workers to contribute towards organisational goals, allow them to exercise skill and responsibility, and where the emphasis will be on non-material incentives.

Obviously, Theory X is akin to the Classical view of human nature and organisational design, whereas Theory Y falls more in the Human Relations tradition. Though McGregor tended to pose his views in neutral terms, it is clear that he favoured Theory Y; he argued, however, that there was nothing deterministic about which approach to adopt. The choice lies with managers. Those who adopt Theory X will create a situation where workers are only able and willing to pursue material needs (as Maslow observed). Such workers will be neither prepared nor in a position to contribute to the wider aims and objectives of the organisation which employs them. Managers who follow Theory Y precepts are likely to receive an entirely different response from their employees; workers will identify more clearly with the general interests of the organisation and be more able and more willing to contribute to their achievement.

Though stressing the element of choice, McGregor, along with other Human Relations adherents, believed that organisations were moving, and should move, more in the direction of Theory Y.

Warren Bennis and 'the death of bureaucracy'

By the 1950s and 1960s, the Human Relations approach and the values it espoused were in the ascendancy. One clear sign of this was the widely held view in the 1960s that bureaucracy was dying and being replaced by more flexible, people-centred organisations which allowed and encouraged personal growth and development.

Warren Bennis (1966) is credited with coining the phrase and making the case for 'the death of bureaucracy'. Bennis argued that every age develops an organisational form appropriate to its time. Bureaucracy was, in his view, appropriate for the first two-thirds of the twentieth century but not beyond that. He believed that bureaucracy emerged because its order, precision and impersonal nature was the correct antidote for the personal subjugation, cruelty, nepotism and capriciousness which passed for management during the Industrial Revolution.

Bureaucracy, he stated, emerged as a creative and wholesome response to the needs and values of the Victorian Age. Up to this point, there is little to distinguish Bennis from Weber; however, he then went on to argue that the Victorian Age, and its needs, were past and that new conditions were emerging to which bureaucracy was no longer suited.

These conditions were:

- *Rapid and unexpected change. Bureaucracy's strength lies in its ability to manage efficiently the routine and predictable; but its pre-programmed rules and inflexibility make it unsuitable for the rapidly changing modern world.*

- *Growth in size. As organisations become larger, then bureaucratic structures become more complex and unwieldy, and less efficient.*

- *Increasing diversity. Rapid growth, quick change and an increase in specialisation create the need for people with diverse and highly specialised skills; these specialists cannot easily or effectively be fitted within the standardised, pyramid structure of bureaucratic organisations.*

- *Change in managerial behaviour. The increasing adoption of the Human Relations approach by managers challenges the simplistic view of human nature put forward by the Classical school, which underpins bureaucracy. If coercion and threats administered in a depersonalised, mechanistic fashion are counter-productive as a way of controlling people in organisations, then the case for bureaucracy is severely diminished.*

For Bennis and others such as Bell (1974) and Toffler (1970), bureaucracy was rightly dying and being replaced by more diverse, flexible structures which could cope with the needs of the modern world.

Job Design: operationalising Human Relations

Though intellectually strong, the Human Relations school remained operationally weak up to the 1950s and 1960s because, unlike the Classical school, it lacked a clear set of operational definitions and guidelines which allowed organisations to understand and implement it in the same way that they could with Scientific Management or bureaucracy. The advent of the Job Design movement in both the USA and Europe rectified this.

In the last thirty years, Job Design, or work humanisation as it has also been called, has become a powerful technique for rolling back the worst excesses of the

Classical school, especially in the area of manual work, where Scientific Management and its clones have had such an impact. It was in America in the 1950s that Davis and Canter (1955), influenced by the work of the Human Relations school, questioned the Tayloristic basis of job design and work organisation. They suggested that it would be possible to design jobs which satisfied not only human needs but also organisational ones as well. They argued that increased job satisfaction and increased performance went hand in hand. Since then many other writers, especially in Europe, have contributed to the development of Job Design theory (Davis *et al*, 1955; Guest, 1957; Hackman and Oldham, 1980; Likert, 1961; Trist *et al*, 1963; Warr, 1987).

Job Design is a direct attack on the precepts of the Classical approach. Whereas Taylorist tradition seeks to fit people to rigidly defined and controlled jobs, Job Design theorists argue that jobs can and should be fitted to human needs. The basic tenets of Job Design are relatively straightforward and follow on from the work of the proponents of the Human Relations approach, especially Maslow. It is argued that the Classical approach to jobs, with its emphasis on fragmenting jobs and reducing workers' autonomy and discretion, is counter-productive to both individual fulfilment and organisational performance. This is because boring, monotonous and meaningless jobs lead to poor mental health and feelings of dissatisfaction. In turn, this can result in lack of motivation, absenteeism, labour turnover and even industrial unrest.

The solution to these problems follows from the analysis. If Tayloristic trends in job design are counter-productive, then they should be reversed and 'variety, task completeness and, above all, autonomy' should be built into jobs (Wall *et al*, 1984:15). Such a move would increase workers' mental health and job satisfaction, bringing in turn increased motivation and performance. Just as Taylor believed his approach would benefit both workers and management, so too do the proponents of Job Design; the difference is that the benefit to the worker is personal fulfilment rather than increased wages, though in both systems the benefit to management is increased productivity (Friedman, 1961; Hackman and Lawler, 1971; Herzberg *et al*, 1959; Kelly, 1982 a and b).

In practice, there are three main variants of Job Design:

- *Job enlargement – which concentrates on increasing work variety by combining previously fragmented tasks together, or by rotating people between different types of work (Guest, 1957).*

- *Job enrichment – concentrates on increasing workers' control over what they do by rearranging work so that some of the responsibilities previously borne by supervisors and support staff are given to individuals or, more often, semi-autonomous work groups (Herzberg, 1968).*

- *Socio-technical systems theory – a variant on Job Design involving a shift of focus from the individual job to the organisation as a whole. Socio-technical systems theory sees organisations as being composed of interdependent social and technical systems. The theory argues that there is little point in*

> *reorganising the social system in isolation from the technology being used,*
> *and that performance is dependent on the degree of fit between the two.*
> *This view sees technology as acting as a limitation on the scope for*
> *redesigning individual jobs (Davis, 1979; Trist et al, 1963).*

Since the 1950s, most European countries have initiated some form of officially-sponsored 'Work Humanisation' programme. Not surprisingly, Norway and Sweden with their traditions of industrial co-operation and democracy have led the way in terms of financial and legal backing, but other countries, notably what was West Germany, have also initiated government-financed programmes. Some of the Job Design initiatives in these countries were inspired by Norwegian researchers like Einar Thorsrud, who propagated the concept of semi-autonomous work groups. Others derived from the work on the socio-technical systems approach carried out by the Tavistock Institute in London (Auer and Riegler, 1990). In the UK, however, despite the presence of the Tavistock Institute and the establishment of the Work Research Unit in 1974, official backing has been noticeably lukewarm. Indeed, even the modest expenditure devoted to the Work Research Unit was cut back considerably in the 1980s, and the unit has now been disbanded. The UK government now shares the American view that 'quality of working life' programmes are the purview of individual organisations rather than something to be promoted by government. Despite this, there can be little doubt that Job Design precepts have permeated Western society on a significant scale, and provide the main operational alternative to the Classical approach (Burnes, 1989).

The Human Relations approach: summary and criticisms

Though many tend to associate the Human Relations movement exclusively with the work of Mayo, the above shows that it is a much more diverse school of thought. Indeed, some have argued that to call it a school owes more to academic convenience than to reality (Rose, 1988). Nevertheless, there are continuing and overlapping themes in the work of the writers cited above which strongly bond them together. The first, and most obvious, is their almost total rejection of the Classical movement's mechanistic-rational approach towards people and organisation structures. The second and more fundamental feature is that while approaching the issues involved from different perspectives and emphasising separate aspects, they create an organisational model which possesses both coherence and plausibility.

The Human Relations model stresses three core elements:

- *leadership and communication;*
- *intrinsic job motivation (as well as extrinsic rewards);*
- *organisation structures and practices which facilitate flexibility and involvement.*

These elements are underpinned by two central propositions:

- *Organisations are complex social systems and not mechanical contrivances.* Therefore, they cannot effectively be controlled by close supervision, rigid rules and purely economic incentives.

- *Human beings have emotional as well as economic needs.* Organisation and job structures need to be designed in such a way as to enable workers to meet both their material and non-material needs. Only in this way will workers perform efficiently and effectively in the best interests of the organisation.

It is not difficult to see why the Human Relations approach proved popular. In a period when many people were becoming increasingly worried about the growth of impersonal bureaucracies, it provided an attractive alternative. It is an approach which stresses that human beings are not mere cogs in a machine but that they have emotional needs: humans want to 'belong', achieve recognition, and develop and fulfil their potential. As mentioned earlier, the Depression of the 1930s and World War Two and its aftermath created, in the USA and Europe, a greater sense of collectivism and community than had hitherto been the case; another reason why the Human Relations doctrine found such a ready audience. Furthermore, it offers implicitly an approach to change management which has a surprisingly modern ring to it. The stress on organisations having clear objectives, effective communication systems and proactive leadership, coupled with the need to obtain the willing cooperation of employees, are central to many modern approaches to change management.

Despite its attractiveness and plausibility, a substantial and often vitriolic body of opinion came to be ranged against the Human Relations approach in the 1950s and 1960s (Rose, 1988). Economists rejected the argument that non-material incentives have a potentially stronger motivating influence than material incentives. The emphasis placed by the proponents of Human Relations on people's needs for 'togetherness' and 'belonging' was seen by some as a denial of individualism. Others thought that it belittled workers and portrayed them as irrational beings who, given the chance, would cling to management as a baby clings to its mother. It was also attacked from both a management and a trade union viewpoint. Some of the former felt that its supposedly powerful manipulative techniques were either useless or inoperable; while representatives of the latter saw Human Relations as a vehicle for manipulating labour, and undermining – or attempting to eliminate – trade unions. Sociologists criticised it for attempting a sociological analysis of organisations without taking into account the larger society within which each organisation exists (Kerr and Fisher, 1957; Landsberger, 1958; Rose, 1988; Whyte, 1960).

Many of the criticisms were clearly directed at the work of Mayo and his colleagues, including inconsistencies between them. Landsberger (1958), for example, was one of the first to point out the difference between Mayo's (1933) interpretations of the Hawthorne Experiments and his colleagues', Roethlisberger and Dickson, (1938) account . However, by no means were all the criticisms levelled at Mayo and his colleagues. Maslow's work, a key theoretical cornerstone of the

Human Relations approach, was found to lack empirical substance when researchers attempted to validate it (Lawler and Suttle, 1972; Hall and Nougaim, 1968). Similarly, Bennis' views were attacked. The Aston Studies in the 1960s (Pugh *et al* 1969 a and b) showed that bureaucracy was growing rather than declining. Miewald (1970) also argued that Bennis did not understand the nature of bureaucracy; in his view, far from being rigid, it could and did adapt to changing and dynamic environments. Kelly (1982b) also attacked the proposition that increased job satisfaction leads to increased performance.

There is one further criticism of the Human Relations approach, one which it shares with the Classical approach: it claims for itself the title of the 'one best way'. Yet, the question was posed, how can any approach claim that there is only one method of structuring and managing organisations, and that it holds good for all organisations and for all time? Indeed, the seed of this criticism can be found in Bennis' (1966) work, where he argued that organisations in the last third of the twentieth century would experience rapid and unexpected change, continue to increase in size – with the problems of complexity which this brings – and become more diverse and specialised. Clearly, while not explicitly advocating it, Bennis was making the case for an approach to organisations which recognised not only that they face different situations but also that these are not stable over time. Similarly, Trist *et al*'s (1963) argument regarding the need to fit social systems to technical ones can also be seen as making a case for a situationalist approach to job design. Indeed, the most telling argument against the 'one best way' approach is that presented by Davis and Canter (1955), mentioned earlier. If jobs and work organisation are social inventions designed to meet the needs of societies and organisations at particular points in time, then there can never be a one best way for all organisations and for all times. What is needed, instead, is an approach which links approaches to work design to the particular context to which they are best suited. In the 1960s and 1970s such an approach emerged.

THE CONTINGENCY THEORY APPROACH

....

Contingency Theory emerged in the 1960s out of a number of now classic studies of organisation structure and management (*see* Child, 1984; Mullins, 1989; Scott, 1987). Since the 1970s, it has proved – as a theory at least – to be more influential than either the Classical or Human Relations approach. In essence, Contingency Theory is a rejection of the 'one best way' approach previously sought by managers and propounded by academics. In its place is substituted the view that the structure and operation of an organisation is dependent ('contingent') on the situational variables it faces – the main ones being environment, technology and size (Burnes, 1989). It follows from this that no two organisations will face exactly the same contingencies; therefore, as their situations are different, so too should their structures and operations be different. Consequently the 'one best way' for *all* organisations is replaced by the 'one best way' for *each* organisation.

As Scott (1987:23) pointed out, one of the clear distinctions between Contingency Theory and its predecessors is that:

The previous definitions tend to view the organisation as a closed system, separate from its environment and comprising a set of stable and easily identified participants. However, organisations are not closed systems, sealed off from their environments but are open to and dependent on flows of personnel and resources from outside.

As Robbins (1987) noted, there is wide agreement that the systems approach offers important insights into the working of an organisation. Systems theory is not new: it has been used in the natural and physical sciences for years. Its application to business organisation, however, only really emerged in the 1960s. The systems approach views the organisation both as a whole, and as part of a larger environment. The idea is that any part of an organisation's activities affects all other parts. Organisations, rather than being closed (as previous theories assumed), are viewed as open systems operating within a wider environment and having multiple channels of interaction (Mullins, 1993). Therefore, organisations are not in complete control of their own fate; they can be, and often are, affected by the environment in which they operate, and this can and does vary from organisation to organisation.

One of the earliest writers to lay the groundwork for Contingency theorists was Herbert Simon. Writing in the 1940s (Simon, 1957), he criticised existing approaches as providing managers with nothing more than proverbs or lists of 'good practice' based on scant ideas, many of which contradicted each other. He argued that organisation theory needed to go beyond superficial and over-simplified precepts, and instead study the conditions under which competing principles could be applied.

Nevertheless, it was not until the 1960s that a considered approach emerged, which broke with the Classical and Human Relations movements' attempts to establish a universal approach suitable to all organisations. The former had concentrated on the formal structure and technical requirements of organisations, and had attempted to establish sets of general principles. The latter, the Human Relations movement, focused on the informal aspects of organisations and the psychological and social needs of their employees. As with the Classical approach, this produced lists of good practice and desired objectives, but lacked precise guidance on how these should be applied.

Contingency theorists adopted a different perspective, based on the premise that organisations are open systems whose internal operation and effectiveness is dependent upon the particular situational variables they face at any one time, and that these vary from organisation to organisation. This is consistent with evidence that not all organisations – or even all successful ones – have the same structure, and that even within organisations, different structural forms can be observed (Mintzberg, 1979). Though many situational variables, such as the age of the organisation and its history, have been put forward as influential in determining structure, it is generally agreed that the three most important contingencies are:

● *Environmental uncertainty and dependence.* It is argued that the management of any organisation is undertaken in circumstances of uncertainty and dependence, both of which change over time. Uncertainty arises because of our inability ever to understand and control events fully, especially the actions of others, whether outside or inside an organisation. Because of this, forecasting is an inexact and hazardous enterprise. Similarly, the dependence of management upon the goodwill and support of others, whether they be internal or external groupings, makes an organisation vulnerable, and may in some circumstances even threaten its very existence. Levels of uncertainty and dependence will vary, but can never be totally eliminated, and must therefore be taken into account – treated as a contingency – when designing organisational structures and procedures (Burns and Stalker, 1961; Child, 1984; Lawrence and Lorsch, 1967; Pugh, 1984; Robbins, 1987; Thompson, 1967).

● *Technology.* The argument for technology being a key variable follows similar lines to that of environment. Organisations creating and providing different products and services use different technologies. Indeed, even those producing similar products may use differing techniques. Given that these technologies can vary from the large and expensive, such as a car assembly line, to the relatively small and cheap, such as a personal computer, the form of organisation necessary to ensure their efficient operation will also vary. If so, there is a need to treat technology as a contingent variable when structuring organisations. However, there are distinct variants of the case for technology, which reflect the different definitions of technology that theorists and researchers have employed. The two best developed approaches are found in Woodward's (1965 and 1970) studies of 'operations technology' and Perrow's (1967 and 1970) analysis of 'materials technology'. The former refer to the equipping and sequencing of activities in an organisation's work flow, while the latter refer to the characteristics of the physical and informational materials used. Woodward's work tends to relate more to manufacturing organisations, whereas Perrow's is more generally applicable (Hickson et al, 1969; Thompson, 1967; Zwerman, 1970).

● *Size.* Some would argue that this is not just a key variable but the key variable. The case for size being a significant variable when designing organisations has a long antecedence within organisation theory, being first cited by Weber in the early part of this century when making the case for bureaucracy (Weber, 1947). The basic case is quite straightforward. It is argued that the structure and practices necessary for the efficient and effective operations of small organisations are not suitable for larger ones. For small organisations, centralised and personalised forms of control are claimed to be appropriate, but as organisations grow in size, more decentralised and impersonal structures and practices become more relevant (Blau, 1970; Mullins, 1989; Pugh et al, 1969 a and b; Scott, 1987).

The main figures in developing and establishing Contingency Theory were academics in Britain and the USA, among whom the pioneers were Burns and Stalker.

Tom Burns and Graham Stalker and the importance of environment

The first major study to establish a relationship between organisations' environment and their structure was carried out by Burns and Stalker (1961) in Britain. They examined 20 firms in a variety of industries in order to assess how their structures responded to the environment in which they operated. Their findings were to have a major impact on organisation theory, and provide concrete evidence for rejecting a universal, 'one best way', approach to organisational structure and practice. They identified five different types of environment, based upon the level of uncertainty that was present, ranging from 'stable' to 'least predictable'. They also identified two basic or ideal forms of structure: 'Mechanistic' and 'Organic'. Their data showed that mechanistic structures were more effective in stable environments, while organic ones were better suited to less stable, less predictable environments.

The mechanistic structure, which is akin to the Classical approach, is characterised by:

- *the specialisation of tasks;*
- *closely defined duties, responsibilities and technical methods;*
- *a clear hierarchical structure with insistence on loyalty to the organisation and obedience to superiors.*

In contrast, the organic form, which has some resemblance to the Human Relations approach, is characterised by:

- *much greater flexibility;*
- *adjustment and continual redefinition of tasks;*
- *a network structure of control, authority and communication;*
- *lateral consultation based on information and advice rather than instructions and decisions;*
- *commitment to the work group and its tasks;*
- *importance and prestige being determined by an individual's contribution to the tasks of their work group rather than their position in the hierarchy.*

As can be seen, Burns and Stalker neither reject nor accept what went before. Instead, they argued that both the Classical approach and the Human Relations approach can be appropriate, but that this depends on the nature of the environment in which the organisation is operating. In this respect, they not only built on the past rather than rejecting it, but also restored responsibility to managers. Instead of being called on to adopt blindly the orthodoxy with regard to structure, managers would in future have to assess their organisation and its needs, and then adopt the structure and practices suitable to its situation (Child, 1984; Mullins, 1989; Scott, 1987).

Paul Lawrence and Jay Lorsch and the case for environment continued

Burns and Stalker's findings on the relationship between organisational environment and structure were examined and developed by a number of researchers in Europe and the USA. One of the most significant pieces of work was that carried out by Lawrence and Lorsch (1967) in the USA. Their work went beyond that of Burns and Stalker, in that they were interested not only in the relationship between environment and a company's overall structure, but also how individual departments within companies responded to, and organised themselves to cope with, aspects of the external environment which were of particular significance to them. They undertook a study of six firms in the plastics industry, followed by a further study of two firms in the container industry and two in the consumer foods industry. The structure of each of the firms was analysed in terms of its degree of 'differentiation' and 'integration'.

Differentiation refers to the degree to which managers and staff in their own functional departments see themselves as separate and have distinct practices, procedures and structures from others in the organisation. Integration refers to the level and form of collaboration that is necessary between departments in order to achieve their individual objectives within the environment in which the firm operates. Therefore, differentiation is the degree to which departments are distinct from each other, while integration refers to the degree to which they have common structures, procedures, practices and objectives at the operational level. Generally, the greater the interdependence among departments, the more integration is needed to co-ordinate their efforts in the best interests of the organisation as a whole; however, this may not always be easy to achieve. In a rapidly-changing environment, the conditions faced by individual departments may differ greatly, and a high degree of differentiation may be necessary. In such a situation, the need for integration is also likely to be great, but the diversity and volatility of the environment are likely to make this difficult to achieve (Cummings and Huse, 1989).

In their study of the plastics industry, Lawrence and Lorsch (1967) found clear differentiation between key departments such as research, production and sales. Research departments were more concerned with long-term issues and were under pressure to produce new ideas and innovations. These departments, in Burns and Stalker's terminology, tended to adopt an Organic form of structure. Production departments on the other hand were, for obvious reasons, concerned with short-term performance targets relating to output, costs, quality and delivery. Such departments tended to operate in a fairly stable environment and had Mechanistic structures. Sales departments tended to fall in between research and production in terms of environment and structure. They operated in a moderately stable environment and were concerned more with getting production to meet deliveries than with long-term issues.

Whilst highlighting the degree of differentiation between key departments, the study also found that the degree of integration was critical to a firm's overall performance. Indeed, the two most successful firms in their sample were not only amongst the most highly differentiated, but also had the highest degree of integration. These findings were confirmed by their studies of the container and consumer foods industries, which showed that differentiation and integration in successful companies vary with the demands of the environment in which they operate. The more diverse and dynamic the environment, the more the successful organisation will be differentiated and highly integrated. In a more stable environment, the pressure for differentiation is less, but the need for integration remains. Therefore, Lawrence and Lorsch found that the most effective organisations had an appropriate fit between the design and co-ordination of departments and the amount of environmental uncertainty they faced. The most successful firms, however, were the ones which, while operating in an environment that required a high level of differentiation, also managed to achieve a high level of integration.

Clearly, in a situation where departments have dissimilar structures, practices and procedures, achieving integration is not easy or conflict-free. Indeed, in such situations, organisational politics can be rife. Lawrence and Lorsch found that the effective firms avoided such a situation by openly confronting conflict, and by working problems through in the context of the overall needs of the organisation. In addition, in firms which dealt successfully with conflict, the success of those responsible for achieving integration was based mainly on their knowledge and competence rather than their formal position. This was because their colleagues in the different departments respected and responded to their perceived understanding of the issues involved. It follows that to achieve high levels of integration and differentiation, an organisation cannot rely solely on the formal managerial hierarchy. This must be supplemented with liaison positions, task forces and teams, and other integrating mechanisms.

As with Burns and Stalker, Lawrence and Lorsch did not reject the Classical and Human Relations approaches *per se*, but instead saw them as alternative options, depending on the environment in which an organisation operated. In looking at the internal operations of organisations in this way, Lawrence and Lorsch raised the issue of dependence as well as uncertainty. This was a subject that James Thompson tackled in greater depth.

James Thompson and environmental uncertainty and dependence

Thompson's (1967) influential work took the environmental perspective forward in three important ways. The first was to argue that although organisations are not rational entities, they strive to be so because it is in the interests of those who design and manage the organisation that its work be carried out as effectively and efficiently as possible. In order to achieve this, organisations attempt to insulate their productive core from the uncertainty of the environment. However, it is not possible to seal off all, or perhaps even any, parts of an organisation, given that it must be open to and interact with its environment if it is to secure resources and sell its products. This leads on to Thompson's second major contribution: different levels of an organisation may exhibit, and need, different structures and operate on a more rational or less rational basis. Thompson's third contribution was to recognise that organisational effectiveness was contingent not only on the level of external environmental uncertainty, but also on the degree of internal dependence present. This echoes Lawrence and Lorsch's argument for integration and differentiation; but Thompson made this point much more explicitly and related it to different structural forms. He formulated a three-type classification in relation to internal dependence:

- *Pooled interdependence. This is where each part of an organisation operates in a relatively autonomous manner, but by fulfilling their individual purposes they enable the organisation as a whole to function effectively.*

- *Sequential interdependence. This is where overall effectiveness requires direct interaction between an organisation's separate parts.*

- *Reciprocal interdependence. This is where the outputs from one part of an organisation constitute the inputs for other parts of the system.*

Thompson went on to argue that the type of interdependence could be related to the degree of complexity present: simple organisations rely on pooled interdependence; more complex organisations demonstrate both pooled and sequential interdependence; and in the most complex organisations, all three forms of interdependence may be present. Thompson envisaged that each form of interdependence would require distinct methods for co-ordinating activities. Pooled interdependence would be characterised by standardisation through the use of rules and procedures. Sequential interdependence would require the use of detailed plans and written agreements, while reciprocal interdependence would achieve co-ordination by means of personal contact and informal agreements between members of those parts of the organisation involved.

Therefore, in a nutshell, Thompson's main arguments are as follows:

- *Different sections of an organisation will be characterised by varying levels of complexity, rationality and formalisation, depending on the extent to which managers can shield them from the level of uncertainty present in the environment.*

- *The higher both the overall level of uncertainty and that faced by each area of an organisation, the greater will be the dependence of one area on another.*

- *As this interdependence increases, co-ordination through standardised procedures and planning mechanisms will become less effective and the need for more personal contact and informal interaction will grow.*

- *The more that co-ordination is achieved through mutual reciprocity in this manner, the less rational will be the operation of the organisation.*

Thompson's work is of seminal importance in the development of organisation theory, not only because of the case he made for linking external uncertainty to internal dependence, but also, as a number of writers have observed (*see* Robbins,

1987; Scott, 1987), because of the attention he drew to the fact that technology can influence organisation structures as well as environmental factors. Thompson's contribution in this respect lay in creating a classification scheme for technology, and arguing that technology determines the selection of the specific structural arrangements for reducing the effect of uncertainty on the various functions of an organisation. The issue of technology and structure had been raised earlier in a major study by Joan Woodward published in 1965.

Joan Woodward and the case for technology

In the 1960s, Joan Woodward carried out a major study of 100 UK manufacturing firms in south-east Essex, in order to establish the validity of the claims made by advocates of the Classical approach that the adoption of a bureaucratic-mechanistic structure was essential for organisational success (Woodward, 1965 and 1970). After much work, Woodward concluded that no such correlation existed; what she found, however, was that the more successful companies adopted an organisational form that varied according to their main production technology. By technology, Woodward meant not only the machinery being used, but also the way it was organised, operated and integrated into a distinct production process. From her sample, she identified three distinct types of production technology, ranging from the least to the most complex:

- *Small batch (or unit) production – where customers' requirements were for one-off or small-volume specialist products.*
- *Large batch (or mass) production – where standardised products were made in large numbers to meet a forecast demand.*
- *Process production – where production was in a continuous flow such as an oil refinery.*

When the firms were grouped in this manner, a pattern emerged which showed that though they apparently differed considerably in terms of their organisational structure, many of the variations for the more successful firms could be explained by reference to the technology employed. Among firms engaged in small batch production, the most appropriate structure appeared to be one with relatively few hierarchical levels and wide middle management spans of control. Woodward noted that technology became more complex as firms moved from small batch to large batch and finally to process production. In turn, structures became taller and more narrowly based, with smaller middle management and larger chief executive spans of control. Within each category of technology, the best performing companies were those closest to the median in the type of structure adopted. Therefore, Woodward's work clearly established a link between technology, structure and success which ran counter to the notion that there was a 'one best way' for all organisations.

Though qualified by later studies (*see* Child, 1984; Handy, 1986; Smith *et al* 1982), Woodward's research remains a milestone in the development of Contingency

Theory. In particular, she demonstrated the need to take into account technological variables in designing organisations, especially in relation to spans of control. Nevertheless, a major drawback of her work was the difficulty of applying it to non-manufacturing companies. This was remedied by the work of Charles Perrow.

Charles Perrow and the case for technology continued

In the USA, Charles Perrow (1967 and 1970) extended Joan Woodward's work on technology and organisation structure by drawing attention to two major dimensions of technology:

- *the extent to which the work being carried out is variable or predictable;*
- *the extent to which the technology can be analysed and categorised.*

The first, *variability*, refers to the incidence of exceptional or unpredictable occurrences, and the extent to which these problems are familiar and can be easily dealt with, or are unique and difficult to solve. For example, an oil refinery should experience few non-routine occurrences, while an advertising agency will encounter many unpredictable and exceptional occurrences. The second major dimension, *analysis and categorisation*, refers to the extent to which the individual task functions can be broken down and tightly specified, and also whether problems can be solved by recourse to recognised, routine procedures or if non-routine procedures have to be invoked. Bringing these two major dimensions of technology together, Perrow constructed a technology continuum ranging from routine to non-routine. With the latter, there are a large number of exceptional occurrences requiring difficult and varied problem-solving techniques to overcome them. Routine technology, on the other hand, throws up few problems, which can be dealt with by recourse to standard, simple techniques.

Perrow argued that by classifying organisations according to their technology and predictability (routine to non-routine) of work tasks, it is then possible to identify the most effective form of structure in any given situation or for any activity. Perrow's routine–non-routine continuum can be equated with Burns and Stalker's mechanistic and organic dimensions for organisation structures. In routine situations, where few problems arise and those that do are easily dealt with, a mechanistic structure is more effective because of the stable and predictable nature of the situation. However, in a dynamic and unpredictable situation, a more flexible, organic form of structure will be more effective in dealing with the non-routine and difficult problems which occur. By formulating Perrow's work in this manner – i.e. by combining technology and predictability – it became possible to apply it to non-manufacturing situations. Therefore, Perrow's work both reinforced and extended Woodward's case for recognising technology as a key situational variable to be taken into account when designing organisations. Nevertheless, while Perrow was developing his ideas, a further group of researchers was making the case for yet another 'key' contingency – size.

The Aston Group and the case for size

Though there are many proponents of the case for organisational size being a key contingency (*see* Child, 1984; Robbins, 1987), perhaps the earliest and most ardent were a group of British researchers based at the University of Aston in Birmingham (who became known as the Aston Group). In the 1960s, they carried out a series of studies to examine and identify the relationship between different forms of organisational structures and their determinants (*see* Pugh *et al*, 1969 a and b). The Aston Group began in the early 1960s by examining a sample of 87 companies, and, as the work developed, further samples were added to their eventually very impressive database. In analysing their results, the Aston Group found that size was the most powerful predictor of specialisation, use of procedures and reliance on paperwork. In effect, what they found was that the larger the organisation, the more likely it was to adopt (and need) a mechanistic (bureaucratic) structure. The reverse was also found: the smaller the organisation, the more likely it was to adopt (and need) an organic (flexible) structure.

This was clearly a major finding. Not only did it support (at least in terms of larger organisations) Weber's earlier work on bureaucracy, but it also struck a blow against those, such as Bennis, who saw bureaucracy as dysfunctional and dying. The work of the Aston Group, along with that of others such as Blau and Schoenherr (1971), who also argued that size is the most important condition affecting the structure of organisations, gave bureaucracy if not a new lease of life then, at least, a new lease of respectability. Bureaucracy, according to the Aston results, was both efficient and effective, at least for larger organisations; and, given the tendency for the average size of private-sector companies and public bodies to increase throughout the twentieth century, its applicability would grow.

There are two explanations for the relationship between size and bureaucracy, both of which have similar implications for organisational efficiency and effectiveness. The first argues that increased size offers greater opportunities for specialisation – the Adam Smith argument, in effect. This will manifest itself in terms of greater structural differentiation and a high degree of uniformity among sub-units. In the first instance, this will make managerial co-ordination more difficult, especially with the emergence of functional autonomy. To counter this, senior managers will move to impose a system of impersonal controls through the use of formal procedures, standardised reporting and control systems, the written recording of information, etc. The second argument reaches similar conclusions, by pointing out that the difficulty of directing ever larger numbers of staff makes it highly inefficient to continue to use a personalised, centralised style of management. Instead a more decentralised system, using impersonal control mechanisms, has to be adopted. The introduction of such a system inevitably leads to the expansion of the administrative core (the bureaucracy) in organisations (Child, 1984).

As with all the Contingency theorists, those who argued for size as the key situational variable were not attempting to re-invent the 'one best way' approach for *all* organisations. Rather they were rejecting it in favour of an approach which saw organisational performance as dependent upon the appropriateness of the organisation's structure for its size. Therefore, like all the Contingency theorists, the Aston school adopted an approach which stressed that there is a 'one best way' for *each* organisation.

Contingency Theory: summary and criticisms

The Contingency approach can be considered much more a cohesive school of thought than either the Classical or Human Relations approaches. It has three unifying themes:

- *Organisations are open systems.*
- *Structure, and therefore performance, is dependent upon the particular circumstances, situational variables, faced by each organisation.*
- *There is no 'one best way' for all organisations.*

The attractions of Contingency Theory are obvious. First, it was in tune with the times in which it emerged – the 1960s and 1970s. This was a period of rapid economic and technological change, a tendency towards much larger organisations, and a significant increase in domestic and international competition. In this situation, Contingency Theory offered a plausible explanation of not only why these events were causing problems for organisations, but also how to resolve them (Burnes, 1989). Second, on the surface at least, it was simpler to understand and apply than the Human Relations approach. Finally, while rejecting the Classical Approach, it was, in the main, a rational approach, based on matching known structural options to identifiable contingencies – size, technology and environment.

The approach to change management offered by Contingency Theory was, it follows, similar to that of the Classical school. In a rational fashion, managers should collect and analyse data on the situational variables the organisation faces and match these to the appropriate structural option. The theory then implies that for employees, faced with a plan for change based on such a 'scientific' approach, the only rational course of action is to accept the validity of the situation and co-operate with managers to achieve the required structural changes. However, it is at this point – the attempt to apply Contingency Theory rationally and mechanically – that problems and drawbacks emerge which give rise to a number of major criticisms of this approach.

- *The difficulty in relating structure to performance.* A number of writers have pointed out that there is no agreed definition of 'good performance', and it therefore becomes difficult to show that linking structure to situational variables brings the benefits claimed (Hendry, 1979 and 1980; Mansfield, 1984; Terry, 1976). Indeed, there are a wide range of factors other than structure which can influence performance, not least of which is luck. Davis and Star (1993) showed that seven of the twelve most profitable firms in the world are pharmaceutical companies, and that three of these are producers of anti-ulcer drugs. They conclude that the profitability of the pharmaceuticals sector is attributable less to the nature of these organisations than to governments' over-generosity – clearly a case of an industry that is in the right place at the right time.

● *No agreed definition of key variables.* Despite the length of time that Contingency Theory has been in circulation, there is still no agreed or unchallenged definition of the three key situational variables – environment, technology and size. The literature gives a wide and conflicting range of definitions of these, making it difficult not only to establish a link between them and structure, but also to apply the theory (Dastmalchian, 1984; Mullins, 1989; Pugh and Hickson, 1976; Robbins, 1987; Warner, 1984; Wood, 1979).

● *Impact of link between size and structure unclear.* While, as argued above, a relationship has been established between size and structure, it has proved difficult to show that this relationship has an appreciable impact on performance. Some researchers have suggested that the link between size and structure relates to preferred systems of control, which may have more to do with the political and cultural nature of organisations than any attempt to improve performance (Allaire and Firsirotu, 1984; Child, 1984; Mansfield, 1984; Pugh and Hickson, 1976; Salaman, 1979).

● *Informal structures ignored.* In examining the link between structure and contingencies, researchers use the organisation's formal organisational structure for comparison purposes. Yet, as the Hawthorne Experiments showed, the actual operation of an organisation may depend more on the informal structures created by workers than the formal ones laid down by management. This was a point made by Woodward (1965) in her study of technology and structure. She noted that organisation charts failed to show important relationships which, taken together, can have a significant impact on performance (Argyris, 1973; Burawoy, 1979; Selznick, 1948).

● *Structure and associated practices and policies may be strongly influenced by external forces* (Mullins, 1993). In the UK, recently privatised utilities are subject to regulation and face restrictions which have a significant influence on how they are structured and operate. Similarly, in the UK financial service organisations are required to establish 'chinese walls' between different parts of their business to avoid market-sensitive information being passed from one area to another.

● *Rather than managers being the virtual prisoners of organisational contingencies when making decisions regarding structure, the reverse may be the case.* Managers may have a significant degree of choice and influence over not only structure but also the situational variables. Whether this is called 'strategic choice' (Child, 1972), 'organisational choice' (Trist *et al*, 1963) or 'design space' (Bessant, 1983), the meaning is the same: those senior managers responsible for such decisions can exercise a high degree of freedom in selecting and influencing the technology to be used, the environment in which they operate and even the size of the organisation. Indeed, one of the architects of the technology–structure hypothesis, Charles Perrow, now argues that technology is chosen and designed to maintain and reinforce existing structures and power relations within organisations rather than the reverse (Perrow, 1983). Other writers make the case for size and environment being manipulated in similar ways (Abell, 1975; Clegg, 1984; Hendry, 1979; Leifer and Huber, 1977; Lorsch, 1970).

● *Presence of conflicting objectives.* It is assumed that organisations pursue clear-cut, well-thought-out, stable and compatible objectives which can be fitted into a Contingency perspective. Researchers and practising managers argue, however, that this is not the case – in fact, even two of the proponents of Contingency Theory, Lawrence and Lorsch (1967), highlighted the presence and danger of conflicting objectives. In reality, objectives are often unclear, and organisations may pursue a number of conflicting goals at the same time. Clearly, the objectives of an organisation will impact on its situation and its structure. If these objectives are arbitrary, conflicting or open to managerial whim, it becomes difficult to apply a Contingency approach (Abodaher, 1976; Edwardes, 1983; Hamel and Prahalad, 1989; Mintzberg, 1987; Sloan, 1986).

● *Too mechanistic an approach.* The last criticism is that Contingency Theory is too mechanistic and deterministic, and ignores the complexity of organisational life. As argued by the Human Relations school, organisations are by no means the rational entities many would like to believe (a point also made by Thompson (1967) in his support of Contingency Theory). There is a need to see organisations as social systems, with all the cultural and political issues which this raises. In this view, structure is the product of power struggles between individuals and groups within the organisation, each arguing and fighting for their own perspective and position (Allaire and Firsirotu, 1984; Buchanan, 1984; Morgan, 1986; Hickson and Butler, 1982; Pfeffer, 1981; Robbins, 1987; Salaman, 1979).

Therefore, despite its attractiveness, Contingency Theory, like the Classical and Human Relations approaches, fails to provide a convincing explanation for the way in which organisations do and should operate.

CONCLUSIONS
....

For organisations, if not for academics, the key purpose of any organisation theory or approach is to help them analyse and rectify the weaknesses and problems of their current situation, and to assist them in bringing about the changes necessary to achieve their future objectives. Over the past 100 years, the design and management of organisations has moved from an *ad hoc* process based on at best guesswork, to one that is highly complex and informed by a host of practical and theoretical considerations. To the uninitiated, it might appear that this has made running organisations an easier and more certain process; yet a close examination of most organisations will reveal that this is far from being the case. Not only are organisations, in general, larger and more complex than in the past, but also the practical and theoretical reference points on which managers can draw are diverse and give conflicting and confusing signals.

Not surprisingly in such a situation, many managers look for simple, foolproof solutions: often ones which, as Douglas McGregor noted, appeal to their own basic orientation – whether that be Theory X or Theory Y. This is one of the reasons why the Classical approach, with its deep roots in the Industrial Revolution and its straightforward mechanical approach to organisations and their members, has proved so enduring, despite strong evidence of its lack of suitability in many situations. This search for simple, often quick-fix solutions, to the problems of organisational life has been manifested in many ways in the last decade, not least the emergence of a series of 'panaceas' such as new technology, human resources management, Total Quality Management, culture change, etc. This is not to deny the benefits these can bring but, taken on their own, at best they encourage a fragmented approach, and at worst they create an atmosphere of resignation within organisations as one 'flavour of the month' is succeeded by yet another, and none is given the time necessary to prove itself. Clearly, in such situations, without an overall, long-term plan, the result of these various 'solutions' is to make the situation worse rather than better (Burnes, 1991; Burnes and Weekes, 1989).

Organisations clearly need to reject a short-term piecemeal approach, and instead see themselves in their totality and adopt a consistent and long-term approach. But which approach should they choose? We have seen in this and the previous chapter that well thought out and well supported cases exist for a number of different approaches, but each has its drawbacks and critics. It may well be that each is capable of assisting organisations to analyse and understand the strengths and weaknesses of their present situation. However, whether they can provide more effective organisational arrangements for the future is more debatable. Similarly, it is not obvious how organisations should actually achieve the process of transformation.

The Human Relations movement offers pertinent advice with regard to having clear objectives, good communication and leadership, but is less forthcoming on how change objectives should be set, and the concomitant changes planned and implemented. Contingency Theory though does give a procedure for setting objectives. It stresses the need to identify and analyse the situational variables an organisation faces in order to choose the most appropriate structure. However, it is also silent on the issues of planning and implementation, other than to imply that rational workers will accept rational propositions for change. In addition, even if organisations do manage to implement the recommendations of the Human

Relations or Contingency advocates, it is not clear what degree of benefit they would derive from this, given the criticisms of these approaches.

In short, neither of the approaches discussed in this chapter appears to be the solution to all known organisational ills that their proponents seem to claim. They fail to reflect and explain the complexities of day-to-day organisational life which we all experience. In particular, the issue of organisational culture (Allaire and Firsirotu, 1984) gets short shrift; yet, over the last decade, its importance as both a promoter of and a barrier to organisational competitiveness has become apparent. Nor do they appear to take account of national differences and preferences, or for that matter pay regard to many of the wider societal factors which now impact on our lives, such as the need to show greater social responsibility, whether it be in the area of 'green' issues or equal opportunities. Yet, it is clear that enormous changes are already taking place in the world, and others may be necessary if some of the worst predictions for the future are to be avoided. The next chapter describes two new perspectives on organisational life which, as the old approaches are perceived as inadequate, have become increasingly influential in the West in the last decade and a half.

Chapter 3

WEST v EAST: NEW PARADIGMS – OLD QUESTIONS

INTRODUCTION

It was TB Kuhn (1962), in his book *The Structure of Scientific Revolutions*, who gave a new importance to the word 'paradigm'. A paradigm is a conceptual framework, a way of looking at the world, a set of assumptions, theories and models that are commonly accepted and shared within a particular field of activity at a particular point in time. As situations change and people's perceptions change, existing paradigms lose their relevance and new ones emerge. As Handy (1986:389) noted:

> **When Copernicus suggested that the earth was not at the centre of the universe he was, though he knew it not, a paradigm revolutionary. But it was the minds of men that changed, not the motions of the planets, and the way in which they now viewed that same universe had a profound effect on their beliefs, values and behaviour.**

In the previous two chapters we discussed the paradigms that, in the West at least, have emerged and become common currency in the field of management and organisational theory. Though these paradigms have their adherents as well as critics, increasingly managers and academics have experienced real difficulties in applying and defending them in today's turbulent, complex and diverse business world.

Old certainties are being challenged and new orthodoxies are arising. The challenge from the East, particularly Japan, to European and American industrial power has sent shock waves through Western economies. Rather like Copernicus, Japan has made the West see the world, and its place in it, from a new perspective.

Organisations are becoming increasingly aware that in the last 10 to 20 years, the world has turned on its axis. The days of the mass production of standardised products appear to be over; the key words for the future are variety, flexibility and customisation. As Perez (1983) and Freeman (1988) argued, a new techno-economic rationale is emerging. This new rationale has three main features:

- *a shift towards information-intensive rather than energy- or materials-intensive products;*

- *a change from dedicated mass-production systems towards more flexible systems that can accommodate a wider range of products, smaller batches and more frequent design changes – 'economies of scale' are being replaced by 'economies of scope';*

- *a move towards the greater integration of processes and systems within companies and between suppliers and customers which permits a more rapid response to market and customer requirements.*

It is not that the nature of organisations themselves have changed fundamentally, though significant changes in size, technology and complexity have certainly taken place. It is rather that, like those who listened to Copernicus, we are seeing their role in the established order from a different perspective and beginning to see new possibilities and new challenges.

It is the emergence of these new possibilities and challenges which is driving Western organisations to undertake a fundamental reassessment of their objectives and operations, rather than a mere change in fashion or managerial whim (though this is obviously present as well). In effect, what we can see from the beginning of the 1980s is the emergence of a paradigm shift. It seems as if the changes taking place in the business environment are so enormous and rapid that existing paradigms, whatever their past merits, are breaking down and new ones emerging.

In this chapter, we examine the two paradigms which have come to dominate Western managerial thinking and writing over the last decade: the Culture–Excellence approach and the Japanese Management approach. The former is very much a Western development and has taken root only in the last decade or so. Its principal exponents (Tom Peters and Robert Waterman, 1982; Rosabeth Moss Kanter, 1989; and Charles Handy, 1989) are attempting both to predict and to promote how successful (excellent) companies will and should operate in the future.

The Japanese Management paradigm is a very different animal. It has been developed in Japan over the last 40 years, and not only is it being extensively practised there, but its success is not disputed. Because of the success of the Japanese economy and Japanese companies since the 1970s, the Japanese approach has attracted much interest in the West. This is especially the case in the UK, where Japanese inward investment (by household names such as Honda, Nissan and Toyota) has generated a great deal of debate regarding the impact and merits of 'Japanisation' (Ackroyd *et al*, 1988; Dale and Cooper, 1992; Hannam, 1993; Turnbull, 1986; Whitehill, 1991). This is also the case in the USA, where Japan and Japanese methods are seen, in turn, as either a threat or a lifeline to American industrial pre-eminence (Pascale and Athos, 1982; Kanter *et al*, 1992; Peters, 1992; Schonberger, 1982).

Though the two approaches have some similarities, for example the resemblance between the Japanese passion for quality and the Culture–Excellence school's fervent advocacy of the pursuit of excellence, the two – as will be shown – also have significant differences. While the Japanese approach has clearly influenced the Culture–Excellence thinkers, there is little indication that the reverse has been the case. The two may be competing paradigms in the West, but certainly are not in Japan. Nevertheless, both are dynamic and developing paradigms, with some common elements, and consequently, a merging or a blending of the two in the West is not beyond all possibilities. Though management practices in Japan are changing, however, a continuing and distinct Japanese approach to management seems by far the most likely outcome there.

In addition, it will be argued in the conclusion to this chapter that, although these paradigms offer new possibilities, they also raise familiar controversies, not least regarding the role and treatment of people. Therefore, though new paradigms, they still have to answer old questions. The following discussion of the two approaches will allow readers to make their own judgment.

THE CULTURE–EXCELLENCE APPROACH

Though predominantly a North American perspective, the Culture–Excellence approach has also found its adherents in Europe. Therefore, the examination of this approach will draw on the work of key writers from both sides of the Atlantic, namely Tom Peters and Robert Waterman, Rosabeth Moss Kanter and Charles Handy. The writers are all practising and internationally recognised management consultants, though Handy and Kanter are distinguished academics as well. Consequently, though their work is attempting to predict and promote the way firms will or should operate in the future, it is firmly based on what they believe the best companies are doing now or planning to do in the future.

These three perspectives form the spearhead of the movement that is simultaneously charting and creating the new organisational forms that have begun to appear. Their work – though both complementary and distinct – is of profound influence in shaping our understanding of what the future holds in the field of management. This work will now be examined in detail, starting with the American perspectives of Peters and Waterman, and Kanter, and concluding with Handy's British perspective.

Tom Peters and Robert Waterman's eight attributes of excellent companies

Both Peters and Waterman are leading management consultants. Indeed, Peters is reputed to be the most highly paid consultant in the world. They are also the authors of one of the earliest and most discussed contributions to the emergence of new forms of organisations, *In Search of Excellence: Lessons from America's Best-Run*

Companies (Peters and Waterman, 1982). The origins of the book lie in a major study of the determinants of organisational excellence, which Peters and Waterman carried out when working for the management consultants McKinsey and Company.

From their study of 62 of America's most successful companies, Peters and Waterman argue that there are eight key attributes which organisations need to demonstrate if they are to achieve excellence. These attributes are largely opposed to the rational theories of management described in previous chapters. They argue that the rational approach is flawed because it leads to:

- *Wrong-headed analysis* – *situation or information analysis that is considered too complex to be useful and too unwieldy to be flexible. This is analysis that strives to be precise about the inherently unknowable.*

- *Paralysis through analysis* – *the application of the rational model to such an extent that action stops and planning runs riot.*

- *Irrational rationality* – *where rational management techniques identify the 'right' answer irrespective of its applicability to the situation in question.*

In the light of these criticisms, Peters and Waterman argue that the analytical tools which characterise the rational approach should only be used as an aid to, rather than a substitute for, human judgment. They believe that it is the freedom given to managers and employees to challenge the orthodox and to experiment with different solutions which distinguishes the excellent companies from the also-rans. This can clearly be seen by looking at their eight attributes of excellence:

1 A bias for action
2 Close to the customer
3 Autonomy and entrepreneurship
4 Productivity through people
5 Hands-on, value-driven
6 Stick to the knitting
7 Simple form, lean staff
8 Simultaneous loose-tight properties.

These are discussed in more detail below.

1 A bias for action

One of the main identifiable attributes of excellent companies is their bias for action. Even though they may be analytical in approach, they also favour methods which encourage rapid and appropriate response. One of the methods devised for achieving quick action is what Peters and Waterman term 'chunking'. Chunking is an approach whereby a problem that arises in the organisation is first made manageable (i.e. broken into 'chunks') and then tackled by a small group of staff brought together specifically for that purpose. The main reason for the use of such groups, variously called project teams, taskforces or quality circles, is to facilitate organisational fluidity and to encourage action. Key characteristics of these groups are:

- *They usually comprise no more than ten members.*
- *They are voluntarily constituted.*
- *The life of the group is usually between three to six months.*
- *The reporting level and seniority of the membership is appropriate to the importance of the problem to be dealt with.*
- *The documentation of the group's proceedings is scant and very informal.*
- *These groups take on a limited set of objectives, which are usually determined, monitored, evaluated, and reviewed by themselves.*

Chunking is merely one example of the bias for action that exists in excellent companies and reflects their willingness to innovate and experiment. These companies' philosophy for action is simple: 'Do it, fix it, try it.' Therefore, excellent companies are characterised by small, *ad hoc* teams applied to solving designated problems which have first been reduced to manageable proportions. Achieving smallness is the key, even though the subject or task may be large. Smallness induces manageability and a sense of understanding, and allows a feeling of ownership.

2 Close to the customer

Excellent companies really do get close to the customer, while others merely talk about it. The customer dictates product, quantity, quality and service. The best organisations are alleged to go to extreme lengths to achieve quality, service and reliability. There is no part of the business that is closed to customers. In fact, many of the excellent companies claim to get their best ideas for new products from listening intently and regularly to their customers. The excellent companies are more 'driven by their direct orientation to the customers rather than by technology or by a desire to be the low-cost producer. They seem to focus more on the revenue-generation side of their services' (Peters and Waterman, 1982:197).

3 Autonomy and entrepreneurship

Perhaps the most important element of excellent companies is their 'ability to be big and yet to act small at the same time. A concomitant essential apparently is that they encourage the entrepreneurial spirit among their people, because they push autonomy markedly far down the line' (Peters and Waterman, 1982:201). Product champions are allowed to come forward, grow and flourish. They are not blue-sky dreamers, or intellectual giants. The champion might even be an ideal thief. But above all, the champion is the pragmatist; the one who latches on to someone else's idea, and doggedly brings something concrete and tangible out of it.

In fostering such attitudes, the excellent companies have what they label 'championing systems,' consisting of:

- *The Product Champion – a zealot or fanatic who believes in a product.*

- *A Successful Executing Champion – one who has been through the process of championing a product before.*

- *The Godfather – typically, an ageing leader who provides the role model for champions.*

The essence of this system is to foster, promote, and sustain the budding entrepreneur. It is claimed that the three elements of the championing system are essential to its operation and credibility.

Another key part of this system is that, in some companies, product champions tend to be allocated their own 'suboptional divisions'. These are similar to small, independent businesses and comprise independent new venture teams, run by champions with the full and total support of senior management. The suboptional division is independent in that it is responsible for its own accounting, personnel activities, quality assurance and support for its product in the field. To encourage entrepreneurship further, teams, groups and divisions are highly encouraged by the companies' reward structures to compete amongst themselves for new projects.

Autonomy and entrepreneurship are also encouraged by the type of no-holds-barred communications procedures adopted by excellent companies. These exhibit the following characteristics:

- *Communication is informal.* Even though there are lots of meetings going on at any one time, most meetings are informal and comprise staff from different disciplines gathering to talk about and solve problems.

- *The communication system is given both physical and material support* . Blackboards, flip-charts and small tables that foster informal small group discussions are everywhere. The aim is to encourage people to talk about the organisation: what needs changing; what is going on; and how to improve things around the place. There are also people, variously described as dreamers, heretics, gadflies, mavericks, or geniuses, whose sole purpose is to spur the system to innovate. Their job is to institutionalise innovation by initiating and encouraging experimentation. They can also call on staff in other divisions of the organisation to assist them in this process, as well as having financial resources at their disposal.

- *Communication is intensive.* Given the freedom, the encouragement and the support (financial, moral and physical) in the organisations, it is no wonder that the level of communication between and amongst workers is not only informal and spontaneous but also intense. This is borne out by the common occurrence of meetings without agendas and minutes. Furthermore, when presentations are made in these meetings, questioning of the proposal is unabashed and discussion is free and open. Those present are expected to be fully involved in such meetings and there are no 'sacred cows' that cannot be questioned.

This intense communication system also acts as a remarkably tight control system, in that people are always checking on each other to see how each is faring. This arises out of a genuine desire to keep abreast of developments in the organisation rather than any untoward motive. One result of this is that teams are more prudent in their financial expenditure on projects. Another is that the sea of inquisitors act as 'idea generators', thereby ensuring that teams are not dependent entirely on their own devices to innovate and solve problems. This usually also ensures that all options are considered before a final decision is made. The concomitant result of this fostering of creativity is that senior management is more tolerant of failure, knowing full well that champions have to make many tries, and consequently suffer some failures, in the process of creating successful innovations.

4 Productivity through people

A cherished principle of the excellent companies is that they treat their workers with respect and dignity; they refer to them as partners. This is because people, rather than systems or machines, are seen as the primary source of quality and productivity gains. Therefore, there is 'tough-minded respect for the individual and the willingness to train him, to set reasonable and clear expectations for him, and to grant him practical autonomy to step out and contribute directly to his job' (Peters and Waterman, 1982:239). There is a closeness and family feeling in such companies; indeed many of the 'partners' see the organisation as an extended family. The slogans of such companies tend to reflect this view of people: 'respect the individual', 'make people winners', 'let them stand out', 'treat people as adults'.

5 Hands-on, value-driven

Excellent companies are value-driven; they are clear about what they stand for and take the process of value-shaping seriously. There is an implicit belief that everyone in the organisation, from the top to the bottom, should be driven by the values of the organisation; hence the great effort, time and money spent to inspire people by, and inculcate them with, these values.

> ... these values are almost always stated in qualitative, rather than quantitative, terms. When financial objectives are mentioned, they are almost always ambitious but never precise. Furthermore, financial and strategic objectives are never stated alone. They are always discussed in the context of the other things the company expects to do well. The idea that profit is a natural by-product of doing something well, and not an end in itself, is almost always universal. (*Peters and Waterman, 1982:284*)

Implanting these values is a primary responsibility of the individual members of the management team. They set the tone by leading from the front. Coherence and homogeneity must first be created among senior management, however, by regular meetings (both formal and informal). The outcome of this is that management speak with one voice. They are passionate in preaching the organisation's values. They unleash excitement, not in their offices, but mainly on the shopfloor where the workers are. Inculcating these values, however, is a laborious process and persistence is vital in achieving the desired goal.

6 Stick to the knitting

Acquisition or internal diversification for its own sake is not one of the characteristics of excellent companies. They must stick to the knitting – do what they know best. But when they do acquire, they do it in an experimental fashion; by first dipping a 'toe in the waters'. If the water does not feel good, they get out fast. Acquisitions are always in fields related to their core activities and they never acquire any business that they do not know how to run. As a general rule, they 'move out mainly through internally generated diversification, one manageable step at a time' (Peters and Waterman, 1982: 279).

7 Simple form, lean staff

A guiding principle in excellent companies is to keep things simple and small. Structurally, the most common form is the 'product division'. This form, which is rarely changed, provides the essential touchstone which everybody understands and from which the complexities of day-to-day life can be approached. Since the use of teams, groups and task forces for specific projects is a common stock-in-trade of these companies, most changes in structure are made at the edges, such as by allocating one or two people to an *ad hoc* team. By this approach, the basic structure is left in place, while all other things revolve and change around it. This gives these organisations great flexibility but still enables them to keep their structures simple, divisionalised and autonomous.

Such simple structures only require a small, lean staff at the corporate and middle management levels. This results in there being fewer administrators and more doers: '... it is not uncommon to find a corporate staff of fewer than 100 people running a multi-billion-dollar enterprise' (Peters and Waterman, 1982:15). Therefore, in excellent companies, flat structures, with few layers, and slimmed-down bureaucracies – which together allow flexibility and rapid communication – are the order of the day.

8 Simultaneous loose-tight properties

This is the 'firm and free' principle. On the one hand, it allows the excellent companies to control everything tightly, while on the other hand allowing and indeed encouraging individual innovation, autonomy and entrepreneurship. These properties are jointly achieved through the organisation's culture – its shared values and beliefs. By sharing the same values, self-control and self-respect result in each person becoming their own, and everyone else's, supervisor. The individual members of the organisation know they have the freedom, and are encouraged, to experiment and innovate. They also know, however, that their actions will be scrutinised and judged, with the utmost attention paid to the impact they have on product quality, targets, and above all, the customer. The focus is on building and expanding the frontiers of the business. The ultimate goal is to be the best company, and in the final analysis, this is the benchmark against which the discipline and flexibility of the individual will be measured.

Therefore, Peters and Waterman maintain that the main attributes of excellent companies are flat, anti-hierarchical structures; innovation and entrepreneurship; small corporate and middle management staffs; reward systems based on contribution rather than position or length of service; brain power rather than muscle power; and strong, flexible cultures.

Peters and Waterman's vision of the organisation of the future, based on their study of leading American companies, has proved extremely influential, not only in the business world but in academia as well. This is not to say – as will be shown later – that they are without their critics; there is little doubt, however, that they laid the groundwork, especially in highlighting the important role played by culture, for other leading thinkers whose work draws on and gels with theirs.

Their vision of the future has not stood still. In particular, Peters has spent the last decade as a consultant and writer developing and implementing their approach. Though not fundamentally changing his view of the need for excellent organisations, Peters (1989) argues that, as yet, none exist in the USA. In his latest book, *Liberation Management* (Peters, 1992), he also places more emphasis on the need to break organisations into smaller and more independent and more flexible units. Only by doing this, he argues, will managers be 'liberated', and thus able to achieve their – and their organisation's – full potential.

Peters (1992) believes that the age of the large corporations such as IBM and General Motors is over. He sees such companies as outmoded and uncompetitive dinosaurs, which are doomed to extinction unless they change rapidly and irreversibly. Peters argues that only rapid structural change can create the conditions for entrepreneurial cultures to emerge which both liberate managers and empower workers. Indeed, his later work is nothing short of an out-and-out attack on the very existence of corporate America.

Though the tone of his work has become more strident and zealot-like, in essence he is still promoting the concepts first developed in *In Search of Excellence*. The main difference, however, is that while the earlier book saw these concepts as a recipe for saving corporate America (and thus maintaining the USA as the premier industrial nation), Peters (1992) now believes that corporate America needs to be destroyed in order for America to survive.

Rosabeth Moss Kanter's post-entrepreneurial model

Kanter is one of America's leading management thinkers. As well as being a professor at the Harvard Business School and editor of the Harvard Business Review, she is also a leading and influential management consultant. Her work complements and develops that of Peters and Waterman by attempting to define what organisations need to be like in the future if they are to be successful. Kanter calls for a revolution in business management to create what she terms post-entrepreneurial organisations. She uses this term:

> ... because it takes entrepreneurship a step further, applying entrepreneurial principles to the traditional corporation, creating a marriage between entrepreneurial creativity and corporate discipline, cooperation, and teamwork. (*Kanter, 1989:9–10*)

Kanter believes that:

> If the new game of business is indeed like Alice-in-Wonderland croquet, then winning it requires faster action, more creative manoeuvring, more flexibility, and closer partnerships with employees and customers than was typical in the traditional corporate bureaucracy. It requires more agile, limber management that pursues opportunity without being bogged down by cumbersome structures or weighty procedures that impede action. Corporate giants, in short, must learn how to dance. (*Kanter, 1989:20*)

In her (1989) book, *When Giants Learn To Dance: Mastering the Challenges of Strategy, Management, and Careers in the 1990s*, she argues that today's corporate elephants need to learn to dance as nimbly and speedily as mice if they are to survive in our increasingly competitive and rapidly changing world. Companies must constantly be alert and on their guard, and keep abreast of their competitors' intentions. By evaluating the response of modern organisations to the demands placed upon them, Kanter has produced her post-entrepreneurial model of how the organisation of the future should operate. She sees post-entrepreneurial organisations as pursuing three main strategies:

1 Restructuring to find synergies.
2 Opening boundaries to form strategic alliances.
3 Creating new ventures from within: encouraging innovation and entrepreneurship.

These are detailed below.

1 Restructuring to find synergies

Synergy occurs where the whole adds up to more than the sum of its constituent parts. In an age where resources are scarce, one of the priorities of organisations is to make every part of the business add value to the whole. In practice this means selling off a company's non-core activities and ensuring that what remains, especially at the corporate and middle management levels, is lean and efficient. Nevertheless, it is not sufficient merely to have a strategy of reducing the size of the organisational bureaucracy. Companies must also ensure that the essential tasks which these people previously carried out are still undertaken. This can be accomplished in a number of ways, such as the use of computers to carry out monitoring and information-gathering, devolving greater responsibility and power down to individual business units, and contracting out services and tasks previously carried out in-house.

The essence of this approach is to identify and concentrate on the core business areas and to remove all obstacles and impediments to their efficient and effective operation. Therefore, all non-core activities are eliminated, and authority is devolved to the appropriate levels of the business – those in the front line. The result is to create flatter, more responsive and less complex organisations which have a greater degree of focus than in the past. Kanter argues, however, that such radical changes need to be well-planned, and executed with care and in a way which ensures that employee motivation is increased, not eliminated.

2 Opening their boundaries to form strategic alliances

With the slimming-down of the organisation and the contracting-out of some of its functions, there arises the need to pool resources with other organisations; to band together to exploit opportunities and to share ideas and information. These alliances take three forms: service alliances, opportunistic alliances and stakeholder alliances. The first, a *service alliance*, is where two or more organisations form a cross-company consortium to undertake a special project with a limited lifespan. Such alliances are usually considered when the resources of the various partners are insufficient to allow them to undertake the project by themselves. For this reason, and not surprisingly, many such alliances involve research and development (R&D) projects. Ford and General Motors collaborating on research into the development of new materials for making cars is an example of this. This approach allows organisations to mobilise resources, often on a large scale, while limiting their exposure and protecting their independence. It is the limited purpose of the consortium which makes it possible even for competitors to join together for their mutual benefit.

The second form, an *opportunistic alliance*, comprises a joint venture whose aim is to take advantage of a particular opportunity which has arisen: '… the two principal advantages behind this kind of alliance are competence-enhancing ones: technology transfer or market access or both' (Kanter, 1989:126). An example of such an alliance is the link-up between the Rover Group and Honda Motors; the former gained access to Japanese know-how, while the latter gained greater access to the European market. As Kanter (1989:126) has pointed out, however, such alliances are not always equally beneficial: '… once one of the partners has gained experience with the competence of the other, the alliance is vulnerable to dissolution – the opportunity can now be pursued without the partner.'

The third form, a *stakeholder alliance*, unlike the previous two, is seen as a continuing, almost permanent partnership between an organisation and its key stakeholders, generally considered to be its employees, customers and suppliers. There is a growing awareness among employees, trade unions and management of the need to see each other as partners in the same enterprise rather than rivals. A similar case is made for treating customers and suppliers as partners too. The main reason for the organisation to exist is to serve its customers; therefore, there is a need to keep close to them, not only to be aware of their present concerns and future needs, but also to gain ideas regarding potential joint product development. In the same way, the organisation relies on its suppliers, who will in any case want to get closer to them as their customers. Stakeholder alliances have gained a growing band of adherents in Britain in recent years, especially, though not exclusively, among Japanese companies such as Nissan Motors (Wickens, 1987; Partnership Sourcing, 1991). As Kanter points out, major innovations in technology and organisational systems require longer-term investments. Companies can only enter into such investments if they are secure in the knowledge that their key stakeholders are themselves committed to the same aims and approach.

The result of these alliances is that structures and positions within organisations will change, sometimes quite dramatically. This is especially the case among senior and line managers, but even previously protected groups – such as R&D specialists – will also see their roles and responsibilities change. They will have to work more closely not only with colleagues internally, but also with external groupings.

3 Creating new ventures from within: encouraging innovation and entrepreneurship

Traditional organisations face a difficult balancing act between gaining the full benefits from existing mainstream business, and, at the same time, creating new activities which will become the mainstream business of the future. Kanter argues that there is a feeling in many traditional companies that opportunities are being missed owing to their inability to give staff the flexibility to pursue new ideas and develop new products. The job of creating new products or ventures used to be the sole domain of the strategic planners or the R&D departments. In the post-entrepreneurial organisation, however, this will no longer be the case; innovation will move from these specialised domains to the centre stage. As the case studies in Part 3 will show, some organisations are deliberately forming new, independent units or entirely restructuring themselves to nurture innovation and entrepreneurship. New cultures are being created which encourage and aid innovation, and old barriers and restrictions are being eradicated. As a result of such changes, the innovative potential of employees is being and will be tapped, and a proliferation of new ideas, products and ways of working is emerging.

The consequences of the post-entrepreneurial model

There is no doubt that the post-entrepreneurial model carries profound implications for both organisations and their employees. Kanter, however, unlike Peters and Waterman, does not see these new developments as being an unalloyed blessing, especially in the case of employees. In particular, she draws attention to three areas where the changes will have a major impact on employees: reward systems, career paths and job security, and lifestyle.

Reward systems

Employers and employees will more and more come to look for new and more appropriate ways of rewarding and being rewarded. Indeed, with the advent of performance-related pay, in both the private and public sectors, there is already a gradual change from determining pay on the basis of a person's position and seniority to basing it on their contribution to the organisation. These changes are being driven by four main concerns.

1 *Cost.* The concern is that the present system is too expensive for companies that must conserve resources to be competitive.

2 *Equity.* Organisations are concerned that the present system does not reward employees fairly for their efforts.

3 *Productivity.* The worry here is that the present system is inadequate to motivate high performance from employees.

4 *Entrepreneurial pressure.* Companies are aware that the present system does not always adequately reward entrepreneurs for their efforts.

These concerns are being approached through the application of three different, though not necessarily mutually exclusive, payment methods. The first is *profit-sharing*, whereby the pay of the employee is pegged to a company's performance. This means that salaries are not fixed but instead are related, by the use of a predetermined formula, to the profit of the organisation over a given period of time, usually the previous financial year. The second method is the use of *performance bonuses*, which are paid on top of basic salary and are related to a pre-determined performance target. This method has the advantage of enabling individuals to establish a direct correlation between their personal effort and the bonus payment they receive. Though this method is not new, the sums involved are – sometimes as much as twice basic salary. The last is the *venture-returns method*, which represents perhaps the most radical break with the past. This is a scheme whereby entrepreneurs and inventors within an organisation are given the opportunity to earn returns based on the performance, in the market place, of the particular products or services for which they are responsible. Through this mechanism, the entrepreneur or inventor remains within the corporate fold but is paid on a similar basis to the owner of a small, independent business. The advantage is that they get the personal satisfaction and reward of running their 'own' business, while the larger organisation benefits from having highly motivated and innovative people in charge of part of its operations.

The picture created by new reward systems is not, of course, totally rosy. Where there are winners, there may also be losers; not everyone will have the opportunity or drive to be an entrepreneur, or will be in a position that lends itself to some form of bonus system. Furthermore, many people who currently benefit from reward systems based on seniority and position may find they lose out. Older workers, established in organisations and well down their chosen career path, could be particularly adversely affected by such changes. In addition, such payment systems may be divisive and create conflict. Kanter stresses the need for teamwork, yet a situation where some members of the team are receiving high bonuses is bound to create tensions which undermine co-operation and collaboration. It may be that profit-sharing schemes, which encompass everyone in the organisation, overcome this threat to teamworking, but if everyone receives the same share of the profits irrespective of their individual contribution, the motivating effect is likely to be diminished. The result of these various approaches to pay could be minimal in terms of motivation, or could even be demotivating and indeed drive out the most experienced people in the organisation.

Careers and job security

As organisations become slimmer and more tasks are contracted out, organisation structures will become flatter as entire layers of hierarchy are dispensed with. The resultant effect may well be the demise of traditional forms of career path. Kanter argues that the idea of staying with one organisation and climbing the corporate career ladder is being replaced by hopping from job to job, not necessarily in the same organisation. Therefore, instead of people relying on organisations to give shape to their career, in future the onus will be on individuals to map out and pursue their own chosen route.

This change will also affect skill development in organisations. It will no longer be sufficient just to be skilled in a particular job or specialism, because these will certainly change over time or even entirely disappear. In future, individuals may find that the concept of job security is replaced by 'employability security' – the ability to adapt and enhance one's skills so as to be able to perform well in different types of jobs and organisations. Careers, therefore, will be shaped by professional and entrepreneurial principles: the ability to develop and market one's own skills and ideas, rather than by the sequence of jobs provided by one company. People will join organisations or accept particular jobs not, as in the past, because of job security or career progression, but in order to develop their skills, add to their knowledge and enhance their future employability.

Kanter argues that:

> **... what people are increasingly working to acquire is the capital of their own individual reputation instead of the organisational capital that comes from learning**

one system well and meeting its idiosyncratic requirements. For many managers, it might be more important, for example, to acquire or demonstrate a talent that a future employer or financial investor might value than to get to know the right people several layers above in the corporation where they currently work. *(Kanter, 1989:324)*

Having painted this picture, it must also be acknowledged that there are contradictions and dilemmas which need to be resolved. What is being created are organisations and cultures which facilitate innovation and entrepreneurship, and change and flexibility. These will be organisations where employability and loyalty are transient concepts and what matters, almost exclusively, is the individual's present performance rather than their past or potential future contribution. The two main dilemmas from the organisational perspective are, therefore, how to reconcile the above with their stated objective of treating employees as long-term partners, and how to motivate employees to work in the organisation's interest rather than their own interest. This is an especially pointed dilemma in the case of the champions and entrepreneurs on whom it is argued the future of organisations depends. This is because it is this group of highly-marketable individuals who are most likely to see their careers in terms of many different jobs and organisations.

Workers' lifestyle

The future type of organisation is likely to be one where people will be given greater freedom to innovate and experiment, where there will be strong financial rewards for increased performance levels and where people will be given greater control over their area of the business. There is little doubt that in such situations people will be expected, and indeed will wish, to work longer hours and centre what social life they have around their work. Nevertheless, where there are benefits, there may also be disbenefits:

The workplace as a centre for social life and the workmate as a candidate for marriage mate is, on one level, a convenience for overloaded people who have absorbing work that leaves little time to pursue a personal life outside. It is also an inevitable consequence of the new workforce demographics. But on another level, the idea is profoundly disturbing. What about the large number of people whose personal lives are not contained within the corridors of the corporation? What about the people with family commitments outside the workplace? *(Kanter, 1989:285)*

We already know the adverse cost that such work patterns can have on people's physical and mental health and on their family life. In the case of the latter, one might expect to see an increase in the already high divorce rates. Indeed, Kanter believes unmarried or divorced executives are already thought to be preferred to their married counterparts by some companies because it is assumed they can focus more on their job given their lack of home life. Therefore, the line between motivation and exploitation may be a narrow one, and crossing it may benefit neither the individual nor the organisation.

Much of Kanter's work supports the view of Peters and Waterman in terms of the need for and direction of organisational change. Certainly, on the issues of innovation and entrepreneurship, culture and flexibility, and structure and jobs, there is much common ground. To an extent we might expect this, given that they are both writing from an American perspective, and basing their views on the experience and plans of leading American companies. Where they differ, however, is that Kanter takes a much more critical view of these developments. In particular, she draws attention to the contradiction that lies at the heart of the post-entrepreneurial model: are people – their skills, motivation and loyalty – central to the success of the organisation of the future, or are they just another commodity to be obtained and dispensed with as circumstances and their performance require?

Like Peters, Kanter has developed her earlier work, but concentrating mainly on the issue of managing change. She and her co-authors (Kanter *et al*, 1992:383) put forward their 'Ten Commandments for Executing Change' :

1 Analyse the organisation and its need for change.

2 Create a shared vision and a common direction.

3 Separate from the past.

4 Create a sense of urgency.

5 Support a strong leader role.

6 Line up political sponsorship.

7 Craft an implementation plan.

8 Develop enabling structures.

9 Communicate, involve people and be honest.

10 Reinforce and institutionalise change.

Looking at approaches to change, Kanter *et al* (1992) distinguished between 'Bold Strokes' and 'Long Marches'. The former relate to major strategic decisions or economic initiatives. These, they argue, can have a clear and rapid impact on an organisation, but they rarely lead to any long-term change in habits or culture. The Long March approach, on the other hand, favours relatively small-scale and operationally focused initiatives which are slow to implement and whose full benefits are achieved in the long term rather than the short term. However, the Long March approach can impact on culture over time. Bold Strokes are initiatives taken by a few senior managers, sometimes only one; they do not rely on the support of the rest of the organisation for their success. The Long March approach, does, however. Without the involvement and commitment of the majority of the work force, such initiatives cannot succeed.

Kanter *et al* argue that these can be complementary, rather than alternative, approaches to change, though in practice companies appear to favour one or the other. Nevertheless, companies may need both the Bold Stroke and the Long March if they are to succeed in transforming themselves.

In the next (and last) section on Culture–Excellence, we will examine the emergence of new organisational forms from the perspective of a leading British theorist: Charles Handy.

Charles Handy's emerging future organisations

Handy has been an oil executive, an economist and a professor at the London Business School. He has also acted as a consultant to a wide range of organisations in business, government, the voluntary sector, education and health. He is now considered as one of Britain's leading management thinkers. In his book *The Age of Unreason* (1989), Handy argues that profound changes are taking place in organisational life:

> **The world of work is changing because the organisations of work are changing their ways. At the same time, however, the organisations are having to adapt to a changing world of work. It's a chicken and egg situation. One thing, at least, is clear: organisations in both private and public sectors face a tougher world – one in which they are judged more harshly than before on their effectiveness and in which there are fewer protective hedges behind which to shelter. (Handy, 1989: 70)**

He asserts that British companies are fast moving away from the labour-intensive organisations of yesteryear. In future, new knowledge-based structures, run by a few smart people at their core who will control a host of equally smart computerised machines, will be the order of the day. Already, he notes, leading British organisations are increasingly becoming entities which receive their added value from the knowledge and the creativity they put in, rather than from the application of muscle power. He contends that fewer, better motivated people, helped by clever machines, can create much more added value than large groups of unthinking, demotivated ones ever could.

As with the two perspectives we have already examined, Handy believes that the emerging future organisations will be smaller, more flexible and less hierarchical. Similarly, he also believes that the new organisations will need to treat people as assets to be developed and motivated, rather than just so much industrial cannon fodder. He does not assume, however, that the future will be without diversity in relation to the organisational forms that emerge. Unlike Peters and Waterman, and to a lesser extent Kanter, he recognises that companies will continue to face differing circumstances and will need to respond in different manners. Therefore, instead of trying to re-establish a new 'one best way' for all organisations, with all the contradictions that arise from such attempts, Handy identifies three generic types of organisation which he argues will dominate in the future:

1 the Shamrock organisation;

2 the Federal organisation;

3 the Triple I organisation.

These are again detailed below.

1 The Shamrock organisation

This form of organisation, like the plant of the same name which has three inter-locking leaves, is composed of three distinct groups of workers who are treated differently and have different expectations: a small group of specialist 'core' workers; a contractual fringe; and a flexible labour force.

The *core workers* are the first leaf, and the main distinguishing feature of the Shamrock form of organisation. These are a group of specialists, professional workers which form the brain, the hub or what we might call the 'nerve centre' of the organisation. These are people who are seen as being essential to the organ-isation. It is in the hands and heads of these few intelligent and articulate personnel that the secrets of the organisation reside. They are both specialists and generalists, in that they run the organisation and control the smart machines and computers that have replaced, to a large extent, much of the labour force. This '… all puts pressure on the core, a pressure which could be summed up by the new equation of half the people, paid twice as much, working three times as effectively' (Handy, 1989: 118–19).

In their well-rewarded jobs, they are expected to be extremely loyal to the organisation, and to live and breathe their work. It is their responsibility to drive the organisation forward to ever greater success; to be flexible enough to meet the constantly changing challenge of competitors and the equally changing and sophist-icated needs of customers. Core workers operate as colleagues and partners in the organisation, as opposed to superiors and subordinates. In a very real sense, it is their company, and as such they expect to be recognised and rewarded for their roles and achievements, rather than the position they occupy on the organisation's ladder. It follows that they are managed differently – by consent, asked and not told what to do.

The *contractual fringe* is the second leaf of the Shamrock. A central feature of such organisations is their smallness in relation to their productive capacity. This is ach-ieved by two methods: first, as mentioned above, the use of machines to replace people; and second, the contracting-out to individuals and other organisations of services and tasks previously done in-house. This leads to the creation of a con-tractual fringe, who may or may not work exclusively for the company in question. They are contracted to carry out certain tasks, for which they are paid a fee based on results, rather than a wage based on time taken. The arguments put forward in favour of such arrangements are numerous, but tend to boil down to three main ones:

1 *It is cheaper* – companies only pay for what they get.
2 *It makes management easier* – why keep the people on the payroll with all the attendant human management problems if it is not necessary?
3 *Workload balancing* – when business is slack, it is the contractor who bears the impact of the reduced workload.

The *flexible labour force* is the third and fastest-growing leaf of the Shamrock and comprises a pool of part-time workers available for use by organisations. These are people with relevant skills who are not in need of, or who cannot obtain, full-time employment, but who are prepared to work on a part-time basis.

Increasingly, among this group of flexible workers are housewives who left their skilled jobs to raise families, but who are willing to return to work on a part-time basis, while still maintaining their child-rearing commitments. Included in this also is the growing army of young and retired executives, who prefer to hop from one job to another, doing bits and pieces of work on a part-time basis. These workers are sometimes referred to as temps (temporaries) or casuals. The growth of this group can be measured by the proliferation of employment agencies, catering solely for these groups, which have been established in the United Kingdom since the early 1980s. However, the flexible workforce never:

> ... have the commitment or ambition of the core. Decent pay and decent conditions are what they want, ... They have jobs not careers and cannot be expected to rejoice in the organisation's triumphs any more than they can expect to share in the proceeds, nor will they put themselves out for the love of it; more work, in their culture, deserves and demands more money. (*Handy, 1989:80-81*)

The picture, therefore, of the Shamrock organisation is one where structure and employment practices allow it to be big in terms of output, while being small in terms of the number of direct employees. For the latter reason, it is lean with few hierarchical layers and even less bureaucracy. It achieves this by the application of smart machines and a combination of part-time staff and subcontractors, whose work can be turned on and off as circumstances dictate. In a departure from past practice, however, the people involved may be highly skilled and competent. This also has the advantage of requiring much less office and factory accommodation than more traditionally organised companies. Other than the core staff, the rest are all scattered in different organisations or their own homes, often linked through sophisticated communication systems.

Such organisations, with their flexibility and skills, are well-suited to the provision of high-performance products and services to demanding and rapidly changing markets. The beauty of it all, as Handy argues, is that they do not have to employ all of the people all of the time or even in the same place to get the work done. According to Handy, small is not only beautiful but also increasingly preferable.

2 The Federal organisation

This is the second type of generic organisation which Handy sees as becoming dominant in the future. He defines this type of organisation as a variety of individual groups of organisations allied together under a common flag with some shaped identity. Federations arise for two reasons. The first is that, as Shamrock organisations grow bigger, the core workers begin to find the volume of information available to them to make decisions increasingly difficult to handle. Second, federations constitute a response to the constantly changing and competitive environment of the business world. Modern organisations need not only to achieve the flexibility that comes from smallness, but also to be able to command the resources and power of big corporations.

As Handy (1989:110) puts it:

> It [Federalism] allows individuals to work in organisation villages with the advantages of big city facilities. Organisational cities no longer work unless they are broken down into villages. In their big city mode they cannot cope with the variety needed in their products, their processes, and their people. On the other hand, the villages on their own have not the resources nor the imagination to grow. Some villages, of course, will be content to survive, happy in their niche, but global markets need global products and large confederations to make them or do them.

Federalism, therefore, implies the granting of autonomy to Shamrocks. Autonomy requires that Shamrocks are headed by their own separate Chief Executives, supported by a team of core workers, who take full responsibility for running the company. In such situations the Shamrocks become separate, but related entities, under the umbrella of the Federal Centre. With the devolving of power to the Shamrocks, who still remain in the Federal portfolio, the Federal Centre is left to pursue the business of providing a common platform for the integration of the activities of the Shamrocks. The Federal Centre has the role of generating and collating ideas from the different Shamrocks and making them into concrete, achievable strategic objectives. Therefore, the Federal Centre is concerned mainly with the future; with looking forward, generating ideas, and creating scenarios and options of what the future will look like. All this is done with the ultimate aim of moving the organisation forward and keeping it ahead not only of its rivals, but also of its time.

Another feature of the Federal organisation is what Handy refers to as the 'inverted do'nut'.

> The do'nut is an American doughnut. It is round with a hole in the middle rather than the jam in its British equivalent. ... This, however, is an inverted American do'nut, in that it has the hole in the middle filled in and the space on the outside; ... The point of the analogy begins to emerge if you think of your job, or any job. There will be a part of the job which will be clearly defined, and which, if you do not do, you will be seen to have failed. That is the heart, the core, the centre of the do'nut ... [but] ... In any job of any significance the person holding the job is expected not only to do all that is required but in some way to improve on that ... to move into the empty space of the do'nut and begin to fill it up. *(Handy, 1989:102)*

Through this approach, the Federal organisation seeks to maximise the innovative and creative potential of staff members. It does this by specifying the core job, the target and the quality standard expected of a given product or service. However, outside of this specified domain – within the do'nut's empty space – staff members are given enough room and latitude to challenge and question existing ideas, to experiment and to come up with new methods of doing things, and new products or services. The aim is to encourage enquiry and experimentation that lead to higher standards. It follows from this that the essence of leadership under a Federal system is to provide a shared vision for the organisation; one which allows room for those whose lives will be affected by it – either directly or indirectly – to modify it, ponder over it, expand it, accept it and then make it a reality. Leadership in such situations is about providing opportunities for staff to grow and test their potential to the limit.

3 The Triple I organisation

This is the third of Handy's new organisational forms, although in fact it comprises a set of principles rather than a structural model. From the above, it is clear that both Shamrock and Federal organisation types introduce new dimensions into the world of work. Traditional perspectives are being transformed, and the established criteria for judging organisational effectiveness are being re-evaluated. Issues such as the definition of a productive contribution to work, reward systems, managerial skills and many more are being examined in the light of new management ideas. Indeed, we appear to be on the verge of a revolution in management thought and practice.

An examination of the attributes of the core workers in both Shamrock and Federal organisations gives an indication of what will constitute the new formula for success and effectiveness in tomorrow's companies. The core workers, as seen by Handy, use their *Intelligence* to analyse the available *Information* to generate *Ideas* for new products and services. Thus we find that Handy's first two organisational forms contain the seeds to produce his third form, the Triple I – organisations based on Intelligence, Information and Ideas. Since the three Is constitute the prime intellectual capital of the new organisations, clearly the Triple I principle applies most importantly to the core group of workers who are in a position to possess these attributes.

In future, it is argued, the equation for organisational success will be Triple I = AV, where Triple I = Intelligence, Information and Ideas, and AV = Added Value, either in cash or kind. This will be an organisation 'obsessed with the pursuit of truth, or, in business language, of quality' (Handy, 1989:113). This will not depend solely on human ability but will be a combination of smart people and smart machines. Therefore, organisations of the future will increasingly have to:

- *invest in smart machines to remain competitive and effective;*
- *recruit skilled and smart people to control the machines; and,*
- *ensure that this group of skilled people is rewarded equitably.*

For the Triple I organisation to emerge and remain successful, it must keep the skills, knowledge and abilities of its staff up to date. This means that it must become a learning organisation; one that provides a conducive environment for the development of its intellectual capital. Time and effort must be consciously and officially devoted to learning and study, at all levels of the organisation. The core, especially, must spend more time than their equivalents in more traditional companies on thinking and study: meeting with other external professionals and experts, going on study tours and listening more to 'partners' within the organisation, all with the objective of improving the organisation's human capital. The new organisations will be dynamic, interactive societies where information is open to all, freely given and freely received. In the Triple I organisation, everyone will be expected to think and learn as well as to do. Nevertheless, it is the core worker from whom most will be demanded. Such people will be increasingly:

> **... expected to have not only the expertise appropriate to his or her particular role, but will also be required to know and understand business, to have the technical skills of analysis and the human skills and the conceptual skills and to keep them up to date.** (*Handy, 1989:124*)

This is one of the key features which make the Triple I organisation unique; it is a hotbed of intellectual discourse, where the prevailing culture is one of consent rather than instruction. Staff are unsupervised in the traditional sense, and instead are trusted to do what is right and given room to experiment with new ideas and concepts. Finally, the flexibility of such organisations, and the unpredictability of the environments in which they operate, mean that careers will become more variegated and less permanent.

As can be seen, therefore, Handy's view of the future shape of organisations does not appear dissimilar to that of Kanter, and Peters and Waterman. However, he does depart from their views in at least two crucial respects. First, he explicitly acknowledges that not all organisations will adopt the same form or move at the same pace. His three generic forms indicate that organisations will have to exercise choice and judgment in order to match their particular circumstances to the most suitable form. Furthermore, it is clear that he views this as an evolutionary as well as a revolutionary process – companies cannot immediately become a Triple I type of organisation; they have to develop into one over time. Second, he explicitly states what is only hinted at by the other writers, namely that in the new organisations where each person is to be treated as an equal 'partner', some will be more equal than others – i.e. the core workers will be treated and rewarded in a more preferential manner than the contractual fringe or the flexible labour force.

Handy does not as such give guidance as to how existing organisations can adapt themselves to take on these new forms. Though he does indicate that the lack of empowerment and self-belief among individuals in organisations presents a major obstacle to change. In an earlier work (1986), however, Handy does state very clearly that fundamental change is a long-term process and that people tend to react psychologically rather than rationally to change.

In his latest book, *The Empty Raincoat* (Handy, 1994), he returns to and restates many of the themes of his earlier book. There are two differences, however. First, he explicitly acknowledges that the types of careers that these new organisational forms will create will have a severely adverse effect on the home life of employees, especially senior managers. They will be called on to be company men and women above all else, including their families.

Second, there is an almost evangelical feel to the book. This is especially noticeable in the latter section of the book, where Handy argues that the modern world has taken meaning out of people's lives and that, while the pursuit of profit may motivate senior managers:

> **Not many in the lower realms of the organisation can get excited by the thought of enriching shareholders. 'Excellence' and 'quality' are the right sort of words, but they have been tarnished by repetition in too many organisations. (*Handy, 1994:265*)**

Handy calls for a new sense of purpose for individuals, organisations and society. He wants to see a strong ethical approach to business and society, and a recreation of the concept that people exist to help and serve each other rather than themselves. Unfortunately, he fails to show how the organisational developments he predicts/ advocates will aid this search for meaning. Indeed, the reader is left with a feeling that the sort of organisations described by Handy may well have the opposite effect.

Culture–Excellence: summary and criticisms

The Culture–Excellence approach to organisations is radically different from what has gone before; although we might note in passing that the new forms, especially Handy's Shamrock type, bear an interesting resemblance to the first budding of organisational life during the Industrial Revolution. The entrepreneurial style of management, the stress on a privileged core of skilled workers, and the contracting-out of whole areas of organisational activities are all hallmarks of the early industrial organisations. However, the big differences between then and now relate to the level of sophistication and complexity of the new organisations which are emerging, the degree of integration of both internal functions and external relationships, the grade of intelligence and skill required of all staff, whether they be core or peripheral – and, of course, the conditions of employment. For Watson (1986:66), who coined the term Culture–Excellence school to describe proponents of this approach, there is one further and crucial difference:

> **[In these new organisations] What brings the activities of the organisational members to focus upon those purposes which lead to effective performance is the existence of a strong and clearly articulated culture. (*Watson, 1986:66*)**

It is this which makes it clear that the Culture–Excellence approach that has been developing over the last decade or so is remarkably different from most of the theory and practice that has grown up in the last 100 years.

Peters (1992), Kanter *et al* (1992), and Handy (1994) argue that organisations are entering a new age, where familiar themes are taking on different meanings and are being expressed in a new language. Contrasting the old with the new, they argue that what is important in the new is not muscle power, but brain power: the ability to make intelligent use of information to create ideas that add value and sustain competitiveness. The new organisation is flatter in structure, though it might be more accurate to say that structure is decreasing in importance and that its role as a directing and controlling mechanism is being taken over by cultures that stress the need for, and facilitate, flexibility and adaptation (though in passing we should note that Peters (1992) also sees the dismembering of hierarchical structures as an important step in creating these new cultures). The Culture–Excellence approach is sounding the death knell of hierarchical organisations and the concept of promotion through the ranks. Careers and skills are taking on new meanings, as are established ideas of reward.

In future, it is argued, careers are likely to depend on the individual and his/her ability to remain employable. In turn, the skills needed for 'employability' will tend to be generic and broad-based rather than organisation- or function/specialism-specific. Likewise, career paths and promotion will no longer be shaped by the particular employing organisation and its structures and criteria, but will be driven more by individuals creating their own opportunities by taking on new roles and responsibilities, either in one organisation or, more likely, by moving from company to company. As for pay, it seems that this will take the form not so much of a wage related to the particular post occupied, but more that of a fee paid for actual performance.

On human relations, the message being transmitted is that the new forms of organisations will treat their employees in a more responsible and humane fashion than has been the norm. Employees will be seen and treated as 'partners', capable of making a substantial contribution to the growth of the organisation. This approach, it is argued, will manifest itself in a tough-minded respect for the individual, who will receive training, be set reasonable and clear objectives, and be given the autonomy to make his/her own contribution to the work of the organisation. The new organisations will seek to develop open, flexible and pragmatic cultures, which help to maintain a learning environment that promotes creativity and entrepreneurship amongst all employees.

Another feature of the new organisational forms, it is claimed, will be their ability to grant autonomy and encourage flexibility and initiative while at the same time keeping a tight control of their operations. Like so much else, this is to be achieved through culture rather than structure, and values rather than rules. Everything is to be monitored closely, not by the watching eye of superiors, but by creation of a homogeneous environment in which all take an equal responsibility for, and legitimate interest in, the work of their colleagues.

Clearly, the new organisation forms which are being promoted offer much that is admirable and worth supporting. Equally clearly, their adherents and promoters raise more questions than they answer. To an extent this is inevitable, given that we are dealing with something that is emerging rather than an existing and concrete reality. Nevertheless, it would be remiss to ignore or gloss over the questions and dilemmas that seem apparent. Many writers have drawn attention to the short-comings of the Culture–Excellence approach. Carroll (1983) and Lawler (1985) were both scathing about the methodological shortcomings of the research on which Peters and Waterman's (1982) book was based. Wilson (1992), however, in re-viewing the Culture-Excellence approach, is perhaps the most scathing critic, claiming that it lacks any apparent empirical or theoretical foundations. Though Wilson's criticisms may seem somewhat exaggerated, it is certainly arguable that the Culture-Excellence approach does have serious weaknesses, especially in three areas that are crucial to the operation of organisations:

1 *People*. There are serious concerns and contradictions regarding the role and behaviour of people in the new organisations. On the one hand, they are proclaimed as the chief asset of the new organisations. On the other hand, there are clearly different grades of employee, from core to periphery, and these different grades will be treated and rewarded in a markedly dissimilar manner (though none of the different grades can expect any real job security). The new organisations will only value employees as long as they and their areas perform to the highest of standards. Not only does this pit individual against individual, but also one part of the organisation against another. While healthy competition may enhance organisational competitiveness, it is not clear that the Culture–Excellence approach is that healthy.

2 *Politics*. Though Western companies traditionally either deny the existence of internal struggles or argue that such behaviour is perverse, it is clear that the struggle for resources, power and survival is as great within organisations as it is between them (Kanter *et al*, 1992; Pfeffer, 1981; Robbins, 1986). As stated above, the recommendations of the Culture–Excellence school would seem to exacerbate this tendency between individuals and groups, yet in the main they ignore this drawback to their approach, even though it is potentially damaging to both organisational and individual performance.

3 *Culture*. The proponents of Culture–Excellence are advocating a 'one best way' (one best culture) approach for all organisations, irrespective of their size, environment and other circumstances. Furthermore, as Wilson (1992) points out, it assumes a simple causal relationship between culture and performance.

Nevertheless, for the proponents of the Culture–Excellence school, culture is the great cure-all – the creation of a culture of excellence is seen as answering all questions and solving all problems. This assumes that the creation of new cultures will itself be unproblematic. As Chapter 4 will show, culture and organisational politics appear to be the Achilles' Heel of all organisation theories.

There is one final concern which is wider than the Culture–Excellence approach *per se* or its impact on organisations. The move towards creating segmented workforces of the type described by Handy (1989) and the emphasis on the temporary nature of employment championed by Peters and Waterman (1982) and Kanter (1989) is part of a continuing trend in the West towards worsening job security and conditions of service, in order to create a vast pool of under-employed, especially part-time, labour that can be turned on or off as the situation dictates.

In the UK in 1993, for example, some 9.7 million workers (38 per cent of all UK workers) were either part-time, temporary, self-employed, on a Government training scheme, or unpaid family workers – an increase of 1.25 million since 1986. Similarly, the proportion of men in employment who are part of the flexible workforce has risen from 18 per cent in 1981 to 27.5 per cent in 1993 (Watson, 1994). This tallies with Hutton's recent argument (1995) that the UK is now more socially divided than at any time since the Industrial Revolution. In particular, he argues that the UK is a 30/30/40 society – the marginalised, the newly insecure and the advantaged – and that this not only raises the spectre of increased social tensions, but is a positive disadvantage to wealth creation. Contrast this with the case of Japan, discussed next, where at government and organisation level, full employment takes precedence over profit and underpins its voracious appetite for economic expansion (Holden and Burgess, 1994).

Despite these concerns and criticisms, the Culture–Excellence approach has become increasingly influential in the USA and Europe, as is apparent from the many articles on its merits and case studies of its use that appear regularly in management journals. During the past four decades, however, the Japanese have been developing an alternative approach to structuring and managing organisations which is not only markedly different from the Culture–Excellence one but also has a proven track record of success.

THE JAPANESE APPROACH TO MANAGEMENT

The last 40 years have seen the rebirth of Japan. Reduced almost to ashes at the end of the Second World War, Japan has now become an industrial power second only to the USA. Though writers have suggested many reasons for Japan's success, ranging from culture to economic institutions, time and again, its approach to managing organisations is cited as the key factor (Hunter, 1989; Schonberger, 1982; Smith and Misumi, 1989; Whitehill, 1991).

Before proceeding to examine what is meant by the Japanese approach to management, it is useful briefly to trace Japan's industrial development. Up to the middle of the nineteenth century, Japan was an intensely nationalistic society which practised a deliberate policy of isolating itself from the outside world. Therefore, for most of its inhabitants, Japan was the world. It was a feudal country which laid strong emphasis on obligation and deference, and where obedience to authority in general, and to the Emperor in particular, was unquestioned (Sheridan, 1993).

For all its deliberate isolation, Japan was a sophisticated and well-educated country with a high degree of literacy. Education was based on a set of Confucian principles which stressed unquestioning obedience to the family, total loyalty to one's superiors and reverence for education and self-development. The abiding influence of these can still be seen in Japanese society today, and underpins the strength of Japanese organisations (Smith and Misumi, 1989). From the mid-nineteenth century, however, Japan began to experience internal tensions. The feudal aristocracy experienced escalating financial difficulties while the merchant class, considered social inferiors, began to prosper. At the same time, it became clear that the growing military might of other countries posed a potential threat to Japan. In response to these developments, Japan adopted a twin-track policy of economic and military growth, not dissimilar to that being developed in Germany at this time (Hunter, 1989).

Missions were dispatched abroad to study and bring technologies and practices back to Japan. In the early years of this century, there was a rapid and enthusiastic adoption of Taylor's Scientific Management principles and allied approaches to work study and production management (McMillan, 1985). By the 1920s, Japan had moved from being an agrarian economy to one dominated by industry. Like many Western countries, industrialisation was accompanied by considerable industrial conflict, sometimes violent (Urabe, 1986). Unlike most Western countries, however, this was not accompanied by a growing democratisation of society. Instead, democratic tendencies were quashed by a growing coalition between industry and the military which promoted intense nationalism and led, almost inexorably, to the Second World War. After Japan's defeat, its shattered society was occupied by the USA, which stripped the Emperor of his traditional powers and replaced these with democratically elected and controlled institutions (Sheridan, 1993; Whitehill, 1991).

Given the state of the Japanese economy after the Second World War, the success of its reconstruction is nothing short of miraculous. The Korean War in the 1950s proved a stroke of good fortune for Japan, in that the USA used Japan as an important staging post for troops and supplies. This injected billions of American dollars into Japan's economy. Despite this, though, there is little doubt that the main credit for Japanese success can be attributed to hard work rather than good fortune, especially the distinctive Japanese approach to developing and managing enterprises (Fruin, 1992; Pascale and Athos, 1982; Smith and Misumi, 1989).

What is the Japanese approach to management?

As one might expect, it is difficult to find an all-embracing definition of the Japanese approach to management which satisfies all commentators or can be found in all Japanese companies. In particular, there are distinct differences between larger and smaller enterprises in Japan, and in the treatment of full-time and part-time, and male and female employees in all enterprises (Cole, 1979). Indeed, such are these differences that some argue there is no such thing as a distinctive Japanese approach to management (Dale, 1986). Nevertheless, the vast majority of observers do seem to agree that it does exist and can, broadly, be defined (Abegglen and Stalk, 1984; Ackroyd *et al*, 1988; Hatvany and Pucik, 1981; Holden and Burgess, 1994; Pascale and Athos, 1982; Smith and Misumi, 1989)

Wickens (1987) believes the Japanese approach can be characterised by three factors: teamwork, quality-consciousness and flexibility. McKenna (1988) believes that the key elements are: lifetime employment, the seniority principle with regard to pay and promotion, and enterprise unionism. Pang and Oliver (1988) agree with McKenna but also draw attention to training and education, company-based welfare schemes, quality circles and manufacturing methods such as Just-in-Time production. Keys and Miller (1984) point to long-term planning, lifetime employment, and collective responsibility as being the hallmarks of Japanese management. Other commentators have also come up with similar lists (*see* especially Pascale and Athos's seven Ss (1982)). The factors identified by these writers can be separated into two categories: those relating to personnel/industrial relations issues and those relating to business/manufacturing practices.

Personnel issues

The dedication, commitment and ability of Japanese workers is seen as a major factor in the success of Japanese companies. Though much credit for this has been given to the culture of Japanese society, especially its Confucian tradition of obedience and loyalty, similar levels of motivation have been reproduced in Japanese companies operating in the West (Wickens, 1987), which would imply that other factors are also at work. Chief among these is the crucial role played by the personnel policies prevalent in many Japanese enterprises, especially the larger ones. The core of the Japanese approach to personnel comprises a group of practices and policies designed to socialise and bind employees to the organisation, and promote their long-term development and commitment. The principle practices and policies concerned are:

1 *Lifetime employment.* Many employees are recruited straight from school or university, and expect, and are expected, to spend the rest of their working lives with the same organisation. This 'guarantee', based as it is on an age-old sense of mutual obligation and belonging, creates an intense sense of loyalty to and dependence on the organisation. Indeed, Holden and Burgess (1994) observed that while a Japanese worker might survive the loss of his family, the collapse of his employing organisation would be unbearable. Therefore, lifetime employment is a central feature of the Japanese approach and supports so much else, including the willingness to change and the maintenance of a stable organisational culture. However, the fact that organisations prefer to recruit school or university leavers also makes it difficult for individuals, who might wish to, to move between companies

once they have accepted an appointment. It follows that if someone is fired, their chances of securing other employment are negligible.

2 *Internal labour markets.* Most positions are filled from inside the company. This is a corollary to lifetime employment which demonstrates to the employee that satisfactory performance will bring promotion, and it eliminates the potential for tension which can be brought about by the recruitment of outsiders.

3 *Seniority-based promotion and reward systems.* Employees are ranked and rewarded primarily, but not exclusively, on their length of service, and independent of the precise nature of the job they perform.

4 *Teamwork and bonding.* Although Japanese employees are made to feel part of the organisation and see it as some sort of extended family, they are first and foremost a member of a particular workgroup or team. The group is not just a collection of individuals, it is constructed and developed in such a way that it comprises a single entity which takes collective responsibility for its performance. Japanese companies use a variety of techniques, both at work and in a social setting, for bonding team members to each other and to the organisation.

5 *Enterprise (single company) unions.* Unlike the West, Japanese companies tend only to allow one union to represent the interests of the workforce. In addition, Japanese unions tend to be company or enterprise unions. Indeed, in the Western sense, they are not so much trade unions as company associations. This is illustrated by the practice of senior managers, at some stage in their careers, being expected to serve as union officials.

6 *Training and education.* Extensive and continuous training and education form an integral part of Japanese personnel policies. This emphasis on the continual development of employees to enable them to carry out their work better and prepare them for promotion represents a significant investment by Japanese companies in their human capital. Much of the training is done on the job and is always geared to the twin aims of improving organisational performance and individual development. Though encouraged by the company, employees are expected to take responsibility for their own self-development.

7 *Company welfarism.* Many Japanese companies provide a wide range of welfare benefits for their employees. These can cover medical treatment, education for children and even housing. Some of the larger companies are almost mini welfare states in themselves.

Many other practices and policies could be added to the list but these appear to be at the core. They are designed to instil in employees:

- *loyalty and gratitude to the company and a commitment to its objectives;*
- *a sense of security;*

- *a strong commitment to hard work and performance improvement;*
- *an atmosphere of co-operation and not conflict;*
- *a belief in self-development and improvement.*

These are the cornerstone of Japanese company life; their presence is the reason why Japanese national culture is often cited as being at the heart of the ability of the Japanese to compete in a world market. These operate within organisation structures which, to Western eyes at least, appear complex, highly formalised and very hierarchical (Whitehill, 1991). However, these personnel issues cannot be seen in isolation from the working practices which Japanese companies use or the objectives they pursue. It is the combination of the two which makes Japanese companies so effective (Wood, 1991). Without overall direction and the appropriate work systems, even the best skilled and motivated workers are ineffective. This is why Japanese business practices and work systems should receive as much attention as personnel issues.

Business practices and work systems

The Japanese ability to satisfy customers, and thereby capture markets, by developing and producing products to a higher specification and lower cost than their competitors, is staggering considering the state of their industry in the 1940s and 1950s. Indeed, even as recently as the 1960s, 'Made in Japan' was synonymous with poor quality. What has changed, or rather what has come to fruition, has been the methods they apply to all aspects of business but especially to manufacturing (Hannam, 1993). The fact that some of these methods have, quite naturally, Japanese names (such as Hoshin Kanri – policy deployment; Genba Kanri – workshop management; Kaizen – continuous improvement; Kanban – a paperless form of scheduling) tends, for the Western audience, to cloak and mystify the core principles and systems being used, and also to disguise how much of these have been adopted from the West. Leaving aside the jargon and terminology, Japanese business practices and work systems can be characterised by three interrelated elements: long-term planning, timeliness and quality.

Long-term planning. This will be discussed further in Chapter 5, but for now, in brief, let us say that the timescale on which Japanese enterprises operate is far longer than many of their Western competitors', and their focus on building a strong market position similarly contrasts with the short-term profit maximisation objectives prevalent in the USA and UK in particular (Hamel and Prahalad, 1989). Needless to say, this is an enormous advantage when considering investment decisions, whether this be for products, processes or people (Smith and Misumi, 1989).

Timeliness. The Japanese have an ability to develop products and bring them to market faster than most of their competitors. Part of the explanation for this relates to *teamwork*. While many Western companies are still designing and developing products on a sequential basis (whereby one part of the design is completed before another is begun), the Japanese work in teams to undertake these tasks simultaneously. Not only does this cut the overall time required, but it also leads to less errors and misunderstandings because all the relevant parties are involved (Womack *et al*, 1990). Another major contribution to the timeliness of the Japanese is a series of practices designed to cut manufacturing lead times. The main one is *Just-in-Time production*. Under Just-in-Time, parts are supplied and used only as and when required. It reduces stock and work-in-progress and thus reduces cost. However, to achieve this (as proponents of lean/agile manufacturing have stressed) requires everything to be 'right first time', otherwise such a system would quickly grind to a halt for lack of usable parts (Kidd and Karwowski, 1994; Lamming, 1993). Therefore, it is necessary to drive waste and inefficiency out of the system, and the key mechanism for achieving this is the Japanese commitment to quality (Dale and Cooper, 1992).

Quality. The Japanese commitment to quality is now legendary. Their approach owes much to the inspiration of three Americans – MacArthur, Deming and Juran (Wilkinson, 1991). General MacArthur, who (on behalf of the USA) virtually ruled Japan in the early post-war years, encouraged Japanese industry to improve production quality as part of the rebuilding of their shattered industrial base. Deming (1982) showed the Japanese that statistical process control (SPC), and other such techniques, are powerful methods of controlling quality. Juran (1988) showed the Japanese that quality was determined by all departments in an organisation, and thus set them on the road to developing *Total Quality Management*. Though imported, the Japanese developed the original concepts considerably. In particular, they introduced the concept of continuous improvement – *Kaizen*. Despite the widespread acceptance of the need for improved quality in the West, the Japanese appear to be the only nation so far capable of diffusing successfully the ideas and practices throughout their industry (Dale and Cooper, 1992; Hannam, 1993; Schonberger, 1982; Womack *et al*, 1990).

In any investigation of the Japanese approach to long-term planning, timeliness and quality, it is necessary to recognise the role played by employees in decision-making. Most discussions of Japanese management emphasise the occurrence of upward influence, particularly through the *ringi system*. This is a procedure whereby proposals for new policies, procedures or expenditure are circulated throughout the firm for comment. The proposal is circulated in written form, and is then sent to all who might be affected if it were to be implemented, in ascending order of seniority. The proposal is modified in line with comments, and only when all agree is it implemented. This joint approach to decision-making is also operated through production councils and quality circles, and covers the planning and scheduling of production, work allocation, changes to production methods, problem-solving, etc (Inagami, 1988). This system of involving large numbers of people in decision-making is the reason why the Japanese are notorious for the slowness with which they make decisions, and famous for their ability to get it right first time (Hannam, 1993; Smith and Misumi, 1989).

One factor only mentioned briefly so far is the importance – or not – of culture to the Japanese approach to management. Certainly, early studies laid great stress on the relationship between Japanese culture and business success (Abegglen, 1958). The argument emerged that it was the nature of Japanese society and its impact on individuals and companies which gave Japan its competitive edge. For this reason, it was argued, the West would never be able to replicate Japanese practices and competitiveness successfully. Obviously, as Hofstede (1980 and 1990) showed, national cultures do impinge on organisational practices. However, whether or not this means that such practices cannot successfully be adopted in other societies is another question. Recent work has undermined the argument for considering the Japanese approach to management to be dependent on Japanese culture. It has been shown that many of the distinctive practices of Japanese companies are relatively new and not embedded in Japanese history, that the role of culture is less influential than other factors, and that the Japanese approach can be successfully replicated outside Japan (Ackroyd *et al*, 1988; Buckley and Mirza, 1985; Cole, 1979; Marsh and Mannari, 1976; Pascale and Athos, 1982; Smith and Misumi, 1989; Urabe, 1986; Wickens, 1987).

The Japanese approach: summary and criticisms

It can be seen, therefore, that there are distinctive practices and policies which have a coherence and can be described as 'the Japanese approach to management'. However, it is not simply the merits of the individual practices which have given the Japanese their competitive edge. Rather it is that they are devised and adopted in such a way that they are integrated and mutually supportive of each other; in particular, Japanese companies have a unique way of combining hard and soft practices (Pascale and Athos, 1982). This is not to say that this approach is universal in Japan or that all elements are present in those companies who do practise it. There is sufficient evidence available, however, to justify stating that it is the dominant approach in Japan at the moment, and has been since at least the 1960s.

This does not imply that it will not change. Indeed, given that most of these practices have been evolving over the last 40 years, it would be surprising if they did not continue to develop and change (Smith and Misumi, 1989; Whitehill, 1991). Already, there is strong evidence to show that even in large companies, such as Toyota and Honda, policies of lifetime employment and the reluctance to recruit staff mid-career are breaking down, owing to the need to recruit skills which are in short supply, and because of economic and social pressures. These include especially the pressures for equal opportunities for men and women, the implications of an ageing population, and the need to recruit foreigners (Dawkins, 1993 and 1994; Thomas, 1993).

Given that lifetime employment is central to the notion of the Japanese enterprise as an extended family, its elimination, as opposed to its modification, could shatter the very basis of Japanese corporate life. Therefore, though the dynamic and innovative nature of Japanese organisations and their passionate devotion to competitiveness are likely to lead to changes in the way organisations are run, it is unlikely that these changes will undermine the core construct of mutual obligation between organisation and employee that lies at the heart of the Japanese system. It also seems more than likely that the changes which are taking place and will take place in the future will enhance, rather than detract from, Japan's economic strength.

The Japanese approach has delivered impressive economic results, but there are those who would question the social cost involved. Japanese workers work longer hours than their Western counterparts, and in addition are expected to participate in many work-related social events (Clark, 1979). There is also considerable evidence to show that Japanese workers are less satisfied with their lot than their Western counterparts, especially in relation to working hours and pay (Kamata, 1982; Lincoln and Kalleberg, 1985; Luthans *et al*, 1985; Naoi and Schooler, 1985; Odaka, 1975).

In many respects this is not surprising. From a Western standpoint at least, Japanese companies appear to operate very oppressive and authoritarian regimes which, through the combination of the personnel practices and work systems discussed above, together with peer group pressure, leave workers little option but to conform and perform to very high standards (Kamata, 1982; Smith and Misumi, 1989). This accounts, in part at least, for the common observation that the Japanese are a nation of workaholics. However, there are other serious criticisms of the Japanese approach:

- *Most companies operate a two-tier labour market, whereby a significant minority of the workforce have good conditions and lifetime employment, at the expense of less well paid and less secure jobs for the majority, especially women.*

- *Even those with lifetime employment are little more than slaves to the corporation because they cannot move to other jobs.*

- *The merits of teamwork are only gained thanks to the unremitting peer group pressure on individuals continually to improve their performance.*

- *The lack of independent trade unions leaves workers defenceless in the face of managerial pressure to work ever harder.*

Whatever the merits or demerits of the Japanese approach, there is little doubt that it has had a significant impact on organisational performance; consequently, attempts are being made to introduce 'Japanisation' into many Western companies (Ackroyd *et al*, 1988; Hannam, 1993; Pang and Oliver, 1988; Pascale and Athos, 1982; Schonberger, 1982; Turnbull, 1986).

CONCLUSIONS
....

This chapter has examined two organisational paradigms which present approaches to managing and structuring organisations which contrast sharply with the three organisational theories discussed in Chapters 1 and 2. This does not mean there are not some similarities, which is hardly surprising given that Japan has borrowed heavily from American and European practices. For example, the Japanese use the industrial engineering concepts developed by Taylor and his contemporaries to study and design jobs. However, the context in which they are deployed (the lack of payment by results, the use of teamwork and worker involvement, and above all else, guaranteed jobs) is markedly different. In the same way, the Culture–Excellence approach can be seen to bear some similarities with the Human Relations movement, especially the emphasis on leadership and communication. However, the emphasis on culture, individual achievement and all-round excellence make it a distinct approach.

There are also points of contact between the Japanese approach and the Culture–Excellence approach (the stress on excellence, the importance of culture), but, again, there are marked differences. Lifetime employment and loyalty to the organisation contrast strongly with the stress on the temporary nature of jobs proposed by the proponents of Culture–Excellence. As an example, contrast the threat to thousands of jobs posed by the merger of the Halifax and Leeds building societies in the UK (in order to form the UK's fourth largest bank) with the case of the merger of the Mitsubishi Bank and the Bank of Tokyo in Japan (to form the world's largest bank) where it was stated that maintaining all jobs was a matter of honour (Hughes, 1995; Rafferty, 1995). Likewise, payment by seniority and payment by performance are significant points of departure (though there is some small-scale use of performance pay in Japan). It is noticeable as well that the Culture–Excellence approach does not really concern itself with the sort of hard, manufacturing/quality practices so common in Japan. Finally, the Culture–Excellence school seems obsessed with down-sizing and arguing for smallness. The Japanese, on the other hand, are committed to growth. As Ferguson (1988:57) remarked, the USA is not being outperformed by small, nimble organisations, but by 'high industrial complexes embedded in stable, strategically co-ordinated alliances often supported by protectionist governments ...'.

In essence, these are competing paradigms. The Japanese approach, with its combination of tried and tested, hard and soft techniques, provides a coherent and comprehensive approach to organisations which stresses both innovation and stability. The Culture–Excellence approach, on the other hand, is relatively new, tends to emphasise soft techniques, stresses innovation, dynamism and unpredictability, but leaves unanswered questions regarding its coherence and staying power. This does not mean that if Western organisations become more adept at adopting Total Quality Management and other such techniques, and if Japanese companies broaden their use of external labour markets, the two may not coalesce. At the moment, however, they remain competitors rather than collaborators.

Nevertheless, neither approach is without its drawbacks or criticisms. In particular, there are five concerns which should be highlighted, on the issues of structure, people, politics, culture and change management.

Structure Much of Part 1 of this book has been concerned with approaches to managing and structuring organisations. The one clear message which has emerged so far is to beware of any theory or proposition which assumes that one form or type of approach is going to be suitable for all situations and organisations. Yet both the Culture–Excellence school and the Japanese Management approach appear to advocate just this.

People The Culture–Excellence and the Japanese approaches also leave much to be desired with regard to people. Both approaches rely on a workforce split into a privileged core and a relatively unprivileged periphery. Under both approaches there is a strong emphasis on commitment to the organisation taking precedence over all else, even family life. Therefore, long hours and short holidays are the norm under both systems. The Japanese approach appears to offer more job security, at least for the privileged core. The price of this, however, is that competition for jobs in the better organisations begins, quite literally, at birth. To get a job with the best companies, applicants have to have been to the best universities; to enter those, one has to have been at the best schools; and to enter the best schools, one has to have been at the best nurseries (Bratton, 1992; Fruin, 1992). One cannot escape the conclusion that the social cost of achieving excellence, in either West or East, is high.

Politics The issue of organisational power and politics has received extensive attention over the last 15 years (Kotter, 1981; Pfeffer, 1981 and 1992; Minett, 1992; Willcocks, 1994). Given that organisations are social entities and not machines, power struggles and political infighting are inevitable. They may not always be prominent, but tend to come to the fore in situations where resources are scarce or organisations are in transition (Morgan, 1986). It is perhaps here that Peters and Waterman, with their notion of total openness and trust to the extent of employees effectively allowing others to monitor their work, could most easily be accused of being out of touch with reality. There is a tendency in the West to treat politics and conflict as illegitimate; but, as Pascale (1993) and Thompkins (1990) argued, conflict is part and parcel of the creative process, and political skills may be a key competence for managers if they are to be successful leaders and persuaders. To ignore the presence of conflict or underestimate its tenacity is usually a recipe for disaster (Kanter *et al*, 1992; McLennan, 1989; Robbins, 1986).

In both the Japanese and Culture–Excellence approaches, however, little is said on the subject of organisational politics and conflict. As far as the Culture-Excellence perspective is concerned, there appears to be an assumption that employees working in smaller business units, having greater autonomy and more satisfying jobs, will work with each other, pursuing a common purpose. As Chapter 4 will show, this is perhaps an unrealistic expectation. It may well be that in Japanese organisations, with their consensual and open approach to decision-making, strong commitment to organisational goals, high peer group pressure and, for some at least, lifetime employment, conflict is either minimised or channelled into creative directions; though Ishizuna (1990), Kamata (1982) and Sakai (1992) have shown that this is not always the case. In the West, however, with companies reshaping their businesses, where job security is being eroded, where an individual's current performance outweighs all other considerations, and where only the fittest and fleetest of foot can expect to survive, it is foolish to deny or underestimate the importance of power and politics or to believe that culture can act as a cure-all.

Culture This bring us to the next concern to which these two approaches give rise. Proponents of both approaches treat culture in a rather subordinate fashion. For the Culture–Excellence school, all problems are resolved through the creation of strong, flexible, pragmatic cultures which promote the values of trust, co-operation and teamwork. There is no real discussion or acknowledgement of the difficulties in defining or changing culture, despite much evidence to the contrary (Allaire and Firsirotu, 1984; Schein, 1985; Wilson, 1992). Nor do those who seek to promote the Japanese approach treat the subject of culture any more thoroughly. Either it is portrayed as an immutable feature of Japanese companies which prevents the West from adopting the Japanese approach or, more frequently these days, the Japanese approach is seen as somehow independent of culture (Smith and Misumi, 1989). Very few writers acknowledge that Japanese companies, like their Western counter-parts, can find themselves with apparently inappropriate cultures which they wish to change (Ishizuna, 1990). Both approaches clearly leave themselves open to the accusation that they gloss over the difficulty of changing culture. The role of organisational culture will be returned to in Chapter 4.

Change management There is one last issue which should be touched on: the management of change. Organisation theories are also theories of change. All organisation theories claim to show organisations how to identify where they are and where they should be. They also, either explicitly or implicitly, address the issue of change management.

For the Classical school, change management is relatively easy: it tells organisations what they should be and, because managers and workers are rational beings, they should accept any concomitant changes because it's the logical thing to do! A similar approach is adopted by the Contingency Theorists. The Human Relations movement, on the other hand, sees change as more problematic. Organisations are social systems; change is not a rational process; emotions come into play as well. Therefore, persuasion and leadership play a key role in changing organisations.

The Culture–Excellence approach has little to say about how change should be achieved, despite acknowledging the radical transformation it is advocating. Peters (1992) advocated a 'Big Bang' approach to change – 'change radically and do it quickly' seems to be his advice. Handy (1986), on the other hand, seemed to adopt a more gradualist approach to change – big changes over long periods. Kanter *et al*

(1992) advocated a combination of both; they argue that major changes, especially in behaviour, can only be achieved over time. They also believe, however, that dramatic gestures are also necessary to improve performance in the short term. Therefore, their approach to change is a combination of 'Bold Strokes' and 'Long Marches'. Taken as a whole, the message from the Culture–Excellence school is somewhat mixed and the process and details are lacking, notwithstanding Kanter *et al*'s (1992) book on change.

The Japanese approach, however, is more specific. They advocate creating a vision of the future and moving towards it in incremental steps (*Kaizen*) at all levels of the organisation. The Japanese are extremely able at this process, which has given them the reputation as a nation which makes ambitious long-term plans which are slowly, relentlessly and successfully achieved. It is debatable, however, whether this approach could work in many Western countries. In the USA and UK in particular, competitive pressures appear to require radical change over a short timescale, while at the same time there appears to be a built-in aversion to long-term thinking, especially among the financial institutions who play a pivotal role in the life of most firms.

Therefore, though both the Japanese and Culture–Excellence approaches have their merits, they also have their drawbacks, at least as far as Western companies are concerned. This is not necessarily a cause for despair. Emerging paradigms by their very nature will contain dilemmas and contradictions which can only be resolved with experience and the passage of time. Nevertheless, this is not a case for ignoring them; rather the reverse. The future is not, hopefully, immutable. Managers are not powerless, they do have some freedom of choice and action, and the possibility does exist to influence the future shape of work by promoting the good and avoiding the bad.

Parts Two, Three and Four of this book will consider managerial choice, and the issues and concerns raised above, in more detail in order to give a realistic view of how organisations operate and what firms can do to shape their future. Before moving on to this, however, the final chapter in Part One will round off the review of organisation theory by examining the role of culture, power and politics in managing and shaping organisations.

Chapter 4

ORGANISATION THEORY AND MANAGERIAL CHOICE

The role of culture, power and politics

INTRODUCTION

The previous three chapters have described the development of organisations and organisation theory from the Industrial Revolution through to the present day. What has emerged is a somewhat confusing picture of theories which claim, each in their own way, to be the answer to all organisational ills, yet which are all open to potentially damning criticism. All the theories we have examined are aimed at giving practical and coherent advice to managers on how to structure and run their organisations. Yet it is in their limited applicability to the range and complexity of situations found in everyday organisational life that these theories are most open to criticism:

● *The tendency to assume a unitary frame of reference, in which workers' and managers' interests either coincide or can be easily reconciled, is a clear shortcoming in all these theories.*

● *The belief of the Classical school and the Human Relations movement that contextual factors, the external environment, size, technology, etc., are irrelevant is another obvious flaw.*

● *Similarly, the assumption by both the Contingency theorists and the proponents of Culture–Excellence that managers are powerless to change the situational variables they face is not borne out in reality.*

● *Perhaps the most serious drawback is that only the Culture–Excellence school, and to a lesser extent the Japanese approach, gives any importance to the role of organisational culture – and even then it is treated in a simplistic fashion. None of the theories acknowledge the role of power and politics in influencing decision-making in organisations.*

This chapter will address this final point by undertaking a review of organisational culture and politics, in order to understand the role they play in shaping the structure and behaviour of organisations. The first part of the chapter deals with organisational culture. Many organisations lack a cohesive culture which bonds them together in a common purpose; and even where strong cultures exist, they may be inappropriate, or undermined owing to the absence of clear or uncontested organisational goals. This section concludes that although the possession of an appropriate culture is important, there is little agreement about the nature of culture, whether it can be changed or the benefits to be gained from attempting to do so. Furthermore, instead of culture being seen as an all-important and malleable determinant of performance, organisational life in many cases is dominated by political-power battles which may be more influential than culture in shaping key decisions.

Consequently, the second part of the chapter moves on to examine the nature of power and politics in organisations. It is argued that, rather than being the prisoners of organisational theories or contingencies, managers (potentially) have considerable freedom of choice over the structure, policies and practices of their organisations, and even over the constraints under which they operate. In exercising choice, managers are influenced less by organisational theories than by their concern to ensure that the outcome of decisions favours, or at least does not damage, their personal interests. The chapter concludes by arguing that, whether illegitimate or useful, political behaviour is an ever-present part of organisational life, which is particularly important in shaping major decisions regarding resource allocation and change.

THE CULTURAL PERSPECTIVE

What is organisational culture?

As can be seen from the discussion in Chapter 3 of the Culture–Excellence school and, to a lesser extent, the Japanese approach to running organisations, many writers argue that managers and employees do not perform their duties in a value-free vacuum. Their work and the way it is done are governed, directed and tempered by an organisation's culture – the particular set of values, beliefs, customs and systems which are unique to that organisation. So influential has this view become that, as Wilson (1992) has noted, culture has come to be seen as the great 'cure-all' for the majority of organisational ills.

The current fascination of business with organisational culture began in the 1980s with the work of writers such as Allen and Kraft (1982), Deal and Kennedy (1982), and above all Peters and Waterman (1982). However, academics, had drawn attention to its importance much earlier (*see* Eldridge and Crombie, 1974; Turner,

1971). Indeed, Allaire and Firsirotu (1984) showed that, over 20 years before the work of Peters and Waterman, there was already substantial academic literature on organisational culture. Blake and Mouton (1969), for example, were already arguing that there was a link between culture and excellence in the late 1960s. For all this it remains a highly contentious topic whose implications are far-reaching.

Turner (1986) traced the 'culture craze' of the 1980s to the decline of standards in manufacturing quality in the USA and the challenge to its economic pre-eminence by Japan. He comments that the concept of culture holds out a new way of understanding organisations, and has been offered by many writers as an explanation for the spectacular success of Japanese companies. Bowles (1989), among others, observed that there is an absence of a cohesive culture in advanced economies in the West, and that the potential for creating systems of beliefs and myth within organisations provides the opportunity for promoting both social and organisation cohesion. The case for culture was best summed up by Deal and Kennedy (1983), who argued that culture rather than structure, strategy or politics is the prime mover in organisations.

Silverman (1970) contended that organisations are societies in miniature and can therefore be expected to show evidence of their own cultural characteristics. However, culture does not spring up automatically and fully formed from the whims of management. Allaire and Firsirotu (1984) argued that it is the product of a number of different influences: the ambient society's values and characteristics, the organisation's history and past leadership, and factors such as industry and technology.

Culture, as Eldridge and Crombie (1974:78) stated, refers 'to the unique configuration of norms, values, beliefs, ways of behaving and so on, that characterise the manner in which groups and individuals combine to get things done'. Culture defines how those in the organisation should behave in a given set of circumstances. It affects all, from the most senior manager to the humblest clerk. Their actions are judged by themselves and others in relation to expected modes of behaviour. Culture legitimises certain forms of action and proscribes other forms. This view is supported by Turner (1971), who observed that cultural systems contain elements of 'ought' which prescribe forms of behaviour or allow behaviour to be judged acceptable or not.

Handy (1986:188) observed that 'There seem to be four main types of culture ... power, role, task and person'. He relates each of these to a particular form of organisational structure.

- A *power culture, he states, is frequently found in small entrepreneurial organisations such as some property, trading and finance companies. Such a culture is associated with a web structure with one or more powerful figures at the centre, wielding power.*

- A *person culture is, he argues, rare. The individual and his or her wishes are the central focus of this form of culture. It is associated with a minimalistic structure the purpose of which is to assist those individuals who choose to work together. Therefore, a person culture can be characterised as a cluster or galaxy of individual stars.*

- *A **role** culture is appropriate to bureaucracies, and organisations with mechanistic, rigid structures and narrow jobs. Such cultures stress the importance of procedures and rules, hierarchical position and authority, security and predictability. In essence, role cultures create situations in which those in the organisation stick rigidly to their job description (role), and any unforeseen events are referred to the next layer up in the hierarchy.*

- ***Task** cultures, on the other hand, are job- or project-orientated; the onus is on getting the job in hand (the task) done rather than prescribing how it should be done. Such types of culture are appropriate to organically-structured organisations where flexibility and team working are encouraged. Task cultures create situations in which speed of reaction, integration and creativity are more important than adherence to particular rules or procedures, and where position and authority are less important than the individual contribution to the task in hand.*

Handy (1986) believes that it is these last two forms of culture, *role* and *task*, which are most frequently found in organisations. Relating these two types of culture to Burns and Stalker's (1961) structural continuum, with mechanistic structures at one end and organic at the other, we can see that Handy is in effect seeking to construct a parallel and related cultural continuum, with role cultures at the mechanistic end and task cultures at the organic end. This categorisation certainly accommodates the four Western approaches to organisation theory discussed in the previous chapters. However, it is difficult to accommodate Japanese organisations within this frame- work, as their cultures contain elements of each extreme. As was described in Chap- ter 3, Japanese companies have very tightly structured jobs, especially at the lower levels; they are very hierarchical and deferential, while at the same time achieving high levels of motivation, initiative and creativity in problem-solving. They tend to be heavily group/team-orientated, with such teams having a great deal of autonomy.

One criticism of Handy's categorisation of culture is that he fails to give sufficient weight to the influence of national cultures on the types of cultures which predominate in particular countries. Hofstede (1980 and 1990) suggested that national cultures can be clustered along the lines of their similarities across a range of dimensions:

- *the prevailing sense of individualism or collectivity in each country;*
- *the power distance accepted in each country (the degree of centralisation, autocratic leadership and number of levels in the hierarchy);*
- *the degree to which uncertainty is tolerated or avoided.*

Based on these dimensions, Hofstede's research found that industrialised countries could be classified into four broad clusters:

1 *Scandinavia (primarily Denmark, Sweden and Norway)*. These cultures are based upon values of collectivity, consensus and decentralisation.

2 *West Germany (prior to unification), Switzerland and Austria*. These are grouped together largely as valuing efficiency – the well-oiled machine – and seeking to reduce uncertainty.

3 *Great Britain, Canada, the USA, New Zealand, Australia and the Netherlands*. These lie somewhere between 1 and 2 but cluster on the value they place on strong individuals and achievers in society.

4 *Japan, France, Belgium, Spain and Italy*. These are clustered on bureaucratic tendencies – the pyramid structure – favouring a large power distance.

Wilson (1992:90) argued that: 'The similarity of the factors in [Hofstede's] national culture study to Handy's (1986) four organizational forms is striking'. However, while one can see that Scandinavia can be classed as exhibiting task culture characteristics, and the group containing West Germany can be seen as exhibiting role culture characteristics, the other two groupings (Great Britain *et al* and Japan *et al*) are more difficult to place. Rather than placing Great Britain and the USA in one category, according to where they are positioned on Hofstede's dimensions, it might be more accurate to follow Handy's own lead and say that both task and role cultures tend to predominate. This still leaves us with where to place Japan *et al*. From the point of view of Hofstede's dimensions, Japan appears to exhibit characteristics of Handy's role culture. As pointed out above, however, this is only part of the story of Japanese organisational life.

Handy's categorisation of types of culture is nevertheless very useful, in that it takes us beyond vague generalisations and gives us a picture of differing cultures. As with the other writers discussed, however, it serves to highlight both the difficulty of clearly defining cultures, and also the profound implications of the cultural approach to organisations. These implications fall under four main headings:

1 Deal and Kennedy (1983) argued that behaviour, instead of reacting directly to intrinsic and extrinsic motivators, is shaped by shared values, beliefs and assumptions about the way an organisation should operate, how rewards should be distributed, the conduct of meetings, even how people should dress.

2 If organisations do have their own identities, personalities or cultures, are there particular types of cultural attributes which are peculiar to top-performing organisations? As discussed in Chapter 3, the Culture–Excellence school gives a resounding Yes! to this question.

3 Sathe (1983) argued that culture guides the actions of an organisation's members without the need for detailed instructions or long meetings to discuss how to approach particular issues or problems; it also reduces the level of ambiguity and misunderstanding between functions and departments. In effect, it provides a common context and a common purpose for those in the organisation. This is only the case, however, when

an organisation possesses a strong culture, and where the members of the organisation have internalised it to the extent that they no longer question the legitimacy or appropriateness of the organisation's values and beliefs.

4 One of the most important implications is that, as Barratt (1990:23) observed, 'values, beliefs and attitudes are learnt, can be managed and changed and are potentially manipulable by management'. O'Reilly (1989) is one of those who clearly believes this is the case. He argued that it is possible to change or manage a culture by choosing the attitudes and behaviours that are required, identifying the norms or expectations that promote or impede them, and then taking action to create the desired effect.

This last implication is particularly contentious, with many writers supporting this view but others arguing strongly against it.

Changing organisational culture: the arguments in favour

That cultures do change is not in question. No organisation's culture is static: as the external and internal factors which influence culture change, so culture will change. However, given that culture is locked into the beliefs, values and norms of each individual in the organisation, and because these are difficult constructs to alter, this type of organic cultural change will be slow, unless perhaps there is some major shock to the organisation (Burnes, 1991). This in itself may not be problematic for organisations, provided that other factors change in an equally slow fashion. However, the argument put forward by the proponents of Culture–Excellence is that a successful culture is one based on values and assumptions appropriate to the environment in which it operates. In addition, like Handy (1986), Allaire and Firsirotu (1984) argued that, to operate effectively and efficiently, an organisation's culture needs to match or be appropriate to its structure. Given that an organisation's environment can change rapidly, as can its structure, situations will arise where an organisation's culture may be out of step with changes that are taking place in the environment, structure and practices of the organisation.
As Handy (1986: 188) commented:

> **Experience suggests that a strong culture makes a strong organisation, but does it matter what sort of culture is involved? Yes, it does. Not all cultures suit all purposes or people. Cultures are founded and built over the years by the dominant groups in an organisation. What suits them and the organisation at one stage is not necessarily appropriate for ever – strong though that culture may be.**

Flynn (1993) described how, with the introduction of a more market-orientated philosophy, such a situation has arisen across organisations in the public sector in Britain. Many similar cases can be found in the private sector (*see* Dobson, 1989). In such situations, rather than facilitating the efficient operation of the organisation, it may obstruct it.

Therefore, for a variety of reasons, organisations may find that their existing culture is inappropriate or even detrimental to their competitive needs. In such a situation, many organisations have decided to change their culture. A survey of the UK's 1000 largest public and private sector organisations, carried out in 1988 by Dobson (1989), revealed that more than 250 of them had been involved in culture change programmes in the preceding five years. Dobson states that these organisations sought to change culture by shaping the beliefs, values and attitudes of employees.

Based on the actions taken by these companies, Dobson identified a four-step approach to culture change:

Step 1 Change recruitment, selection and redundancy policies to alter the composition of the workforce so that promotion and employment prospects are dependent on those concerned possessing or displaying the beliefs and values the organisation wishes to promote.

Step 2 Reorganise the workforce to ensure that those employees and managers displaying the required traits occupy positions of influence.

Step 3 Effectively communicate the new values. This is done using a variety of methods such as one-to-one interviews, briefing groups, quality circles, house journals, etc. The example of senior managers exhibiting the new beliefs and values is seen as particularly important.

Step 4 Change systems and procedures, especially those concerned with rewards and appraisal.

Cummings and Huse (1989:428–30) identified what they considered to be the crucial steps necessary to bring about cultural change. Though wider in scope in that their approach sets change in a strategic context, the actual mechanics are very similar to those adopted by the organisations Dobson studied.

1 *A clear strategic vision.* Effective cultural change should start from a clear vision of the firm's new strategy and of the shared values and behaviour needed to make it work. This vision provides the purpose and direction for cultural change.

2 *Top management commitment.* Cultural change must be managed from the top of the organisation. Senior managers and administrators need to be strongly committed to the new values and the need to create constant pressure for change.

3 *Symbolic leadership.* Senior executives must communicate the new culture through their own actions. Their behaviours need to symbolise the kind of values and behaviours being sought.

4 *Supporting organisational changes.* Cultural change must be accompanied by supporting modifications in organisational structure, human resource systems, information and control systems, and management style. These

organisational features can help to orientate people's behaviours to the new culture.

5 *Organisational membership.* One of the most effective methods for changing culture is to change organisational membership. People can be selected in terms of their fit with the new culture, and provided with an induction clearly indicating desired attitudes and behaviour. Existing staff who cannot adapt to the new ways may have their employment terminated, for example, through early retirement schemes. This is especially important in key leadership positions, where people's actions can significantly promote or hinder new values and behaviours.

Many writers advocating culture change adopt a similar approach. Some of these, including Peters and Waterman (1982) with their seven steps to excellence, take a very prescriptive line. Others appear greatly to underestimate the difficulty involved in changing culture. An example of this is a recent article in *Management Today* (Egan, 1994) which took just four pages to show how organisations could quickly, and with apparent ease, identify and change their cultures. Regardless of how its supporters interpret or apply it, however, this type of generic approach to culture has been criticised as being too simplistic, and putting forward recommendations which are far too general to be of use to individual organisations (Gordon, 1985; Hassard and Sharifi, 1989; Nord, 1985: Uttal, 1983).

There are other writers, however, who, while sharing the belief that culture can be changed, take a more considered view. One of the more influential, Schein (1985), believed that before any attempt is made to change an organisation's culture, it is first necessary to understand the nature of its existing culture and how this is sustained. According to Schein, this can be achieved by analysing the values that govern behaviour, and uncovering the underlying and often unconscious assumptions which determine how those in the organisation think, feel and react. Difficult though he acknowledges this to be, he argues that it can be achieved by:

- *analysing the process of recruitment and induction for new employees;*
- *analysing responses to critical incidents in the organisation's history, as these are often translated into unwritten, but nevertheless very strong, rules of behaviour;*
- *analysing the beliefs, values and assumptions of those who are seen as the guardians and promoters of the organisation's culture;*
- *discussing the findings from the above with those in the organisation, and paying especial attention to anomalies or puzzling features which have been observed.*

Schein's approach, therefore, is to treat culture as an adaptive and tangible learning process. His approach emphasises the way in which an organisation communicates its culture to new recruits. It illustrates how assumptions are translated into values and how values influence behaviour. Schein seeks to understand the mechanisms used to propagate culture, and how new values and behaviours are learned. Once these mechanisms are revealed, he argues, they can then form the basis of a strategy to change the organisation's culture.

In a synthesis of the literature on organisational culture, Hassard and Sharifi (1989) proposed a similar approach to that advocated by Schein. In particular, Hassard and Sharifi (1989: 11) stress two crucial aspects of culture change:

- *Before a major [cultural] change campaign is commenced, senior managers must understand the implications of the new system for their own behaviour; senior management must be involved in all the main stages preceding change.*

- *In change programmes, special attention must be given to the company's 'opinion leaders'.*

Schwartz and Davis (1981), on the other hand, adopted a different stance with regard to culture. They suggest that, when an organisation is considering any form of change, it should compare the strategic significance (the importance to the organisation's future) of the change with the cultural resistance that attempts to make the particular change will encounter. They term this the 'cultural risk' approach. They offer a step-by-step method for identifying the degree of cultural risk involved in any particular change project. From this, they argue, it is then possible for an organisation to decide with a degree of certainty whether to ignore the culture, manage round it, attempt to change the culture to fit the strategy, or change the strategy to fit the culture. Although Schwartz and Davis' method relies heavily on managerial judgment, they maintain that it constitutes a methodical approach to identifying, at an early stage, the potential impact of strategic change on an organisation's culture, and *vice versa*.

It should, of course, be pointed out that though the approach of Schein and that of Schwartz and Davis are different, this does not mean they are in conflict or are not compatible. Indeed, both could be considered as different aspects of the same task: deciding whether culture needs to be changed, and, if it does, in what way.

No one should dispute the difficulty of changing an organisation's culture. The work of Schein (1985), Schwartz and Davis (1981), Cummings and Huse (1989) and Dobson (1989) provides organisations with the guidelines and methods for evaluating the need for and undertaking cultural change. Schein's work shows how an organisation's existing culture, and the way it is reinforced, can be revealed. Schwartz and Davis' work shows how the need for cultural change can be evaluated and the necessary changes identified. Finally, the work of Cummings and Huse (1989) and Dobson (1989) shows how cultural change can be and is implemented.

Changing organisational culture: some reservations

One of those who sounded a cautious note regarding the feasibility or advisability of culture change was Edgar Schein. Though Schein (1984 and 1985) believes that culture can be changed, he also argues that there is a negative side to creating (or attempting to create) a strong and cohesive organisational culture. Shared values, particularly where they have been seen to be consistently successful in the past, make organisations resistant to certain types of change or strategic options, regardless of their merit.

Schein (in conversation with Luthans, 1989) was also critical of the idea that culture change can be achieved by a top-down, management-led approach. Schein (1989) appears to advocate a contingency or context-specific view of culture. He argues that an organisation may need a strong culture in its formative years to hold it together while it grows. It may reach a stage, however, where it is increasingly differentiated geographically, by function and by division. At this stage, managing culture becomes more a question of knitting together the warring factions and sub-cultures. In such a case, a strong culture may outlive its usefulness.

Salaman (1979) also pointed out that while there may be a strong or dominant culture in an organisation, there will also be sub-cultures, as in society at large. These may be peculiar to the organisation or may cut across organisations. An example of the latter are professional groups, such as accountants, who have their own cultures which extend beyond the organisation. This may also be the case with other white- and blue-collar staff. These sub-cultures will exist in a complex and potentially conflicting relationship with the dominant culture. If that dominant culture is seen by some groups to have lost its appropriateness (and thus legitimacy), then potential conflicts can become actual conflicts. The reverse can also be the case: cultural values and methods of operation which one group adopts may be seen as out of step with 'the way we've always done things'. This in turn can lead to an undermining of the authority of managers and specialists – endangering the efficient operation of the organisation (Morieux and Sutherland, 1988).

Uttal (1983) is another who expressed caution with regard to the difficulties and advisability of culture change. In particular, he observed that even where it is successful, the process can take anywhere from 6 to 15 years. Meyer and Zucker (1989) went further, arguing that while managing cultural change may result in short-term economic benefits, in the longer term it may result in stagnation and demise.

Though Schein and other writers question the advisability of culture change and strong cultures in some situations, there are also writers who believe that culture cannot be changed or managed at all. Meek (1982:469–470) commented that:

> **Culture as a whole cannot be manipulated, turned on or off, although it needs to be recognised that some [organisations] are in a better position than others to intentionally influence aspects of it ... culture should be regarded as something an organisation 'is', not something it 'has': it is not an independent variable nor can it be created, discovered or destroyed by the whims of management.**

In a similar vein, Filby and Willmott (1988) also questioned the notion that management has the capacity to control culture. They point out that this ignores the way in which an individual's values and beliefs are conditioned by experience outside the workplace – through exposure to the media, through social activities, as well as through previous occupational activities.

A further factor in the case against the feasibility of managing/changing culture is the ethical dimension. Van Maanen and Kunda (1989) argued that behind the interest in culture is an attempt by managers to control what employees feel as well as what they say or do. Their argument is that culture is a mechanism for disciplining emotion – a method of guiding the way people are expected to feel. Seen in this light, attempts to change culture can be conceived of as Taylorism of the mind. Frederick Taylor sought to control behaviour by laying down and enforcing strict rules about how work should be carried out. Van Maanen and Kunda were in effect arguing that culture change programmes attempt to achieve a similar end through a form of mind control.

Changing organisational culture: conflicts and choices

As in so much else to do with organisations, there is no agreement among those who study culture as to its nature, purpose or malleability. Certainly, few writers doubt its importance but beyond that there is little agreement. The Culture–Excellence proponents argue that there is only one form of culture which matters in today's environment – a strong and flexible culture – and that organisations should adopt it quickly or face the consequences. Schein (1984, 1985 and 1989) agreed that culture is important and that in certain cases a strong culture is desirable. In other situations, however, shared values and strong cultures may have a negative effect by stifling diversity and preventing alternative strategies arising. He also doubts that managers acting in isolation from the rest of an organisation have the ability themselves to change the existing culture or impose a new one. Salaman (1979) also drew attention to the presence and role of sub-cultures, particularly their potential for creating conflict. Meek (1988) took the view that culture is not amenable to conscious managerial change programmes at all.

Despite the lack of consensus among writers, there are two main conclusions we can draw from the above review of the culture literature. First, in the absence of unambiguous guidelines on organisational culture, managers must make their own choices based on their own circumstances and perceived options as to whether to attempt to change their organisation's culture.

Second, in the absence of strong or appropriate cultures which bind their members together in a common purpose and legitimate and guide decision-making, managers may find it difficult either to agree among themselves or to gain agreement from others in the organisation. As Robbins (1987) argued, in such a situation, there is a tendency for conflict and power battles to take place. Where clear and unambiguous goals are present and where rational decision-making is possible, managers may well place (or be constrained to place) the best interests of the organisation above personal or sectional interest.

Therefore, in understanding how organisations operate and the strengths and weaknesses of the theories we have been discussing in the previous chapters, it is necessary to examine the political perspective on organisations.

THE POWER-POLITICS PERSPECTIVE

Political behaviour in organisations

The cultural perspective on organisational life reinforces the argument developed in earlier chapters that organisations are not rational entities where everyone subscribes to, and helps to achieve, the organisation's overarching goals. Instead, organisations can be seen as coalitions of groups and individuals who come together to perform certain agreed tasks (Robbins, 1986 and 1987). The extent to which agreement exists about these tasks, and the extent to which members of the organisation are committed to achieving them, will be affected by the strength and the perceived legitimacy of the organisation's culture. However, the importance of the power-politics perspective is that it shows that, even where a strong culture may be present, the cohesiveness, willingness and stability of these coalitions is unlikely to be uniform either across an organisation or over time. Rather the degree of co-operation and commitment they exhibit will vary with the degree to which they perceive the goals they are pursuing as broadly consistent with their own interests (Mullins, 1993). As Pfeffer (1978:11–12) commented:

> **It is difficult to think of situations in which goals are so congruent, or the facts clear-cut that judgment and compromise are not involved. What is rational from one point of view is irrational from another. Organizations are political systems, coalitions of interests, and rationality is defined only with respect to unitary and consistent ordering of preferences.**

It might be comforting to believe that individuals and groups within organisations are supportive of each other, that they work in a harmonious and co-operative fashion. Such a non-political perspective portrays employees as always behaving in a manner consistent with the interests of the organisation. In contrast, as Robbins (1986:283) remarked, 'a political view can explain much of, what may seem to be, irrational behaviour in organizations. It can help to explain, for instance, why employees withhold information, restrict output, attempt to "build empires"...'

Handy (1986) also observed the tendency for individuals and groups to pursue courses of action which promote their interests, regardless of the organisation's formal goals and objectives. He notes that where individuals perceive that the actual or proposed goals of the organisation or the tasks they are asked to perform are out of step with their own interests, they will seek where possible to bring the two into line. In some cases, individuals and groups may be persuaded to change their perceptions; in others, they may seek to change or influence the goals or tasks. It is this phenomenon of individuals and groups, throughout an organisation, pursuing differing interests, and battling with each other to shape decisions in their favour, that has led many commentators to characterise organisations as political systems (Mintzberg, 1983; Morgan, 1986; Pfeffer, 1981 and 1992; Pettigrew, 1985 and 1987).

Zaleznik (1970) stated that where there are scarce resources (which is the case in most organisations), the psychology of scarcity and comparison take over. In such situations, possession of resources becomes the focus for comparisons, the basis for self-esteem and, ultimately, the source of power. Such situations will see the emergence not only of dominant coalitions but also, Zaleznik argues, of unconscious collusion based on defensive reaction. Therefore, while some individuals will perceive their actions as 'political' or self-interested, others may act in the same manner, but believe they are pursuing the best interests of the organisation.

Drory and Romm (1988) argued that those in managerial/supervisory positions are less likely than those in non-supervisory positions to define (or recognise) their actions as political. This may be explained by findings by Gandz and Murray (1980) that supervisory staff are more involved in political behaviour, and therefore tend to see it as a typical part of organisational life. If this is the case, it could be argued that the more individuals and groups are involved in political behaviour, the more it becomes the norm, and they become blind to its political nature and see it merely as 'standard' practice. Those less involved in such behaviour, on the other hand, recognise its political nature because it stands out from their normal practices. It is also the case that those lower down the organisation, while affected by resource allocation decisions, are less likely, on a regular basis, to be in a position to influence such decisions. For managers, however, arguing for additional resources or allocating existing resources is the normal currency of everyday life.

Morgan (1986) offered a model of interests, conflicts and power whereby diversity of interests can create conflict. In such circumstances, power and influence are, he suggests, the major means of resolving conflict. Willcocks (1994:31) took the view that diverse interests are part of organisational culture. They include, he argues, 'for example, the goals, values and expectation of the organizational participants and have been described as cognitive maps or personal agendas.'

Power, politics and legitimacy

Though it is relatively easy to provide simple definitions of power (the possession of position and/or resources) and politics (the deployment of influence/leverage), it is more difficult to distinguish between the two, as was shown by Drory and Romm (1988). They argue that the two concepts are often used interchangeably and that the difference between the two has never been fully settled. Indeed, a brief examination of each shows the difficulty, and perhaps danger, in separating them. First, however, it is also necessary to understand the difference between power and authority.

Robbins (1987:186) drew an important distinction between authority and power:

> ... we defined authority as the right to act, or command others to act, toward the attainment of organizational goals. Its unique characteristic, we said, was that this right had legitimacy based on the authority figure's position in the organization. Authority goes with the job ... When we use the term power we mean an individual's capacity to influence decisions...the ability to influence based on an individual's

legitimate position can affect decisions, but one does not require authority to have such influence.

In support of his view, Robbins quotes the example of high-ranking executives' secretaries, who may have a great deal of power, by virtue of their ability to influence the flow of information and people to their bosses, but have very little actual authority.

On the other hand, Robbins (1987:194) defines organisational politics as the:

... efforts of organizational members to mobilize support for or against policies, rules, goals, or other decisions in which the outcome will have some effect on them. Politics, therefore, is essentially the exercise of power.

Robbins' argument is, then, that power is the capacity to influence decisions while politics is the actual process of exerting this influence. This view, that politics is merely the enactment of power, is held by many writers. Gibson *et al* (1988:44), for example, stated that organisational politics comprises 'those activities used at all levels to acquire, develop or use power and other resources to obtain individual choices when there is uncertainty or disagreement about choices'.

Many writers refer to organisational politics as games. Pfeffer (1981), in his major work on power in organisations, took the view that decisions in organisations are the result of games among players with different perceptions and interests. This was a theme developed by Mintzberg (1983) in his comprehensive review of power and politics in organisations. He lists 13 political games that are common in organisations, the key ones being: games to resist authority, games to counter resistance, games to build power bases, games to defeat rivals, and games to change the organisation.

Like all games, political ones have their particular tactics or ploys associated with them. Research into political behaviour has identified the seven most common ploys used by managers when seeking to influence superiors, equals and subordinates (Kipnis *et al*, 1980; Kipnis *et al*, 1984; Schilit and Locke, 1982), which are as follows:

- *Reason – facts and information are used selectively to mount seemingly logical or rational arguments.*
- *Friendliness – the use of flattery, creation of goodwill, etc., prior to making a request.*
- *Coalition – joining forces with others so as to increase one's own influence.*
- *Bargaining – exchanging benefits and favours in order to achieve a particular outcome.*
- *Assertiveness – being forceful in making requests and demanding compliance.*
- *Higher authority – gaining the support of superiors for a particular course of action.*

● *Sanctions – using the promise of rewards or the threat of punishment to force compliance.*

Robbins (1986) observed that the most popular tactic or ploy is the selective use of reason, regardless of whether the influence was directed upwards or downwards. Although cloaked in reason, arguments and data are deployed in such a way that the outcome favoured by those using the tactic is presented in a more favourable light than the alternatives. Therefore, though reason may be deployed, it is not done so in an unbiased or neutral fashion; it is used as a screen to disguise the real objective of the exercise.

Kipnis *et al* (1984) identified four contingency variables which affect the choice of tactic by managers: the manager's relative power, the manager's objectives in seeking to influence others, the manager's expectations of the target person's/group's willingness to comply, and the organisation's culture.

Politics – whose best interests?

Though this gives us a clearer picture of what power and politics are, it leaves uncertainty over the distinction between the legitimate and illegitimate use of power. Thompkins (1990) firmly believed that the use of politics is a direct contravention of or challenge to the legitimate rules of an organisation. However, many, see organisational politics as existing in a grey area between prescribed and illegal behaviour (Drory and Romm, 1988). Porter *et al* (1983) differentiated between three types of organisational behaviour: prescribed, discretionary and illegal. They believe that political behaviour falls within the discretionary rather than the illegal category. Therefore, the most common view is that the use of politics in organisations can best be described as non-sanctioned or informal or discretionary behaviour, rather than behaviour which is clearly prohibited or illegal (Farrell and Petersen, 1983; Mayes and Allen, 1977). This definition of politics helps to distinguish between the formal and legitimate use of officially sanctioned power by authorised personnel, and power that is exercised either in an illegitimate manner by authorised personnel or used by non-authorised personnel for their own ends.

In the main, most organisations and many writers see political behaviour as dysfunctional (Drory and Romm, 1988). Batten and Swab (1965), Pettigrew (1973) and Porter (1976) believed that political behaviour goes against and undermines formal organisational goals and interests. Thompkins (1990) argued, however, that political manoeuvring in organisations is due to a failure by senior managers to set and implement coherent and consistent goals and policies in the first place. This results in uncertainties, which in turn lead to conflict between groups and individuals. In such a situation, Thompkins (1990:24) argues:

> **Management is then left without top level guidance to run company operations. They will, then, by their own nature of survival, over a period of time, make decisions that**

will perpetuate their own safety and security. This is the beginning of political power, where legitimate discipline begins to decline and illegitimate discipline begins to strangle the organisation. In short, the tail begins to wag the dog. 'Politics' in this form is created by the neglect of top executive management.

Pfeffer (1981) took a different view of organisational politics. Rather than their being caused by the lack of clear-cut goals and policies, he suggests that the construction of organisational goals is itself a political process. Mintzberg (1983) developed this argument further. He maintains that, when used in moderation, political games can have a healthy effect by keeping the organisation on its toes. Mayes and Allen (1977) took a similar view. Pascale (1993) went further, putting forward the view that conflict and contention are necessary to save an organisation from complacency and decline. However, Mintzberg cautions that, when carried too far, such games can turn the whole organisation into a political cauldron and divert it from its main task.

To an extent, the degree to which the balance between positive and negative benefits is tipped one way or the other in an organisation is dependent on the type of power deployed and how it is used. Etzioni (1975) identified three distinct types of power used in organisations:

- *Coercive power – the threat of negative consequences (including physical sanctions or force) should compliance not be forthcoming.*

- *Remunerative power – the promise of material rewards as inducements to co-operate.*

- *Normative power – the allocation and manipulation of symbolic rewards, such as status symbols, as inducements to obey.*

Robbins (1986) went further by identifying not only types of power but also the sources of power. To Etzioni's three types of power he adds a fourth – *knowledge power*: the control of information. Robbins suggests that these types of power stem from four separate sources: a person's position in the organisation, personal characteristics, expertise, and ability to receive and obstruct information.

All four types of power can be and are deployed in organisations. However, the degree to which they will be effective is likely to depend upon the source from which they spring. Coercive power is usually the prerogative of those in senior positions, while even quite junior members of an organisation may, in particular circumstances, control or possess information which enables them to exert knowledge power. The interesting point to note is that the use of knowledge power – the selective and biased use of information (often deployed under the guise of reason) – is shown to be effective in gaining willing compliance and co-operation from those at whom it is directed. As argued by many observers, however, the use of remunerative and coercive power is often counter-productive because those on the receiving end of such power tend to view it negatively and resent it (Bachman *et al*, 1968; Student, 1968; Ivancevich, 1970; Robbins, 1986).

This is perhaps why the most damaging outcomes from the deployment of power come when people feel they are being coerced into a particular course of action which goes against their beliefs or self-interest. Therefore, irrespective of the source or type of power, it is perhaps the willingness to use it in situations where there will be clear winners and losers, and where the covert activities of warring coalitions turn into open warfare, that leads to the more dysfunctional and damaging consequences. Such battles, where groups and individuals fight to influence key decisions and in so doing bolster their own position, especially where the stakes are high, can end with senior figures either leaving or being forced out of the organisation. This was the case with Pehr Gyllenhammar, the man who ran Volvo for more than two decades. His 1993 attempt to merge Volvo with Renault, the French state-controlled car company, was opposed by a coalition of shareholders and managers, who felt that it was not so much a merger of equals as a takeover by Renault. Both shareholders and managers felt that in such a situation their interests would be damaged, and a very public power struggle ensued, with both sides claiming to act in Volvo's best interests (Done, 1994). Similarly, the recent battle for control of the advertising agency Saatchi & Saatchi, which resulted in the founders leaving, seems another example of a power struggle which leaves the organisation damaged (Barrie, 1995; Donovan, 1995).

Clearly, the deployment of coercive power seen in the Volvo and Saatchi & Saatchi cases is very damaging; however, other forms of power can also have adverse effects, though perhaps in a more insidious fashion. Thus the use of remunerative power by senior managers in the recently privatised utilities (gas, water and power) in the UK is a case in point. On the one hand, they used their power to give themselves extremely generous remuneration packages; while, on the other hand, they cut jobs and wages for many staff elsewhere in their organisations (Smithers, 1995). The issue is not so much whether the way they distributed the rewards in their organisations was fair or not, but the corrosive effect such a blatant use of power might have on employee morale and customer support.

These very public manifestations of power battles in organisations represent merely the tip of the iceberg. They illustrate the tendency for such battles to be fought under the banner of 'the best interests of the organisation'. Political in-fighting, the seeking of allies, the influencing of decisions, and/or the protection/promotion of one's own or one's group's interests are nearly always justified by recourse to the best interests of the organisation (just as the parties involved in any armed struggle always seem to justify it on the grounds that they have justice on their side). It is not that they necessarily believe their own propaganda, though often they do; it is that, without it, they would find it very difficult to justify, to themselves and their allies, the use of blatantly illegitimate tactics such as challenging, undermining or explicitly ignoring their organisation's official goals and policies.

Therefore, in opposing or promoting a particular decision or development, those indulging in even a low level of political behaviour rarely openly declare their own personal interest in the outcome. As Pfeffer (1981) maintained, a major characteristic accompanying political behaviour is the attempt to conceal its true motive.

This is because, as Allen *et al* (1979), Drory and Romm (1988) and Frost and Hayes (1979) have observed, those involved believe that it would be judged unacceptable or illegitimate by others in the organisation and as such resisted. Accordingly, a false but acceptable motive is presented instead.

POWER, POLITICS AND CHANGE: BRINGING BACK CHOICE

We can see from the above why writers have found it difficult to separate power from politics. While it is possible to examine the potential for power without also examining how power is or might be exercised, for students of organisational life this is rather a sterile endeavour. For the purpose of understanding what makes organisations tick, how decisions are arrived at, why resources are allocated in a particular way and why certain changes are initiated and others not, we have to comprehend both the possession and exercise of power, whether it be by official or political means.

Though Robbins rightly draws a distinction between formal authority and the possession/deployment of power, we should not fall into the trap of assuming that there is not a close relationship between the two. An examination of the ability to exert influence (power) over key decisions and the possession of position (authority) shows that these tend to lie within dominant coalitions rather than being spread evenly across organisations (*see* Pfeffer, 1978, 1981 and 1992; Robbins, 1987). The dominant coalition is the one which has the power to affect structure. The reason why this is so important is that the choice of structure will automatically favour some groups and disadvantage others. A person or group's position in the structure will determine such things as their influence in planning, their choice of technology, the criteria by which they will be evaluated, allocation of rewards, control of information, proximity to senior managers, and their ability to exercise influence on a whole range of decisions (Morgan, 1986; Perrow, 1983; Pfeffer, 1981 and 1992; Robbins, 1987).

It also follows that political activity is likely to be most prevalent during periods of change (especially change which may challenge the status quo). Murray (1989:285), reporting on a major study of the introduction and use of information technology commented that: 'the use of new technology is subject to processes of organizational decision-making and implementation characterized by often conflicting managerial objectives, rationalities and strategies developed through the mobilization of organizational power'. Therefore, as far as Morgan (1986), Murray (1989), Pfeffer, (1981), Robbins (1987) and many others are concerned, the process of organisational change is inherently a political one.

This view that the choice of structure, and other key decisions, is the outcome of a political process rather than the application of rational analysis and decision-making has significant implications for organisation theory. While it does not necessarily invalidate the appropriateness or otherwise of particular approaches, it does mean that managerial aspirations and interests are seen as more important than might otherwise be the case. It also means that, rather than being the prisoners of organisation theory (as some might suppose or hope), managers do exercise significant choice with regard to structure and other organisation characteristics.

In his review of the influence of power and politics in organisations, Robbins (1987) noted that no more than 50 to 60 per cent of variability in structure can be explained by strategy, size, technology, and environment. He then went on to argue that a substantial portion of the residual variance can be explained by those in positions of power choosing a structure that will, as far as possible, maintain and enhance their control. He points out that other determinants of structure, size, technology, etc., assume that organisations are rational entities:

> **However, for rationality to prevail an organisation must have either a single goal or agreement over the multiple goals. Neither case exists in most organisations. (*Robbins, 1987:200*)**

Consequently, structural decisions are not rational. Such decisions arise from a power struggle between special-interest groups or coalitions, each arguing for a structural arrangement that best suits them. Robbins (1987:200) believes that while strategy, size, technology and environment define the minimum level of effectiveness and set the parameters within which self-serving decision choices will be made: 'both technology and environment are chosen. Thus, those in power will select technologies and environments that will facilitate their maintenance of control.'

Many other writers have also challenged the view of management as rational and neutral implementers of decisions determined by objective data. In particular, the detailed case studies of organisational decision-making and change at ICI and Cadbury Ltd carried out, respectively, by Pettigrew (1985 and 1987) and Child and Smith (1987) lend a great deal of weight to the view that management in general, and the management of change in particular, is inherently a political process. Pettigrew (1987) concluded that the process of change is:

> **... shaped by the interests and commitments of individuals and groups, the forces of bureaucratic momentum, gross changes in the environment and the manipulation of the structural context around decisions ... structures, cultures and strategies are not just being treated here as neutral, functional constructs connectable to some system need ... the constructs are viewed as capable of serving to protect the interests of the dominant groups ... the context of strategic change is thus ultimately a product of a legitimation process shaped by political/cultural considerations, though often expressed in rational/analytical terms (*quoted in Murray, 1989:287*).**

Murray (1989) made the telling point that, given the insecurity of many managers' positions, particularly during periods of major upheaval and change, it is not surprising that managers and other groups attempt to influence decisions in order to protect, enhance or shore up their position in the organisation.

Linking the arguments by Robbins, Pettigrew and Murray regarding managerial choice of structure to the discussion on culture, two very interesting points arise. First, it was argued by Allaire and Firsirotu (1984), and others, that culture and structure need to be mutually supportive if an organisation is to operate efficiently and effectively. If, as the power-politics perspective argues, structure is the outcome of self-interested choice by the dominant coalition, the degree of congruence between the two may be due more to accident than choice. Second, it was also argued above that organisational culture is the product of long-term social learning in which dominant coalitions play a key role. This clearly opens up scope for choices over both structure and culture. However, the development of culture and approaches to changing it are long-term processes. Dominant coalitions, on the other hand, change their composition and priorities over time. Therefore, although it can be argued that the possibility exists for managers to choose both the structure and culture that best suit their own self-interests, this is only likely to result in a balanced and effective structure-culture if the dominant coalition holds sway and is consistent in its aims over time. As many observers have noted, while these conditions may exist in some Western companies (e.g. GEC, Hanson Trust), these are the exception. In any case, as the recent battle between Tiny Rowland and his successor at Lonrho has shown, such situations often rely on dominant individuals to hold coalitions together; when they go, the dominant coalition falls apart, and in some cases so too does the organisation.

The Japanese experience appears at first glance to follow a similar pattern. Dominant coalitions often rely on one key person. In their case, however, when that person departs, the organisations appear to maintain the unity of purpose of the dominant coalition (Fruin, 1992; Pascale and Athos, 1982; Whitehill, 1991). Yet, even the Japanese are not immune from problems when changing leaders. For example, Nissan's appointment of a new Chief Executive in 1985 was followed by an attempt to change its culture in order to overcome what were seen as major mistakes by the previous incumbent (Ishizuna, 1990).

CONCLUSIONS

In reviewing the main approaches to organisation theory, this first part of the book has shown that, by succeeding stages, these have moved from the mechanical-rational outlook of the Classical school to the cultural perspective of the Culture–Excellence school (passing through the social perspective of the Human Relations school and the rational perspective of the Contingency theorists). They all argue for a 'one best way' approach (though the Contingency theorists believed in this for 'each' rather than 'all' organisations). Because of this approach they all, in effect, seek to remove choice from managers: do as we tell you, or else! Indeed, it was one of the main claims of the Classical school that it removed discretion not only from workers, but also from managers. The role of managers, from these perspectives, is to apply rationally the dictates of the particular theory promoted. To do otherwise would be sub-optimal and irrational.

What this chapter has sought to do is to move managerial choice back to centre stage. The first part of the chapter examined the case for culture. Is it important? Can it be changed? Should it be changed? What emerged was that culture is a more elusive and less malleable concept than the advocates of the Culture–Excellence school would have us believe. In particular, important though it is in influencing behaviour, there are those who question the usefulness of strong cultures in all situations; diversity and conflict rather than uniformity and consensus may be necessary for organisational survival. Furthermore, the degree to which culture influences behaviour is dependent upon the presence of clear and consistent organisational goals. If these are not present, which appears to be the case in many companies, conflict and disagreement emerge regardless of the nature of the culture. In such situations, it is the political perspective on organisational life which offers the better opportunity for understanding how and why organisations manage and structure themselves in particular ways, or follow particular courses of action.

The examination of organisational politics and power which has covered the second half of this chapter added further weight to the criticisms of the approaches to organisation theory considered in previous chapters, particularly concerning the scope for decision-making and choice. To an extent the key issue was raised when discussing Contingency Theory, namely the question as to whether managers are the prisoners of the situational variables they face, or whether they can influence or change these. Certainly the critics of Contingency Theory argue that managers can, partly at least, influence or choose the contingencies they face. This casts doubts not only about the deterministic nature of Contingency Theory but about all organisational theories, because – either openly or implicitly – they are all founded on the notion that organisations face certain immutable conditions which they cannot influence and to which they must therefore adapt.

This does not necessarily mean that the various theories and their attendant structures and practices we have discussed so far in this book are invalid, unhelpful or inapplicable. It does mean, however, that it may be possible for organisations to decide upon the structure and behaviours they want to promote, and then shape the conditions and contingencies to suit these, rather than vice versa. Indeed, as far as the public sector in the UK is concerned, this appears to be exactly what the government has done. The UK government took the view that they wanted managers in the public sector to be cost-focused and entrepreneurial, and have shaped the conditions in which the public sector operates (i.e. its environment) in order to promote those attributes (Flynn, 1993).

Clearly, if decisions are not formulated on the basis of objective theories or measurable contingencies, one then has to ask what factors do influence the decisions taken. The review of the power–politics literature showed organisations as shifting coalitions of groups and individuals seeking to promote policies and decisions which enhanced or maintained their position in the organisation. From the literature, a persuasive argument is mounted for seeing politics and power – usually promoted under the cloak of rationality, reasonableness and the organisation's best interests – as central determinants of the way organisations operate.

In particular, though political behaviour appears to be an ever-present feature of organisational life, politics comes to the fore when major issues of structural change or resource allocation are concerned. Such decisions have crucial importance for achieving and maintaining power or position, or even – when the chips are down – for keeping one's job when all around are losing theirs.

Therefore, it is surprising that organisational theory, which after all is primarily concerned with major decisions concerning structure and resource allocation, seems to dismiss or gloss over power and politics. Nevertheless, what is clear from this chapter is that managers have a far wider scope for shaping decisions than most organisation theories acknowledge, and that the scope for choice and the deployment of political influence is likely to be most pronounced when change, particularly major change, is on the managerial agenda.

Having examined the merits and drawbacks of the main organisational theories, and in particular having raised the issue of the way in which major decisions are decided upon and implemented, the time is now right to make an in-depth examination of change management.

PART 2

MANAGING CHANGE: APPROACHES AND CHOICES

Chapter 5

STRATEGIC MANAGEMENT

Managerial choice and constraints

INTRODUCTION

It has become the accepted view that, for society at large, the magnitude, speed, unpredictability and impact of change are greater than ever before. Certainly, new products and processes are appearing at an ever-increasing rate. Local markets are becoming global markets. Protected or semi-protected markets and industries are being opened up to fierce competition. Public bureaucracies and monopolies are either being transferred to the private sector or, as in the case of the UK National Health Service, having the market transferred into them.

Is it actually true, however, that the degree and magnitude of change are the greatest yet? The Industrial Revolution led to enormous changes in society. The rapid growth of welfare provision and the advent of 'Big Government' was a phenomenon experienced by most Western countries before and, especially, just after the Second World War. In Scandinavia, it was connected with the advent of social democracy; in the USA it came through Roosevelt's New Deal; and in the UK, the creation of the Welfare State was the major work of the postwar Labour Government. Whatever the cause, in each case it transformed the role of government and led to an unparalleled expansion of the public sector. The rapid growth of industry and competition, especially at an international level, in the 1950s and 1960s also saw large-scale changes in societies. This was especially the case in Asia where some countries, such as South Korea, Malaysia, Hong Kong and Singapore, industrialised at a furious pace.

So although we egotistically tend to see the present level of change as being unprecedented, the history of the past 200 years could well be characterised as successive periods of unprecedented change. Indeed, given that it was the ancient Greeks who coined the phrase, 'change is the only constant', we should perhaps remember that the history of the human race is one of massive change and dislocation. Each generation seems to yearn for some golden past which has been swept away by progress, and each generation, building on past knowledge, develops new ways of coping with and managing change. If this is the case, perhaps the main issue is not whether we are experiencing an unprecedented era of change. Instead, we should be asking:

● *Are all organisations affected to the same degree?*
● *How can each organisation best cope with the degree of turbulence it faces?*

In Part One, we discussed the options open to organisations in terms of their structures, cultures and practices. By examining the development of organisational theory in the 200 years since the Industrial Revolution, we saw that, in the beginning, management was almost exclusively concerned with strict labour discipline and long working hours. The methods used to pursue these were *ad hoc*, erratic, short-term and usually harsh and unfair. As the period progressed, more structured and consistent approaches came to the fore. Up to the 1960s, it was the Classical and Human Relations approaches which dominated organisational thinking. With the advent of these two approaches, the emphasis moved to the effectiveness and efficiency of the entire organisation, rather than focusing purely on discipline and hours of work.

Both these approaches tended to dwell on internal arrangements and to assume that organisation structures and practices were in some way insulated from the outside world. The development of Contingency Theory in the 1960s, with its underlying Open Systems perspective, changed all this. The nature of the environment (both internal and external) in which organisations operated emerged as a central factor in how they should structure themselves. This theme has been continued with the advent of the development of new paradigms in the 1980s and 1990s, and the importance of the situational variables, especially environmental turbulence, which companies and firms face is now an accepted fact.

As argued in Chapter 4, however, the degree to which organisations are the prisoners of these situational variables (as opposed to being able to exercise influence and choice) is certainly open to debate. Similarly, the credibility of the rational approach to decision-making has been considerably undermined in the last two decades. The political perspective, discussed in Chapter 4, is increasingly influential in explaining how and why decisions are taken in organisations. It is obvious that organisations cannot cope successfully with the modern world and all its changing aspects purely on an *ad hoc* and piecemeal basis. Whether decision-makers operate on the basis of rationality or are influenced by personal considerations or organisational cultures, for organisations to succeed there must be a consistency and coherence to the decisions taken.

As this chapter will show, since the 1950s, organisations have begun to take a strategic perspective on their activities. They have increasingly sought to take a long-term overview in order to plan for and cope with the vagaries of the future. In many respects, the development of strategic management has tended to mirror the development of organisational theory. Initially, strategic management only considered one aspect of an organisation's activities – the external environment. It tended to seek rational, mathematical approaches to planning. With the passing of time, more intuitive and less rational approaches to strategic management have been developed which claim to incorporate the totality of organisational life, especially its political dimension.

In this chapter, we shall examine the development and shortcomings of the main approaches to strategy which have been put forward in the last 50 years. The tools and techniques associated with these will also be examined. The chapter concludes by arguing that far from managers being the prisoners of mathematical models and rational approaches to decision-making, they have considerable freedom of action and a wide range of options from which to choose. They are not totally free agents, however; their freedom of action is seen as being constrained or shaped by the unique set of organisational, environmental and societal factors faced by their particular organisation. Fortunately, these constraints are not immutable. As argued in Part One, it is possible for managers to manipulate the situational variables they face with regard to structure. Therefore, in a similar fashion, managers can also exert some influence over strategic constraints and, potentially at least, can select the approach to strategy which best suits their preferences.

THE ORIGINS OF STRATEGIC MANAGEMENT

It is commonly believed that our concept of strategy has been passed down to us from the ancient Greeks. Bracker (1980:219) argued that the word strategy comes from the Greek *stratego*, meaning 'to plan the destruction of one's enemies through the effective use of resources'. However, the Greeks developed the concept purely in relation to the successful pursuit of victory in war. The concept remained a military one until the nineteenth century when it began to be applied to the business world, though most writers believe the actual process by which this took place is untraceable (Bracker, 1980; Chandler, 1962). Chandler (1962) put forward the view that the emergence of strategy in civilian organisational life resulted from an awareness of the opportunities and needs – created by changing population, income and technology – to employ existing or expanding resources more profitably.

Hoskin (1990) largely agreed with Chandler's view of the development of modern business strategy since the Industrial Revolution. However, he does take issue with both Chandler and Bracker on two crucial points. First, he argues that the modern concept of organisational strategy bears little resemblance to military strategy, at least as it existed up to the First World War. Second, he challenges the view that the origins of business strategy are untraceable. When investigating the emergence of modern strategy he did find a link with the military world, though it was not quite the link that others have proposed. He argues – like Chandler – that one of the most significant developments in business management in the nineteenth century occurred in the running of the US railways; Hoskin gives the credit for initiating business strategy to one of the Pennsylvania railway's executives, Herman Haupt. He states that Haupt:

> ... changes the rules of business discourse: the image in which he reconstructs business, on the Pennsylvania Railroad, is that of the proactive, future-oriented organization, which is managed by the numbers ... How does he do so? By importing the practices of writing, examination and grading ... On the Pennsylvania Railroad we find for the first time the full interactive play of grammatocentrism [writing and recording] and calculability [mathematical analysis of the recorded data]. (*Hoskin, 1990:20*)

This approach created the bedrock on which strategic management grew in the United States, especially after the Second World War. It also ensured that strategic management became a quantitatively-orientated discipline, whose focus was on the use of numerical analysis to forecast market trends in order to plan for the future. Hoskin also points out that Haupt was a graduate of the US military academy at West Point, which pioneered the techniques of 'writing, examination and grading' in the military world. From there its graduates, particularly Haupt, took the techniques out into the business world – hence the link between military and civilian management techniques.

It is possible, therefore, to see why strategic management developed in the way it has – as a quantitative, mathematical approach. We can also see that there are links between the military and business world, but that they are not as some have argued. Management strategy has not developed from the approach to military campaigns of the ancient Greeks; instead it has adopted and made its own the techniques of record-keeping and analysis that were developed at West Point in order to measure the performance and suitability for military life of the US army's future officer class.

The contribution of the American armed forces to this quantitative approach to strategy did not end with West Point or in the nineteenth century. After the Second World War, the development and use of strategy in business was given a significant impetus when some of the personalities involved in the United States Air Force's strategic studies returned to civilian life – most notable amongst whom was Robert McNamara, who became Chairman of the Ford Motor Company, Secretary of State under John F Kennedy and President of the World Bank (Moore, 1992). Their main vehicle for influencing business was the Harvard Business School's approach to business policy teaching, which steadily moved the focus of management away from a preoccupation with internal organisational issues (as proposed by the Classical and Human Relations schools) towards an external orientation. This was best exemplified by the development of two important concepts: *marketing*, with its emphasis on analysing demand and tailoring products to meet it; and *systems theory*, with its emphasis not only on the interconnectedness of different parts of an organisation, but also the links between internal and external forces.

In the intervening years, first in the USA and later across the Western world, these techniques and approaches have become more widely disseminated and used

(Bracker, 1980). Much credit for this must go to three key figures – Kenneth R Andrews, Alfred D Chandler and H Igor Ansoff – for their work in developing and fleshing out the concept of strategic management, and especially for demonstrating the importance of product–market mix. Nevertheless, in highlighting the importance of the outside world, and thus breaking managers' Classical School-inspired fixation with internal structures and practices, they can be criticised for not making the link between the two. As a result, managers moved from believing that internal arrangements alone would bring success to believing that an external, market focus was the key.

This will be explored further below. In addition, the main definitions of strategic management will be discussed.

DEVELOPMENT AND DEFINITION OF STRATEGY

As mentioned above, though the origins of strategic management can be traced to the middle years of the nineteenth century, it was not until after the Second World War that strategic management began to be more widely used, and then only in the United States. Initially, organisations tried to cope with the new and rapidly-changing technological, economic and organisational developments through a form of long-range planning. This necessitated first defining the firm's objectives, then establishing plans in order to achieve those objectives, and finally, allocating resources, through capital budgeting, in line with the plans. A key objective of this process was to reduce the gap that often occurred between a firm's aspirations and plans and the extrapolation of existing trends (Fox, 1975).

The use of long-range planning, in this manner, to formulate strategy, ran into problems when it became increasingly evident that forecasting past trends into the future could not produce accurate results or achieve the firm's desired objectives. Growth was not steady; it could slow down, increase or be interrupted in an unpredictable and violent manner. In addition, new opportunities and threats, which nobody had envisaged, could and did emerge. Furthermore, it became evident that closing the planning gap was not necessarily the most critical aspect of strategy formulation. Volatile markets, over-capacity, and resource constraints have taken over as dominant management considerations since the early 1970s. Consequently, long-range planning has been replaced by strategic management, which incorporates the possibility that changes in trends can and do take place, and is not based on the assumption that adequate growth can be assured (Elliot and Lawrence, 1985). In addition, strategic management focuses more closely on winning market share from competitors, rather than assuming that organisations can rely solely on the expansion of markets for their own growth.

Therefore, long-range planning was essentially concerned with plotting trends and planning the actions required to achieve the identified growth targets, all of which were heavily biased towards financial targets and budgetary controls. Strategic management, on the other hand, focuses more on the environmental assumptions that underlie market trends (Mintzberg and Quinn, 1991).

Bearing these developments in mind, it is now possible to achieve a clearer definition of what is meant by strategic management. However, we should note the injunction of one of the founders of the strategy school, Igor Ansoff (1987), who warns that strategy is an elusive and somewhat abstract concept. This is perhaps why, like many other concepts in the field of management, there is no agreed, all-embracing definition of strategic management. This must be expected, however, when dealing with an area that is constantly developing. Nor should this inhibit the search for a definition, because in doing so we can see how strategic management is developing and where the main areas of dispute lie.

Ansoff (1965), in his early work, regarded strategic management as primarily concerned with the external, rather than internal, concerns of the firm, especially the choice of product-mix and markets. Chandler (1962) defined strategic management as the determination of the basic long-term goals and objectives of an enterprise and the adoption of courses of action and the allocation of resources necessary for carrying out these goals. Hofer and Schendel (1978) defined it as the basic characteristics of the match an organisation achieves with its environment.

The crucial difference between Ansoff, Hofer and Schendel on the one hand, and Chandler on the other, is that the former three regard strategy as almost exclusively concerned with the relationships between the firm and its environment, while Chandler takes a broader view. His definition includes internal as well as external factors. In particular, he sees issues such as organisational structures, production processes and technology as being essentially strategic. The point he makes is that the external and internal cannot be separated, as the Open Systems theorists would be the first to point out (*see* Scott, 1987). The external affects the internal, and vice versa. Therefore, strategic management must encompass the totality of the organisational domain and must not be restricted to one aspect, such as determining the product–market mix (Andrews, 1980).

This brings us a little nearer a definition but still leaves us with a hazy concept. Mintzberg *et al* (1988) identified five interrelated definitions of strategy: *Plan, Ploy, Pattern, Position* and *Perspective*.

- *Strategy as a Plan. According to this view, strategy is some form of consciously intended course of action which is created ahead of events. This can either be a general strategy or a specific one. If specific, it may also constitute a ploy.*

- *Strategy as a Ploy. This is where strategy is a manoeuvre to outwit an opponent. An example of this is when a firm threatens to lower its prices substantially to deter new entrants into its market. It is the threat of lower prices which is the consciously intended course of action, and not any actual plan to do so.*

- *Strategy as a Pattern. This is where we observe, after the event, that an organisation has acted in a consistent manner over time; i.e. whether consciously or not, the organisation exhibits a consistent pattern of behaviour. We can say from this that an organisation has pursued a particular strategy. It could be argued that this reflects a conscious plan. However, this is often not the case.*

● *Strategy as a Position. From this perspective, strategy is about positioning the organisation in order to achieve or maintain a sustainable competitive advantage. Mintzberg et al argue that most organisations try to avoid head-on competition. What they seek to achieve is a position where their competitors cannot or will not challenge them. In this sense, strategy is also seen as a game, groups of players circling each other, each trying to gain the high ground.*

● *Strategy as a Perspective. This definition sees strategy as a somewhat abstract concept which exists primarily in people's minds. For members of an organisation, the actual details of its strategy, as such, are irrelevant. What is important is that everyone in the organisation shares a common view of its purpose and direction which, whether people are aware of it or not, informs and guides decision-making and actions. Consequently, without the need for detailed plans, the organisation, through a shared understanding, pursues a consistent strategy/purpose.*

Mintzberg *et al* (1988) do not argue that one definition should be preferred to the others. In some senses they can be considered as alternatives or complementary approaches to strategy. Furthermore, they are useful in adding important elements to the discussion of strategy. They draw our attention to the distinction between conscious and unconscious strategy, and between emergent and planned strategy. They also highlight the role of the organisation's collective mind in developing and implementing strategy.

These multiple definitions also help us to make sense of the confusion of terms which litter the strategy literature and which different writers use in different ways. Many writers seem to treat corporate planning, long-range planning, strategic planning and formal planning as synonymous. However, not all would agree. Naylor (1979), for example, defined strategic planning as long-range planning with a time horizon of three to five years. Litschert and Nicholson (1974) disagreed: they state that strategic and long-term planning are not synonymous. They argue that strategic planning is a process which involves making a sequence of interrelated decisions aimed at achieving a desirable future environment for an organisation. Andrews (1980), similarly, defined strategy as a:

... pattern of decisions in a company that determines and reveals its objectives, purposes, or goals, produces the principal policies and plans for achieving those goals, and defines the range of business the company is to pursue, the kind of economic and human organisation it is, or intends to be, and the nature of the economic and non-economic contribution it intends to make to its shareholders, employees, customers and communities. (*Quoted in Smith, 1985:10*)

What we can see from the above is that, knowingly or not, writers are using different definitions of strategy and thus interpreting particular terms or phrases in the light of their own implicit or explicit definition. Nevertheless, in the use of these various terms, a certain consensus of opinion does emerge with regard to the basic features regarding strategic management and strategic decisions. In the main, most of the writers would agree with Johnson and Scholes (1993) who described strategy as:

- *concerning the full scope of an organisation's activities;*
- *concerning the process of matching the organisation's activities to its environment;*
- *concerning the process of matching its activities to its resource capability;*
- *having major resource implications;*
- *affecting operational decisions;*
- *being affected by the values and beliefs of those who have power in an organisation;*
- *affecting the long-term direction of an organisation.*

In defining strategic management, especially bearing in mind Mintzberg *et al*'s (1988) group of definitions, there are two further issues which need to be considered:

1 Is strategy a process or the outcome of a process?

2 Is strategy an economic/rational phenomenon or is it an organisational/social phenomenon?

Taking these two questions together, it can be seen that there is a body of opinion which sees strategy as an intentional, prescriptive process, based on a rational model of decision-making (Ansoff, 1965; Steiner, 1969; Argenti, 1974). However, there is an equally insistent body which argues that it is the outcome of the complex social and political processes involved in organisational decision-making (Hamel and Prahalad, 1989; Miles and Snow, 1978; Mintzberg, 1987; Pettigrew, 1980; Quinn, 1980).

The former group represents the early work in the field of strategic management. They not only see strategy as an economic/rational process, but also consider its options and usefulness as primarily restricted to issues relating to market share and profit maximisation (Porter, 1980). The latter group, which represents the new face of strategic management, increasingly views strategy not as a process, but as an outcome of a process. Their emphasis is not on the construction of detailed plans, which in any case they believe to be an unworkable approach, but on the organisational and social aspects of strategy formation. The argument here is that the capabilities of an organisation, in terms of its structure, systems, technology and management style, restrict the range of strategic options the organisation can pursue. Consequently, in a very real sense, it is the day-to-day stream of decisions regarding the development of its capabilities which determines an organisation's strategic direction, rather than the reverse. (Miles and Snow, 1978).

One of the often cited examples for this view is that of Japanese management. Pascale and Athos (1982) and Hamel and Prahalad (1989) argued that Japanese business success is not based on well thought out strategies *per se*, but on the commitment of Japanese managers to create and pursue a vision of their desired future. The vision is then used to bind an organisation together and give it a common purpose to which all can contribute. A key part of this common purpose is the identification and development of the core competences and capabilities necessary for the achievement of the organisation's vision.

This theme has been taken up by other Western writers on strategy. Kay (1993) used the term 'distinctive capabilities' rather than 'core competences', but is clearly describing the same thing. He argues that a firm's distinctive capabilities fall under four headings: reputation, architecture (i.e. internal and external structures and linkages), innovation and strategic assets. Kay believes that an organisation's competitiveness is dependent not upon any strategic plan *per se*, but upon the uniqueness and strength of its capabilities. It is these that allow an organisation to take advantage of opportunities and avoid threats, whether foreseeable or not. In a similar way, Stalk *et al* (1992) used the term 'core capability' in referring to an organisation's practices and business routines; and Grant (1991b) proposed a framework for analysing a firm's competitive advantage in terms of its resources and capabilities.

To an extent, the case made by Kay, Stalk *et al* and Grant is complementary to Mintzberg's (1987) concept of emergent strategy. Based on the many Western companies he had studied, Mintzberg argued that successful companies do not start out with detailed strategic plans. Instead, their strategies emerge over time from the pattern of decisions they take on key aspects of their activities. Clearly, there are similarities between the Japanese approach, Mintzberg's and that of Kay, etc. The Japanese consciously work out their shared vision and consciously pursue it. The emergent approach, at least in its pure form, lacks the concept of 'vision' and doubts the presence of conscious intent. Mintzberg (1994:25), however, wrote of organisations pursuing:

... umbrella strategies: the broad outlines are deliberate while the details are allowed to emerge within them. Thus emergent strategies are not bad and deliberate ones good; effective strategies mix these characteristics in ways that reflect the conditions at hand, notably the ability to predict as well as the need to react to unexpected events.

Kay (1993) took a similar view. While doubting the efficacy of corporate vision *per se*, he does stress that the development of capabilities is a conscious and planned process.

A further approach which has attracted a great deal of interest in recent years is *Chaos Theory* (Stacey, 1993). Originally a concept developed in the natural sciences, it is now being applied to business (Prigogine and Stengers, 1984). The applicability of Chaos Theory to organisations is based on the notion that the environment in which organisations operate has become more and more chaotic and unpredictable (Nonaka, 1988). In such a situation, it is dubious whether organisations possess the ability to plan their future in any meaningful way. For Chaos Theorists, strategy is about achieving beneficial change. Stacey (1991) argued that change falls into two categories: closed and contained change, where outcomes are predictable and achievable; and open-ended change, where the process is unpredictable and outcomes are unknowable. In the case of closed and contained situations, structured approaches to strategy and change are appropriate and can be effective. When it comes to rapid, open-ended situations where outcomes are unpredictable and unknowable, planned and structured approaches are impractical. Instead, what is necessary is an approach which can create 'organisational order' out of 'environmental chaos'.

The Chaos Theorists argue that organisations can only counter a situation of environmental chaos by creating internal chaos (Stacey, 1993). Weick (1987:56) argued that:

> ... it may be necessary for the organizational process to be chaotic in order to match adequately the chaotic nature of the environment. We can understand what we have done only through meaningful experiments, i.e. acts.

Stacey (1990) stated that visions and plans are counter-productive in trying to manage open-ended change; they merely lead to unintended and counter-productive consequences. For companies to succeed in a chaotic environment, according to Stacey (1990:15), they must:

> ... focus on single strategic issues and challenges, usually one by one, they develop explicit dynamic strategic agendas, they focus organizational attention on issues and challenges at many levels, they make experimental energy and resources. In this way, they develop their business organically and dynamically.

Hannan and Freeman (1988) and Williamson (1991), however, took issue with the notion that success can be assured by consciously matching strategies to circumstances. Their argument is that the modern business environment is so unpredictable, unstable and hostile that survival cannot be planned; luck may be more important than good judgment.

Pettigrew (1985 and 1987), and Child and Smith (1987) through their respective studies of ICI and Cadbury, also offered important insights and perspectives on approaches to strategic management. Pettigrew argues that there is a need for a change theory which sees organisations and how they operate in their entirety – one that recognises the importance and influence of the wider environment and appreciates the dynamic nature of strategy development and change. He is critical of theories based on the concept that organisations are rational entities, and which believe that change is undertaken in pursuit of their best interests. Instead, he argues that organisations have to be understood in the context of the constraints and possibilities offered by the environment in which they operate.

Pettigrew, whose views on the pervasive influence of power were discussed in Chapter 4, sees organisations primarily as political systems in which groups and individuals, under the guise of rationality, seek to mobilise support for, and legitimate the pursuit of, strategies and actions which promote or sustain their personal or sectional interests. Particular groups or individuals may achieve a position of dominance, but that dominance is always subject to prevailing intra-organisational and environmental conditions. Therefore, Pettigrew rejects the view that strategy is a rational process of deliberate calculation and analysis. Instead he believes that organisational strategy – though often cloaked in rational and analytical terms – is in reality the outcome of a combination of internal political struggles, between groups and individuals seeking to influence policy in their favour, and external environmental pressures and constraints.

Child and Smith's (1987) firm-in-sector perspective had some similarities with Pettigrew's work; they argue, however, for a stronger determining link between the individual firm and the sector in which it operates, and a lesser role for organisational politics. They suggest three areas of firm–sector linkage which shape and constrain the strategies organisations pursue:

1 *The 'objective conditions' for success.* Though each firm within the sector may pursue a different strategy, these will all tend to focus on or be determined by similar success factors such as customer satisfaction, quality, profitability, etc.

2 *The prevailing managerial consensus.* Within and across a sector, regardless of the organisation in which they work, managers are likely to develop a common and (implicitly at least) agreed view of how firms should operate, the key factors in their industry and the basis on which they compete with one another.

3 *The collaborative networks operating in the sector.* These may be with customers, suppliers, outside experts or even competitors.

Child and Smith's (1987) view draws on economic theories of the firm and suggests that the sector, particularly when strongly competitive, determines the path a firm must take for its future success. Though not denying a role for organisational politics, they claim that, unless the strategic decisions a firm takes are consistent with the conditions prevailing in its sector, success may be jeopardised. Therefore, Child and Smith appear to exhibit a greater faith in a rational and linear progression from market sector analysis to strategy formulation and implementation than Pettigrew and many other writers.

Understanding strategy: choices and constraints
....

The above is somewhat confusing. Clearly there is a distinction between the long-range planning approach of the 1960s and the strategic intent/competences approach of the 1980s and 1990s. What is not clear, however, is the degree to which a common understanding and perspective exists among those advocating the strategic intent/competences approach. Certainly, a number of writers have tried to argue that a common perspective does exist. Brown and Jopling (1994) believed that the main distinction lies between the writers of the 1950s and 1960s who, they argue, saw strategy as basically concerned with fitting the organisation to its environment, and the writers of the 1980s and 1990s who, they argue, see strategy as focusing on internal issues, mainly to do with the development of core competences. They base their case on a contingency perspective. The earlier approach was suitable to organisations operating in relatively stable and predictable environments, who had a limited product range, and where competition was restricted. With the advent of greater competition and more unstable environments, this approach was no longer viable, and firms had to look internally at how they could organise themselves to cope with the new situation. To an extent, this is an attractive analysis. However, though it is true that the earlier writers on strategy – Ansoff and company – did concentrate on product – market mix issues, it is also true that later they came to appreciate the link between the outside and the inside (Moore, 1992). Furthermore, while Mintzberg and others have concentrated on internal capabilities, the Japanese approach has been to see the internal and external as two sides of the same coin, which is why they emphasise the importance of the strategic outward-looking vision driving the development of internal capabilities.

Obviously, the development and categorisation of strategy is more complex than a straightforward attempt to fit writers into two camps, whether they be early and late, external and internal. The multiple-definition view of strategy argued by Mintzberg *et al* (1988), and particularly their proposition that these are both competing and complementary definitions, offer another perspective. Strategy can be considered as either a process or an outcome. It can also be considered as either a rational approach or a political/social phenomenon. The various approaches to strategy do not reflect some underlying truth; rather they are different approaches which organisations can choose (consciously or not) to adopt, depending on their circumstances, objectives and management.

While the above discussion of approaches to and perspectives on strategy cannot claim to be exhaustive, it does cover the key protagonists in the area. What it does not do, however, is to provide a classification or taxonomy of the various approaches. Whittington (1993) attempted to make sense of the many definitions and categories of strategy by identifying four generic approaches to strategy: the Classical, Evolutionary, Processual and Systemic.

The Classical approach

This is the oldest and most influential approach to strategy. It portrays strategy as a rational process, based on analysis and quantification, and aimed at maximising an organisation's long-term advantage. It argues that, through rigorous planning, senior managers can predict and shape both the external environment and the organisation itself.

The Evolutionary approach

As the name implies, this uses the analogy of biological evolution to describe strategy development. It believes that organisations are at the mercy of the unpredictable and hostile vagaries of the market. Those organisations which survive and prosper do so not because of their ability to plan and predict, which is impossible, but because they have been lucky enough to hit on a winning formula. From this perspective, successful strategies cannot be planned but emerge from the decisions managers take to align and realign their organisations with the changing environmental conditions.

The Processual approach

This perspective views organisations and their members as shifting coalitions of individuals and groups with different interests, imperfect knowledge and short attention spans. Markets are similarly capricious and imperfect but, because of this, do not require organisations to achieve a perfect fit with their environment in order to prosper and survive. Strategy under these conditions is portrayed as a pragmatic process of trial and error, aimed at achieving a compromise between the needs of the market and the objectives of the warring factions within the organisation.

The Systemic approach

The core argument of this perspective is that strategy can be a deliberate process, and planning and predictability are possible, but only if the conditions within the host society are favourable. Therefore, to an extent, this is a contingency approach to strategy which can accommodate situations where firms do not seek to maximise profit or bow to market pressures. If the conditions within the host society are supportive, markets can be manipulated, financial considerations can become a secondary issue and stability and predictability can be achieved. Furthermore, under such conditions, the objectives managers seek to pursue may be related more to their social background, degree of patriotism or even professional pride, than to profit maximisation. Therefore, from the Systemic perspective, the strategy an organisation adopts and the interests managers pursue reflect the nature of the particular social system within which it operates.

Whittington's categorisation of generic approaches to strategy is extremely useful in making sense of the plethora of approaches on offer. As one would expect, it is not perfect; some writers, such as Mintzberg, could fall under more than one heading, while others, Child and Smith, are difficult to locate. Nevertheless, the Classical approach would clearly incorporate the work of Ansoff (1965) and the other early Western writers on strategy. The Evolutionary approach is akin to the work of Hannan and Freeman (1988) and Williamson (1991); Mintzberg's (1994) work might also fall under this heading. The Processual approach could also cover Mintzberg's work and certainly includes Pettigrew's (1985 and 1987) work on organisational politics. The Systemic perspective clearly owes much to the Japanese approach to strategy as described by Hamel and Prahalad (1989).

Whittington (1993) also categorises these four approaches to strategy in terms of how they view outcomes and processes. He argues that the Classical and Evolutionary approaches see profit maximisation as the natural outcome of strategy. The Systemic and Processual approaches, on the other hand, believe other possible outcomes are both possible and acceptable. With regard to processes, the groupings change. Here the Classical and Systemic both agree that strategy can be a deliberate process. The Evolutionists and Processualists see strategy as emerging from processes governed by chance and confusion.

Whittington's four categories of strategy can be summarised as follows. Classicists see strategy as a rational process of long-term planning aimed at maximising profit. Evolutionists also believe that the purpose of strategy is profit-maximisation, but regard the future as too volatile and unpredictable to allow effective planning. Instead, they advise organisations to focus on maximising chances of survival today. The Processualists are equally sceptical of long-range planning, and see strategy as an emergent process of learning and adaptation. Finally, the Systemic perspective argues that the nature and aims of strategy are dependent upon the particular social context in which the organisation operates.

To an extent, the four approaches to strategy have some symmetry to the four Western approaches to organisation theory. The Classical, Evolutionary and Processual approaches are clearly 'one best way' or 'only possible way' approaches whereas the Systemic approach offers a Contingency perspective on strategy. They also share some common ground with organisation theory on the issue of rationality. The Classical and Systemic approaches argue that strategy is or can be rational in its development and objectives. The Processualists believe that it is rational in neither aspect, while the Evolutionists take a similar view of process but appear to adopt a rational perspective on outcomes in that profit-maximisation is seen as the only outcome which guarantees survival.

In their view of the scope for managerial choice and judgment, however, three of these four approaches to strategy do appear to be more permissive than organisation theory. Clearly, the Classical strategy theorists leave little scope for either: their instruction seems to be to follow the textbook in terms of outcomes and processes or else. However, both the Evolutionists and the Processualists emphasise the need for managers to be fleet of foot and percipient in making key decisions responding to opportunities or threats; although the Evolutionists (rather like Napoleon in his view of generals) appear to believe that, at the end of the day, a lucky manager may be more desirable than an able one. For advocates of the Systemic approach, choice and judgment are important, but tend to be constrained by the limits and objectives of the society in which they are located.

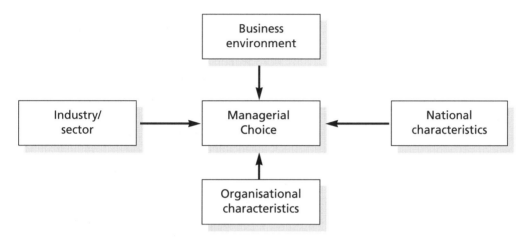

Fig. 5.1 Constraints on managerial choice

It would appear, therefore, that managerial choice, preference and judgment, for all but the Classicists, do have a role to play in determining not just the organisation's strategy, but also the particular approach to strategy it adopts. In our examination of the strategy literature, however, it is clear that choice is constrained and can only be exercised within limits (from some perspectives, very narrow limits indeed). As Fig. 5.1 shows, these limits or constraints, which are suggested by or inferred from the literature, can be classified under four headings.

National objectives, practices and cultures

The case for country-specific constraints very much follows the argument of the Systemic perspective on strategy. This view sees the operation of organisations as strongly influenced by the social system in which they operate. In some cases, such as in Japan and Germany, patriotism, national pride and a collectivist ethos have created a business environment that supports the pursuit of long-term national objectives. This is reflected in the behaviour of individual firms and financial institutions which favour stable growth over the medium to long term, rather than short-term profit maximisation. In Britain and the USA, on the other hand, the climate is far more supportive of individual endeavour and short-term profit maximisation rather than the national interest *per se*.

The difference between these two approaches is neatly summed up in the old saying that 'What's good for General Motors is good for America'. The Japanese would, of course, transpose this to read 'What is good for Japan is good for Toyota'.

This view also draws support from Hofstede's (1980 and 1990) work on national cultures discussed in Chapter 3. The implication, therefore, is that organisations ignore national norms at their peril: the pursuit of short-term profit maximisation in Japan and Germany is likely to be as difficult, and perhaps counter-productive, as the pursuit of a long-term strategy of growing market share, which ignores short-term profitability, would be in the UK or the USA. Nevertheless, these constraints are open to manipulation and avoidance. The move by many British companies – GEC, GKN, Lucas – to manufacture outside the UK is an example of this, as is the Japanese trend to establish manufacturing plants in the USA and Europe in order to avoid high production costs on the one hand and import quotas on the other. Another example is the lobbying of governments and national and international bodies for changes in laws and regulations which particular organisations or industries see as operating against their interests.

Industry and sector practices and norms

This follows from Child and Smith's (1987) firm-in-sector perspective. As discussed earlier, they believe that the objective conditions operating in a sector, managers' understanding of the dynamics of the sector, and the nature and degree of inter-firm collaboration all combine to determine the path a firm must take for its future success. This is especially the case where the sector is highly competitive. In effect, Child and Smith's argument is that firms must stick to the rules of engagement in their sector or perish. However, they do concede that, where competition is less intense, then managers have a greater degree of freedom with regard to the selection of strategy. Indeed, the low level of competition may explain how Japanese companies were able to change the rules of engagement to their advantage in many industries in the 1960s and 1970s (Hamel and Prahalad, 1989); although it is also the case that Japanese companies pay less attention to today's sectoral constraints and more to reshaping the rules of the game to create competitive conditions more favourable to themselves (Turner, 1990). Another method of overcoming sectoral constraints and conditions is, as illustrated by Allaire and Firsirotu (1989), by diversifying into new products and different sectors.

Business environment

For nearly all the approaches to strategy which we have discussed, their proponents assume, explicitly or implicitly, that they are operating in a particular type of environment. The Classical approach to strategy is clearly predicated on the existence of a relatively stable and predictable environment. If this exists, then predicting the future and planning accordingly is a much less hazardous exercise than would otherwise be the case. The Systemic view also seems to assume a degree of environmental stability. As Japan and Germany show, however, stability is actively promoted by government–industry co-operation rather than by the invisible hand of the market. For Processualists and even more so the Evolutionists, the environment is a hostile, unpredictable and uncertain place. Planning is almost impossible, and success comes either from continually adapting to changes in the environment, or from being in the right place at the right time.

For three of these perspectives, the environment is a given, even if they disagree about exactly what is given. For those advocating a Systemic approach, however, the environment is not a given; it can be changed. This coincides with those critics of Contingency Theory who argue that contingencies can be manipulated. The implications from this are that though many companies may have to adjust their strategic approach to environmental conditions, some companies may be able to do the reverse, especially with active government backing. The UK National Health Service is a good example of this. As Burnes and Salauroo (1995) noted, the NHS operated prior to 1990 as a typical government bureaucracy. The government allocated resources and gave policy direction, while the NHS centrally planned how resources would be allocated and policies operationalised (i.e. the Classical approach to strategy). This meant that there was considerable stability and predictability in its environment. However, the government wanted the NHS to operate in a more cost-conscious and entrepreneurial mode. To facilitate and encourage this, it changed the way funds were provided and distributed. Rather than funds being given as of right to service providers (e.g. hospitals), they were reallocated to service purchasers (e.g. local doctors) who could decide what to buy and from whom. This creation of a market for the provision of medical services has destabilised the environment and made planning and prediction very hazardous exercises (thus making an Evolutionary or Processual approach to strategy more relevant).

Normally, attempts at manipulating the environment are in the other direction: to reduce, or at least cope with rather than increase, uncertainty. Allaire and Firsirotu (1989) identified three ways of coping with uncertainty. The first of these is to predict and plan (the Classical approach). The second is to restructure for flexibility (the Contingency approach). The third, however, is to manipulate or control the environment. Allaire and Firsirotu cite the examples of Boeing and IBM, who created and subsequently dominated their environments. Another major approach they identify is the use of co-operative strategies – collusion, market-sharing and other methods of reducing competition. A recent example of this in the UK is the agreement by the main companies in the milk industry to 'carve up the country so they stop competing with each other' for doorstep sales (Cowe, 1995: 40). It is definitely possible, therefore, to change/control/manipulate the environment in which an organisation operates, and thus either necessitate or make possible a particular approach to strategy.

Organisation characteristics

Obviously, there are many organisation characteristics which act to constrain and thus facilitate managerial choice. However, there do appear to be four which have particular importance – *structure, culture, politics* and *managerial style*. Apart from the latter, these have been reviewed extensively in Chapters 3 and 4 and can be

discussed relatively briefly. An organisation's structure and culture have clear implications for managerial choice in the area of strategy. Organisations with organic
structures and task cultures are likely to be resistant to or incapable of operating a
Classical form of strategy. Similarly, organisations with mechanistic structures and
role cultures are likely to view Processual or Evolutionary approaches to strategy in
a somewhat hostile fashion. Moving on to the issue of organisational politics: where
decisions are heavily influenced by individual and group self-interest, as opposed to
organisational objectives, it is unlikely that a Classical or Systemic approach to
strategy would be successful. A Processual or Evolutionary approach, though, would
have clear applicability.

There remains the subject of managerial style. Burnes and James (1995), building
on the work of Beatty and Lee (1992) and Gibbons (1992), identified two basic
organisational states: *convergent* – a stable state – and *divergent* – where predictability and stability are absent. For each of these states, they argue, there is an
appropriate managerial style. Convergent states require managers with a *transactional style* – ones who are good at optimising the performance of the organisation
within the confines of existing policy. Divergent states, however, require managers
with a *transformational style* – ones who challenge the status quo and create new
visions. It follows from this that Transactional managers will prefer approaches to
strategy which stress continuity and predictability (i.e. the Classical or, in some
circumstances, Systemic approach), while transformational managers will be more
comfortable with a Processual or Evolutionary type of approach. Managerial style
will be further discussed in Chapter 11.

As was the case with the other three forms of constraint, organisational characteristics can be amended. The debate on structure and culture has been well covered
already, but politics are also open to change, not least either by developing a transparent decision-making process, such as the Japanese ringi system, or by doing
precisely the reverse. Managerial style operates somewhat differently, because
managers tend in any case to change organisations to fit their style.

It should be borne in mind that the particular mix of these four forms of constraint
will vary from organisation to organisation, even where these operate in the same
country and industry. Furthermore, it needs to be recognised that these constraints
are as likely to conflict with each other as they are to complement each other. (For
example, car companies operating in the UK may find that the culture of the UK's
financial institutions favours short-term profit maximisation, while the car industry
appears to require long-term investment in building market share. This may be one
reason why the UK motor industry is now foreign-owned.) In addition, it should be
noted that while managers are not obliged to take account of the constraints they
face, they may well pay a price for this in terms of the performance of their
organisation. Successful firms are likely to be ones which have managers who are
aware of, and can balance, the various constraints they face. This obviously raises
the issue of managerial ability and competence, an issue we shall explore in some
depth in Chapter 11.

The key point to emerge from the majority of writers is that the type of strategic approach adopted is a matter of managerial choice, but that choice is constrained by a variety of organisational, environmental, sectoral and national factors. As was argued in Part One, organisations and managers may be able to influence or change the constraints they face.

However, both the case for managerial choice and the argument for manipulating constraints need to be taken with a pinch of salt. The fact of the matter is that in the West, as Whittington (1993) noted, the Classical approach to strategy is still dominant. Furthermore, as Cohen *et al* (1972) noted, decisions are often not taken but happen. They suggest that decisions occur when four independent streams meet: problems, solutions, participants and choice opportunities. They argue that when a *problem* becomes severe it demands attention. *Solutions*, on the other hand, are answers looking for a problem. *Participants* are the people in the organisation possessing problems and/or solutions while *choice opportunities* are occasions when organisations are required to make a decision. When these four elements come together, decisions occur. Seen in this way, decision-making is not conscious, rational or systematic; on the contrary, decisions are haphazard, accidental and unplanned. Nelson and Winter (1982) took a similar view, seeing decision-making as being almost unconscious and automatic, based on a repertoire that individuals develop over time of responses to particular situations. This is similar to Ashforth and Fried's (1988) observation that there is a tendency in some organisations for behaviour to become almost mindless – employees and managers, as a result of organisational socialisation and experience, respond automatically to events in a prescribed fashion. Consequently, though the potential for choice exists, the reality is that many managers appear not to exercise it, preferring instead to stick to tried and tested, routine, orthodox, textbook approaches – regardless of their suitability.

Nevertheless, it is important to note that, in the academic world, the weight of the argument appears to be shifting from seeing strategy as a rational, mathematical process, to seeing it as the outcome of the ability of an organisation's management to utilise its strengths and competencies in the competitive pursuit of success. There are some writers, however, who believe the reverse is true of the business world, and that more and more firms are opting for rational decision-making approaches to strategy based on value-maximising financial techniques (Grant, 1991a). Whatever the truth or otherwise of this view, as the following shows, the main strategies available to organisations are still, though no longer exclusively, market- and quantitatively-orientated, and certainly give greater credence to rational decision-making than to more qualitative approaches.

TYPES OF STRATEGIES

There is a wide, and often confusing, variety of types of strategy that organisations can adopt. One important way of categorising these, and thus reducing the confusion, is to recognise that there are three levels of strategic decision-making in organisations:

- *The corporate level. Strategy at this level concerns the direction, composition and co-ordination of the various businesses and activities that comprise a large and diversified organisation, such as the Hanson Trust or Lonrho.*

- *The business level. Strategy at this level relates to the operation and direction of each of the individual businesses within a group of companies, such as Nissan's car assembly plant at Sunderland.*

- *The functional level. Strategy at this level concerns individual business functions and processes such as marketing or personnel.*

Each of these levels, though interrelated, has its own distinct strategic concerns and each can draw on a different battery of strategic weapons, or types; although there are strategies at the corporate level which have their counterparts at the business level, and likewise at the functional level.

At the *corporate* level, strategy deals with the 'game plan' for managing diversified enterprises whose activities cut across several lines of business. It concerns itself with questions such as:

- *What is the mission of the organisation?*

- *How should the business portfolio be managed?*

- *Which existing businesses should be disposed of and which new ones acquired ?*

- *What priority and role should be given to each of the businesses in the current portfolio?*

According to Thompson and Strickland (1983), the central strategic concerns at the individual *business* level are:

- *How should the firm position itself to compete in distinct, identifiable and strategically relevant markets?*

- *Which types of products should it offer to which groups of customers?*

- *How should the firm structure and manage the internal aspects of the business in support of its chosen competitive approach?*

Functional (or *operational*) level strategy concerns itself with issues such as:

- *How can the strategies formulated at the corporate and business levels be translated into concrete operational terms in such a way that the individual organisational functions and processes (marketing, finance, R&D, manufacturing, personnel, finance, etc.) can pursue and achieve them?*

- *How should the individual functions and processes of the business organise themselves in order not only to achieve their own aims, but also to ensure that they integrate with the rest of the business to create synergy?*

Given the different concerns of these three levels, it becomes possible to appreciate why there are so many types of strategy available and at which level they are most appropriate. The need to integrate the strategies and structures of these three levels also becomes clear. Otherwise, for example, the corporate level may pursue a strategy of diversification while the individual businesses are busy concentrating their efforts on fewer products and markets. Nevertheless, it would be wrong to see this as a mechanical process which begins at the corporate level and moves in a linear fashion through to the functional level. Strategy formation is inherently iterative, and aims to optimise the operation of the organisation in its entirety rather than maximising the product of any one particular part. These issues, and the main differences in scope and focus of the individual levels, can clearly be seen by a brief examination of the types of strategy that are pursued at the corporate and business levels. Functional level strategies will not be examined because these flow from and facilitate the other two levels.

Corporate level strategy

A review of the literature broadly reveals six basic types of strategy at this level:

Stability strategy (also known as maintenance strategy)

As its name implies, strategies under this heading are designed to keep organisations quiet and stable. They are most frequently found in successful organisations, operating in medium-attractiveness industries, who are faced with unpredictable circumstances outside the range of their normal business experience. Because of their markets and products, such organisations believe they have no need to make sudden changes and have the time and position to allow events to unfold before making any response (Wheelen and Hunger, 1989).

Growth strategy

This is possibly the most common form of all corporate strategies, and involves either concentrating on dominating one industry or growing by diversification across a number of industries. As a number of writers have suggested (*see* Argenti, 1974; Byars, 1984), its basic attraction is twofold. First, there is a strong correlation between increased turnover and increased profit. Second, the performance of senior managers tends to be measured in terms of the annual increase in turnover and profit. However, there are those who point out that increases in turnover are not necessarily matched by increases in profits and that, given the need to invest to achieve growth in turnover, growth may actually weaken a company's financial health (Byars, 1984; Drucker, 1974).

Portfolio extension

This is another variant of the growth strategy but is achieved through mergers, joint ventures or acquisitions, rather than organic growth. The first two of these allow growth or development to take place, without the organisations involved having to invest the level of resources that would be necessary if they were operating in isolation. The latter, acquisition, is usually resource-intensive but brings immediate gains in the form of an established and, hopefully, profitable business (Byars, 1984; Little, 1984; Leontiades, 1986).

Retrenchment strategy

This strategy is usually only embarked upon when an organisation is in trouble or, because of adverse market conditions, sees trouble ahead. It usually involves a process of cutting back on numbers employed and activities undertaken – downsizing, to use Peters and Waterman's (1982) phrase. In some situations this may lead to selling off the entire enterprise. However, the general aim is to cut back in order to match expenditure to projected income, and refocus the organisation so as to be able once again to attain prosperity in the future (Bowman and Asch, 1985; Thompson and Strickland, 1983).

Harvesting strategy

This involves reducing investment in a business or area of activity in order to reduce costs, improve cashflow and capitalise on whatever residual competencies or areas of advantage still remain. This approach can be implemented at different rates depending on the urgency of the situation. Slow harvesting means to reduce financial support at such a slow rate that it almost appears to be a maintenance strategy; at the other extreme, fast harvesting can result in budgets being cut at such a rate that it seems almost indistinguishable from liquidation (Harrigan, 1980; Kotler, 1978; Porter, 1980).

Combination strategy

The above strategies are not mutually exclusive, and can be linked together in whatever combination seems appropriate given the circumstances of the organisation in question. However, combination strategies are clearly more appropriate, or at least more necessary, in large multidivisional organisations where the circumstances faced by the different activities are likely to vary. Therefore, in such situations, organisations may experience a constant flurry of change where some parts are being run down and/or disposed of while new units are being acquired and other areas of the business rapidly expanded (Glueck, 1978; Pearson, 1977).

The above list is not exhaustive, nor can it be, given that each organisation is free to develop its own strategic variant in relation to its own circumstances. However, as argued above, it is the circumstances of the particular organisation in question which should dictate the type of strategy adopted by its managers, rather than any attempt to copy what has been successful elsewhere. Nevertheless, it should be noted that all except the first, maintenance strategy, imply fundamental restructuring of the internal operations of the organisation. In such situations, there are likely to be winners and losers, and managers may be more concerned with preserving their jobs and power than choosing the best strategy for the organisation.

Business level strategy

While corporate level strategies are mainly concerned with managing diversified enterprises whose activities span a number of different areas, business level strategies relate to the different ways that an individual business unit can compete in its chosen market(s). It must be remembered, however, that they are chosen and deployed within the framework of an overall corporate strategy and not in isolation from it. Just as at the corporate level, the available business level strategies are many and varied. To attempt to describe them all would be time-consuming, confusing and unnecessary. Instead, we shall examine the main variants through an examination of the work of one of the leading authorities on business level strategies, Michael Porter.

Porter (1980) argued that there are only three basic business level strategies: cost leadership, product differentiation and specialisation by focus.

Cost leadership

The aim of this strategy is to achieve overall lower costs than one's competitors, without reducing comparable product quality. To do this requires a high volume of sales in order to allow organisations to structure themselves in such a way that they can achieve economies of scale. This strategy, to quote Porter, requires the:

> ... **aggressive construction of efficient scale facilities, vigorous pursuit of cost reductions from experience, tight cost and overhead control, avoidance of marginal customer accounts, and cost minimisation in areas like R&D, services, sales force and so on. (*Porter, 1980:15*)**

Product differentiation

This is based on achieving industry-wide recognition of different and superior products and services compared to those of other suppliers. This recognition can be accomplished through the design of special brand images, technology features, customer service or higher quality, all of which have implications for the structure and operation of companies. Achieving differentiation is likely to result in insulation against competitive rivalry due to securing customer loyalty. The resultant competitive advantage also leads to increased returns, sometimes through making customers less sensitive to high product price.

Specialisation by focus

In this case the strategy is concerned with selecting (focusing upon) only certain markets, products or geographic areas in which to compete. Porter argues that by focusing in this way, it becomes feasible for a firm to dominate its chosen area(s). The method of achieving domination could either be through cost advantage or product differentiation. According to Porter (1980:15), however, such niche markets must have certain characteristics which separate them out from the market in general:

> **... the target segment must either have buyers with unusual needs or else the production and delivery system that best serves the target must differ from that of the other industry segments.**

If the niche market grows, or is incorporated, into a larger market, then market dominance is unlikely to be retained. In such circumstances, the previously dominant organisation will find itself having to compete for market share with others. In effect, the rules of the game have changed and a different strategy is required – either attempting to gain cost leadership across the entire market, or adopting a product differentiation policy which neutralises other competitors' cost advantage.

Porter's assertion concerning these three strategies is that they are distinct and cannot be mixed. That is to say, it is not possible to pursue successfully a cost leadership strategy and a product differentiation strategy at the same time because each requires different organisational arrangements to be successful. Furthermore, if a firm does not achieve cost leadership, product differentiation or specialisation in its products, services or market, it is bound to produce low profitability and have below-average performance. He refers to this sort of firm as 'stuck in the middle'. Many others share Porter's view (*see* White, 1986). A study by Dees and Davis (1984) also broadly supported Porter but, contrary to Porter's assertion, they found that there is some evidence to show that businesses with both a low cost and a high differentiation position can be very successful.

While there are, then, certain generic strategies that can be adopted at the corporate and business levels, the appropriateness of any of them for a particular firm is, as argued earlier, strongly related to the nature of the societal, sector, environmental and organisational constraints it faces. These include the stage of product–market evolution, the competitive position the firm has, the competitive position it seeks, the business strategies being used by rival firms, the internal resources and distinctive competencies at a firm's disposal, the prevailing market threats and opportunities, the type and vigour of competition, customer needs, and the conditions which financial institutions place on capital availability, to mention only the more obvious ones (Thompson and Strickland, 1983).

In addition, it must be acknowledged that generic strategies will always give rise to a host of variants and, therefore, at any one time the choice of the most suitable strategy will be a highly complex task. Indeed, this is what one would expect. If choosing and implementing strategy were easy, then all firms would be successful. By definition of success, however, not everyone can be successful; therefore, strategy formulation will and must remain fraught with danger and complexity.

A major point to note, however, is that almost without exception, all these forms of strategy require organisations to adopt appropriate structures, practices and cultures. Contrary to the views of earlier writers on strategy (such as Ansoff, 1965), it is the internal arrangements that need to be changed, often radically, in order to achieve the desired market place objectives. This clearly raises the issue of functional level strategies; but once again, these do not stand in isolation from the other levels of strategy. There is no need to discuss these here, however, because, by and large, the main ones are either products of corporate and business level strategies – such as market and product strategies – or, like personnel and structural strategies, received ample exposure in Part One.

Miles and Snow (1978) developed an important variant of the argument on types of strategy. Rather than attempting to classify the types or levels of strategies that organisations can adopt, they classify the organisations themselves as strategic types, based on the rate at which an organisation changes its products or markets. Miles and Snow identified four strategic types:

- *Defenders. These seek internal stability and efficiency by producing only a limited set of products, directed at a narrow but relatively stable segment of the overall market, which they defend aggressively. Such organisations are characterised by tight control, extensive division of labour and a high degree of formalisation and centralisation.*

- *Prospectors. These are almost the opposite of defenders. They aim for internal flexibility in order to develop and exploit new products and markets. To operate effectively in a dynamic environment they have loose structure, low division of labour and formalisation, and a high degree of decentralisation.*

- *Analysers. These types of organisations seek to capitalise on the best of both the preceding types. They aim to minimise risk and maximise profit. They move into new markets only after viability has been proved by Prospectors. Their internal arrangements are characterised by moderately centralised control, with tight control over current activities but looser controls over new undertakings.*

- *Reactors. This is a residual strategy. These types of organisations exhibit inconsistent and unstable patterns caused by pursuing one of the other three strategies erratically. In general, Reactors respond inappropriately, perform poorly, and lack the confidence to commit themselves fully to a specific strategy for the future.*

Before moving on to examine the strategic tools that organisations have at their disposal, it is important to remember that the concept of strategy (whether at the functional, business or corporate level) is contentious. The earlier section in this chapter on understanding strategy showed that there are many influential writers who do not believe in strategy as a conscious and planned process (e.g. Mintzberg, 1994; Pettigrew, 1985 and 1987; and Stacey, 1993). This does not invalidate corporate, business or functional strategies *per se*, but it does mean that they occupy a problematic and contested terrain.

STRATEGIC PLANNING TOOLS
....

The above shows that there are distinct approaches to strategy and a wide variety of strategies which organisations can adopt. This section briefly reviews the main tools that organisations use to select and construct their strategies. In the main, these tools tend to be either qualitative or quantitative. In the past it was the quantitative tools (mathematical models) which tended to dominate. This is, to a large extent, a product of the preference for quantification, especially in the financial arena, in the USA where many of the leading tools of and approaches to strategy originated (Grant, 1991a; Moore, 1992). It should be noted, however, that other leading industrial nations, especially Germany and Japan, place less reliance on financial and other quantitative measures in determining strategy (Carr *et al*, 1991; Whittington, 1993). Indeed, the Japanese electronics giant, NEC, never uses discounted cash flow; and though Toyota does calculate cash flows, it does not take account of them for decision-making purposes (Williams *et al*, 1991). Nevertheless, even in the USA and UK where financial considerations appear paramount, there has been some movement away from the sole reliance on quantitative techniques, and a growing interest in softer, qualitative tools such as scenario-building. This follows the move away from quantification and towards the use of more qualitative techniques in organisational theory in general.

Three of the main tools being used are as follows:

1 The PIMS (Profit Impact on Marketing Strategy) model
2 The Growth-Share Matrix
3 The Scenario construction approach.

The first two focus on corporate and business level strategies, but the latter can be applied to the functional level as well.

PIMS

This technique originated in 1960 as a research project at GE (General Electric) of America. GE began by analysing its operations with the aim of identifying those factors responsible for business success. In 1975 the work was moved to the Harvard

Business School, where it was located in the Strategic Planning Institute (SPI), which was specifically set up to manage it. By the early 1980s, the project had grown to encompass some 200 corporations, covering more than 2,000 individual business units (McNamee, 1985).

The rationale underlying the PIMS model is that certain characteristics of a business and its markets determine profitability. Consequently, understanding these characteristics and acting upon them will aid a company to become more profitable. Using company and industry data, the PIMS model seeks to provide individual companies with answers to questions such as:

- *What profit rate is 'normal' for a given business?*
- *What strategic changes are likely to improve performance?*
- *Given a specific contemplated future strategy, what are its effects on matters such as profitability and cash flow, both in the short and long term?*

There has been much discussion as to the success of the PIMS model. Certainly, some of its users, as well as academic observers, regard it as having only a limited use (Ford, 1981; Mitroff and Mason, 1981). The main criticisms levelled against PIMS are:

- *It is flawed because it uses historic data, without consideration for future changes. The argument is that, as organisations operate in a dynamic environment, to use the past to explain the future can be a dangerous exercise. Indeed, PIMS seems to be useful only in a stable environment, where companies stick to doing what they know best. It is even questioned whether PIMS can be regarded as a tool for policy in a strategic sense, since it can be argued that the 'variables' it so relies on, such as market share, are performance variables, not strategic ones (Abell, 1977).*
- *It is highly analytical, but very limited in solving problems. In addition, because PIMS has to use a very large data base for its analysis, it is argued that this creates a major problem for managers in terms of absorbing all the data generated. In turn, since the statistical errors in its output are rarely openly discussed, there is a tendency for managers not to question its findings because 'the computer is always right' (Andrews, 1971).*
- *Its assertion that profitability is closely linked to market share, and that an improvement in market share can be associated with a comparable increase in return on investment, is of dubious validity. It could equally be argued that both are due to common factors, such as low costs and good management (Smith, 1985).*
- *Most of the factors which govern the forecasts of the model are beyond the control of individual companies. Therefore, since PIMS relies heavily on this data, whatever conclusions it reaches about the fate of a company are final. It is not comforting, or even particularly useful, to be told you cannot do anything to turn a negative forecast around, because the factors responsible are out of your hands (Anderson and Paine, 1978).*

- *It assumes that a rather large set of quantitative variables, primarily of a financial nature, are sufficient to capture the state of a business and from this determine a realistic strategy (Naylor, 1981).*

- *It is based on the premise that business problems are orderly or well-structured. PIMS thus assumes that the determination or classification of the level of the organisation or business unit, the customer group, the competition, the market and the product line to which the analysis applies are all either well-known or well-specified. It is, therefore, not equipped to handle imprecise, let alone conflicting, definitions of business problems (Naylor, 1981).*

In summary, the main criticisms of PIMS are that it is too mechanistic, overly complex, based on unreliable data, and cannot cope adequately with dynamic and unpredictable environments. Yet, despite the criticisms levelled against it, many researchers still believe that PIMS is a useful tool. The PIMS method has also been praised for the insight it has given into the true nature of the relationships between strategic variables. Obviously, managers must deal with these variables and their relationships on a daily basis, but attempts at conceptualising these relationships had been lacking until the advent of the PIMS research programme (Anderson and Paine, 1978; Ford, 1981; Mitroff and Mason, 1981).

The Growth-Share Matrix

This was the brainchild of the Boston Consulting Group (BCG) in the USA. It is based on the assumption that all except the smallest and simplest organisations are composed of more than one business. The collection of businesses within an organisation is termed its business portfolio. Using pictorial analogies, it puts forward that businesses in an organisation's portfolio can be classified into stars, cash-cows, dogs and problem children (Smith, 1985).

- *Stars are business units, industries or products with high growth and high market share. Because of this, stars are assumed to use and generate large amounts of cash. It is argued that as they, generally, represent the best profit and investment opportunities, then the best strategy for stars, usually, is to make the necessary investments to maintain or improve their competitive position.*

- *Cash-cows are defined as former stars whose rate of market growth is in decline. They were once market leaders, during the early days when the market was rapidly growing, and have maintained that position as the growth tapered off. They are regarded as businesses with low growth but high market share. Because they are entrenched in the market, they have lower costs and make higher profits than their competitors. These businesses are cash rich; therefore the appropriate strategy for such businesses is to 'milk' them in order to develop the rest of the organisation's portfolio.*

- *Dogs are businesses that have low market share and which operate in markets with low growth potential. Low market share normally implies poor profit, and because the market growth is low, investment to increase market share is frequently prohibitive. Furthermore, in such situations, the cash required to maintain a competitive position often exceeds the cash generated. Therefore, dogs often become cash traps. It follows from this that, generally, the best strategy is for dogs to be sold off.*

- *Problem children or question marks, as they are sometimes labelled, are regarded as having a high growth rate and low market share. They have high cash requirements to keep them on course, but their profitability is low because of their low market share. They are so named because, most of the time, the appropriate strategy to adopt is not clear. With their high growth rate, it might be possible to turn them into stars, by further investment. On the other hand, because of the uncertainty that surrounds this type of businesses, the best strategy might be to sell them off altogether.*

The originators of the Growth-Share Matrix see it as a dynamic tool. As growth in their industries slows down, the original stars are expected to move into the position of cash-cows, as long as they keep maintaining their high market share; otherwise they will become dogs, and so on with changes in the other characteristics. This means the Growth-Share Matrix can be used to forecast the development of a business portfolio over a period of time. There are two basic assumptions underlying the matrix: first, that those industries, products or businesses that have a high growth rate can be differentiated from those that have a low growth rate; secondly, that those that have a high competitive position/market share can be differentiated from those that have a low competitive position/market share. Based on these assumptions, the matrix classifies business units or activities according to the growth rate of the industry of which they are a part and by their market share.

Over the years, the Growth-Share Matrix has attracted its fair share of criticisms as well as praise. One of the glaring objections to the matrix is the labels it employs for the classification of businesses. Andrews (1980) described these labels as a 'vulgar and destructive vocabulary'. There are, however, other more serious criticisms concerning the assumptions underlying, and the operation of, the Boston Model. The main one is that the uniqueness of an organisation and its problems may not be adequately captured by this or any other tight classification scheme. This is reflected in the views of Mitroff and Mason (1981), who argue that the critical assumptions underlying the matrix are tautologous and simplistic. They summarise these assumptions as follows:

- *that the classification scheme applies to all businesses, because all businesses can be classified as one of the four basic types;*

- *that the classification scheme is relevant to all businesses, meaning that all businesses should be able to be classified as one of the four types;*

● *that the model and its recommendations for action are universally applicable to all businesses, no matter what the characteristics of a particular business may be.*

In addition, a wide range of researchers have drawn attention to the difficulty in defining and measuring the major variables on which the matrix relies. In this respect, the criticisms are similar to those raised against PIMS. As examples, Hax and Majluf (1982) argue that the definition of market share used in the matrix is unrealistic. Similarly, Hax and Nicholson (1983) point out that a product/market segment can be defined in a variety of ways, and that, in reality, there is a whole hierarchy of product/market segments. Another reservation, expressed by Fawn and Cox (1985), is that the concept of what constitutes a single business is difficult to operationalise.

There is also some concern as to the validity of the indicators of profitability used: market share and industry growth. Hax and Nicholson (1983) pose two interesting and vital questions in this respect: 'Is market share really the major factor determining profitability?', and 'Is industry growth really the only variable that fully explains growth opportunities?' These reservations are echoed by Smith (1985). A further concern is that the matrix assumes that a good portfolio analysis should identify the competitive strengths and the industry attractiveness of each business unit. Alternatives to the Growth Share Matrix, however, reject this assertion. Instead they start by assuming that these two dimensions cannot be revealed by a single measurement, but require a wider set of critical factors for reliable positioning of the business units (Hax and Majluf, 1982; Hofer and Schendel, 1978). Perhaps the most telling criticism is that many of the companies who have used the matrix found, to their alarm, that all their component businesses were dogs even though these businesses were actually profitable!

In the face of such criticisms, a number of modifications have been made to the original Growth Share Matrix. General Electric, for example, in association with McKinsey and Co. of the United States, have developed a nine-way matrix instead of the original four-way classification (Hax and Nicholson, 1983). A similar system called the Directional Policy Matrix (DPM) has also been developed by Shell Chemicals in the UK (Hussey, 1978). Many other organisations have, in their turn, developed or employed similar schemes to meet their organisational needs (Patel and Younger, 1978). Nevertheless, portfolio models, possibly because they seek to cover all possible types of businesses, do seem severely flawed (Turner, 1990).

Regardless of the merits of these criticisms, few would dispute that, like PIMS, the Growth Share Matrix is primarily suited to well-structured planning problems in which the basic definition of a business unit, product or competition is not an issue (Bowman and Asch, 1985). Unfortunately, because of the uncertain and rapidly changing nature of business today, such situations are becoming less and less common. This, to an extent, may account for the increase in the popularity of the next approach.

The scenario-building approach

As a way of overcoming some of the criticisms of the above quantitative approaches, the use of scenario-building techniques emerged in the 1970s. The aim of the scenario approach is to enable an organisation to picture and make various assumptions about future events and trends which might affect the operations of the organisation. Organisations, like individuals, are unique and complex. As argued above, this can undermine the effectiveness of models or general principles as tools for strategic planning. If this is the case, rather than applying standard, but inappropriate, tools, each organisation must consider its own individual requirements. This process should be based on an intensive examination of its unique features and needs by a personally concerned, involved and experienced analyst. It is this that scenario-building attempts to do (Linneman and Klein, 1979).

The scenario approach has been defined in a number of ways. McNulty (1977) defined it as a quantitative or qualitative picture of a given organisation or group developed within the framework of a set of specified assumptions. Kahn and Weiner (1978) defined it as a hypothetical sequence of events constructed for the purpose of focusing attention on causal processes and decision points. To Kahn and Weiner, the purpose of scenarios is to display, in as dramatic and persuasive a fashion as possible, a number of possibilities for the future. To Norse (1979), scenarios are a means of improving our understanding of the long-term global, regional or national consequences of existing or potential trends or policies and their interaction. All these definitions are useful in the sense that they portray the different uses (national, international, corporate level, business level) to which scenarios can be put.

Essentially, building scenarios can be regarded as making different pictures of the future (business or otherwise) through the construction of case studies, either quantitatively or qualitatively. The quantitative variant of scenario-building, sometimes called the hard method, uses mathematics, models and computers to make pictures of the future, through the production of a vast array of numbers and figures. However, the main approach is the qualitative, or soft, method which is essentially intuitive and descriptive; it is based on the resources of the human mind and derived from the methods of psychology and sociology. The two main scenario-building approaches which have been established are the *Delphi Method* and the *Cross Impact Method*. In recent years, however, another approach has become increasingly influential: *vision-building*. Though this bears some relation to other scenario-building techniques, it comes from a different tradition. Underpinning the scenario-building approach is the concept of double-loop learning.

Single-loop learning is where individuals and groups respond to changes in the external and internal environments by detecting errors and modifying strategies within the existing norms of the organisation. Double-loop learning occurs when, in response to environmental changes, individuals and groups question the efficacy of the existing strategies and norms themselves (Argyris, 1977; Bateson, 1972). Therefore, one of the main functions of scenario-type approaches is that they enable organisations to question the very foundations of their existence, to examine the usefulness of their values and norms. Instead of asking how they can improve what they are doing, they begin to ask: Why are we doing this at all? What alternatives are there? This questioning of basic assumptions is something which is alien to the quantitative tools discussed above, especially given that most managers do not understand the basic assumptions built into such models in the first place. Indeed, quantitative models appear to remove the necessity for managers to think by providing them with 'answers' rather than information. The three main qualitative approaches, on the other hand, are designed specifically to make managers think radically about their organisation, its purpose and its future.

The Delphi Method

This uses a panel of experts, who are interrogated about a number of future issues within their area of expertise. In the classic application, the interrogation is conducted under conditions whereby each respondent is unknown to the others, in order to avoid effects of authority and the development of a consensual bandwagon. After the initial round of interrogations, the results are reported to the panel and another round of interrogations is conducted. Several rounds may be carried out in this manner.

Results produced from these interrogations may be amenable to statistical treatment with a view to yielding numbers, dates and ranges from them. At the end of the process, depending on whether a quantitative or qualitative approach is taken, either a detailed numerical forecast of the future is obtained, or a more descriptive and richer picture. In both cases, the central tendencies of majority opinion and the range of minority disagreements will also be presented (McNulty 1977; Zentner 1982).

The Cross Impact Method

This is a variation of the Delphi Method. It uses essentially the same interrogation method as the Delphi, i.e. a panel of experts; the difference, however, lies in what they are asked to do. The Delphi requires the experts to identify a number of future issues that they think will affect the organisation or business within their area of expertise. The Cross Impact Method, on the other hand, asks its panel of experts to assign subjective probabilities and time priorities to a list of potential future events and developments supplied by the organisation. The emphasis is on identifying reinforcing or inhibiting events and trends, to uncover relationships and to indicate the importance of specific events. The accruing data from this exercise is processed to yield curves of the probabilities for each event as a function of time (Lanford, 1972).

Like all approaches to strategic planning, the scenario-building approach has attracted criticism. One criticism is its reliance on subjectivity. The fact that any five management specialists can interpret the same situation in totally different ways is an oft-quoted example of this type of criticism. Furthermore, this approach is prone to retrospection. People's ideas of the future are informed by their knowledge and experience of the past. Since experience is not always the best teacher, scenarios may be based on false assumptions.

Another claimed drawback is that scenario development cannot be carried out by novices. It requires experts in the field concerned to be able to look into the future and make judgments about the likelihood of what might happen. In a survey of US industrial companies using scenarios in 1979, a senior Vice-President claimed that 'The major problem is the amount of time and quality of personnel required to prepare meaningful scenarios.' Others in the same survey complained that 'multiple anything is more work than single anything, especially if the need for the multiple is questionable.' A further respondent said, 'As no one is clairvoyant, to develop more than a most probable scenario is counter-productive and an exercise of mental gymnastics.' Most concluded that 'it is a waste of time and effort, since it mostly deals with the improbable' (Keshavan and Rakesh, 1979:57–61).

Nevertheless, in a study conducted in 1984 to review the extent of the use of multiple scenarios in Europe, the researchers discovered that 46 per cent (of a sample of 100 companies) said they would increase their use of the method in the future and only 12 per cent stated that they would make less use of the method. Companies in the same report stated that scenario construction was useful in controlling the 'uncertainty and unpredictability of the corporate environment'. It also helped them to 'organise co-operation between different levels of management and participation in creating the company's future, and thus improved not only planning, but the whole strategic management' (Malaska *et al*, 1984:48). Finally, Shell, a company which pioneered the use of scenarios in corporate strategy and which has, since 1973, adopted it as a permanent strategy tool, regards the use of scenarios as a way out of the ills associated with predicting the future. Shell asserts that the use of scenarios in planning has provoked better strategic thinking throughout the company and has increased flexibility (Leemhuis, 1990; Smith, 1985).

Vision-building

This has gained in popularity in recent years, especially in the United States. While it certainly bears a resemblance to the other scenario-building techniques, and is therefore open to the same criticisms, it is influenced more by Japanese management practices than by those in the West (Cummings and Huse, 1989; Hamel and Prahalad, 1989). It is a much less structured approach than the other two scenario-building techniques, and relies more on a company's own management. The major elements of vision-building are:

● *the conception by a company's senior management team of an 'ideal' future state for their organisation;*

● *the identification of the organisation's mission, its rationale for existence;*

● *a clear statement of desired outcomes and the desired conditions needed to achieve these.*

This is an iterative process which is designed to move from the general (the vision) to the specific (desired outcomes and conditions), and back again. By going round the loop in this manner, according to Cummings and Huse (1989), an ambitious yet attainable future can be constructed and pursued. This owes much to the Japanese, who pioneered the concept of Strategic Intent on which vision-building is based.

The work of Hamel and Prahalad (1989) is of particular importance in this respect. They argued that the strategic approach of Japanese companies is markedly different to that of their Western counterparts. Rather than attempting to lay down a detailed plan in advance, Japanese companies operate within a long-term framework of strategic intent. They create a vision of their desired future – their 'intent' – which they then pursue in a relentless but flexible manner. Hamel and Prahalad quote examples of leading Japanese companies who, in the 1960s, when they were insignificant in world terms, set out to dominate their markets. Honda's strategic intent was to be the 'Second Ford', Komatsu's to 'Encircle Caterpillar' and Canon's to 'Beat Xerox'. These companies then mobilised their resources towards achieving their individual strategic intent. In this, the prime resource they deployed was the commitment, ingenuity and flexibility of their workforces.

CONCLUSIONS
....

As can be seen from this chapter, the concept of strategic management has developed considerably since it began to be widely used in America in the 1950s and 1960s. No longer is strategy purely about the external world; no longer is it solely seen as a rational, quantitative process. Indeed, writers and practitioners from different backgrounds and countries, such as Hamel and Prahalad (1989), Mintzberg and Quinn (1991), Ohmae (1986) and Stacey (1993), have argued that it is not a process at all, but the outcome of a process: an outcome that is shaped not by mathematical models but by human creativity.

The move towards this new perspective on strategy has been brought about by the mounting criticisms against the Classical approach to strategy. The main criticisms are that it is mechanistic, prescriptive, inflexible, and reliant on quantitative tools and techniques of dubious validity. The result is that organisations who attempt to construct strategies using the Classical approach fall foul of what Peters and Waterman (1982) described as 'paralysis through analysis' and 'irrational rationality'. In effect, organisations contort themselves in a vain attempt to make the real world fit the constraints and limitations of their mathematical models, rather than vice versa.

The alternative view, and one that is gaining adherents, is that organisations should move away from exclusive reliance on mathematical models. Instead, human creativity should be brought into play. Senior managers should create a vision of the organisation's future – establish its strategic intent. This should then be pursued relentlessly by the organisation. In the process of doing so, the strategy emerges from the decisions that are taken with regard to resource allocation, organisation structure and the other key areas of operation. From different perspectives, a number of writers have come to the same conclusion. For successful companies, strategy is not a pre-conceived and detailed set of steps for achieving a coherent package of concrete goals within a given timescale. Nor is it a rational process which is amenable to mathematical modelling. Rather, it is the outcome of a process of decision-making and resource allocation that is embarked upon in pursuit of a vision (though even here there is disagreement about how conscious this process is). Such an approach is inherently irrational, inherently unplannable – it cannot be modelled or quantified, though it can and must be pursued with rigour and determination.

In this chapter, we have suggested a third approach, one which sides with neither the quantitative nor qualitative schools of thought. Instead, it has been argued that the approach to strategy which organisations adopt is or can be the outcome of managerial choice and preference. However, choice in this respect, as most others, is constrained. The key constraints identified were societal, sectoral, environmental and organisational. While on the face of it this appears to impose severe restraints on the degree of freedom managers have with regard to the choice of strategy, it was also argued that managers can influence or manipulate the constraints they face.

This follows on from Part One, where it was claimed that managers are not the passive creatures portrayed by much of organisation theory. Instead of having to adapt their organisations to the circumstances in which they find themselves, they can attempt to amend the circumstances. Therefore, managers in organisations faced by a dynamic and unpredictable environment could seek to change markets and/or products, influence the behaviour of competitors, or change customers' perceptions, in order to reduce uncertainty and increase predictability. By so doing, an organisation could still function efficiently at the more mechanistic end of the mechanistic–organic spectrum, if that were the type of structure preferred by its managers.

This argument would seem equally applicable to the constraints managers face when choosing an approach to strategy. Some managers might prefer an Evolutionary or Processual approach to strategy, either because it suits their own temperament or because they believe that a hostile and turbulent environment suits them better than their competitors (the move by Rupert Murdoch's newspapers in the UK to start a price-cutting war is an example of this). On the other hand, constraints might be manipulated or changed for ideological reasons, such as the UK government's introduction of market forces into the National Health Service. The point is that the possibility does exist for managers to choose not only the approach to strategy but also, to an extent at least, the constraints they face.

To choose an approach to strategy is one thing; to implement it is an entirely different matter. Therefore, just as this chapter has reviewed the main arguments with regard to strategy, so the next will review the strengths and weaknesses of the main approaches to change management.

Chapter 6

APPROACHES TO CHANGE MANAGEMENT

INTRODUCTION

This chapter takes over where the previous one left off. Chapter 5 was essentially concerned with approaches to determining and charting an organisation's strategic direction. It identified four generic perspectives on strategy development: Classical, Evolutionary, Processual and Systemic. Each of these perspectives has differing implications for the management of change. Broadly speaking, the Classical and, to an extent, the Systemic perspectives see change management initiatives arising from and contributing to the achievement of an organisation's strategy. The Evolutionary and Processual perspectives, on the other hand, see strategy, to a large extent, as arising from the day-to-day decisions (changes) that an organisation makes in attempting to adapt to and cope with environmental and other pressures and constraints. However, all four perspectives view change management as vitally important, whether it be for strategy implementation or development.

Consequently, this chapter focuses on the approaches to planning and implementing the changes required to achieve, or shape, strategic objectives. It begins by investigating the theoretical foundations of change management. In particular, it is shown that the three main theories that underpin approaches to change management can be distinguished by their respective concentration on individual, group and organisation-wide issues. This leads on to an examination of the two main approaches to change management: planned change and emergent change.

The *planned* approach to change has dominated the theory and practice of change management for the past 50 years. Based on the pioneering work of Kurt Lewin, this approach views organisational change as essentially a process of moving from one fixed state to another through a series of predictable and pre-planned steps. The *emergent* approach, which came to the fore in the 1980s, starts from the assumption that change is a continuous, open-ended and unpredictable process of aligning and realigning an organisation to its changing environment. Advocates of emergent change argue that it is more suitable to the turbulent environment in which modern firms now operate because, unlike the planned approach, it recognises the need for organisations to align their internal practices and behaviour with changing external conditions. Proponents of planned change, however, dispute this criticism and argue for its continuing relevance.

So despite the large body of literature devoted to the topic of change management, and the many tools and techniques available to change agents, there is considerable disagreement regarding the most appropriate approach. In an effort to bring clarity to the issue, the chapter concludes by arguing that neither the emergent nor planned approach is suitable for all situations and circumstances. Instead, it proposes a model of change which incorporates both approaches and, like the previous chapter, stresses the potential for managers to influence the constraints and conditions under which their organisations operate.

Nevertheless, neither strategy nor change management would be considered particularly important if products and markets were stable and organisational change was rare. However, that is not the case, nor – as Chapter 1 showed – has it ever been so. Change is an ever-present feature of organisational life, though many would argue that the pace and magnitude of change have increased significantly in recent years. The Institute of Management (IM), formerly the British Institute of Management, which regularly carries out surveys of its members, has certainly found this to be true. In 1991, the IM reported that 90 per cent of organisations in its survey were becoming 'slimmer and flatter' (Coulson-Thomas and Coe, 1991:10). In 1992, it reported that 80 per cent of managers responding to its survey had experienced one or more corporate restructurings in their organisations in the previous five years (Wheatley, 1992). In its latest survey (Institute of Management, 1995), 70 per cent of respondents reported that their organisations had restructured in the previous two years. A similar picture emerged from a recent study carried out at the University of Manchester Institute of Science and Technology (UMIST). This study found that 51 per cent of respondents' organisations were experiencing major transformations (Ezzamel *et al*, 1994). Therefore, we can see that over a very short timespan, most organisations and their employees have experienced or are experiencing substantial changes in what they do and how they do it.

Undoubtedly, the way such changes are managed, and the appropriateness of the approach adopted, have major implications for the way people experience change and their perceptions of the outcome. In both the latest IM study and the UMIST study, managers appear to report considerable levels of dissatisfaction with the outcome of change. The Institute of Management (1995) study found that, as a result of recent organisational changes, managers' workloads had increased greatly and that one in five was working an extra 15 hours per week. Many also reported that increased workloads were preventing them from devoting adequate time to long-term strategic planning or to their own training and development needs. The UMIST study found that while most managers supported the case for change, many were anxious not only about the outcome of change but also about the process of change itself (Ezzamel *et al*, 1994).

Given the vast literature on the topic, it may appear strange that many managers have doubts about both the approach to and outcome of change. Yet the reality, according to many observers, is that organisations can and do experience severe problems in managing change effectively (Howarth, 1988). It is clear that to manage change successfully, even on a small scale, can be complex and difficult. The literature abounds with examples of change projects which have gone wrong, some disastrously so (*see* Burnes and Weekes, 1989; Cummings and Huse, 1989; Kanter, 1992; Kelly, 1982 a and b). Therefore, there is substantial evidence that managers are right to be anxious about organisational change.

Organisational change comes in all shapes, sizes and forms and, for this reason, it is difficult to establish an accurate picture of the degree of difficulty firms face in managing change successfully. However, there are three types of organisational change which, because of their perceived importance, have received considerable attention: the introduction of new technology in the 1980s; the adoption of Total Quality Management (TQM) over the last decade; and, in recent years, the application of Business Process Re-engineering (BPR). All three, in their time, were hailed as 'revolutionary' approaches to improving performance and competitiveness.

The impact of the (so-called) Microelectronics Revolution of the 1980s, which saw the rapid expansion of computers and computer-based processes into most areas of organisational life, was the subject of a great many studies. These found that the failure rate of new technology change projects was anywhere between 40 per cent and 70 per cent (Kearney, 1989; Bessant and Haywood, 1985; McKracken, 1986; New, 1989; Smith and Tranfield, 1987; Voss, 1985).

The move by European countries to adopt Total Quality Management began in the mid-1980s. At its simplest, TQM is an organisation-wide effort to improve quality through changes in structure, practices, systems and, above all, attitudes (Dale and Cooper, 1992). Though seen as pre-eminently a Japanese innovation, the basic TQM techniques were developed in the USA in the 1950s (Crosby, 1979; Deming, 1982; Juran, 1988; Taguchi, 1986). Though TQM appears to be central to the success of Japanese companies, the experience of Western companies has been that it is difficult to introduce and sustain. Indeed, one of the founders of the TQM movement, Philip Crosby (1979), claimed that over 90 per cent of TQM initiatives by American organisations fail. Though a 90 per cent failure rate seems incredibly high, studies of the adoption of TQM by companies in the UK and other European countries show that they too have experienced a similarly high failure rate – perhaps as much as 80 per cent or more (Kearney, 1992; Cruise O'Brien and Voss, 1992; Economist Intelligence Unit, 1992; Whyte and Witcher, 1992; Witcher, 1993; Zairi *et al*, 1994).

Business Process Re-engineering has been hailed as 'the biggest business innovation of the 1990s' (Mill, 1994:26). Wastell *et al* (1994:23) stated that BPR refers to 'initiatives, large and small, radical and conservative, whose common theme is the achievement of significant improvements in organisational performance by augmenting the efficiency and effectiveness of key business processes'. Though relatively new, and therefore less well documented than either new technology or TQM, Wastell *et al* (1994:37) concluded from the available evidence that 'BPR initiatives have typically achieved much less than they promised'. Other studies of BPR have come to similar conclusions (Coombs and Hull, 1994; Short and Venkatraman, 1992).

Therefore, even well-established change initiatives, for which a great deal of information, advice and assistance is available, are no guarantee of success. This is perhaps why, in a recent survey, managers identified their ability (or inability) to manage change as the number one obstacle to the increased competitiveness of their organisations (Hanson, 1993).

Organisations have been and still are changing radically. Some are choosing to follow the prescriptions of writers such as Handy (1989), Kanter (1989), and Peters and Waterman (1982), while others are seeking to emulate Japanese experience as popularised by writers such as Hamel and Prahalad (1989) and Whitehill (1991). However, whatever particular form change takes and whatever objectives it seeks to achieve, organisations cannot expect to achieve success unless those responsible for managing it understand the different approaches on offer and can match them to their circumstances and preferences. On this basis, understanding the theory and practice of change management is not an optional extra but an essential requisite for survival.

CHANGE MANAGEMENT: THEORETICAL FOUNDATIONS

Change management is not a distinct discipline with rigid and clearly defined boundaries. Rather, the theory and practice of change management draws on a number of social science disciplines and traditions. Though this is one of its strengths, it does make the task of tracing its origins and defining its core concepts more difficult than might otherwise be the case.

The task is complicated further by the simple fact that the social sciences themselves are interwoven. As an example, theories of management education and learning, an important component of change management, cannot be fully discussed without reference to theories of child and adult psychology. Nor can these be discussed without touching on theories of knowledge (epistemology), which are themselves a veritable philosophical minefield.

The challenge, then, is to range wide enough to capture the theoretical foundations of change management, without straying so far into its related disciplines that clarity and understanding suffer. In order to achieve this delicate balance, the examination will be limited to the three schools of thought which form the central planks on which change management theory stands:

- *The Individual Perspective school*
- *The Group Dynamics school*
- *The Open Systems school*

The Individual Perspective school

The supporters of this school are split into two camps: the Behaviourists and the Gestalt-Field psychologists. The former view behaviour as resulting from an individual's interaction with their environment. Gestalt-Field psychologists, on the other hand, believe that this is only a partial explanation. Instead, they argue that an individual's behaviour is the product of environment and reason.

In Behaviourist theory, all behaviour is learned; the individual is the passive recipient of external and objective data. Among the earliest to work in the field of conditioning of behaviour was Pavlov (1927). In an experiment which has now passed into folklore, he discovered that a dog could be 'taught' to salivate at the ringing of a bell, by conditioning the dog to associate the sound of the bell with food. Arising from this, one of the basic principles of the Behaviourists is that human actions are conditioned by their expected consequences. Behaviour that is rewarded tends to be repeated, and behaviour that is ignored tends not to be. Therefore, in order to change behaviour, it is necessary to change the conditions which cause it (Skinner, 1974).

In practice, behaviour modification involves the manipulation of reinforcing stimuli so as to reward desired activity. The aim is to reward immediately all instances of the wanted behaviour, but to ignore all instances of the unwanted behaviour (because even recognition can act as a reinforcer). This is based on the principle of extinction; a behaviour will stop eventually if it is not rewarded (Lovell, 1980). Not surprisingly, given the period when it emerged, the Behaviourist approach mirrors in many respects that of the Classical school, portraying humans as cogs in a machine, who respond solely to external stimuli.

For Gestalt-Field theorists, learning is a process of gaining or changing insights, outlooks, expectations or thought patterns. In explaining an individual's behaviour, this group takes into account not only a person's actions and the responses these elicit, but also the interpretation the individual places on these. As French and Bell (1984: 140) explain:

> **Gestalt therapy is based on the belief that persons function as whole, total organisms. And each person possesses positive and negative characteristics that must be 'owned up to' and permitted expression. People get into trouble when they get fragmented, when they do not accept their total selves ... Basically, one must come to terms with oneself, ... must stop blocking off awareness, authenticity, and the like by dysfunctional behaviours.**

Therefore, from the Gestalt-Field perspective, behaviour is not just a product of external stimuli; rather it arises from how the individual uses reason to interpret these stimuli. Consequently, the Gestalt-Field proponents seek to help individual members of an organisation change their understanding of themselves and the situation in question, which, they believe, in turn will lead to changes in behaviour (Smith *et al*, 1982). The Behaviourists, on the other hand, seek to achieve organisational change solely by modifying the external stimuli acting upon the individual.

Both groups in the Individual Perspective school have proved influential in the management of change; indeed, some writers even advocate using them in tandem. This is certainly the case with advocates of the Culture–Excellence school, who recommend the use of both strong individual incentives (external stimuli) and discussion, involvement and debate (internal reflection) in order to bring about organisational change (*see* Chapter 3).

This combining of external and internal motivators owes much to the work of the Human Relations school, which (through the work of Maslow, 1943) stresses the need for both forms of stimuli in order to influence human behaviour. Though acknowledging the role of the individual, however, the Human Relations school also draws attention to the importance of social groups in organisations, as does the Group Dynamics school.

The Group Dynamics school

As a component of change theory, this school has the longest history (Schein, 1969). Its emphasis is on bringing about organisational change through teams or work groups, rather than individuals (Bernstein, 1968). The rationale behind this, according to Lewin (1958), is that because people in organisations work in groups, individual behaviour must be seen, modified or changed in the light of groups' prevailing practices and norms.

Lewin (1958) postulated that group behaviour is an intricate set of symbolic interactions and forces which not only affect group structures, but also modify individual behaviour. Therefore, he argued that individual behaviour is a function of the group environment or 'field', as he termed it. This field produces forces and tensions which emanate from group pressures on each of its members. An individual's behaviour at any given time, according to Lewin, is an interplay between the intensity and valence (whether the force is positive or negative) of the forces impinging on the person. Because of this, he asserted that a group is never in a 'steady state of equilibrium', but is in a continuous process of mutual adaptation which he termed 'quasi-stationary equilibrium'.

To bring about change, therefore, it is useless to concentrate on changing the behaviour of individuals, according to the Group Dynamics school. The individual in isolation is constrained by group pressures to conform. The focus of change must be at the group level and should concentrate on influencing and changing the group's norms, roles and values (Bell and French, 1984; Cummings and Huse, 1989; Smith *et al*, 1982).

Norms are rules or standards that define what people should do, think or feel in a given situation. For the Group Dynamics school, what is important in analysing group norms is the difference between implicit and explicit norms. Explicit norms are formal, written rules which are known by, and applicable to, all. Implicit norms are informal and unwritten, and individuals may not even be consciously aware of them. Nevertheless, implicit norms have been identified as playing a vital role in dictating the actions of group members.

Roles are patterns of behaviour to which individuals and groups are expected to conform. In organisational terms, roles are formally defined by job descriptions and performance targets, though in practice they are also strongly influenced by norms and values as well. Even in their work life, individuals rarely have only one role. For example, a production manager may also be secretary of the company's social club, a clerical officer may also be a shop steward, and a supervisor may also be the company's safety representative. A similar situation exists for groups. A group's main role may be to perform a particular activity or service, but it might also be expected to pursue continuous development, maintain and develop its skills, and act as a repository of expert knowledge for others in the organisation. Clearly, where members of a group and the group itself are required to conform to a number of different roles, the scope for role conflict or role ambiguity is ever present. Unless roles are both clearly defined and compatible, the result can be sub-optimal for the individual – in terms of stress, and for the group – in terms of lack of cohesion and poor performance.

Values are ideas and beliefs which individuals and groups hold about what is right and wrong. Values refer not so much to what people do or think or feel in a given situation; instead they relate to the broader principles which lie behind these. Values are a more problematic concept than either norms or roles. Norms and roles can, with diligence, be more or less accurately determined. Values, on the other hand, are more difficult to determine because group members are not always consciously aware of, nor can they easily articulate, the values which influence their behaviour. Therefore, questioning people and observing their actions is unlikely to produce a true picture of group values. Nevertheless, the concept itself is seen as very important in determining, and changing, patterns of behaviour.

Despite its limited focus, the Group Dynamics school has proved to be very influential in developing both the theory and practice of change management. This can be seen by the very fact that it is now usual for organisations to view themselves as comprising groups and teams, rather than merely collections of individuals (Mullins, 1989).

As French and Bell (1984:127–9) pointed out, the importance given to teams is reflected in the fact that:

> ... **the most important single group of interventions in OD [Organisation Development] are team-building activities the goals of which are the improved and increased effectiveness of various teams within the organization. ... The ... team-building meeting has the goal of improving the team's effectiveness through better management of task demands, relationship demands, and group processes. ... [The team] analyzes its way of doing things, and attempts to develop strategies to improve its operation.**

In so doing, norms, roles and values are examined, challenged and – where necessary – changed.

Nevertheless, despite the emphasis that many place on groups within organisations, others argue that the correct approach is one that deals with an organisation as a whole.

The Open Systems school

Having examined approaches to change which emphasise the importance of groups and individuals, we now come to one whose primary point of reference is the organisation in its entirety. The Open Systems school (as mentioned in Chapter 2) sees organisations as composed of a number of interconnected sub-systems. It follows that any change to one part of the system will have an impact on other parts of the system, and, in turn, on its overall performance (Scott, 1987). The Open Systems school's approach to change is based on a method of describing and evaluating these sub-systems, in order to determine how they need to be changed so as to improve the overall functioning of the organisation.

However, this school does not just see organisations as systems in isolation; they are 'open' systems. Organisations are seen as open in two respects. First, they are open to, and therefore, interact with, their external environment. Second, they are open internally: the various sub-systems interact with each other. Therefore, internal changes in one area affect other areas, and in turn have an impact on the external environment, and vice versa (Buckley, 1968).

The objective of the Open Systems approach is to structure the functions of a business in such a manner that, through clearly defined lines of co-ordination and interdependence, the overall business objectives are collectively pursued. The emphasis is on achieving overall synergy, rather than on optimising the performance of any one individual part *per se* (Mullins, 1989).

Miller (1967) argues that there are four principal organisational sub-systems:

- *The organisational goals and values sub-system. This comprises the organisation's stated objectives and the values it wishes to promote in order to attain them. To operate effectively, the organisation has to ensure that its goals and values are compatible not only with each other, but also with its external and internal environments.*

- *The technical sub-system. This is the specific combination of knowledge, techniques and technologies which an organisation requires in order to function. Once again, the concern here is with the compatibility and appropriateness of these in relation to an organisation's particular circumstances.*

- *The psychosocial sub-system. This is also variously referred to as organisational climate and organisational culture. In essence, it is the fabric of role relationships, values and norms that binds people together and makes them citizens of a particular miniature society (the organisation). It is influenced by an organisation's environment, history and employees, as well as its tasks, technology and structures. If the psychosocial sub-system is weak, fragmented or inappropriate, then instead of binding the organisation together, it may have the opposite effect.*

- *The managerial sub-system. This spans the entire organisation. It is responsible for relating an organisation to its environment, setting goals, determining values, developing comprehensive strategic and operational plans, designing structure and establishing control processes. It is this sub-system that has the responsibility for consciously directing an organisation and ensuring that it attains its objectives. If the managerial sub-system fails, so does the rest of an organisation.*

The Open Systems school is concerned with understanding organisations in their entirety; therefore, it attempts to take a holistic rather than a particularistic perspective. This is reflected in its approach to change. According to Burke (1980), this is informed by three factors:

1 *Sub-systems are interdependent.* If alterations are made to one part of an organisation without taking account of its dependence or impact on the rest of the organisation, the outcome may be sub-optimal.

2 *Training, as a mechanism for change, is unlikely to succeed on its own.* This is because it concentrates on the individual and not the organisational level. As Burke (1980:75) argues, 'although training may lead to individual change and in some cases to small group change, there is scant evidence that attempting to change the individual will in turn change the organisation.'

3 *In order to be successful, organisations have to tap and direct the energy and talent of their workforce.* This requires the removal of obstacles which prevent this, and the provision of positive reinforcement which promotes it. Given that this is likely to require changes to such things as norms, reward systems and work structures, it must be approached from an organisational, rather than individual or group, perspective.

Though the Open Systems perspective has attracted much praise, attention has also been drawn to its alleged shortcomings. Butler (1985:345), for example, while hailing it as a major step forward in understanding organisational change, points out that: 'Social systems are extremely dynamic and complex entities that often defy descriptions and analysis. Therefore, one can easily get lost in attempting to sort out all the cause-and-effect relationships.' Beach (1980:138), in a similar vein, argues that Open Systems theory:

> **... does not comprise a consistent, articulated, coherent theory. Much of it constitutes a high level of abstraction. To be really useful to the professional practice of management, its spokesmen and leaders must move to a more concrete and operationally useful range.**

Despite these criticisms, the level of support for this approach, from eminent theorists such as Burns and Stalker (1961), Joan Woodward (1965) and Lawrence and Lorsch (1967), is formidable. This is why, as explained in Chapter 2, it has proved so influential.

Summary

In looking at the three schools which form the central planks of change management theory, two major points stand out. First, not only do they stand, generally, in sharp contrast to the mechanistic approach of the Classical school towards organisations and people, but also, in their approach to individuals, groups and organisations as a whole, they form a link to the emerging organisational paradigms that were discussed in Chapter 3. Indeed, it might be possible to go further and say that these three schools provide many of the core concepts of the new paradigms. If this is so, the claim (by Kanter, 1989, and others) that these new forms of organisation are a radical break with the past may have to be reconsidered.

Second, though each School puts itself forward as the most effective, if not the only, approach to change, they are not necessarily in conflict or competition. Indeed, it could well be argued that they are complementary approaches. The key task, which will be examined in more detail later, is to identify the circumstances in which each is appropriate: does the problem or the objective of change lie at the level of the organisation, group or individual? Can any of these levels be tackled in isolation from the others?

In practice, the Open Systems perspective may be correct: change at one level or in one area should take into account the effect it will have elsewhere in the organisation. However, whether the perspective adopted is organisation-wide, or limited to groups and individuals, in the final analysis, what is it that is being changed? The answer, surely, is the behaviour of individuals and groups, because organisations are, as the proponents of these perspectives admit, social systems. To change anything requires the co-operation and consent of the groups and individuals who make up an organisation, for it is only through their behaviour that the structures, technologies, systems and procedures of an organisation move from being abstract concepts to concrete realities. This is made even plainer in the remainder of this chapter, where we examine the two main approaches to organisational change.

THE PLANNED APPROACH TO ORGANISATIONAL CHANGE

The practice of change management is dependent on a number of factors, not least the particular school of thought involved. Not surprisingly, therefore, even amongst those advocating planned change, a variety of different models of change management has arisen over the years. Though these were devised to meet the needs of particular organisations, or arose from a specific school of thought, nevertheless, most of the literature on the planned approach to change has been derived from the practice of Organisation Development (OD). OD has been defined as 'a systemwide application of behavioral science knowledge to the planned development and reinforcement of organizational strategies, structures and processes for improving an organization's effectiveness' (Cummings and Huse, 1989:1).

Within the OD field, there are a number of major theorists and practitioners who have contributed their own models and techniques to the development of change management (e.g. Blake and Mouton, 1976; French and Bell, 1984). Most observers seem to agree, however, that these can be related to three basic models of the change process, which in turn arise from the pioneering work of one person – Kurt Lewin. Lewin was a prolific theorist, researcher and practitioner in interpersonal, group, intergroup and community relationships. In 1945 he founded and became the first director of the hugely influential Research Centre for Group Dynamics. The models of the change process which emerged from his work are:

- *The Action Research model*
- *The Three-Step model*
- *The Phases of Planned Change model*

Action Research

This term was coined by Lewin (1946) in an article entitled 'Action Research and Minority Problems'. Action Research was designed as a collective approach to solving social and organisational problems. Though American in origin, soon after its emergence it was adopted by the Tavistock Institute in Britain, and was used to improve managerial competency and efficiency in the, then, newly nationalised coal industry. Since then it has acquired strong adherents on both sides of the Atlantic (French and Bell, 1984).

According to French and Bell (1984:98–9):

> **Action Research is research on action with the goal of making that action more effective. Action refers to programs and interventions designed to solve a problem or improve a condition ... Action Research is the process of systematically collecting research data about an ongoing system relative to some objective, goal, or need of that system; feeding these data back into the system; taking action by altering selected variables within the system based both on the data and on hypotheses; and evaluating the results of actions by collecting more data.**

Action Research is based on the proposition that an effective approach to solving organisational problems must involve a rational, systematic analysis of the issues in question. It must be an approach which secures information, hypotheses and action from all parties involved, as well as evaluating the action taken towards the solution of the problem. It follows that the change process itself must become a learning situation: one in which participants learn not only from the actual research, the use of theory to investigate the problem and identify a solution, but also from the process of collaborative action, problem-solving (Bennett, 1983).

An Action Research project usually comprises three distinct groups: the organisation (in the form of one or more senior managers), the subject (people from the area where the change is to take place), and the change agent (a consultant who may or may not be a member of the organisation). These three distinct entities form the learning community in and through which the research is carried out, and by which the organisation's or group's problem is solved.

The three entities must all, both individually and collectively, agree to come together, as a group, under mutually acceptable and constructed terms of reference. This usually small face-to-face group constitutes the medium through which the problem situation may be changed, as well as providing a forum in which the interests and ethics of the various parties to this process may be investigated. It is a cyclical process, whereby the group analyses and solves the problem through a succession of iterations. The change agent (consultant), through skills of co-ordination, links the different insights and activities within the group, so as to form a coherent chain of ideas and hypotheses (Heller, 1970).

The method of data gathering, analysis and diagnosis is dependent on the nature of the problem; but in all cases, these are carried out participatively. The change agent provides the methods of investigation in accordance with his or her understanding of the problem. The organisation contributes its understanding of the specific situation and its idiosyncrasies. This data is then presented to the subject for consideration. The response is fed back to the other two parties, and a series of iterations begins. The knowledge and understanding gained from this exchange of views and perceptions of the issues often result in a redefinition of the situation and of the problem. This in turn demands new action planning, if the outcome is to be followed up, fed back and evaluated. From this fact-finding process, hypotheses are framed, the line of action decided upon, implemented and evaluated. All this happens within the group and with the consent of every member.

Action Research is, therefore, a two-pronged process. First, it emphasises that change requires action, and is directed at achieving this. Second, it recognises also that successful action is based on analysing the situation correctly, identifying all the possible alternative solutions (hypotheses) and choosing the one most appropriate to the situation at hand (Bennett, 1983). This two-pronged approach, by stressing action as well as research, overcomes the 'paralysis through analysis' syndrome that can occur with some techniques (*see* Peters and Waterman, 1982). The theoretical foundations of this approach lie in Gestalt-Field theory, which stresses that change can only successfully be achieved by helping individuals to reflect on and gain new insights into their situation. However, it also has a strong affinity with Group Dynamics, given that it uses teams to solve problems and stresses the involvement of all those concerned. This is not surprising given Lewin's role in developing both Action Research and Group Dynamics.

Nevertheless, though Action Research has enjoyed a large following over the years, one of the barriers to its use is the need to gain the commitment of both the organisation and the subject of the change. This becomes especially difficult when dealing with large organisations. A common strategy is to use a top-down approach; establishing senior management agreement as a first step. This does not always work, however, as compliance at the top does not always guarantee co-operation at other levels in the organisation (Clark, 1972).

Co-operation, though, is not enough. There has also to be a 'felt-need'. Felt-need is an individual's inner realisation that change is necessary. The need must be felt by all those involved if progress is to be made. If felt-need is low in the organisation, introducing change becomes problematic – especially where the principles of Action Research are being applied. Furthermore, even when the need for change is accepted, this may not override anxieties about the implications of change. This can be particularly so when there exists a close relationship between personal identity, position at work and social standing, which is threatened by the proposed change (Bennis, 1966).

Even taking these drawbacks into consideration, Action Research is still a highly regarded approach to managing change (Cummings and Huse, 1989). However, this did not prevent its originator, Kurt Lewin, from seeking to improve upon it.

The Three-step model

In developing this model, Lewin (1958) noted that a change toward a higher level of group performance is frequently short-lived; after a 'shot in the arm', group behaviour may soon revert back to its previous pattern. This indicates that it is not sufficient to define the objective of change solely as the achievement of a higher level of group performance. Permanence of the new level should also be included in the objective. A successful change project, Lewin (1958) argued, should involve three steps:

1 *Unfreezing* the present level.
2 *Moving* to the new level.
3 *Refreezing* the new level.

This recognises that before new behaviour can be successfully adopted, the old has to be discarded. Only then can the new behaviour become accepted. Central to this approach is the belief that the will of the change adopter (the subject of the change) is important, both in discarding the old, 'unfreezing', and the 'moving' to the new. This once again stresses the importance of felt-need.

Felt-need is not the only similarity that the Three-step model shares with Action Research. Indeed, it is not too much to argue that the first two steps of the model, unfreezing and moving, roughly approximate to Action Research. This can be seen from the techniques used.

Unfreezing usually involves reducing those forces maintaining the organisation's behaviour at its present level. According to Rubin (1967), unfreezing requires some form of confrontation meeting or re-education process for those involved. This might be achieved through team-building or some other form of management development, in which the problem to be solved (changed) is analysed, or data presented, to show that a serious problem exists (Bowers *et al*, 1975). The essence of these activities is to enable those concerned to become convinced of the need for change. Unfreezing clearly equates with the research element of Action Research, just as the next step, moving, equates with the action element.

Moving, in practice, involves acting on the results of the first step. That is, having analysed the present situation, identified alternatives and selected the most appropriate, action is then necessary to move to the more desirable state of affairs. This requires developing new behaviours, values, and attitudes through changes in organisational structures and processes. The key task is to ensure that this is done in such a way that those involved do not, after a short period, revert back to the old ways of doing things.

Refreezing is the final step in the Three-step model and represents, depending on the viewpoint, either a break with Action Research or its logical extension. Refreezing seeks to stabilise the organisation at a new state of equilibrium in order to ensure that the new ways of working are relatively safe from regression. It is frequently achieved through the use of supporting mechanisms that positively reinforce the new ways of working; these include organisational culture, norms, policies and practices (Cummings and Huse, 1989).

The Three-step model provides a general framework for understanding the process of organisational change. However, the three steps are relatively broad and, for this reason, have been further developed in an attempt to enhance the practicable value of this approach.

Phases of planned change

In attempting to elaborate upon Lewin's Three-step model, writers have expanded the number of steps or phases. Lippitt *et al* (1958) developed a seven-phase model of planned change, while Cummings and Huse (1989), not to be outdone, produced an eight-phase model. However, as Cummings and Huse (1989:51) point out, 'the concept of planned change implies that an organization exists in different states at different times and that planned movement can occur from one state to another.' Therefore, in order to understand planned change, it is not sufficient merely to understand the processes which bring about change; there must also be an appreciation of the states that an organisation must pass through in order to move from an unsatisfactory present state to a more desired future state.

Bullock and Batten (1985) developed an integrated, four-phase model of planned change based on a review and synthesis of over thirty models of planned change. Their model describes planned change in terms of two major dimensions: *change phases*, which are distinct states an organisation moves through as it undertakes planned change; and *change processes*, which are the methods used to move an organisation from one state to another.

The four change phases, and their attendant change processes, identified by Bullock and Batten are as follows:

1 *Exploration phase.* In this state an organisation has to explore and decide whether it wants to make specific changes in its operations and, if so, commit resources to planning the changes. The change processes involved in this phase are: becoming aware of the need for change; searching for outside assistance (a consultant/facilitator) to assist with planning and implementing the changes; and establishing a contract with the consultant which defines each party's responsibilities.

2 *Planning phase.* Once the consultant and the organisation have established a contract, then the next state, which involves understanding the organisation's problem or concern, begins. The change processes involved in this are: collecting information in order to establish a correct diagnosis of the problem; establishing change goals and designing the appropriate actions to achieve these goals; and getting key decision-makers to approve and support the proposed changes.

3 *Action phase.* In this state, an organisation implements the changes derived from the planning. The change processes involved are designed to move an organisation from its current state to a desired future state, and include: establishing appropriate arrangements to manage the change process and gaining support for the actions to be taken; and evaluating the implementation activities and feeding back the results so that any necessary adjustments or refinements can be made.

4 *Integration phase.* This state commences once the changes have been successfully implemented. It is concerned with consolidating and stabilising the changes so that they become part of an organisation's normal, everyday operation and do not require special arrangements or encouragement to maintain them. The change processes involved are: reinforcing new behaviours through feedback and reward systems and gradually decreasing reliance on the consultant; diffusing the successful aspects of the change process throughout the organisation; and training managers and employees to monitor the changes constantly and seek to improve upon them.

According to Cummings and Huse (1989), this model has broad applicability to most change situations. It clearly incorporates key aspects of many other change models and, especially, it overcomes any confusion between the processes (methods) of change and the phases of change – the sequential states which organisations must go through to achieve successful change.

Planned change: summary and criticisms

As with Action Research and the Three-step model, Bullock and Batten's model stresses that change is a cyclical process involving diagnosis, action, and evaluation, and further action and evaluation. Their approach also recognises that once change has taken place it must be self-sustaining (i.e. safe from retrogression). In addition, they also stress the collaborative nature of the change effort: the organisation and the consultant jointly diagnose the organisation's problem and jointly plan and design the specific changes.

It is at this point that there appears to be a change of emphasis in Bullock and Batten's model in comparison with Lewin's Action Research model. Action Research aims to solve organisational problems through social action (dialogue). It seeks the active participation of the change adopter (the subject) in understanding the problem, selecting a solution and implementing it. The change agent is a facilitator, not a director or a doer. More important even than the solution to the problem, the consultant's real task is to develop those involved, and to create a learning environment that allows them to gain new insights into themselves and their circumstances.

Bullock and Batten's model, and to a lesser extent the Three-step model, gives the consultant a more directive and less developmental role. Their model seems to place a greater emphasis on the consultant as an equal partner rather than as a facilitator; the consultant is as free to direct and do as the others involved. Those involved are more dependent on the change agent, not just for his or her skills of analysis but also for providing solutions and helping to implement them. Therefore, the focus is on what the change agent can do for and to those involved, rather than on seeking to get the subjects to change themselves.

Action Research, as mentioned earlier, is an off-shoot of the work of the Gestalt-Field theorists, who believe that successful change requires a process of learning. This allows those involved to gain or change insights, outlooks, expectations and thought patterns. This approach seeks to provide the change adopter with an opportunity to 'reason out' their situation and develop their own solutions (Bigge, 1982). Bullock and Batten's approach, and to a lesser extent the Three-step model as well, on the other hand, appears to owe more to the Behaviourist approach. The emphasis is on the consultant as a provider of expertise that the organisation lacks. The consultant's task is not only to facilitate but also to provide solutions. The danger in this situation is that the learner (the change adopter) becomes a passive recipient of external and objective data, one who has to be directed to the 'correct' solution. Reason does not enter into this particular equation; those involved are shown the solution and motivated, through the application of positive reinforcement, to adopt it on a permanent basis (Skinner, 1974).

Nevertheless, serious though this criticism is, as Burnes and Salauroo (1995) pointed out, there are those who question not only particular aspects of the planned approach to change but also the utility and practicality of the approach as a whole. The main charges levelled against the planned approach to change are as follows.

1 It is based on the assumption that, as Cummings and Huse (1989:51) pointed out, 'an organization exists in different states at different times and that planned movement can occur from one state to another'. However, an increasing number of writers argue that, in the turbulent and chaotic world

in which we live, such assumptions are increasingly tenuous and that organisational change is more a continuous and open-ended process than a set of discrete and self-contained events (Garvin, 1994; Nonaka, 1988; Peters, 1989; Stacey, 1993).

2 On a similar note, a number of writers have criticised the planned approach for its emphasis on incremental and isolated change and its inability to incorporate radical, transformational change (Dunphy and Stace, 1993; Harris, 1985; Miller and Friesen, 1984; Schein, 1985).

3 The planned change approach is based on the assumption that common agreement can be reached, and that all the parties involved in a particular change project have a willingness and interest in doing so. This assumption appears to ignore organisational conflict and politics, or at least assumes they can be easily identified and resolved. Given what was said of organisational power, politics and vested interests in Chapter 4, however, such a view is difficult to substantiate. It also ignores situations where more directive approaches may be required, such as when a crisis, requiring rapid and major change, does not allow scope for widespread involvement or consultation (Dunphy and Stace, 1993).

4 It assumes that one type of approach to change is suitable for all organisations, all situations and all times. Dunphy and Stace (1993: 905), on the other hand, argue that:

Turbulent times demand different responses in varied circumstances. So managers and consultants need a model of change that is essentially a 'situational' or 'contingency' model', one that indicates how to vary change strategies to achieve 'optimum fit' with the changing environment.

There are proponents of planned change who would argue that these criticisms are not valid, that it is a more flexible and holistic approach than its detractors would acknowledge and is capable of incorporating transformational change (Cummings and Huse, 1989; French and Bell, 1990; McLennan, 1989; Mirvis, 1990). Nevertheless, it is the case that a new approach to change has been gaining ground in recent years. Though it has been given a number of different labels, such as continuous improvement or organisational learning, it is more often referred to as the emergent approach to change. The emergent approach tends to see change as driven from the bottom up rather than from the top down, it stresses that change is an open-ended and continuous process of adaptation to changing conditions and circumstances, and it also sees the process of change as a process of learning and not just a method of changing organisational structures and practices (Dawson, 1994; Mabey and Mayon-White, 1993; Wilson, 1992).

THE EMERGENT APPROACH TO ORGANISATIONAL CHANGE

As can be seen from the above, the planned change approach is relatively well developed and understood, and is supported by a coherent body of literature, methods and techniques. The emergent approach, on the other hand, is a relatively new concept which lacks an agreed set of methods and techniques. The proponents of emergent change approach it from different perspectives and tend to focus on their own particular concerns. To this extent, they are much less of a coherent group than the advocates of planned change and, rather than being united by a shared belief, they tend to be distinguished by a common disbelief in the efficacy of planned change.

Dawson (1994) and Wilson (1992) both challenged the appropriateness of planned change in a business environment that is increasingly dynamic and uncertain. They argue that those who believe that organisational change can successfully be achieved through a preplanned and centrally directed process of 'unfreezing', 'moving' and 'refreezing' ignore the complex and dynamic nature of environmental and change processes, and do not address crucial issues such as the continuous need for employee flexibility and structural adaptation. Wilson (1992) also believes that the planned approach, by attempting to lay down timetables, objectives and methods in advance, is too heavily reliant on the role of managers, and assumes (perhaps rashly) that they can have a full understanding of the consequences of their actions and that their plans will be understood, accepted and can be implemented.

The emergent approach, on the other hand, stresses the developing and unpredictable nature of change. It views change as a process that unfolds through the interplay of multiple variables (context, political processes and consultation) within an organisation. In contrast to the pre-ordained certainty of planned change, Dawson (1994), in particular, adopted a processual approach to change which, in particular, is less prescriptive and more analytical and, he argues, better able to achieve a broader understanding of the problems and practice of managing change within a complex environment.

This processual approach to change is akin to the processual approach to strategy discussed in Chapter 5. Advocates of emergent change who adopt this perspective tend to stress that there can be no simple prescription for managing organisational transitions successfully, owing to temporal and contextual factors. Furthermore, as Dawson (1994:181) argued, change cannot be characterised 'as a rational series of decision-making activities and events … nor as a single reaction to adverse contingent circumstances'. Therefore, successful change is less dependent on detailed plans and projections than on reaching an understanding of the complexity of the issues concerned and identifying the range of available options.

The rationale for the emergent approach stems from the belief that change should not be and cannot be solidified, or seen as a series of linear events within a given period of time; instead, it is viewed as a continuous process. Dawson (1994) saw change as a period of organisational transition characterised by disruption, confusion and unforeseen events that emerge over long timeframes. Even when changes are operational, they will need to be constantly refined and developed in order to maintain their relevance.

From this perspective, Clarke (1994) suggested that mastering the challenge of change is not a specialist activity facilitated or driven by an expert, but an increasingly important part of every manager's role. To be effective in creating sustainable change, according to McCalman and Paton (1992), managers will need an extensive and systemic understanding of their organisation's environment, in order to identify the pressures for change and to ensure that, by mobilising the necessary internal resources, their organisation responds in a timely and appropriate manner. Dawson (1994) claimed that change must be linked with the complexity of changing market realities, the transitional nature of work organisation, systems of management control and redefined organisational boundaries and relationships. He emphasises that, in today's business environment, one-dimensional change interventions are likely to generate only short-term results and heighten instability rather than reduce it.

As can be seen, though they do not openly state it, advocates of emergent change tend to adopt a Contingency perspective. For them, it is the uncertainty of the environment which makes planned change inappropriate and emergent change more pertinent. A key competence for organisations is, therefore, the ability to scan the external environment in order to identify and assess the impact of trends and discontinuities (McCalman and Paton, 1992). This includes exploring the full range of external variables, including markets and customers, shareholders, legal requirements, the economy, suppliers, technology, and social trends. This activity is made more difficult by the changing and arbitrary nature of organisation boundaries: customers can also be competitors; suppliers may become partners; and employees can be transformed into customers, suppliers or competitors.

To cope with this complexity, Pettigrew and Whipp (1993) proposed a model of strategic and operational change which involves five interrelated activities: environmental assessment, leading change, coherence, linking strategic and operational change, and developing human resources. By undertaking these activities, organisations can cope with uncertainty by becoming open learning systems, with strategy development and change emerging from the way the company, as a whole, acquires, interprets and processes information about its environment. Clarke (1994) took a similar view, arguing that an organisation's survival and growth depends on identifying environmental and market change quickly, and responding opportunistically. However, as Benjamin and Mabey (1993:181) pointed out:

> ... while the primary stimulus for change remains those forces in the external environment, the primary motivator for how change is accomplished resides with the people within the organization.

Changes in the external environment, therefore, require appropriate responses within organisations. It is a response, the supporters of the emergent approach state, that should promote extensive and deep understanding of strategy, structure, systems, people, style and culture, and how these can function either as sources of inertia that can block change, or alternatively, as levers to encourage an effective change process (Dawson, 1994; Pettigrew and Whipp, 1993; Wilson, 1992). A major development in this respect is the move to adopt a 'bottom-up' rather than a 'top-down' approach to initiating and implementing change. The case in favour of this move is based on the view that the pace of environmental change is so rapid and complex that it is impossible for a small number of senior managers effectively to identify, plan and implement the necessary organisational responses. The responsibility for organisational change is therefore of necessity becoming more devolved. As described in Chapter 2, this is very much what the advocates of Contingency Theory would expect in such a situation.

A bottom-up approach requires a major change in the role of senior managers. Instead of directing and controlling change, their role becomes one of ensuring the organisation's members are receptive to, and have the necessary skills and motivation to take charge of, the change process. Wilson (1992) believed that to achieve this, senior managers must not only change the way they perceive and interpret the world, but achieve a similar transformation among everyone else in the organisation as well. Pettigrew and Whipp (1993) contend that the degree to which organisations can achieve such a difficult task, and create a climate receptive to change, is dependent on four conditioning factors:

- *the extent to which key players in the organisation are prepared to champion environmental assessment techniques that increase openness;*
- *the degree to which assessment occurs and how effectively it is integrated with central business operations;*
- *the extent to which environmental pressures are recognised; and*
- *the structural and cultural characteristics of the organisation.*

Pettigrew and Whipp (1993:6) conclude that there are no universal rules with regard to leading change; rather it involves 'linking action by people at all levels of the business'.

Nevertheless, though the concept of universally applicable rules for change are rejected, supporters of the emergent approach do tend to stress four features of organisations which either promote or obstruct success: structures, cultures, organisational learning and managerial behaviour.

Organisational structure

This is seen as playing a crucial role in defining how people relate to each other and in influencing the momentum for change (Clarke, 1994; Dawson, 1994). Therefore, an appropriate organisation structure can be an important lever for achieving change, but its effectiveness is regarded as dependent upon the recognition of its informal as well as its formal aspects.

The case for developing more appropriate organisational structures in order to facilitate change very much follows the arguments of the Contingency theorists (discussed in Chapter 2) and the Culture–Excellence school (discussed in Chapter 3). Those favouring an emergent approach to change point out that the 1990s are witnessing a move to create flatter organisational structures in order to increase responsiveness by devolving authority and responsibility. An aspect of this is the move to create customer-centred organisations with structures that reflect, and are responsive to, different markets rather than different functions. Customer responsiveness places greater emphasis on effective horizontal processes and embodies the concept that everyone is someone else's customer.

One result of attempts to respond rapidly to changing conditions by breaking down internal barriers, disseminating knowledge and developing synergy across functions is the creation of *network organisations*, or to use Handy's (1989) term, *federal organisations*. Snow *et al* (1993) suggested that the semi-autonomous nature of each part of a network reduces the need for and erodes the power of centrally managed bureaucracies, which, in turn, leads to change and adaptation being driven from the bottom up rather than from the top down. They further argue that the specialisation and flexibility required to cope with globalisation, intense competition and rapid technological change can only be achieved by loosening the central ties and controls that have characterised organisations in the past.

Organisational culture

Johnson (1993:64) suggested that the strategic management of change is 'essentially a cultural and cognitive phenomenon' rather than an analytical, rational exercise. Clarke (1994) stated that the essence of sustainable change is to understand the culture of the organisation that is to be changed. If proposed changes contradict cultural biases and traditions, it is inevitable that they will be difficult to embed in the organisation.

In a similar vein, Dawson (1994) suggested that attempts to realign internal behaviour with external conditions require change strategies that are culturally sensitive. Organisations, he points out, must be aware that the process is lengthy, potentially dangerous, and demands considerable reinforcement if culture change is to be sustained against the inevitable tendency to regress to old patterns of behaviour. Clarke (1994) also stressed that change can be slow, especially where mechanisms which reinforce old or inappropriate behaviour, such as reward, recruitment and promotion structures, continue unchallenged. In addition, if these reinforcement mechanisms are complemented by managerial behaviour which promotes risk aversion and fear of failure, it is unlikely to create a climate where people are willing to propose or undertake change. Accordingly, as Clarke (1994:94) suggested, 'Creating a culture for change means that change has to be part of the way we do things around here, it cannot be bolted on as an extra.'

Therefore, for many proponents of the emergent approach to change, the presence or development of an appropriate organisational culture is essential. However, not all its proponents take this view. Beer *et al* (1993) suggested that the most effective way to promote change is not by directly attempting to influence organisational behaviour or culture. Instead, they advocate restructuring organisations in order to place people in a new organisational context which imposes new roles, relationships and responsibilities upon them. This, they believe, forces new attitudes and behaviours upon people. This view, as discussed in Chapter 3, is also shared by Tom Peters (1993) who advocates rapid and complete destruction of existing hierarchical organisation structures as a precursor to behaviourial change.

Wilson (1992:91), however, took an even more sceptical approach, claiming that:

> **... to effect change in an organization simply by attempting to change its culture assumes an unwarranted linear connection between something called organizational culture and performance. Not only is this concept of organizational culture multifaceted, it is also not always clear precisely how culture and change are related, if at all, and, if so, in which direction.**

Organisational learning

A willingness to change often only stems from the feeling that there is no other option. Therefore, as Wilson (1992) suggests, change can be precipitated by making impending crises real to everyone in the organisation (or perhaps even engineering crises) or encouraging dissatisfaction with current systems and procedures. The latter is probably best achieved through the creation of mechanisms by managers which allow staff to become familiar with the marketplace, customers, competitors, legal requirements, etc., in order to recognise the pressures for change.

Clarke (1994) and Nadler (1993) suggested that individual and organisational learning stems from effective top-down communication and the promotion of self-development and confidence. In turn, this encourages the commitment to, and shared ownership of, the organisation's vision, actions and decisions that are necessary to respond to the external environment and take advantage of the opportunities it offers. Additionally, as Pugh (1993) pointed out, in order to generate the need and climate for change, people within organisations need to be involved in the diagnosis of problems and the development of solutions. Carnall (1990) took this argument further, maintaining that organisational effectiveness can only be achieved and sustained through learning from the experience of change.

Clarke (1994:156) believed that involving staff in change management decisions has the effect of 'stimulating habits of criticism and open debate' which enables them to challenge existing norms and question established practices. This, in turn, creates the opportunity for innovation and radical change. Benjamin and Mabey (1993) argued that such questioning of the status quo is the essence of bottom-up change. They consider that, as employees' learning becomes more valued and visible within a company, then rather than managers putting pressure on staff to change, the reverse occurs. The new openness and knowledge of staff puts pressure on managers to address fundamental questions about the purpose and direction of the organisation which previously they might have avoided. Pettigrew and Whipp (1993:18) also contended that 'collective learning' is one of the main preconditions for sustainable change. They argue that 'collective learning' ensures that the full implications of an organisation's view of its environment can then inform subsequent actions over the long-term and, in turn, the way in which future shifts in the environment are approached.

Managerial behaviour

As was argued in Chapter 1, the traditional view of organisations sees managers as directing and controlling staff, resources and information. However, the emergent approach to change requires a radical change in managerial behaviour. Managers are expected to operate as facilitators and coaches who, through their ability to span hierarchical, functional and organisational boundaries, can bring together and motivate teams and groups to identify the need for, and achieve, change (Mabey and Mayon-White, 1993).

To be effective in this new role, Clarke (1994) believed that managers would require knowledge of and expertise in strategy formulation, human resource management, marketing/sales and negotiation/conflict resolution. The key to success, however, the decisive factor in creating a focused agenda for organisational change is, according to Clarke (1994), managers' own behaviour. If managers are to gain the commitment of others to change, they must first be prepared to challenge their own assumptions, attitudes and mindsets so that they develop an understanding of the emotional and intellectual processes involved (Buchanan and Boddy, 1992b).

For supporters of the emergent approach, the essence of change is the move from the familiar to the unknown. In this situation, it is essential for managers to be able to tolerate risk and cope with ambiguity. Pugh (1993) took the view that, in a dynamic environment, open and active communication with those participating in the change process is the key to coping with risk and ambiguity. This very much follows Clarke's (1994:172) assertion that because 'top-down, unilaterally imposed change does not work, bottom-up, early involvement and genuine consultation' are essential to achieving successful change. This in turn requires managers to facilitate open, organisation-wide communication via groups, individuals, and formal and informal channels.

An organisation's ability to gather, disseminate, analyse and discuss information is, from the perspective of the emergent approach, crucial for successful change. The reason for this, as Wilson (1992) argued, is that to effect change successfully, organisations need consciously and proactively to move forward incrementally. Large-scale change and more formal and integrated approaches to change (such as Total Quality Management) can quickly lose their sense of purpose and relevance for organisations operating in dynamic and uncertain environments. However, if organisations move towards their strategic vision on the basis of many small-scale, localised incremental changes, managers must ensure that those concerned, which could (potentially) be the entire workforce, have access to and are able to act on all the available information. Furthermore, by encouraging a collective pooling of knowledge and information in this way, a better understanding of the pressures and possibilities for change can be achieved, which should enable managers to improve the quality of strategic decisions (Buchanan and Boddy, 1992a; Quinn, 1993).

As well as ensuring the free flow of information, managers must also recognise and be able to cope with resistance to, and political intervention in, change. They will especially need to acquire and develop a range of interpersonal skills that enable them to deal with individuals and groups who seek to block or manipulate change for their own benefit (Buchanan and Boddy, 1992a). In addition, supporting openness, reducing uncertainty, and encouraging experimentation can be powerful mechanisms for promoting change (Mabey and Mayon-White, 1993). In this respect, Coghlan (1993) and McCalman and Paton (1992) advocated the use of Organisation Development (OD) tools and techniques (such as transactional analysis, teamwork, group problem-solving, role playing, etc.) which have long been used in planned change programmes. There is however, an enormous and potentially confusing array of these; Mayon-White (1993) and Buchanan and Boddy (1992b) argued that managers have a crucial role to play in terms of identifying and applying the appropriate ones. The main objective in deploying such tools and techniques is to encourage shared learning through teamwork and co-operation. It is this which provides the framework and support for the emergence of creative solutions and encourages a sense of involvement, commitment and ownership of the change process (Carnall, 1990; McCalman and Paton, 1992).

Nevertheless, it would be naïve to assume that everyone will want to work, or be able to function effectively, in such situations. The cognitive and behavourial changes necessary for organisational survival may be too large for many people, including and perhaps especially managers. An important managerial task will, therefore, be to identify sources of inertia, assess the skill mix within their organisation and, most of all, consider whether their own managerial attitudes and styles are appropriate.

Emergent change: summary and criticisms

The proponents of emergent change are a somewhat disparate group who tend to be united more by their scepticism regarding planned change than by a commonly agreed alternative. Nevertheless, there does seem to be some agreement regarding the main tenets of emergent change:

- *Organisational change is a continuous process of experiment and adaptation aimed at matching an organisation's capabilities to the needs and dictates of a dynamic and uncertain environment.*

- *Though this is best achieved through a multitude of (mainly) small-scale incremental changes, over time these can lead to a major reconfiguration and transformation of an organisation.*

- *The role of managers is not to plan or implement change, but to create or*

193

foster an organisational structure and climate which encourages and sustains experimentation and risk-taking, and to develop a workforce that will take responsibility for identifying the need for change and implementing it.

● *Though managers are expected to become facilitators rather than doers, they also have the prime responsibility for developing a collective vision or common purpose which gives direction to their organisation, and within which the appropriateness of any proposed change can be judged.*

● *The key organisational activities which allow these elements to operate successfully are:*

1 *Information-gathering* – about the external environment and internal objectives and capabilities;

2 *Communication* – the transmission, analysis and discussion of information; and

3 *Learning* – the ability to develop new skills, identify appropriate responses and draw knowledge from their own and others' past and present actions.

Though not always stated openly, the case for an emergent approach to change is based on the assumption that all organisations operate in a turbulent, dynamic and unpredictable environment. Therefore, if the external world is changing in a rapid and uncertain fashion, organisations need to be continually scanning their environment in order to adapt and respond to changes. Because this is a continuous and open-ended process, the planned approach to change is inappropriate. To be successful, an organisation must allow changes to emerge locally and incrementally in order to respond to and take advantage of environmental threats and opportunities.

Presented in this fashion, there is certainly an apparent coherence and validity to the emergent approach. However, it is a fragile coherence and of challengeable validity. As far as coherence is concerned, some proponents of emergent change, especially Dawson (1994) and Pettigrew and Whipp (1993), clearly approach it from the processual perspective on organisations. It is not clear, however, that Wilson (1992) and Buchanan and Boddy (1992 a and b) would fully subscribe to this view. In the case of Clarke (1994) and Carnall (1990), it is clear that they do not take a processual perspective. This is partly explained by the fact that some of these writers (especially Dawson, 1992; Pettigrew and Whipp, 1993; and Wilson, 1992) are attempting to understand and investigate change from a critical perspective, while others (notably Buchanan and Boddy, 1992 a and b; Carnall, 1990; and Clarke, 1994) are more concerned to provide recipes and checklists for successful change. Nevertheless, these differing objectives and perspectives do put a question mark against the coherence of the emergent approach.

The validity or general applicability of the emergent approach to change depends to a large extent on whether or not one subscribes to the view that all organisations operate in a dynamic and unpredictable environment to which they continually have to adapt. The issue of the nature and posited immutability of the environment in which organisations operate has been discussed extensively in previous chapters. The conclusion reached was that not all organisations face the same degree of environmental turbulence and that, in any case, it is possible to manipulate or change environmental constraints. This does not necessarily invalidate the emergent approach as a whole, but it does indicate that some organisations, by accident or action, may find the planned approach to change both appropriate and effective in their particular circumstances.

Obviously, the above raises a major question mark regarding the emergent approach; even without reservations regarding its coherence and validity, however, there would still be serious criticisms of this approach. First, much of it seems to advocate the same approach to organisations as the Culture–Excellence school and is, therefore, open to the same criticisms (see Chapter 3). Second, a great deal of emphasis is given to creating appropriate organisational cultures; but, as Chapter 4 noted, this is neither easy nor, it can be argued, necessarily possible. Indeed, as mentioned earlier, even Wilson (1992) was sceptical about the case for culture. Similar points can be made regarding the 'learning organisation' approach. As Whittington (1993:130) commented:

> **The danger of the purely 'learning' approach to change, therefore, is that ... managers [and others] may actually recognize the need for change, yet still refuse to 'learn' because they understand perfectly well the implications for their power and status. Resistance to change may not be 'stupid'... but based on a very shrewd appreciation of the personal consequences.**

A variant of this criticism relates to the impact of success on managerial learning. Miller (1993:119) observed that, while managers generally start out by attempting to learn all they can about their organisation's environment, over time, as they gain experience, they 'form quite definite opinions of what works and why' and as a consequence tend to limit their search for information and knowledge. So experience, especially where it is based on success, may actually be a barrier to learning, in that it shapes the cognitive structures by which managers, and everyone else, see and interpret the world. As Nystrom and Starbuck (1984:55) observed:

> **What people see, predict, understand, depends on their cognitive structures ... [which] manifest themselves in perceptual frameworks, expectations, world views, plans, goals ... myths, rituals, symbols ... and jargon.**

This brings us neatly to the topic of the role of managers. Though this will be discussed extensively in Chapter 11, for now it should be noted that managers are the ones who appear to have to make the greatest change in their behaviour. As the above quotations indicate, however, they may neither welcome nor accept such a change, especially where it requires them to challenge and change their own beliefs, and where it runs counter to their experience of 'what works and why'. Furthermore, if, as mentioned above, the possibility exists to manipulate environmental variables and constraints to avoid having to change their behaviour, they may perceive this as a more attractive or viable option.

Therefore, though the emergent approach to change has apparent advantages over the planned approach, an examination of it reveals that there are serious question marks over its coherence, validity and applicability.

CONCLUSIONS

This chapter has examined the development and applicability of approaches to change management. It began by reviewing the three main theoretical foundations (relating to individuals, groups and systems) which underpin approaches to change management. It was argued that while these can be viewed as separate theories, as far as managing change is concerned, individuals, groups and systems have to be viewed in a holistic fashion, especially in terms of their interface with the external environment. These separate theories are given life and put into practice through two main approaches to the management of change: the planned approach and the emergent approach.

As a formal subject for study and development, change management began with the development of the planned change approach over 50 years ago. Though elaborated upon and supported by a considerable number of very useful tools and techniques, it has remained essentially true to Lewin's original 'unfreezing', 'moving' and 'refreezing' approach. In the increasingly dynamic and unpredictable business environment of the 1980s, however, writers began to question the appropriateness of a top-down approach which saw the process of change primarily in terms of a 'beginning, middle and end' framework. In place of the planned approach to change, the emergent approach began to gain support. With its emphasis on bottom-up and open-ended change, it appeared to offer a more appropriate method of accomplishing the stream of adaptations organisations believed they needed to make in order to bring themselves back into line with their environment. However, this chapter has shown that emergent change appears to have as many shortcomings as planned change.

The two approaches appear to have some striking similarities, especially the stress they place on the process of change also being a learning process. They also share a common, and major, difficulty which is that, while both claim to be universally applicable, they were developed with particular situations and types of organisation in mind. Though neither acknowledges this limitation as such, the planned approach is clearly predicated on the assumptions that organisations operate in stable or relatively predictable environments, that managers can identify where change is required, that change projects are about moving from one fixed point to another fixed point and that the steps or phases in between are relatively clear and realisable. The planned approach also appears to assume that organisations, managers and employees are open and frank, welcome involvement, and are willing to change, or that these attributes can be achieved with the application of the appropriate tools and techniques.

The emergent approach, on the other hand, assumes organisations operate in unpredictable and uncertain conditions over which they have little control. It further assumes that change is a continuous process of adaptation which managers can neither fully identify nor effectively control. From the emergent perspective, organisations are perceived to be open and fluid systems which are tied to the environment in which they operate; implicitly managers are seen as highly competent and adaptable, capable of switching from being controllers and co-ordinators to becoming facilitators and partners; and employees are believed to be willing to take responsibility for identifying deficiencies and implementing change. The advocates of the emergent approach do not assume that all organisations are like this now, though clearly they believe some are, but they do assume that most can move in this direction.

In many respects, the debate between planned and emergent approaches to change bears certain similarities to the debate between the Classical and Human Relations approaches to organisation design, with both claiming to be the 'one best way'. It may also be that Contingency theory, which helped to clarify the debate over Organisation theory (see Chapter 2), also offers useful pointers in attempting to resolve the debate over approaches to change. If we regard the planned and emergent approaches as equally valid but applying to different organisational circumstances, then, using the Contingency analogy, we can locate them at either end of a business environment continuum (*see* Fig. 6.1) which runs from stability and predictability to turbulence and uncertainty. Based on this, we can begin to construct a model of change which incorporates a range of approaches, each of which is related to a particular type of environment. This concept of a multiplicity of approaches is in line with the call by Dunphy and Stace (1993:905) for '... a model of change that is

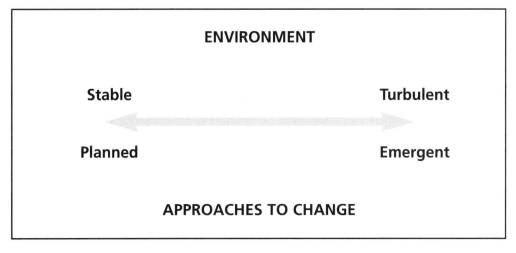

ENVIRONMENT

Stable   **Turbulent**

Planned   **Emergent**

APPROACHES TO CHANGE

Fig. 6.1 The position of the planned and emergent approaches on the business environment continuum

essentially a "situational" or "contingency model", one that indicates how to vary strategies to achieve "optimum fit" with the changing environment'.

Though this approach to change appears to have some merit, it is subject to the same sort of criticisms levelled at Contingency Theory (*see* Chapter 2). If we adopt the perspective developed in the last chapter, however, and see the environment and other organisational constraints as manipulable or subject to managerial choice, many of these criticisms can be answered and new possibilities open up. Some organisations will find that the organisational adjustments required to accommodate their position on the environment continuum coincides with the dominant view in the organisation of how it should operate. In that case, whether the approach to change adopted is planned or emergent, it will fit in with both how the organisation wishes to operate and the needs of the environment. Some organisations will, obviously, find that the dominant view internally of how they should operate is out of step with what is required to align or realign them with their environment. Such organisations face a number of choices ranging from whether to attempt to change their structures, cultures or style of management to accommodate the environment, or whether to attempt to manipulate the environment and other constraints so as to align them more closely with the dominant view within the organisation of how it should operate. Still further, there will be other organisations who face severe problems either because they failed to respond quickly enough or in an appropriate manner to changes in their environment, or because the environment moved too rapidly for an incremental approach to respond adequately. For such organisations, there may be no alternative to a major and radical restructuring, other than to go out of business. As the UK saw in the late 1970s and early 1980s, many organisations fell into the latter category.

The concept of a model which allows approaches to change to be matched to environmental conditions and organisational constraints is clearly attractive. The fact that it incorporates the potential for managers to exercise some choice or influence over their environment and other constraints allows the model to move beyond the limitations of mechanistic and rational perspectives on organisations, and into the heartland of organisational reality. In addition, though not coincidentally, it is in harmony with the approach to strategy developed in the previous chapter.

Nevertheless, though such a model of change has its attractions, its usefulness depends on how well it accommodates the reality of organisational life. To investigate this, Part Three of the book – Chapters 7, 8 and 9 – presents ten case studies of strategy development and change. This is then followed, in Chapter 10, by a comparison of the case studies with this chapter on change management and the previous chapter on strategic management. The intention is to construct a model of change management which incorporates both theory and practice.

PART 3

CASE STUDIES IN STRATEGY DEVELOPMENT AND CHANGE MANAGEMENT

Chapter 7

Case studies in strategic management

Introduction

In Part Two of this book, Chapter 5 examined approaches to strategic management by leading theorists. It described the origins and development of strategic management, showing how it had moved from being considered as a rational perspective solely concerned with product–market issues, to a situation where there are radically differing perspectives on its purpose, function and efficacy. The quantitative rationality of the Classical approach is still very much in evidence, but it has been challenged by the fatalism of the Evolutionists, the pragmatism of the Processualists and the societal perspective of the Systemicists – though no one now appears to doubt the need to view organisations in their entirety, rather than being merely concerned with external variables.

This chapter presents four case studies of organisations which have embarked on strategic management. It describes the experiences of these four organisations and relates these to issues discussed in Chapter 5. The case studies cover a wide range of situations, from rapid and apparently successful transformational change to more hesitant and less successful planned change. They also cover different time frames, ranging from two to three years to 15 years.

The chapter begins with the case of the Danish hearing-aid manufacturer, Oticon, which literally overnight reinvented itself. This is a company singled out as an outstanding example of transformational change by no less a person than Tom Peters (1992:206): '… the transition at Oticon to a radically new form of organization has been smoother than almost anyone would have imagined.' Oticon's story is one that highlights the importance of visionary leadership which is prepared to break out of the industry standard approach and, *de facto*, change the rules of the game.

Case Study 2 could have been invented, though it was not, to show the applicability in the West of the Japanese long-term approach to strategy. It illustrates how a strong leader, with a clear vision, can move an organisation from an apparently hopeless position to one where, 15 years later, it employs nearly six times as many people, has increased turnover more than thirty-fold, and is considered a European leader in its sector. It shows how a combination of consistency of purpose, the adoption of industry best practice, trial and error and, possibly, good fortune can transform an organisation – but not, in this case, overnight.

The third case study, Process Control Inc, is an updated version of one which appeared in the first edition of this book. It has made a reappearance not only because it shows that visionary leadership alone is not enough but also, in its updated form, it shows that new ideas, once rejected, do not always die. They can, if the circumstances are favourable, return and make old opponents into new converts. In addition, the case study illustrates how an organisation's fortunes can ebb and flow with disconcerting rapidity.

The concluding case study, Midshires College of Midwifery and Nursing, concerns the attempt to merge five organisations into one entity. It reveals the problems that can arise when a manager with a traditional, transactional approach to strategy attempts to apply this approach in a rapidly changing and unpredictable environment. The result is a constant chopping and changing of plans and initiatives, which not only demoralise staff but add to rather than reduce the level of uncertainty.

The chapter concludes by discussing the implications of the case studies in the light of the constraints on managerial choice identified in Chapter 5. It is argued that breaking out of constraints and exercising choice, especially where this challenges the *status quo*, requires not only special qualities from a manager but also favourable organisational conditions.

To assist the reader in getting the most out of these case studies, the conclusion is followed by a list of discussion points.

Case study 1

OTICON*

Background

Oticon, the Danish hearing-aid manufacturer, was founded in 1904. In 1979, it was the top hearing-aid manufacturer in the world. In the 1980s, however, its fortunes plummeted and it lost money and market share. In 1987, so poor was the company's performance that it lost half of its equity. The basic problem was that Oticon was a very traditional, departmentalised and slow-moving company. It had a distinguished past but it was a small company operating in a global market. Though it had 15 sites around the world and 95 distributorships, the Head Office, its largest site by far, only employed 145 people. Yet it was operating in a market which had come to be dominated by Siemens, Phillips, Sony, 3M and Panasonic. More importantly, it had the wrong products. Oticon manufactured the standard 'behind-the-ear' hearing aids but customers increasingly preferred the 'in-the-ear' variety. Furthermore, Oticon was strong in analogue technology, while the market and its customers were moving towards digital technology. In addition, though the company was strong in the state-subsidised markets of Scandinavia and Northern Europe, it was weak in the more buoyant markets of America and the Far East.

This began to change with the appointment of Lars Kolind as President of the company in 1988. The fact that he was only the third person to hold this post in the company's history helps to explain its strong attachment to tradition. In his view the company had 'been sleeping for ten years'. In the next two years, he worked hard to turn the situation round, and by 1990 Oticon made a profit of 4 per cent on sales and was growing at 2 per cent per annum. However, the market was growing at 6 per cent. More importantly, Kolind did not think the company had a future. He had been searching for a sustainable competitive advantage for Oticon: 'I looked at technology, audiology. I looked at distribution strength. I looked at everything, but there was nothing we could do better than the competition.' That he arrived at this view is hardly surprising. When competing against the world's leading electronics companies, it is very difficult to see how a small Danish company could, for example, design a better microchip for digital sound processing than Sony.

Nevertheless, he did not give up. On New Year's Day 1990, the solution came to him:

Maybe we could design a new way of running a business that could be significantly more creative, faster, and more cost-effective than the big players, and maybe that could compensate for our lack of technological excellence, our lack of capital, and our general lack of resources.

* I am grateful for the help provided by Ronnie Stronge of Stronge Communications in preparing this case study.

The vision – a knowledge-based organisation

Kolind realised that the industry was totally technology-focused, and that the main thrust was to make hearing aids smaller. He, on the other hand, thought this exclusive focus on technology was short-sighted. He believed Oticon was not in the hearing-aid business *per se*; it was in the business of 'making people smile' – restoring the enjoyment of life that hearing impairment can destroy. Making people smile, he reasoned, means not only giving them a wonderful piece of technology but actually changing people's lives for the better.

To achieve this requires knowledge of their lifestyle and how hearing impairment affects this, and an understanding of the social stigma associated with hearing impairment and the use of hearing aids. He saw that what would allow Oticon to compete and thrive was not selling hearing aids, but providing a new holistic approach to customer care – a system which would allow a hearing clinic to assess hearing loss, to discuss the lifestyle needs of the person concerned, to select the appropriate hearing aid, to programme it, and to interpret the feedback from the user in order to finetune the hearing aid. The intent would be to allow people with hearing difficulties to lead the sort of life they wanted in their situation, whether they preferred classical music or rock music, whether they worked in a noisy environment or a quiet one, whether sound was central to their work or peripheral.

Kolind had the vision for Oticon's role in meeting customers' needs, but he still had to find a way of implementing it. He believed the key lay in the mix of expertise necessary to produce a hearing aid: micromechanics, microchip design, audiology, psychology, marketing, manufacturing, logistics, and all-round service capability. If Oticon were to move away from merely making hearing aids and instead provide a total package of support for people with hearing difficulties, it would have to develop a whole new concept in hearing-aid service. It would need to combine this expertise in a new way and add new areas of expertise to the organisation. In short, they would have to move from a technological orientation to a knowledge orientation, from a technology-based manufacturing company to a knowledge-based service business. They had to build a learning organisation where experts put aside their expertise and work as a team to 'make people smile'.

For Kolind, a knowledge-based or learning organisation:

> ... should not work like a machine, it should work like a brain. Brains do not know hierarchies – no boxes – no job descriptions; what there is is a very chaotic set of thousands of relationships tangled in with each other based on certain knowledge centres, with an interaction which may seem chaotic. It is the reflection of the brain into the organisation that creates companies that are able to manage that knowledge process.

The strategy

Having identified the vision for the organisation, the next step was to set about fleshing out and implementing his strategy for change. Beginning with the Head

Office, which comprised the finance, management, marketing and product development functions, the company decided to abandon the concept of a formal organisation. Formal structures, job descriptions and policies were seen as creating barriers to co-operation, innovation and teamwork rather than facilitating it. Oticon got rid of departments, departmental heads and other managerial and supervisory positions. Job descriptions and titles and anything else which created a barrier between one member of staff and another were also eliminated. The company wanted to get rid of everything associated with traditional organisations, including budgets. The intent was to see what happened when staff were 'liberated' to do what they thought best. They wanted everyone in the organisation, from secretaries to technical experts, to work much more closely together to make things happen more creatively, more quickly and more cost effectively.

The reason for beginning with the Head Office was relatively simple: this was not just where the bulk of Oticon's costs were but, more importantly, where the core of its competence lay. The belief was that if it could get the Head Office functioning effectively, the rest of Oticon's somewhat scattered organisation would follow.

The concept of creating chaos out of organisation and expecting anything other than a disaster to follow seems far-fetched, if not downright lunatic. Oticon also recognised the dangers in the course it was embarking upon. The company realised that if success was to follow, above all else, there were two elements it needed to get right: direction and human values.

Direction Oticon's management was convinced that without a clear direction which everyone understood and believed in, the company would fragment and collapse into a disorientated mass of individuals each pursuing their own course of action. To avoid this, the management and staff openly and at length discussed and debated the new strategy for the company, and the implications for how Oticon would be structured and operate. Kolind commented that:

> ... the entire staff discussed not only where we were going but why we were doing so, and we created a consensus among staff that not only made them know why we were doing it and what we were doing, but we also got as far as having everybody think that this fundamentally made a lot of sense ... so there was consensus on the strategy.

Human Values as well as a consensus about the strategy, Oticon realised it also needed to get a 'fundamental consensus about the basic human values' of its business. After much debate, these were summed up in one sentence:

> We build this company on the assumption that we only employ adults, and everything we do will rest on that assumption, so we will not treat our staff as children – we will treat them as responsible adults.

Underlying this simple statement was a view that adults do not have to be told when to come to work and go home or that those dealing with, for example, the Japanese market will come in later and go home later than those servicing the American market. In a similar fashion, Oticon's management believed that staff would not over-spend or misspend budgets and, therefore, there was no need continually to remind them of this fact or harp on about other company rules or practices.

Implementing the strategy

Oticon now operates on a project basis. Anyone can start a project, provided they have the permission of one of five senior managers. Some projects are also initiated by management. Whomsoever the idea comes from, the main criterion for accept-ance is that a project is customer-focused. Anyone can join a project, provided they have the agreement of the project leader. The basic idea, going back to the concept that Oticon treats everyone as an adult, is that it is the individual's responsibility to fill his or her day usefully. If people do not have anything to do, it's their job to find something useful to do – either by starting a project or by joining one.

Communication is at the centre of this new approach to work. This is partly facilitated by computer. Each desk has a computer, and these list all the projects 'on offer' and the team leader's name along with the tasks involved. Usually the team leader will try and 'recruit' the skills he or she needs, but individuals are also expected to seek out opportunities as well. There are no demarcation lines; if an R&D specialist or a secretary wants to work with a marketing group, then all they have to do is have a chat with the project leader in order to sign on.

The physical embodiment of this new 'structureless' structure is the workplace. Gone are individual offices, gone are corridors – all the walls have been taken out and everyone works in the same open-plan office. Staff gather where they wish to work; there are no individual offices. Instead, everyone has a little filing cabinet on wheels. Staff come in each morning, pick up their mobile office and trundle it to where they are working that day. Oticon is also a genuinely 'paperless office'. All incoming mail is scanned into the computer and then shredded. The reason for this is simple: Oticon wants staff to move around from project group to project group as work requires. It does not want this process hindered by staff having to transport masses of paper as happens in most offices – the solution is to get rid of the paper.

This requires everyone to have access to and to be able to use a computer. The emphasis at Oticon, however, is on face-to-face, informal communication (although, for example, E-mail is used extensively). This is why the office is littered with stand-up coffee bars to encourage small, informal (but short) meetings. Three or four people will meet to discuss an issue or exchange ideas/information and then return to where they are working that day and follow up ideas and suggestions. These are usually fed straight into the computer and are available to everybody else. There is also an expectation not only that all information is open to staff in this manner, but that staff actually want to know the information. Therefore, rather than putting up barriers or operating on a need-to-know basis, Oticon tries to be transparent about all aspects of its business, whether it be new products, staff salaries or finance in general. The view is that the more a person knows, the more valuable they are to the company.

Staff did not take to this way of operating overnight. They were not originally recruited for their project skills, and some have found it hard to come to terms with this new arrangement. Furthermore, there is competition among project leaders for the best staff. Some groups of staff have found it much more difficult than others; receptionists still, mainly, answer the telephone. Nor has this new approach been adopted outside the Head Office, although the manufacturing operation, which is on a different site, has shown some interest.

The outcome

The changes to, or rather the transformation of, Oticon started at 8 am on 8 August 1991. At the beginning it was a catastrophe. It took months before everyone understood their new roles, and the organisation cast off its old ways and began to operate in the fashion Kolind had envisaged. By 1994, however, the results were impressive:

- *Fifteen new products had been launched (twice as many as the company had before).*
- *New product lead time had been halved.*
- *The company's sales were growing at 20 per cent per year, after a period of 10 years without real growth and at a time when the market was shrinking by 5 per cent per year.*
- *Oticon's market share increased from 8 per cent in 1990 to 12 per cent in 1993.*
- *Profit increased from zero in 1991 to $14 million in 1993 and $10 million in the first half of 1994, a return on sales of 17.6 per cent.*

Quite obviously, Oticon must be doing something right, but what? The key to its success appears to lie in five factors:

- **Changing the rules of the game.** *Oticon created a vision of where it wanted to be. Like Japanese companies such as Canon and Honda, this was based not only on ambition but also on a deep understanding of the nature of the market in which it operates. This allowed Oticon to spot the chink in the armour of the big players, and in effect to change the rules of the game – recognising that service delivery in total and not technological development in isolation is what customers really prefer.*
- **Moving to a project-type structure** *which fits the strategy and vision of the business.*
- **Creating a whole-hearted commitment from everyone to working co-operatively and proactively.** *In effect, there appears to have been a wholesale cultural change at Oticon, from the senior management down.*

- *Leadership. Oticon appears to be one of those rare cases of genuine visionary leadership which has transformed an organisation over a short space of time.*

- *Societal values. As has been mentioned several times before, Scandinavia has a long history of industrial and social democracy. Denmark in particular has led the way with the creation of a strong co-operative movement. The changes which have taken place at Oticon appear to be a classic, if somewhat extreme, form of Scandinavian industrial democracy. As such, Oticon's new way of working fits in with the societal values espoused by Denmark and other Scandinavian countries.*

Case study 2

FLAIR ENGINEERING LTD

Background

This UK company was founded in the 1940s as a manufacturer of pressed steel products. In the 1950s it ceased to be an independent company and joined a small, family-owned conglomerate. By the 1960s and early 1970s, it had ceased to produce its own products and tended to specialise in providing pressed parts for the white goods industries. However, with the increasing penetration of the UK market by foreign companies, this work declined. By the late 1970s, it was operating as a 'seller of capacity' to whoever was prepared to buy. Throughout the previous 40 years, it had remained a small company; employment fluctuated between 50 and 150. Its turnover never exceeded £4 million and its profits were equally modest, though even in difficult periods it never made significant losses, nor did it require its parent company to provide much in the way of capital investment.

Therefore, like many small companies, it survived rather than thrived, and it reacted to events rather than seeking to control its own destiny. This all began to change in 1980, however, with the promotion of an existing manager to the post of Managing Director. On taking over, he carried out a strategic review of the company, the first in its history. The review confirmed his worst fears: turnover for 1979/80 was down from £4 million to £2.5 million and the company's main customers were continuing to cut back their orders. Furthermore, in the midst of a world economic recession, there did not seem to be much likelihood of alternative customers filling the gap.

The Managing Director concluded that the company lacked:

- *product differentiation;*
- *distinct competitive strengths;*

- *a low cost base;*
- *modern equipment and manufacturing methods.*

A strategy emerges

The future looked bleak and, as proved to be the case for many companies in a similar state in the early 1980s, the most likely outcome was that they would go out of business. However, the Managing Director was determined that this would not happen. He believed that the company did have a prosperous future, but only if it could be transformed into a modern, competitive manufacturing organisation. This required it to face up to four major challenges:

- *to develop a distinctive product and industry focus;*
- *to reduce its cost base;*
- *to improve quality;*
- *to invest in people and equipment.*

These four challenges went hand-in-hand. Flair could not survive any longer merely as a seller of capacity to whoever required it. It needed to provide a coherent range of products, built around its core competence in pressed metal parts, to an industry or industries whose long-term prospects were secure. In order to achieve this, the company needed to reduce its cost base, improve quality and modernise its production equipment and methods. In addition, it had a loyal, though somewhat apprehensive workforce, whose goodwill and commitment it had to maintain if the company was to be transformed.

The first steps to achieving these challenges were:

1 *To undertake a market survey in order to identify potential and desired customers and products.* This took approximately six months; in the end, the motor vehicle industry was targeted as the preferred market. Though the UK industry was in a poor state at the time – Talbot Motors was about to fold and Rover Group (at this time still called British Leyland) looked as though it could follow – Flair believed its long-term future was secure. This industry proved to be a particularly judicious choice, given the arrival of the Japanese transplants in the UK in the latter half of the 1980s.

2 *To establish how best to organise the company in order to become a credible force in its chosen field.* In effect, the company was undertaking a benchmarking exercise to identify world-class performance. Though benchmarking activities and the search for world-class performance are now commonplace, this was not so in 1980, and shows how the company was beginning to become a trendsetter rather than a follower. In order to establish benchmarks, the Managing Director visited leading companies in Germany and Japan. While he was impressed by the engineering skills of German companies, the way that the Japanese organised and applied themselves was a revelation to him. He found their commitment to quality,

and the way the whole workforce was involved in eliminating waste and increasing effectiveness, particularly impressive. It was clear from this point onwards that if the company were to achieve its vision of becoming a world-class automotive supplier, it was to Japanese standards of excellence that they should aspire.

Having established where they wanted to go, the company now needed to win orders from its target market and establish a long-term relationship with customers. Though Ford and Rover were impressed enough with Flair's plans to give them work on forthcoming models, it was made clear that they would share this work with other suppliers and that future work depended on the company's ability to meet the cost, quality and delivery performance of these other suppliers.

With the Ford and Rover work, the company set itself two objectives: first, to exceed the performance of the other suppliers; and second, to become the single-source supplier for these components. This in essence became the company's strategy for developing partnerships with customers: to outperform the opposition and on that basis take 100 per cent of the available work.

Though it had won the work, it now needed to deliver. The Ford and Rover models were both due to come on stream in 1983. This meant that Flair had two years to organise production. The company had already convinced its parent company of the worth of the strategy; now it needed to get its agreement to raise and spend the £1 million necessary to make this happen. Though reluctant to invest such a large sum in an ailing company, the parent agreed. Persuading the financial institutions to lend the money was more difficult, but this was also achieved.

The new equipment was then installed and though there were continuing teething troubles, the company began delivering parts to Ford and Rover as planned in 1983. In the financial year 1983/4, company turnover increased fivefold over its 1979/80 level, which appeared to justify the relatively large investment.

It was at this point that the parent company, worried about raising the capital for Flair's ambitious plans, agreed to a management buy-out. Finance for this was raised partly from the Directors' own resources, but mainly from venture capitalists. Though this freed the hands of the managers (now the owners) to pursue their own plans, it did not make raising capital for investment any easier. No British banks were prepared to put up money for their investment needs. As a last resort, Flair approached a French bank who were prepared to advance the necessary capital for Flair's investment programme.

The mid-1980s: increasing the pace of change

Despite the success with the Ford and Rover work, the Managing Director still felt that the company's performance was well below what it should be. Once again the senior managers undertook a full review of the company and concluded that:

- *Senior managers were still operating in a reactive rather than proactive mode.*

- *Key operational problems were being 'worked round' rather than analysed and solved.*

- *Costs had grown faster than turnover.*

- *Quality was poor and they were still relying on inspection to detect and correct this.*

Nevertheless, there was good news. The company's reputation as a reliable and innovative supplier was growing and they were attracting additional work from both existing and new customers. Furthermore, the motor industry was beginning to change its view of customer–supplier relationships. Based on the Japanese experience, vehicle manufacturers were coming to see the merits of developing long-term partnerships. In particular, preferred supplier status was emerging, and customers were urging such suppliers to invest in new equipment and processes in order to enhance their competitiveness. Given that the company was already reshaping itself along these lines, it was in advance of many of its competitors.

However, this did not obviate the need to tackle the serious issues identified above. Therefore, the management team set itself six key objectives for 1985/6:

1 Reduce costs.

2 Reduce stocks and work-in-progress.

3 Acquire new customers in order to gain full utilisation of capital equipment.

4 Reorganise sales and purchasing into one operation.

5 Move to Just-in-Time manufacturing.

6 Adopt the Deming/Juran approach to quality, beginning with the introduction of Statistical Process Control (SPC).

The adoption of these objectives, especially the last, began to move the company away from being just another company who had introduced new technology towards one which was truly committed to transforming itself into a world-class performer. In 1985/6 the company's turnover exceeded £12 million, and profits were in excess of £500,000. In addition, it had been chosen as a supplier to the new car factory being established in the UK by Nissan. Statistical Process Control had been introduced throughout the factory, work was continuing on getting processes right, and targets were now in place for all key areas of activity.

The progress made so far had been driven by senior managers, mainly the Managing Director. The management team believed the company needed to move from having a workforce which accepted management initiatives to one which understood and took a proactive approach to its strategic aims. Without this, the Managing Director believed, they would never match Japanese performance levels, especially in terms of quality.

What was to prove the crucial initiative in gaining employee participation began in 1986, with the introduction of cellular manufacture and the move to team working at all levels. On the shopfloor, separate cells (process teams) were created, and these were supported by the other key processes in the company, i.e. engineering, purchasing and finance. The cells were, eventually, given responsibility for their own quality, methods and costs. From the outset, they were encouraged to examine critically all aspects of how the cell operated in order to make improvements.

In retrospect, this turned out to be a key move in terms of achieving a step change in performance, although it was the early 1990s before the cellular approach began to work as anticipated. The main difficulties lay in developing a team mentality and, in particular, appointing suitable team leaders. Furthermore, a major retraining effort was needed to ensure the multiskilling necessary for this approach. A further problem was changing the relationship between the production teams and the other functions to one of support for the cells. In the past, staff in engineering and purchasing had been more used to telling the shopfloor what to do rather than vice versa. As for the finance section, previously they had had little to do with the shopfloor, whereas under the new arrangement they had a central role in supplying information to the cells. Therefore, though the move to cellular manufacture could be characterised as shopfloor reorganisation, it was in fact a sea change for the entire company. The locus of power ceased to be fragmented among the various staff functions and moved to the cells. In particular, the cell managers came to play a pivotal role in orchestrating the day-to-day life of the company.

1991/2: a turning point

Three key events occurred in 1991/2 which were to have a significant impact on the company's strategy and performance.

1 A new Operations Director was appointed. The Managing Director had taken personal responsibility for operations in the past, but it was clear that the volume of work involved would not allow this to continue. The person appointed to this post was both experienced and progressive. Almost his first action was to visit Japan to benchmark the company against the best in the world.

2 One of their key customers, Nissan, asked them to take part in a strategy development programme for senior managers. This took place over six months and allowed them: (a) to undertake a rigorous review of their plans for the company's future; (b) to set clear targets, based partly on the Operations Director's benchmarking exercise; and (c) to focus on achieving world-class status.

3 The Directors, with a great deal of reluctance, decided to sell the company. Flair's ever-greater need for capital, for its ambitious expansion programme, was becoming increasingly difficult to sustain. During this period, capital investment was running at nearly 50 per cent of turnover. Not surprisingly, the venture capitalists who owned a large part of the company were becoming concerned about this. After much debate and many offers – the company was seen as a prize catch in the industry – Flair was sold to a German conglomerate.

The sale of the company did not materially alter Flair's strategy or approach. Nor did the management change; indeed, it was a condition of the sale that they remain in place. What it did do was to remove the financial uncertainty from the company and allow managers to concentrate on building a world-class organisation.

By 1995 the company had been totally transformed from what it was in 1980. Turnover was £80 million (1980 = £2.5 million) and it employed 850 staff (1980 = 150). Its customer base was almost exclusively leading vehicle builders, and its reputation in the industry for quality and performance was high. In addition, an independent survey had shown that it was one of the few UK-based companies which was approaching world-class status.

In some organisations this would have led to complacency, or at least a slackening of the rate of change. Not so for Flair. In 1994, the company's Operations Director spent a month in Japan in order, once again, to benchmark the company against the best in the world. Flair had made significant progress since his last visit (including reducing defects to 10 parts per million and achieving 100 per cent on-time delivery performance). However, the Japanese had not stood still either, and what had appeared to be exceptional performance three years earlier had now become industry standard. In particular, quality and delivery performance were no longer considered as differentiators – these were now prerequisites for doing business with the leading car companies. The Operations Director identified the new differentiators as *cost focus*, *design capability* and *flexibility*. He believed that while Flair could achieve these, it would require the total commitment of all the organisation to continuous improvement.

So although in European terms Flair had moved from being a virtual nobody to become one of the leading companies in its field, in global terms (which is the arena in which it must compete), much remained to be done. The company's performance in meeting both customer requirements and its own strategic objectives continues to improve. One of the key lessons it learnt from acting as a supplier to Nissan was the need to incorporate continuous improvement into all its activities.

The outcome

Any case study that covers such a lengthy period is bound to raise a wide range of issues. Looking at strategy development and change management, there are four areas which seem particularly important.

1 From 1980 onwards, Flair developed and continued to redefine its strategic objectives, which enabled it to take charge of its own destiny.

2 It redefined the role of senior managers. No longer do they expect, or are they expected, to involve themselves in day-to-day decision-making or problem-solving. Instead, they focus on strategic issues rather than operational fire-fighting.

3 The new role for senior managers can only be maintained because of the company's move to focus on processes, and to organisation on a cellular basis. This gives front-line managers and their teams both the responsibility and the authority to deal with day-to-day issues, thus freeing senior managers to concentrate on longer-term strategic issues.

4 The process of change was driven by the vision, ambition and commitment of the Managing Director. There is little doubt that up to the early 1990s, it was this man who, in a somewhat autocratic fashion, dragged and pushed the company along in pursuit of his vision.

There are three points to note with regard to these issues. First, the transformation of Flair took place over more than a decade. The changes involved were not easily devised or implemented, nor did they always work first time. In essence, they emerged from a combination of predetermined strategic objectives, best practices from elsewhere, and trial and error.

Second, though major organisational and technical changes have been achieved, the key changes have been in the behaviour and attitudes of staff at all levels in the company. In effect, the company has experienced a culture change. Changes in attitudes and behaviour throughout the company were not quickly or easily achieved and tended to follow changes in structure, objectives, personnel (the company has taken on over 700 new staff), and senior management behaviour. The two key changes in this respect are that (a) staff now work co-operatively in teams rather than individually in isolation, and (b) they are proactive completers rather than reactive buck-passers. Though this change of culture was necessary in order to achieve greater internal effectiveness, it was not planned as such. It arose from the actions taken to improve competitiveness.

Finally, let us examine the company's approach to strategy. As discussed in Chapter 5, there are many approaches to strategy, but the tendency in the West has been to pursue quantitatively based, resource-driven strategies as opposed to the more vision- and ambition-driven approach of the Japanese. What is interesting in this case is that the company, apparently unconsciously, adopted a Japanese approach. It identified a long-term, ambitious vision for itself. As part of this vision, it determined the core technologies and competencies it would need to develop in order to make this vision a reality. The company did not attempt to plot out its strategy in detail, which would have been impossible given the dynamic environment in which it chose to operate. Rather, it laid down key objectives and milestones which were reviewed and updated on a regular basis. By identifying its preferred customers and products, and determining and developing its core competencies and skills, it put itself in a position to take advantage of opportunities and avoid threats. As Hamel and Prahalad (1989) argued, this approach is the classic Japanese recipe for success. It also, incidentally, fits in with Mintzberg's (1987) theory of emergent strategy.

That the company's approach was appropriate for (or at least worked in) its situation is demonstrated by its dramatic growth in turnover and improvement in all-round performance.

Case study 3

PROCESS CONTROL INC

Background

Process Control Inc (PCI) is the European manufacturing arm of an American conglomerate and is located in the UK Midlands. Although this plant shares the same site as the European Marketing and Technology (product development) divisions of its parent company, the three concerns are operationally separate with very little liaison. PCI's present operation came into being in 1979, through a merger with a subsidiary of a British-owned electronics company. PCI specialises in the production of printed circuit boards (PCBs) and process control equipment. In 1988, PCI's PCB business was significantly expanded when its parent company centred most of its PCB manufacture there, by transferring work from its USA base. By the early 1990s, PCI was producing over 95 per cent of the conglomerate's total PCB needs, and employed a staff of 395.

With the rapid expansion of PCB assembly in 1988, the company began to experience major operational problems relating to quality and delivery. This in turn caused increasing difficulties for the parent company in the USA, who found its own deliveries and quality suffering as a consequence.

Alongside the increase in workload for PCI came a greater dependence on the other two functions on the PCI site, Marketing and Technology. Indeed, it was alleged by PCI that many of its problems were caused by staff in both the Marketing and Technology divisions making erratic and unrealistic demands on them. Managers claimed that volumes and product mix forecasts were rarely accurate, and that PCB designs were often changed by the Technology division during manufacture. The cumulative effect of all these factors was that manufacturing performance was worsening rather than improving, so that a large proportion of its target completion dates could not be met. There were also concomitant quality problems.

When this situation failed to improve, the parent company sacked the plant's British Chief Executive Officer (CEO) and replaced him with an American who was to be seconded to PCI for a one- to two-year period. This came as a shock not only to the CEO but also to the entire workforce. There was widespread feeling, at all levels in the company, that he had been treated shabbily, especially given that he had been with the company, in its various forms, for 25 years. This shock was compounded by the character of the new CEO. He was a colourful and flamboyant person who wore a Mickey Mouse watch, dressed as Father Christmas and the Easter Bunny at the appropriate time of the year, and was given to public soul-searching.

His remit was twofold:

1 to turn the plant around to a position where it could meet its obligations; and

2 to identify an in-house replacement for the time when his secondment came to an end.

The assumption underlying this remit was that PCI's difficulties were all of their own making and that a combination of a new CEO and some relatively minor managerial changes – to improve the CEO's position and communication within the management structure – would shake the company up enough to remedy the situation.

In his first three months, the Chief Executive flattened the management hierarchy. The previous CEO had only three managers reporting directly to him, with a further tier of eight managers reporting to them. The new CEO combined these two layers and created a new 11-person management team responsible to him. This levelling-up created some resentment among the original three team members, which was compounded when two of them were told to switch jobs with their former subordinates. Indeed, at one point there was talk that these managers might resign.

Overall, because of these changes, the newly created management team was anything but a team. The CEO, nevertheless, stuck to his decision. When justifying his action, the CEO said, 'If you've got a business that you expect to change, because the technology and customers are changing rapidly, which is the business we are in, then you have to have a flatter, more flexible organisation.' Another reason advanced for flattening the senior management structure was that the CEO envisaged a team of senior managers who could work together co-operatively. He wanted to, in his own words, 'change the mind set' of the managers so that 'they can know the strength that can come through working in a team'.

In addition, the CEO foresaw the need to broaden his managers' work experience in order to identify and develop a potential successor. This was the rationale behind the moving of some of the managers to 'unfamiliar grounds' and the swopping of roles with their former subordinates.

Developing strategy

By March 1989, the new CEO had come to the conclusion that the problems of PCI were much greater than had been assumed, and that more radical solutions than 'administering a shock to the system' were required. He identified the underlying causes as follows:

- *The organisation structure and the attitudes and skills of both management and employees prevented the company from achieving the high levels of performance and flexibility required of it.*

- *There was a lack of appropriate liaison between PCI, Technology and Marketing – in effect, he claimed that the latter two were acting in such an erratic manner that the company's task was made doubly difficult.*

In a bid to bring the management team closer together and to begin to tackle the underlying problems of the plant, the CEO organised a weekend-long, off-site management seminar. This was led by an outside Organisation Development specialist and was, the CEO said, about soul-searching and team-building. His aim was to deliberate on the state of the organisation and to develop a vision for a 'high performance organisation' and a strategy for achieving this.

At the end of this, he felt that the weekend was a turning-point in the organisation's fortunes. Not only did they emerge as a more coherent and committed team, but they also came up with the bones of a strategic plan which they saw as the solution necessary to pull the organisation out of its predicament. According to the CEO, who introduced the concept and continued to be its main champion, the initial reaction of the management team to the idea of developing a manufacturing strategy was: 'Yes, we need to do planning but we are in a deep mess, we don't have time to do it.' The CEO said that, 'in the end, I had to force the idea of strategic planning on the organisation.' The vision produced by the management team aimed to 'empower the organisation to be a world-class manufacturing unit and thereby achieve customer delight'. The strategic plan to achieve the vision had five elements which were to be developed by small sub-groups of the management team:

1 people involvement;
2 supplier partnering;
3 Just-in-Time;
4 Total Quality;
5 social responsibility.

The middle three of these are in principle recognisable. The first, seen by the CEO as the most important, but also the most difficult and contentious, aimed to restructure the company into high-performance, semi-autonomous work groups on both the shop floor and in the offices, along the lines advocated by writers such as Peters and Waterman (1982). In so doing, however, this plan threatened not only the conventional supervisors, but also, because of its emphasis on breaking down functional barriers, the core skills of managers. It was also the least understood of the five elements. The fifth element, social responsibility, was a declaration that the company wished to do well not only by its employees but also by the community at large – especially in relation to environmental issues.

Throughout the summer of 1989, the management team and its sub-groups met to develop and approve the strategies. However, while some maintained their original enthusiasm, others became more sceptical. Some managers felt the process was being rushed, and that as a consequence the time available for thinking through and discussing the proposals was limited. One example of this was that the sub-groups responsible for developing the five elements of the plan did not have the time to meet and the chairman of each group mainly wrote these with little input from others. Notwithstanding this, by September 1989, the complete strategy was agreed by the management team, along with the priorities and timetables for the next 12 months.

Implementing strategy

The CEO then organised a meeting of all supervisory/middle management staff to brief them on the strategy and to attempt to involve them. This initial meeting was not judged to be particularly successful by the participants. The main reason for this was the sheer volume of information presented. Therefore, a second meeting was organised. The problem, however, with both meetings was that because the organisation was under pressure for quick results to turn its fortunes around, much of the time was spent on the action required to achieve the plan, rather than taking enough time to explain its 'whys' and 'wherefores' and what the outcomes would mean for the workforce. It was left to the members of the management team to explain these to their own subordinates. This would have been acceptable in a situation where the management team were fully conversant with and committed to the plan. In this case, though, some of the managers themselves were unclear or in need of convincing of the merits of the proposed changes. Consequently, rather than giving reassurance, these briefings had the opposite effect – especially when staff compared what different managers were saying.

As is common in such situations, rumours and counter-rumours abounded; complaints focused on attempts by 'some people' to 'Americanise' the plant, the unpreparedness of the workforce for the strategic plan, and the short timescale for the implementation of some aspects of the plan. Furthermore, members of the trade union, usually very supportive of the company, complained about 'the looming prospects of redundancy', while others voiced scepticism about the real motives of the CEO and the tactics being employed to implement the changes. Above all, there were real fears among the supervisors and middle managers about their future in the plant, because the plans involved structural changes which would result in the removal of some of these posts.

The management team's response to this 'uneasiness' among the workforce was to introduce a series of weekend and lunch-break meetings aimed at educating the workforce. These meetings, to an extent, were able to calm the fears of the workforce on the reasons for the strategic plan and some of the structural adjustments taking place. However, overall, they could not fully come to grips with people's worries, because most of the meetings (especially the plant-wide monthly lunch-break meetings) were too large, and so intimate and sensitive questions were not even asked, let alone discussed in the open.

Despite the many unanswered questions about the strategic plan, by December 1989 elements of the strategy were being implemented. However, there was still much to do both in implementing what had been decided and in clarifying what the new organisational structure should look like. Indeed, the question of structure emerged as the main issue of uncertainty and contention in the management team. It became clear that the plan would require a new organisation structure – if only to make sense of the many apparently isolated structural changes taking place. Though the CEO said he was clear what was required, the rest of his team were not. Despite this, the CEO held on to the belief that agreement had been reached to move to a system of 'mini' factories within a new matrix-type structure. This clearly demonstrated the growing gap between the CEO and his team – even those who supported him. The gap was particularly obvious among those managers who controlled support functions such as quality, purchasing and production control, because they felt their specialism would be dismembered and career prospects threatened.

Suspending the strategy

In the week before Christmas 1989, all this was thrown into confusion when the CEO announced he was leaving. He had been offered, and had accepted the chance to take over a more important plant in the company's portfolio in the USA and he felt the opportunity was too good to be missed. At this point, it was not clear who would take over – though there had been an undercurrent of fighting for succession in the management team all along, especially between the Production Manager and the Materials Manager. Before long, it was announced that another 'interim' CEO would be appointed until the time was right for someone in PCI to take the post. There was a delay, however, before the new person could take up his appointment and, in the early months of 1990, he could only make intermittent visits to PCI. This delay, as well as the change in CEO, inevitably led to uncertainty regarding the strategy.

Most of the management team were content to await the arrival of the new CEO rather than continuing with the more controversial elements of the strategy. The Production Manager, however, who had been won over by the Chief Executive's ideas, and who saw himself as a potential successor, began to push the strategy very strongly. This was quickly put down by the rest of the team through non-co-operation. It did, however, have the unexpected side-effect of encouraging other managers to come out openly and express their doubts and misgivings about the strategy. Nevertheless, most managers reverted to their former state of dealing with the day-to-day running of the plant, and the manufacturing strategy, which was of top priority a few weeks previously, now came to play a secondary role.

In March 1990, the new CEO assumed office on a full-time basis. He met a situation completely different from that which faced his predecessor. When the former came in, he met a plant that was behind in its output and with severe quality problems. The new CEO inherited a plant making profit, meeting its completion dates and which had considerably reduced defects in its finished products: although how much of this was due to PCI's own efforts and how much to a reduced demand for its product was difficult to say. A number of managers feared that a resurgence of demand would once again lead to delivery and quality problems. As far as people were concerned, however, according to the new CEO, the management team had lapsed both in its commitment to working as a team and in its enthusiasm for the manufacturing strategy. Given that he saw his role as an interim one, he was content to maintain the status quo and was, in any case, openly critical of the 'revolutionary' approach of his predecessor. He was dubious about the strategy and its implementation and simply wanted to keep the plant running efficiently, until he was recalled to the United States.

There was an upsurge in demand for PCBs, however, and, as some feared, the plant began to lag behind in its performance. By the end of June 1990, barely six months since the departure of the prime mover of the manufacturing strategy, many of the original difficulties re-emerged. The plant and its managers were once again back to square one; fire-fighting the day-to-day problems of the plant in order to keep the order book on schedule. The combination of this and the new CEO's reluctance to become involved in the strategic plan led to a decision to 'suspend' it until the operating difficulties had been sorted out. Nevertheless, there was a feeling that this particular exercise had come to an end and that the suspension would be permanent.

The threat of closure

The manufacturing strategy was occasionally the topic of discussion at management team meetings in 1990 but, given the scepticism of some team members and the passive style of the interim CEO, no decision was taken on its content or implementation. In December, the interim CEO announced he would be leaving and that he would be replaced by the Materials Manager. This news was welcomed by most people, though the Production Manager was extremely upset at being passed over.

When he took office in January 1991, the new CEO surprised most of his colleagues by declaring that he wanted to resuscitate the manufacturing strategy. This was partly as an olive branch to the Production Manager and partly because he recognised that the company had underlying problems which were not being tackled. Given that the company had spent the past year fire-fighting rather than tackling the causes of the fires, the rest of the management team reacted more enthusiastically to this initiative than they would have done 12 months earlier. The Production Manager was also placated by being made 'champion' of the manufacturing strategy.

By June, the strategy had been overhauled and, surprisingly given the past dissension, in its revised form it appeared to have the full support of the management team. Before proceeding with its implementation, however, the CEO decided to present it to his superiors in the USA. This he duly did, but the outcome was totally unexpected. His superiors liked and approved the plan, but announced that they were not convinced that PCI could ever reach a position where it was competitive with the best in the world. Therefore, the American parent company proposed either to close the plant down, or to subcontract out the manufacture of PCBs to the Far East. The latter option would leave a much-reduced PCI responsible for some managerial functions and the assembly of certain larger systems. The CEO was given six months to recommend which course of action to follow, or to make a case for an alternative.

The return of the manufacturing strategy

When he returned and informed his colleagues of the outcome of his visit to the USA, they were obviously distressed. However, there were two causes for guarded optimism. First, the decision by the parent company was not based on hard data but a general perception that others could and did perform better than PCI. The second factor was the manufacturing strategy. The management team felt that it offered enormous scope to cut costs and improve performance, if they were just given the chance to implement it.

Nevertheless, over the next few months the team suspended all development activities, including work on the manufacturing plan, in order to build the case for retaining PCI in its present form. This involved visits to Europe, America and particularly the Far East to gather information from and on potential subcontractors/ competitors. A report arguing the case for retaining the company with its present range of products and responsibilities was prepared.

The report, which was presented to the parent company in October 1991, had three core elements:

1 *A comparison of PCI with similar companies in Europe, the USA and the Far East.* This showed that PCI was ahead of European and USA producers but apparently lagged behind the Far East.

2 *A detailed examination of the products and manufacturing systems of the Far Eastern companies.* This showed that the latter's advantage over PCI could be accounted for by the high-volume, low-complexity nature of the products they were making. PCI, on the other hand, were at the low-volume, high-complexity end of the market.

3 *The manufacturing strategic plan* showing that a step change in performance was possible.

After much debate, the Americans accepted the report, and in addition agreed to provide the company with £10 million to undertake the restructuring necessary to implement the manufacturing strategy.

The outcome

When the CEO returned to his colleagues with this news, they clearly had cause for celebration, but they were also strengthened in their commitment to the manufacturing strategy. As one of his colleagues commented, 'we've been ambivalent to the plan, hostile to the plan, committed to the plan and now without it, we're dead.'

This commitment was not even diminished when, in January 1992, the CEO was promoted out of the company – there was a general feeling that he had saved PCI and deserved his promotion. Nor did the Production Manager seem down-hearted by the fact he was once again overlooked for the post in favour of one of his colleagues; after all, he was still the 'champion' of the manufacturing strategy.

By April 1992, major changes had been accomplished in PCI's manufacturing operations and changes in other areas were under way. These changes had been accomplished on time and with little disruption, and the benefits were beginning to make themselves felt in terms of quality, costs and delivery.

There are four main issues to note with regard to the case of PCI:

● *Though strong and clear leadership appears essential to achieving major change, especially where the status quo is being challenged, there must also be continuity of leadership. Without continuity and consistency, attempts to bring about changes in structure, responsibilities and behaviour will almost certainly meet with resistance and conflict.*

● *Frequent managerial changes are usually, though not always, counter-productive. In particular, unless the criteria for selecting a replacement are clear and/or the actual successor is named at an early stage, fighting for succession can arise, which is nearly always detrimental to performance.*

● *Unless a management team understands and is committed to a particular strategy, its development and implementation are likely to be slow and uncertain. It is also likely to be accompanied by political manoeuvring designed either to slow, speed or shape the process, especially if the climate in the organisation does not favour open and honest debate and dissent.*

● *Mintzberg's (1987) case for seeing strategy as an emergent and iterative process does appear to hold water in this instance. Cohen et al's (1972) view, that decisions occur when problems, solutions, participants and choice opportunities coincide, is also valid. In PCI's case, the problems had existed for some time, and so had the solution (in the form of the strategy) and the participants (the management team). Nevertheless, it was only with the advent of the choice opportunity (the threat of closure) that the four coincided and a decision to adopt and implement the manufacturing strategy emerged.*

Given the on-and-off nature of PCI's commitment to the manufacturing strategy, it would not be surprising if it fell out of favour again. However, this would merely serve to underline the difficult and uncertain conditions under which strategic management is conducted.

Case study 4

Midshires college of midwifery and nursing

Background

The cornerstone of the British welfare state, since its inception after the Second World War, has been the National Health Service (NHS). Such is, or at least was, the NHS's standing that it was often referred to as 'the envy of the world'. However, since the early 1980s, it has experienced successive waves of increasingly contentious change. The most recent of these, heralded by the UK Government's 1989 White Paper 'Working for Patients' (HMSO, 1989), came into operation in 1991. This was aimed at creating an internal market within the NHS, primarily through the division of 'purchasers' and 'providers' of medical and other services into separate, semi-autonomous bodies – e.g. GP Fundholders and NHS Hospital Trusts. The rationale behind this latest reorganisation was, according to two senior figures in the NHS (Carr and Donaldson, 1993:23):

> ... the belief that a market system of care would induce positive behaviour [by managers and professionals] which would work in the interests of patients, and that it would bring accountability and value for money within a proper management framework.

This case study describes how the management and staff within one particular part of the NHS, colleges of midwifery and nursing, are coping with the new NHS. In line with the government's new market-led approach to the NHS, the NHS Executive Board decided that colleges of nursing needed to be able to offer a wider range of services and expertise than in the past, and therefore a programme of merging colleges of midwifery and colleges of nursing to form larger organisations was initiated. In the case in question, it was decided to merge five existing colleges to form the new Midshires College of Midwifery and Nursing. These colleges, between them, serviced hospitals in ten different Health Authorities.

The Health Authorities, in consultation with the Regional Health Authority, appointed a Steering Group of senior managers, drawn from the Boards of Governors of the five colleges, to oversee the merger. The Steering Group comprised General Managers from hospitals (NHS Hospital Trusts) within the Health Authorities, Chief Nursing Officers, and representatives from the Regional Health Authority, some 24 members in all.

The remit of the Steering Group was fairly straightforward: to oversee the amalgamation of the five colleges. There seems to have been no formal acknowledgement that this amalgamation was in any way different from previous ones. However, there were a number of issues related to the changing nature of the NHS

---

* The research for this case study was undertaken with Mohammad Salauroo of the University of Hertfordshire School of Nursing.

which made this process significantly different and inherently more complicated than past amalgamations:

- *There was uncertainty over the demand for nurse education in the future (both in terms of numbers and function).*

- *A potential conflict of interest existed between the General Managers on the Steering Group on the one hand and the new college on the other. The General Managers, under the new purchaser–provider system in the NHS, would in future not be tied to a particular college of nursing in terms of nurse education. They could, if they so wished, put their requirements out to open tender to any college in the country, as one Health Authority/Trust elsewhere in the UK had already done. In addition, and in the short term more probably, they could seek alternative suppliers for post-experience courses, or even provide these courses themselves in competition with the new college. Indeed, two of the Health Authorities had already established their own organisation for delivering post-experience nurse education in competition with the new college. This is perhaps why some members of the Steering Group suggested that the new college should not have in its remit the provision of post-experience courses (with implications for the jobs of some 30 per cent of existing staff in the five colleges to be amalgamated). Therefore, key players in establishing the college found themselves placed in a somewhat ambiguous position with regard to its purpose and remit.*

- *It was expected that qualifications gained at the new college would be validated by a higher education institution and that eventually, as similar colleges were doing, it would actually merge into the university sector.*

It might have been expected that the Steering Group would seek to clarify these key issues before proceeding to resolve the structure and organisation of the new college. After all, how could decisions regarding its structure and functioning be resolved in advance of key decisions on student numbers, course content, areas of operation, and whether or not it would merge with a higher education institution? Nevertheless, the Steering Group avoided tackling these issues prior to commencing the merger process.

Developing the strategy

The Steering Group decided that merging the five colleges could and should be managed as a straightforward and uncomplicated, almost mechanical, process. In November 1992, they appointed a Project Leader, on a fixed-term contract of two years, to complete the task of merging the colleges by October 1994.

The appointee was the Principal of one of the colleges being merged. He had no direct experience of merging colleges, but had only two years' service left prior to retirement. This meant that, unlike the other four college principals, he would not be a potential candidate for the principal's post in the new college. Surprisingly, the

Project Leader was given no budget or dedicated secretarial or administrative support. He could call on the resources of the five colleges, provided that the principals agreed.

Within 48 hours of his appointment, the Project Leader contacted the principals of the other colleges, by fax, and announced both the formation of a Project Board and its membership. The membership included the Project Leader and the principals of the five colleges, including the acting principal from his own college. There were also three external members brought in as advisors to the project group. These were a Finance Manager and a Personnel Manager from the Regional Health Authority and the Education Officer from the English National Board for Nursing.

By the time of the Project Board's first meeting, the Project Leader had produced a plan which, among other objectives, proposed the integration of some administrative processes within a matter of weeks. The plan also called for the centralisation of student recruitment, and outlined steps for the integration of the pre-registration courses for nurse education. The core of the plan was the establishment of four subprojects aimed at integrating the major functions of the five colleges: pre-registration courses for nursing, post-registration courses for nursing, midwifery education, and education support services.

The first meeting of the Project Board discussed its own membership, the Project Leader's project plan, the roles of the Project Board members, communications, the development of new courses, and the accountability of the Project Board to the Steering Group. The Project Leader stated that he had been given clear instructions by the Steering Group, and that the task of the Project Board was to get on with the job of integrating the five colleges as laid down in his project plan. This first meeting set the pattern for the future; the Project Leader would act as the only conduit between the Steering Group and the Project Board, and questions relating to the pace, purpose and form of the proposed merger were not part of the Board's remit. Within these constraints, scope for questions and initiatives existed, but the Project Leader had the final say on all matters.

Time for a rethink

In February 1993, some four months after the first Project Board meeting, a one-day staff conference was organised for everyone employed at the five colleges. The purpose of the day was to brief staff on developments and get feedback from them. It was apparent as the day progressed that, although staff in the colleges were enthusiastic about the change, and indeed appeared to have more enthusiasm and ideas than the Project Board itself, there were key issues which were not being addressed and which were causing increasing concern. The obvious issue for staff was that no one seemed to have a clue as to how many staff would retain their posts in the new college, or what mix of skills would be required. However, staff were just as concerned, if not more so, by the lack of any clear direction for the new college: What was its mission? What products/services would it provide? How would it be structured? Who would make these decisions, when and on what basis? What seemed to shock and dismay many of the staff was that the Project Leader seemed as uncertain and powerless as themselves regarding these issues.

The conference brought home to the Project Leader the lack of progress made towards amalgamation. The sub-groups had met frequently and produced extremely detailed plans; but the ability to turn these plans into actions seemed to elude them, partly because key issues had still not been resolved. For the Project Leader, the conference had crystallised a number of his concerns regarding both the pace of the amalgamation and the effectiveness of the Project Board system.

He also, privately, expressed the view that he had become a 'piggy in the middle' between the Project Board and the Steering Group, having critics in both camps but supporters in neither. It was also the case that some members of the Project Board were meeting informally but regularly to discuss and promote alternative ideas to those of the Project Leader, though whether he was aware of this was unclear. Similarly, Board members were seeing members of the Steering Group informally as well. So a great deal of behind-the-scenes lobbying and jockeying for position were taking place. This was hardly surprising, given the uncertainty – particularly over jobs – which was present.

Shortly after the staff conference, the Project Leader called a one-day Project Board meeting to discuss progress, and he invited the Chair of the Steering Group to be part of the meeting. Though members were told that the meeting was to examine the situation and discuss options, they were in effect presented with a *fait accompli* by the Project Leader. He made a number of major announcements at this meeting which in effect tore up the previous four months' work:

- *The Project Board was to be disbanded and replaced by an interim Management Committee for the new college.*
- *The four existing principals would become part of the Management Committee with specific areas of responsibility.*
- *The role of the existing principals in the five individual colleges would be replaced by the appointment of heads of sites.*
- *The sub-projects were to be abandoned; in their place, the Project Leader announced a structure for the new college which would, he stated, be fully operational by October 1993.*

Despite these changes, decisions had still not been taken regarding the number of students the new college would have in the future, whether it would be allowed to offer post-registration courses, or whether it would be moving into higher education. Without this information, it was almost impossible to determine staffing levels and the skill mix for the new college, or judge the appropriateness of the proposed structure. In such a situation, inevitably, staff morale continued to decline, especially among staff on short-term contracts. One example of this was the high number of staff, especially in managerial positions, who were on long-term sick leave with stress-related illnesses.

January 1994

The creation of the Management Committee appeared to have had little positive impact upon the new college. The new structure still only existed on paper. The reports from the Management Committee were vague, irregular and fragmented. One issue was nevertheless becoming a little clearer: it appeared that the Regional Health Authority had guaranteed the new college the same level of pre-registration work (training student nurses) in 1994 as in 1993. In 1995, however, the guarantee would be reduced to 50 per cent, and in 1996 it would be eliminated altogether. This did not mean that the new college's workload in this area would necessarily decline. It did mean, though, that it could expect to face competition for the work.

The situation with regard to post-registration courses (upgrading the skills of practising nurses), however, was still unresolved, as was the question of the link with higher education. On this latter issue, it had been understood informally that the final decision would be known in December 1993 but, like other deadlines for this decision in 1993 – May, June, July, and September – it came and went with no decision being made.

Therefore, more than one year after the merger process officially began, key issues around which the future of the college revolved had still not been resolved. Most staff still did not know if they would have jobs with the new college, although those on short-term contracts were informed by open fax messages to each of the college's sites that their contracts would not be renewed (this was later rescinded). In a similar vein, a leaked letter from the Project Leader to the Regional Health Authority discussed redundancy arrangements for permanent staff. Not surprisingly, as 1994 progressed, the climate in the organisation deteriorated drastically and any sense of optimism had all but evaporated.

The outcome

This case study shows that the new market-orientated environment in which the NHS is now operating has brought about significant changes in relationships between all parts of the NHS, and not just between purchasers and providers of patient care, although for obvious reasons it is the latter which has been the focus of most attention. The creation of the NHS internal market was not just an attempt to create a more efficient method of distributing resources. It was also seen as a key element in creating a more entrepreneurial culture in the NHS (Carr and Donaldson, 1993; Fullerton and Price, 1991; Rothwell, 1994). However, the process of creating such a culture brings with it a large degree of uncertainty, dislocation and conflict, as the case study illustrates.

In this study, we can see how this conflict of interests, together with a failure to appreciate the implications of the new arrangements within the NHS, acted to undermine the effectiveness of an approach to the management of change which assumed that stability was possible and conflict was absent, or at least easily resolvable. In particular, there are three issues which seem of major significance in understanding the development of the change process in this instance.

1 *The move from a stable to an uncertain environment.* The NHS was no
longer operating in a stable environment. Even leaving aside the question of
the level of overall funding, the introduction of the internal market was
likely to have an enormous impact on the location and flow of resources in
the NHS. It was also apparent that no one could predict who would be the
winners and losers in that particular game, or when – if ever – a stable state
would again emerge. Therefore, the environment for the NHS was becoming
increasingly uncertain and unpredictable. In such a situation, the assumption
by the Steering Group that the merger of the colleges could be conducted in
a planned and, almost, mechanical fashion was clearly flawed.

2 *The Project Leader.* Many of the problems which then arose in the merging
the colleges can be traced to the Steering Group's misconception regarding
the nature of the change process in this instance, and especially the choice of
Project Leader. This job was given to a man who could have been expected
to amalgamate the separate colleges efficiently, almost as if dealing with
model building blocks, if he had been operating in a stable environment with
a bureaucratic culture amenable to his autocratic style. When it became clear
to him that this was not the case, the Project Leader lacked the aptitude
either to win over his own colleagues (who in some cases were apparently
actively working against him) or to confront the Steering Group with its
own indecision. This was not a shortcoming on his part; rather the fault lay
with those who had chosen a manager with a traditional bureaucratic
approach to change to undertake a complicated exercise in an uncertain and,
as it transpired, hostile situation.

3 *Conflict of interests.* It can be seen that the potential conflict of interests
between members of the Steering Group led to key issues concerning the
college's future workload, and thus staffing needs, not being addressed in
advance of (or even during!) the merger process. Instead of resolving issues
regarding student numbers and the scope of its activities, the Steering Group
appointed a Project Leader whose style and track record could almost
guarantee that these issues would not be raised or resolved. Small wonder,
therefore, taking into account the absence of any firm decision about the
new college's role and workload, and the turbulent environment in which it
would be operating, that this approach failed.

The lesson for the NHS, and for other public sector organisations in the UK, is that
conflict and ambiguity are an inevitable outcome of the changing environment in
which they now operate; and that these adjustment difficulties, and the culture
change which is accompanying them, cannot be dealt with as though they either do
not exist or do not matter. Different situations do call for different approaches; a
style of management suited to a stable state situation may, as in this instance, be
totally unsuited to a more dynamic situation. Yet the culture of organisations in the

UK, as Hofstede (1980 and 1990) noted, tends to be one where organisations are seen as well-oiled machines which pursue rational ends and where personal conflicts and ambitions are subjugated to the needs of the organisation. In such situations, it is frequently not seen as legitimate to acknowledge conflicts of interest.

CONCLUSIONS
....

In Part Two, it was argued that the potential exists for managers to exercise a wide degree of choice with regard to almost all aspects of their business, whether that be products, structures, personnel policies or culture. However, this potential freedom is limited by societal, environmental, industry-specific and organisational constraints, many of which may conflict with each other.

This chapter has shown that, despite the formidable constraints on managerial freedom of action, it is possible for organisations to throw off the shackles, strike out in new directions and, in some cases, literally reinvent themselves. The Oticon case study shows how a determined manager can break out of the standard patterns of competition that exist in an industry and rewrite the competitive rule book to his company's advantage. The second case study, Flair Engineering, shows, once again, the ability of a determined manager to transform his organisation: not, this time, by changing the rules, but by changing its markets, products and technologies. In effect, he chose to move into an industry where the Japanese had already changed the rules in order to favour the type of organisation he wished to create. He also broke out of the financial straitjacket that limits so many UK companies' freedom to manoeuvre by borrowing from a French bank and eventually selling the company to a German conglomerate.

Up to this point, it might be assumed that a determined and visionary manager is all that is required for successful change. However, the PCI case study shows that this is not enough. As with both Oticon and Flair, a new Chief Executive was appointed to a business that was experiencing severe difficulties. As with the two previous studies, he developed a vision and tried to sell it to the rest of the organisation. His vision was not met with universal approval either by his fellow managers or the workforce. Whether or not it would have been successful, given time, can be debated, but the fact that he left after little more than a year meant that support for it dwindled. Nevertheless, his vision refused to die because the underlying problems of the organisation also refused to go away. It was resurrected as a key mechanism for saving the company from the threat of closure. Furthermore, the manager who gave it new life was not only previously sceptical of it, but also could not be described as a visionary leader (though he was a very able and effective manager). Therefore, it is not only visionary managers who are capable of breaking the mould: the conditions and context are highly relevant.

Having said that, Case Study 4, Midshires College, shows the problems that arise when a situation which apparently warrants radical change is designated the responsibility of a manager who lacks the ability or aptitude to challenge and change the status quo. The manager, with a brief which assumed that change could be approached in a mechanical, bureaucratic fashion, failed to recognise, or could not cope with, the uncertainties and unpredictability of an environment that was diverging from the stable state conditions that he had come to expect as the norm.

The result was a constant chopping and changing of initiatives but very little progress.

The case studies raise a number of important issues regarding strategic management in general and managerial choice in particular.

- *The particular strategic approach that an organisation (or rather its management) adopts is limited by, and to an extent must accommodate, societal, environmental, sectoral and organisational constraints. However, because these can conflict with each other, or can be manipulated or changed for more favourable conditions, managers do have the freedom to adopt a strategic approach which is more in keeping with their own interests or beliefs. That is to say, under certain conditions and certain circumstances, the world in which they operate can be shaped by their views, rather than vice versa. This certainly appears to be one interpretation of events in the Oticon and Flair case studies.*

- *Nevertheless, as the PCI and Midshires cases show, there are situations where managers either have to accept an approach to strategy which would not be their first choice, or flounder because they cannot adapt their style or beliefs to the needs of the situation.*

- *A clear vision of the future and the strength of character to challenge existing norms seem essential attributes for achieving radical change; yet these are not enough. Managers must also be capable of winning over other managers and the workforce as a whole. In Oticon this seems to have taken approximately 18 months (though much remains to be done). In Flair, managerial co-operation seems to have been achieved at an early stage, but convincing the rest of the workforce, particularly those in support functions, was a much longer process. However, both cases were aided initially by the apparently perilous state of the organisations in question. In PCI, though problems existed, initially at least they seemed to stem from the workload – they were the victims of their own success in winning new business. In the Midshires case, it took managers some time to realise – or at least openly acknowledge – all the dangers the new organisation faced, by which time the manager in charge appeared to have lost support.*

- *In terms of implementing strategy, it is not necessary to work out all the details in advance, but the first few steps must be clear and consistent with the vision (it also helps if they are seen to succeed). This appears to have been the situation for Oticon and Flair, despite the fact that, in Oticon's case, the initial steps also resulted in a degree of chaos – although this may well have been deliberate. For PCI, it appears that initial steps were taken to implement the strategy, especially some structural changes; but because the vision lacked clarity, the changes lacked support. A similar but perhaps more damning conclusion can be drawn from the Midshires study.*

Discussion points

1 Compare the four case studies with the four generic approaches to strategy identified in Chapter 5 (Classical, Evolutionary, Processual and Systemic) and identify the degree to which events in the studies can be explained by any or all of them.

2 To what extent is the case for managerial choice supported by the four case studies?

3 Identify the main constraints on freedom of choice faced by managers in the Oticon and Flair studies, and show how they accommodated or overcame them.

4 Identify the main constraints on freedom of choice faced by managers in the PCI and Midshires case studies, and suggest how they could have accommodated or overcome them.

5 To what extent do any or all of the case studies support or undermine the argument that power and politics should be seen as a dominant factor in decision-making?

6 What evidence exists from the case studies to show that cultural change is a necessary part of organisational transformation?

Chapter 8

CASE STUDIES IN CHANGING INTERNAL RELATIONSHIPS AND ATTITUDES

INTRODUCTION

This chapter presents three case studies of organisations who, for varying reasons of efficiency, effectiveness and competitiveness, attempted to change internal relationships and attitudes across functions and between hierarchical levels. Drawing on the arguments developed in Chapters 5 and 6, the case studies examine why and how the particular decisions relating to change were taken and, especially, whether the resultant implementation programmes could be described as planned or emergent.

Case Study 5 recounts the attempts by Volvo, over a period of more than 20 years, to break with the assembly-line approach to car production and move to a more human-centred approach. The study shows that it is unclear to what extent the move to Job Design precepts could be construed as part of a vision or concerted strategy for the organisation. Other strategic developments within Volvo were certainly in tune with and helped to encourage the move to Job Design. It is nevertheless apparent that, both in its conception and execution, the move to reorganise work at Volvo was emergent rather than planned. Subsequent job redesign initiatives were obviously informed by, and built on, what went before to the extent that a general orientation towards group work and the creation of more satisfying jobs appears to have become embedded in Volvo. However, the particular form of work reorganisation varied from case to case, and was heavily influenced by local circumstances and the orientation of the parties involved; the same applied to implementation and development. Though much effort went into planning the actual changes, it does not appear as though a settled pattern of working arrangements developed on any of the sites. Rather, as circumstances changed, and perhaps the balance of forces shifted, so too did the actual characteristics of jobs and relationships between groups and individuals, groups and other functions and groups and management. Therefore, the move to Job Design at Volvo, though driven by a general predisposition, can be characterised as a process of development, experimentation and learning.

The Rover Group study, Case Study 6, is another attempt by a car company to change internal relationships and attitudes. Unlike Volvo, however, the main focus is not on changing job content or moving away from the assembly line, it is on developing a learning organisation – creating a skilled, committed and empowered workforce. In the Rover case, one can see successive strategies emerging which moved the emphasis away from seeing workers as liabilities and threats, towards seeing them as the company's main competitive edge. This process of change was consciously open-ended and experimental. In its attempts to create a learning organisation, Rover has been prepared to embark upon some initiatives almost as an act of faith rather than in the pursuit of concrete and measurable objectives and ends.

Not all Rover's change projects share this open-ended nature. Rover has also adopted an approach to managing operational changes which very much exemplifies the beginning, middle and end approach developed by Kurt Lewin. Therefore, at Rover we can see that the company operates a range of approaches to change depending on the issues and circumstances involved.

Case Study 7, GK Printers, is an updated version of a study which originally appeared in the first edition of this book. In some respects, it is almost the reverse of the only other study retained from the first edition, Case Study 3 – PCI. While the case of PCI could be characterised as 'victory snatched from the jaws of defeat', GK Printers was nearly a case of 'defeat snatched from the jaws of victory'. The company put a great deal of collective effort into turning around its fortunes, only to see the gains threatened by inertia and conflict between managers.

Fortunately, it managed to rescue the situation in time, but it could so easily have been different. In many respects, it is a company where only in a crisis can existing norms and concepts be challenged and new strategies emerge. The actual implementation process tends towards planned rather than emergent or open-ended change. Despite the fact that the organisation is operating in a changing and highly competitive environment, it is still inclined to view change as a one-off activity rather than a process of continuous improvement.

The chapter concludes by arguing that in modern organisations, facing uncertain and changing environments, it is not just strategy that is emergent but also, in many cases, the implementation process. This does not invalidate the planned approach to change, and certainly not the many tools and techniques associated with it. It does mean, however, that for change projects which are rather experimental in nature and/or open ended, the concept of some form of settled pattern being established, and thus the process of change being concluded, is not valid.

Case study 5

VOLVO'S APPROACH TO JOB DESIGN*

Background

In Chapter 3, we examined the emergence of new organisational paradigms. In reviewing both the Culture–Excellence school and especially the Japanese approach, the emphasis placed on team or group work was striking. Though the importance of group work for both individual well-being and organisational performance has been a central feature of the Job Design literature for many years (*see* Chapter 2), its actual influence on work and organisational design in Western companies has been relatively small. One of the few exceptions to this has been Volvo, the Swedish motor vehicle manufacturer, which has been seen as a leader in innovations in work organisation since the 1970s. Indeed, it is probably not an exaggeration to say that in the 1970s, when it began moving away from traditional methods of car assembly, Volvo was more famous for its commitment to work humanisation than for the actual vehicles it manufactured (Blackler and Brown, 1978).

As will be described below, Volvo's approach to reorganising vehicle production has evolved through three distinct phases: the abandonment of the assembly line in favour of group-based static assembly; the extension of group roles to include more collective responsibility and some decision-making autonomy; and the introduction of self-paced assembly work (Pontusson, 1991).

It is also worth noting that the process of change was initially entirely management-driven (though the unions were involved or consulted on some aspects). However, through the 1980s in particular, the trade unions have taken a more pro-active role. The Swedish Co-determination Law, which came into effect in 1976, obliged firms to involve unions more but, in this instance, it may also have encouraged Volvo to be more radical in extending group work than might otherwise have been the case.

The move to more flexible forms of work organisation at Volvo went hand-in-hand with its move away from corporate bureaucracy and to more decentralised, localised management of its various vehicle operations. In addition, the last 20 years have seen repeated attempts at diversification and alliances by Volvo, aimed at spreading the risks of operating in a highly cyclical industry. With the departure of Pehr Gyllenhammar as Chief Executive, however, all this has been reversed: its interests in other industries and businesses have been sold, and once again Volvo is operating purely as an independent automotive company (Done, 1994).

Despite the benefits of good design and leading-edge technologies, vehicle producers tend to stand or fall by the effectiveness and efficiency of their assembly

---

*The term Job Design is fully explained in Chapter 2. In essence it is the antithesis of Taylorism and involves designing work to fit human needs and abilities.

operations (Womack *et al*, 1990). Therefore, Volvo's move to end assembly-line production was not and is not a marginal activity – it strikes at the very core of its competitiveness. The decision to adopt Job Design at Volvo was and remains driven by management, regardless of later union and legislative encouragement, though to what extent they foresaw how extensively it would develop is not known. What is clear, however, is that in the 1960s Volvo was as committed as any car company to the Classical approach to work organisation espoused by Taylor and embodied in the assembly-line approach to car production devised by Henry Ford. In the 1970s, however, it chose to break away from this industry-standard approach and embark on (what has turned out to be) a long-term programme of increasingly radical work reorganisation.

There are two complementary explanations for Volvo's actions. The first is the explanation given by Pehr Gyllenhammar (1977:73), until 1994 Volvo's Chief Executive, identifying the need to reduce labour turnover, which the company believed was caused by boring and monotonous jobs:

> **The company has to bear the costs of recruiting labour and training employees. The absenteeism and turnover rates also increase the costs for quality control, for maintaining buffer stocks of semifinished goods and components, and for adjustments, tools and machinery. Administrative costs go up when a company must maintain pools of reserve labour to fill requirements during peak periods of absenteeism.**

To flesh Gyllenhammar's explanation out a little, Pontusson (1990) pointed out that Volvo's freedom of manoeuvre in tackling its recruitment and retention problems was limited by the labour market conditions of the time. There was full employment, which made it easier for workers to move jobs; and very effective wage bargaining by unions, establishing industry and sectoral pay rates which made it very difficult for Volvo to offer higher wage rates than other employers. In the presence of full employment and the absence of wage flexibility, Volvo chose to tackle labour turnover and absenteeism by attempting to create more satisfying and varied jobs.

The second explanation was offered by Karlsson (1973). He pointed out that Volvo was, and still remains, one of Sweden's largest and most successful companies. As such, its actions and practices will always be in the public eye. With the increasing interest in Job Design in Scandinavia in general and Sweden in particular in the 1960s and 1970s, it was hardly surprising that Volvo's work organisation methods were the subject of much attention. In particular, Karlsson (1973:34) pointed out that the company was heavily criticised for its 'inhuman principles of organisation' based 'entirely on the scientific management method'.

It appears, therefore, that Volvo's conversion to Job Design was inspired by commercial considerations relating to the costs of absenteeism and labour turnover, allied to pressure from public opinion in Sweden for it to embrace a less 'inhuman' form of work organisation. Although these appear to be the principal reasons for Volvo's management embarking on its commitment to Job Design, since then the process has developed its own momentum, to the extent that (as noted by Auer and

Riegler, 1990:14): 'group work is the basic concept for all changes in the organisation of production work at Volvo'. However, this did not come about overnight, without hesitation and backtracking, or in a fully planned and co-ordinated fashion; rather it has evolved or emerged through three distinct phases.

Three phases of change

Volvo's adoption of Job Design principles began over 20 years ago. It has now reached a stage where group work has become the standard approach to work design, and assembly-line working is not considered appropriate for any new Volvo plant. When dealing with events spanning such a long period, it is often difficult to form an accurate picture of what has taken place and why; particularly when, as in this case, these events have been played out on different sites by different groups of managers and workers. Nevertheless, as Auer and Riegler (1990) and Pontusson (1990) pointed out, by examining major change programmes involving large investments in new or remodelled plants, it is possible to identify three distinct phases in the evolution of Volvo's approach to Job Design.

These three phases are related to major investment projects which occurred in the 1970s and 1980s, namely:

- *Kalmar – This plant opened in 1974 and was the company's first, and most cited, attempt to move away from assembly-line work.*

- *Torslanda – This is Volvo's main car plant which, since the late 1970s, has seen a number of increasingly radical attempts to move away from the traditional assembly-line approach to car production.*

- *Uddevalla – This new assembly plant opened in 1990, and exemplifies Volvo's decisive break with traditional motor industry jobs.*

Phase One – Kalmar

Those committed to challenging the 'inhuman' approach to work, epitomised by the Classical school in general and Henry Ford's moving assembly line in particular, came to look on Volvo's Kalmar car plant as a sort of promised land – a blueprint for the future of work. This was not only because Kalmar was seen as a model of human-centred work organisation, but also because it struck at the very heart of the industry which, through its use of the moving assembly line with its severe division of labour and short cycle times, had taken Taylorist work practices to their ultimate extremes. In addition, and just as importantly, it was heralded as a commercial success. Indeed, Kalmar was famous throughout the world for its 'revolutionary' approach to Job Design even before it opened (Blackler and Brown, 1978).

Perhaps the main reason for the perception that Kalmar was making a decisive break with the past was due to the way Volvo approached its design. The original management concept for Kalmar attempted to incorporate many of the progressive Job Design ideas circulating in the early 1970s. A project team which was composed of managers, production technicians, and architects was given responsibility for designing and building the plant. However, each decision of this team had to be approved by a committee which included trade union representatives, health and safety experts, doctors and outside Job Design experts, including colleagues working with Einar Thorsrud, the noted Norwegian work psychologist.

However, the 'revolutionary' image of Kalmar also owed much to the efficiency of Volvo's own publicity machine. This can be seen from statements about the ethos of the plant made by Pehr Gyllenhammar, Volvo's former Chief Executive, before it opened:

> **The objective of Kalmar will be to arrange auto production in such a way that each employee will be able to find meaning and satisfaction in his work.**
>
> **This will be a factory which, without any sacrifice of efficiency or the company's financial objectives, will give employees opportunities to work in groups, to communicate freely among themselves, to switch from one job assignment to another, to vary the pace of their work, to identify with the product, to be conscious of a responsibility for quality, and to influence their own working environment.**
>
> **When a product is made by people who find meaning in their work, it must inevitably be a product of high quality. (*All quotes are from Aguren et al, 1984:13.*)**

Opened in 1974, Kalmar was Volvo's second largest final assembly plant (the much bigger Torslanda being the largest). It had been planned for an annual capacity of 30,000 cars with around 600 employees. In 1976, it produced 22,000 cars but production fell to 17,000 when demand slumped after the second oil shock in 1977. Production rose again in 1979 but fell back in 1980, when a four-day week was briefly introduced. In 1985, Kalmar produced 32,500 cars, representing about 16 per cent of Volvo's Swedish output of cars. In 1988 the plant had around 960 employees (Aguren *et al*, 1984; Auer and Riegler, 1990).

The difference between Kalmar and a traditional car plant is that, in the latter, the pace of work is determined by the moving assembly line, jobs are extremely fragmented and have cycle times of a few minutes or less, and workers are dedicated to one task only. At Kalmar there is no assembly line, workers operate in teams, with each team having its own dedicated area of the factory. Within the team, workers can move between tasks, and each task has a cycle time of between 20 and 30 minutes. In place of the assembly line, cars are mounted on automated carriers which move around the plant and serve both as a means of transport and as a work platform. This arrangement allowed Kalmar originally to operate two alternatives to the moving assembly line:

- *Straight-line assembly. Work within each team area is split up into four or five work stations placed in a series along the production flow. Two team members work at each station, following the carrier through all the stations and carrying out all the necessary assembly operations.*
- *Dock assembly. This is where one carrier at a time is guided into the 'dock'*

assembly areas where all of the team's tasks are carried out on the stationary carrier by two or three people.

The main difference between the two approaches is that the first, straight-line assembly, still bears some relation to the moving assembly line in that the car carriers move automatically from station to station. In the second approach, the dock system, the car is stationary all the time. Nevertheless, both forms revolve around team work and offer variety and task completeness.

There can be very little doubt that, for its time, Kalmar represented a significant break with the past. However, there are those who question whether the original high hopes for the plant, in terms of the humanisation of work, have been met. Pontusson (1990) argued that the economic consequences of fluctuations in output levels led the plant management to retreat from its original ambitions and, in the latter part of the 1970s, to tighten managerial control over the work process. In particular, he argues, that as dock assembly was abandoned, the potential for workers to influence the pace of work by taking automated carriers out of the main flow was ended.

Blackler and Brown (1978) argued that, with the abandonment of dock assembly, and despite longer cycle times, some fundamental elements of the assembly line (i.e. machine-paced work) have been maintained. Auer and Riegler (1990) made a similar point. They argued that, over time, changes such as new work evaluation methods, the removal of time buffers between stages and the general speeding up of the carriers (which are controlled by a central computer) have intensified the pace of work and have returned the production process much closer to the assembly-line concept than was originally intended.

Before it opened, Kalmar was being hailed as a revolution in Job Design. The reality is that Kalmar does not appear to have represented the dramatic break with the Fordist–Taylorist production process that many had hoped for (Auer and Riegler, 1990; Blackler and Brown, 1978; Pontusson, 1990). However, this does not mean that Kalmar was a failure. Given that Volvo, hitherto very much a traditional car company, was trying to invent a new concept in car assembly, it would have been surprising if it had managed to rewrite the rules of car production at the first attempt. It must be remembered that, although Kalmar was a social experiment, it was also expected to be an economic success. If the social dimension appeared to threaten financial performance, it was the former rather than the latter which would be sacrificed. The true measure of Kalmar's success lies not in the degree to which it achieved its 'revolutionary' goal, but in the extent to which it encouraged Volvo's management to continue with and accelerate the move away from Fordist–Taylorist approaches to work. As Auer and Riegler (1990:27) concluded, despite some disagreement among managers over the effectiveness of the organisation of Kalmar plant, there were sufficient supporters for Volvo to proceed with the development of 'far more progressive' and 'radical' attempts to distance itself from the traditional assembly-line approach to car production.

Phase Two – Torslanda

As well as Kalmar, the late 1970s and early 1980s saw Volvo experimenting with alternatives to the traditional assembly-line at a number of plants. In the main, these were small-scale, and tended to concentrate on bus or truck production rather than car assembly. However, from the late 1970s onwards, a series of increasingly radical attempts were made to transform work organisation at Torslanda, Volvo's main car assembly plant. In 1976, at the central assembly plant, Torslanda management experimented with the use of large, autonomous work groups to assemble an entire car using a dock-assembly approach similar to that being attempted at Kalmar. Due to poor productivity, this was abandoned within six months. Management believed that the workforce lacked the necessary skills to make such an approach work, while the metal workers' trade union felt the experiment was too risky.

In 1979/80, with the opening of the TUN facility at Torslanda to assemble the new 700 series car, management attempted to revive group-based assembly. The TUN workforce was selected from the existing production personnel at Torslanda. The original plan for TUN, initially drawn up without union involvement, envisaged car assembly being carried out by autonomous work groups who would be responsible for their own quality and pace of work. It was planned that work groups would also have responsibility for job rotation, managing material supplies and some maintenance tasks.

The reality though was somewhat less ambitious than originally conceived. The unions, who – when eventually involved – played a larger part in the design of TUN than they had at Kalmar, were highly sceptical of the original concept and this, together with certain practical difficulties in trying to mix indirect tasks with direct production work, led to the scaling-down of the original proposals. TUN is still organised around group-based assembly, and job rotation is still practised, but the pace of work is centrally controlled and workers no longer perform indirect tasks. Nevertheless, workers at TUN see it as being a clear improvement on the traditional approach to car assembly (Auer and Riegler, 1990).

In 1986, once again management began to consider major changes to the organisation of work at Torslanda's central assembly plant. At this time, the plant employed 4000 workers and was mainly organised around Fordist–Taylorist principles. This time the trade unions were involved much earlier and played a more central role. In February 1986, management and unions agreed an 'action plan' which emphasised the transformation of car assembly into an 'attractive alternative' to the traditional methods of car manufacture. In particular, building on the earlier failure, the plan stressed the need for high-quality and continuing training to allow workers to gain the skills necessary for effective group work. The action plan appeared to revive many of the original ideas for TUN (including the provision for direct production workers to carry out indirect tasks). In addition, it envisaged working time being adjusted to employee needs.

Though the full reorganisation of Torslanda is still not complete, some of the individual sections, such as motor and axle assembly, have come on stream. The changes envisaged in the action plan have been introduced, especially those relating to workers controlling the pace of work and undertaking indirect tasks. As might be expected, there have been some difficulties in implementing these. However, the main problem appears to relate to trade union attempts to protect traditional demarcations between direct and indirect tasks and between work groups and supervisors. Maintenance staff still work outside the work group structure, and the foremen's trade union successfully resisted their partial replacement by rotating team leaders. The metal workers' union also wanted to maintain a more hierarchical structure in order to preserve a job ladder between the shopfloor and management. Nevertheless, progress has been made and, though the final form that Torslanda will take is still uncertain, it does appear to promise a more radical break with tradition than occurred at Kalmar (Auer and Riegler, 1990; Pontusson, 1990), especially taking into account the progress already made at the Uddevalla plant.

Phase Three – Uddevalla

This was the first all-new car assembly plant built by Volvo in Sweden since Kalmar. It was designed to employ 1,000 people and have the capability to produce 40,000 cars per year. Many observers believe the plant goes far beyond Volvo's previous attempts at Job Design: 'the only [car plant] in the world where workers build cars from start to finish rather on assembly lines' (McIvor, 1995 1995:37). The design of the plant was the result of a 'modernisation pact' between the plant's management and the metal workers' union, many of whose extensive demands were incorporated into the plant's design (Auer and Riegler, 1990). In accordance with Sweden's Co-determination Law (and Volvo's practice at Torslanda), the unions were involved in the steering group responsible for designing and building the Uddevalla plant. Indeed, three union officials worked full-time on the project between 1985 and 1987.

The completed plant comprised six mini-factories, each containing eight dock assembly areas, each with its own autonomous work group. In theory, each dock can independently assemble an entire car.

Each work group comprises 10 fully trained assembly workers, each of whom can, again in theory, perform all the tasks necessary to assemble an entire car. Each group is responsible for determining its pace of work and internal job rotation. In addition, the groups have responsibility for maintenance, administration and quality control. The role of group leader rotates among the members of each group. The incorporation of so many functions within each group resulted in a very flat hierarchy: there are no layers between the groups and the factory managers. The plant also adopted an equal opportunities policy which reserved at least 40 per cent of production jobs for women and at least 25 per cent for workers over 45 years old.

The plant is clearly at the leading edge of Job Design, at least as far as the car industry is concerned. Nevertheless, as other such initiatives by Volvo have shown, economic and operational concerns could lead to its more radical elements, especially self-paced work, being modified over time. Indeed, the original plan for the plant very much followed the practices adopted at Kalmar. It was only with considerable pressure from the trade unions, and the intervention of Volvo's top management, that more radical ideas were eventually adopted, though even the unions took some convincing that machine-paced assembly might be abandoned altogether (Pontusson, 1990). Unfortunately, the plant opened at a time when car demand was falling dramatically. Despite attempts to keep it open, Volvo closed the plant in 1992 in the face of mounting and considerable losses. Nevertheless, in 1995 the plant was re-opened. Though operating on a smaller scale than originally envisaged, Uddevalla's new Chief Executive appears determined to stick to its original Job Design concept (McIvor, 1995:37).

The outcome

The progress of redesigning jobs at Volvo has been remarkable in comparison with the Taylorist–Fordist nature of the company in the 1960s. The fact that it has continued and intensified over a period of twenty years, and that any organisational changes at Volvo are expected to revolve around group work, speaks volumes for the degree to which it has become embedded in the culture of the company. This is not to say that the result is perfect. It must be remembered that assembling cars and trucks will always be a physically demanding job. Furthermore, Volvo is not an altruistic organisation; it exist to make a profit, and the way it organises work must reflect and facilitate this (regardless of pressures from trade unions, government legislation and public opinion). Nevertheless, as Pontusson (1990:315) observed, the 'stages of workplace reform involve a cumulative process of innovation, with a trajectory which adds up to a more or less definitive break with Fordism.'

Some might also point out that though Volvo has led the way, many other companies have followed – including much of the car industry. However, this would be to miss two important points. First, Volvo's approach is not a copycat or 'flavour of the month' one. Rather, it is a long-standing and still developing approach which now appears to be firmly embedded in the company's culture. Second, though most other car companies have adopted, to a lesser or greater extent, the autonomous/semi-autonomous work group concept, especially the Japanese, no one else has abandoned the assembly line and no one else appears to allow workers to determine the pace of work themselves. Indeed, as recent visits to car assembly plants in the UK have shown, if anything the pace of work on assembly lines now seems more intense in the 1990s than the supposedly bad old days of the 1960s and 1970s.

The changes at Volvo have taken place over an extended timescale, at different sites and under different conditions and, therefore, have been influenced by a wide range of factors. Despite the subsequent advent of the Culture–Excellence approach and the Japanese approach, what has successfully taken place at Volvo is the adoption of practices and principles associated with the Human Relations school and operationalised by the Job Design movement. There are several key factors which appear to have played a major role in terms of influencing Volvo to adopt this approach.

- *For sound economic and business reasons, Volvo needed to reduce absenteeism and high labour turnover.*

- *Full employment and a lack of wage flexibility precluded more traditional 'stick and carrot' measures for dealing with absenteeism and labour turnover. Therefore, Volvo had to look at alternative methods of reducing absenteeism and labour turnover and, instead of trying to alleviate the symptoms, they chose to tackle the boredom and dissatisfaction which gave rise to labour problems in the first place. The decision by Volvo's management to adopt a Job Design approach appears to have come about owing to a combination of intense public pressure on the company to move to a more human-centred approach to assembly work, and managerial preference. It should be noted, though, that Volvo's management have never been unanimous in supporting the more radical aspects of Job Design, as was demonstrated by the disagreement over the success of Kalmar and the need for senior managers to intervene to ensure a more radical approach at Uddevalla.*

- *The parallel move by Volvo to adopt a strategy of decentralising control to plant level (as opposed to its previous centralised, bureaucratic control procedures) both gave local management some freedom to experiment with new ways of working, and allowed management to experience the lessening of control which they were advocating for workers.*

- *Though originally the move away from Fordist–Taylorist work practices was entirely management-inspired, trade unions came to play an increasingly active role in encouraging its adoption. In this, they were aided by both the Co-determination Law which came in to effect in 1976 and the generally favourable climate towards Job Design in Sweden. However, as Torslanda demonstrated, the trade unions – like Volvo's management – are capable of exhibiting conservative tendencies and in need of convincing that some of the more radical elements of group work should be adopted.*

- *While these changes have taken place on different sites and at different times, both management and workers appear to have found a way of capturing the knowledge gained at other plants and lessons learnt for future projects. This process of organisational learning appears to be fundamental to understanding how Volvo has moved (not always in an easy or deliberate fashion) from the limited, though significant, structural changes at Kalmar to the genuine expansion of workers' control seen at Uddevalla. Auer and Riegler (1990:52), who carried out a comprehensive review of work organisation changes at Volvo, commented that:*

Interviews with managers, representatives of trade unions and researchers all confirmed ... Volvo is one of the few companies where management, employees, and trade unions have found broad opportunities for gathering experience in changing the organisation of work and that the company is a place of learning ...

Evidently, the case of Volvo's attempts to move to a radical change in its internal relationships, one which passes significantly greater control of production to workers than had hitherto been considered wise and efficient, is by no means straightforward. Though the intent was there from the start, and though we can argue about why the move to Job Design came about, the actual details have been subject to a process of pragmatism, revision and trial and error over the last 20 years. The new approach to work organisation coincided with Volvo's granting of greater autonomy to plant-level managers, the introduction of the Co-determination Law, and considerable public support for Job Design in Sweden; clearly, these were all influential in what happened at Volvo. However, it should be remembered that Volvo was and is a large and relatively successful private company. If it had wanted to, it could have chosen another course of action: indeed, Volvo's management itself disagreed about the need for and extent of Job Design. The fact that Volvo chose to break the car industry mould at Kalmar, and to keep breaking it at other plants, shows that no matter how powerful or dominant a particular paradigm is, alternatives are always possible. It is also true that, if the move to new ways of working had not allowed the company to develop its competitiveness, the initiative would not have flourished. It may well have been the case that in the atmosphere of the 1970s, Volvo was under great pressure from a number of sources to develop a more human-centred approach to work. However, with the easing of this pressure in the 1980s and 1990s, the company could have chosen quietly to abandon this approach. That it did not clearly demonstrates the belief, especially by Volvo's management, that job redesign works.

Case study 6

ROVER GROUP – BUILDING A LEARNING ORGANISATION*

Background

The announcement in April 1995 that Rover Group had made record profits and that its domestic and export sales were continuing to forge ahead merely confirmed what many observers believed – that Rover has turned itself into one of Europe's leading car companies, and is approaching a position where it can challenge the best in the world. It was this potential for world-class performance which lay behind BMW's purchase of Rover in February 1994. As the BMW Chairman, Bernd Pischetsrieder, commented on BBC TV's *Money Programme* at the time, 'The objective is that BMW and Rover together will be the largest specialist manufacturer worldwide.' The purchase of the company by a German firm renowned for its commitment to quality, flair and financial soundness was a major vote of confidence

*This case study is based on research carried out with Penny West of Edge Hill College.

in Rover, and set the seal on what has been one of the most remarkable turnarounds in British corporate life.

By any stretch of the imagination, Rover Group should not be in business today. Its troubled history of the 1970s and early 1980s, both in terms of industrial relations and serious financial problems, would have been enough to sink many an organisation. It was also plagued with an image of poor quality and design, and high costs, at a time when the Japanese had taken the world motor industry by storm. General Motors and Ford were in serious trouble and Chrysler, once regarded as one of the three leading motor companies in the world, looked likely to sink without trace. If these companies were in trouble, how could Rover survive?

The short answer was that it could not. In 1975, when it was still called British Leyland, it was nationalised by the then Labour government to save it from collapse. Nevertheless, it continued to make substantial losses. By the early 1980s, it had received state aid of £2 billion and had still accumulated losses of £2.6 billion. Margaret Thatcher, then Prime Minister and no supporter of state aid, wanted the company broken up and sold off. She did not get her way, however. Though Unipart (the spares business) and Jaguar were floated off as separate companies (the latter eventually purchased by Ford), and the bus and truck operations were sold to Volvo and DAF respectively, the car business remained intact and continued the task of reshaping itself for future prosperity.

In 1988, to most people's surprise, Rover Group was sold to British Aerospace for £150 million, which, given that the BMW deal valued it at £1 billion, now looks like something of a bargain. Between 1989 and 1994, Rover's transformation continued apace. Thanks partly to collaboration with its long-time partner Honda, it launched a series of best-selling and award-winning cars (the 200, 400, 600 and 800 series and the Discovery were especially successful).

Though this transformation can be attributed to many factors, especially its links with Honda, perhaps its most remarkable aspect is the way that Rover's employees have moved from being seen as its greatest liability to its greatest asset.

The genesis of a learning business

The change in employee relations at Rover came neither overnight nor without accompanying changes in managerial personnel and style. When Michael Edwardes became Managing Director in 1978, the company had become a byword for industrial militancy – a common joke at the time was: 'only Bobby Charlton strikes faster than British Leyland'. One of Edwardes' first priorities was to tackle the industrial relations strife at the company and establish, or re-establish, 'management's right to manage'. Obviously, he did much else, including establishing the link with Honda, but it was his fierce determination to restore managerial authority and end union militancy which characterised his reign.

In 1982, Edwardes left and was replaced by Harold Musgrove. By this time, employee relations were on a less volatile footing. It was under Musgrove that management, strongly influenced by Rover's alliance with Honda, came to recognise that the rapid development of new models and attendant changes in processes and techniques required a substantial retraining of the workforce, and an end to the 'them and us' culture which still dominated the organisation. It was not until 1986, however, with the appointment of Graham Day as Chairman, followed shortly after by the appointment of a new managing director, that 'people' moved to the top of the agenda.

Under Edwardes and Musgrove, Rover's priorities had been profits, products, procedures and people, in that order. Day became convinced that Rover's only hope of long-term survival was to stand the company's objectives on their head. Profit, he argued, would be the result of people concentrating on producing superior products by way of distinctive processes. People came first, profits came later. It is difficult to overestimate how much of a challenge this was to the established view held by managers in Rover. They had spent three or four very painful years in the late 1970s and early 1980s establishing their right to manage, and fully subscribed to the traditional management macho ethos of the British motor industry. Suddenly they were being told that employee initiative was the key to success, that there must be a partnership between managers and workers.

Nevertheless, through a succession of meetings and brainstorming sessions, senior managers began to craft a new personnel approach for the company. The effort began with a new quality initiative in Rover which stressed that 'quality is about people' and a new mission for Rover 'to achieve extraordinary customer satisfaction'. The personnel function also adopted a new mission statement:

> **The purpose of personnel within Rover is to achieve success through people and the purpose of the personnel team is to gain success for the business through the success of its people.**

From this time, as the following quotations demonstrate, senior managers began to speak a new language: 'We want to change the emphasis from training – people having something done to them, to learning – people doing something for themselves'; 'we want to unlock the potential of everyone to make a contribution to the future'; 'we want to bridge the gap between management and workforce'; 'we want to achieve success through people'; 'it's our people's contribution which will give us our competitive edge'. Furthermore, the emphasis moved from managers managing to managers leading: 'We see excellent leadership as the key to unlock those [employees'] contributions so we focus heavily on encouraging our line managers' leadership skills.'

Since 1986, a whole raft of measures and policies designed to open up the opportunities for and to promote learning have been developed. Rover now estimates that, at any one time, over half of all employees are engaged in some form of learning. In order to facilitate this process and create a corporate learning environment, the company has attempted to remove barriers which separate one employee from another. It has flattened its management structure and removed the bewildering plethora of job titles and job descriptions that used to exist. It has committed itself to end the divide between blue-collar and white-collar jobs, and the insecurity that had often been a feature of the former. This commitment was demonstrated in 1992 with the launch of the company's far-reaching 'Rover Tomorrow – The New Deal'. This included:

- *a company undertaking not to make compulsory redundancies, in return for a commitment from employees to continuous improvement and flexibility;*

- *the harmonisation of terms and conditions between white-collar and blue-collar staff;*

- *the coining of a new term – 'associates' – to describe all Rover employees, regardless of what job they did or where they worked;*

- *the expectation that white-collar staff should be prepared to be redeployed onto assembly-line work;*

- *a requirement that all new graduate recruits had to spend their first three months with Rover working on the production lines;*

- *the expectation that all Rover employees, even directors, should wear the same grey overalls.*

In order to accelerate that pace of change at Rover, in 1990 Rover Learning Business was created to bring together and give focus to the company's various learning initiatives.

Rover Learning Business

The idea of creating a separate business within a business to promote organisational learning appears at first strange, especially given the enormous effort Rover put into creating a learning culture between 1986 and 1990. However, senior managers came to believe that the push for continuous improvement through the provision of opportunities for continuous learning could lead to a mass of fragmented and unco-ordinated initiatives, unless a group was established with the sole purpose of directing, co-ordinating and developing the company's learning initiatives. This view was strengthened by the evidence from employee attitude surveys, which the company had conducted for a number of years. These had consistently shown that (a) employees did not feel the best use was being made of their talents, and that they were prepared for faster and more radical change than the company had so far experienced; and (b) employees felt they were not well enough informed about opportunities for involvement, development and progression within Rover. Consequently, there was a strong view among both managers and workforce that the pace of change could and should be accelerated and, despite past efforts, that a more coherent, co-ordinated and publicised approach to learning was required. Rover Learning Business (or RLB, as it is generally referred to in Rover) was launched on 14 May 1990. It was given a budget of around £30 million, and a remit to help Rover Group achieve a number of specific objectives:

- *to distinguish Rover Group as the best in Europe for attracting, retaining and developing people;*
- *to emphasise the view that people are its greatest asset;*
- *to gain recognition by its own employees that the company's commitment to every individual had increased;*
- *to unlock and recognise employee talents and to make better use of these talents;*
- *to improve the competitive edge of the company.*

In addressing the first RLB Open Conference in 1993, Sir Graham Day, Rover Group's Chairman, summed up the philosophy that underpins the work of RLB:

Neither the corporate learning process nor the individual one is optional. If the company seeks to survive and prosper, it must learn. If the individual, at a minimum, seeks to remain employed, let alone progress, learning is essential.

The work of RLB is overseen by a Board of Governors, comprising senior managers from Rover and leading educationalists from the UK and beyond. Over the past five years, the Governors have seen RLB expand its activities to include car dealerships and suppliers as well as Rover employees. RLB has also received much media attention for its innovative role.

Its main activities remain focused on internal activities and relationships within Rover. Its core learning products, as it refers to them, are as follows:

REAL (Rover Employee Assisted Learning)

This programme provides employees with £100 per year to spend on personal development. Originally, staff could spend it on whatever learning activity they chose (many people used it to develop leisure pursuits such as scuba diving or archery). The reasoning behind it was that people whose experience of education had not been positive, or who had been out of education for many years, needed to gain confidence in their own ability to learn. REAL money can now only be spent on work-related learning activities (though this is very broadly defined). REAL is increasingly used to fund team building activities whereby work groups and teams, on their own initiative, combine their REAL money to go on team building courses together.

Personal Development Files (PDFs)

These were launched as a result of the inadequacies of traditional approaches to appraisal and performance review. PDFs are designed not only to review past performance, but also to identify future learning objectives for individuals, and match these to the company's business objectives. So far, more than 70 per cent of the workforce have asked for PDFs, though the interest from managers, supervisors and team leaders seems to be much greater than from shopfloor associates.

GLEN (Group Learning Exchange Network)

This comprises an extensive computer database of information and case studies developed to assist Rover associates to improve and develop the manner in which they carry out their work. As well as being able to access GLEN, staff are also expected to put information into it. As an example, when staff carry out an improvement activity, they are encouraged to write it up and put it into GLEN so that others can learn from their experience.

The Change Management Process

RLB has put a great deal of effort into assisting staff in Rover to plan and implement change. Out of this, they have developed an approach to change which is both rigorous and effective. The approach is based on teamwork, and stresses the need to seek information on best practice and benchmarking, and to involve those most closely affected. The process is driven by business needs, and takes the change team step-by-step through the various stages necessary to plan and implement change. RLB point out that it is also a learning tool. Once a project has been completed, the team evaluate what worked and did not work, and what lessons they can learn for the future.

On a recent visit by the author to Land Rover, staff explained how they had used the process successfully to plan and implement the introduction of a new production line for the Discovery. They had assembled a team and had gone off-site for four days. They were accompanied by a fellow manager who was familiar with the RLB Change Management Process and who acted as a facilitator. At the end of the four days, they not only had a plan for introducing the new Discovery line, including a timetable and resource implications, but had also developed a presentation to explain to managers and other associates what they intended to do. One of the team members commented that it was the smoothest and quickest change project he had ever been involved in. In addition, the team had managed to introduce the new line at no cost to the company and with no additional resources or loss of production.

On the same visit to Land Rover, staff at all levels were enthusiastic and complementary about the changes which had taken place at Rover, and especially the opportunities for learning.

The outcome

Rover's strategy is to stimulate changes on a broad front, aimed ultimately at achieving a competitive advantage through the efforts of all managers and employees. The view it takes is that in an industry of fast followers, those who learn fastest will be the winners. So Rover does not necessarily need to invent new methods and new processes itself; however, it must be capable of identifying them and utilising them more quickly and better than its competitors. For Rover, the emphasis is not on technology (though that is important to the company), production methods (though the Honda link has put Rover at the forefront in these), or design (though its cars are extremely well thought-out and designed), all of which can be copied relatively quickly. The emphasis is on developing people as the key to achieving a competitive edge, and on creating a learning organisation which can draw on ideas from a wide range of industries and sources and adapt them to Rover's needs.

The result of this has been to transform relationships and working practices in Rover Group. The 'them and us' philosophy which permeated the company has been replaced, though probably not in everyone's mind, with a much more team- and company-orientated approach. Perhaps the most dramatic example is that not only was the company prepared to ask white-collar staff to take shopfloor jobs, but some actually have.

In cases such as this, where companies receive a great deal of media attention, it is important to try to separate the hype from the reality. What can be seen objectively is that Rover has changed out of all recognition since it was rescued by the UK government in 1975. Though the foundations for this were laid in the Edwardes' era (especially the link with Honda), the step change in performance appears to have come in the last ten years, with the development of a new attitude towards staff, and the move to creating a learning organisation.

A number of important issues can be discerned from the Rover experience:

● *The strategic development of Rover as a learning organisation emerged over time in response to the specific needs of the business as perceived by senior managers.*

● *The move to change management–worker relations (and indeed, manager–manager and worker–worker relations) was not driven by any altruistic belief in the goodness of human nature. Rather it was driven by the commercial reality of the world in which Rover operates. Managers realised that they could not beat the opposition by competing on technology or cost alone. However, they could build a better organisation, one which was smarter and faster than the opposition.*

● *In effect, Rover chose to compete on different grounds, to focus on different competences, to the opposition. This was by no means the obvious or easiest route for Rover, but managers chose it because they felt it would give them a genuine competitive edge over the opposition. In effect, they decided to change the organisational environment in which they operated.*

● *Though driven by management, this strategy also required changes to management. It was developed by successive management teams, each of which found it slightly easier than the last to move down this route: so, just as Musgrove succeeded Edwardes, so co-operation succeeded conflict; and, as Day succeeded Musgrove, so partnership succeeded co-operation. It is important to note that changes in managerial personnel and style preceded changes in Rover's internal and external relationships.*

● *Though this was an emergent process, and in some elements experimental, it was neither* ad hoc *nor unplanned. Instead, managers spent considerable time thinking through the implications and planning the implementation of the changes. In particular, because Rover regularly surveyed opinion among its workforce, it ensured that changes were geared towards eliminating discontent and promoting desired behaviour. In creating Rover Learning Business, the company also recognised the danger of fragmentation and loss of ownership which can occur if a large number of initiatives are launched in a short space of time. RLB has allowed Rover to give ownership and focus to its learning initiatives, and ensure that they are driven by business needs. In addition, because the RLB Board has a significant outside representation, it can act as a ginger group to encourage Rover to take more ambitious and perhaps innovative steps than might otherwise be the case.*

Case study 7

GK PRINTERS LTD – CHANGING SYSTEMS AND ATTITUDES

Background

GK Printers Ltd is a small, family-run printing business. It was established just after the Second World War by the present Managing Director's father. The company was originally a jobbing printers; which is to say it would print anything. 'No job too large or too small', might well have been its motto, although in fact, the mainstay of its business was producing stationery, business cards and publicity brochures for local companies.

This work was moderately profitable and provided a reasonable living for the owners and their workforce, some 20 people. By the beginning of the 1980s, however, this situation began to change. First, the recession had a strong negative effect on its traditional customer base, and orders began to fall off dramatically. Second, the advent of newer, computerised printing techniques, which GK had not adopted, meant that rivals could offer a quicker, cheaper and often better-quality service. Third, the advent of small printing bureaux (such as Prontaprint), often situated in prime city centre locations, and portraying an up-to-date image, further eroded GK's business. Finally, it was clear that many of its customers were no longer going to a printer directly. Instead, in the image-conscious 1980s, they were putting their work out to graphic designers who, having finalised the design, would then sub-contract out the printing. In such a situation, there was no guarantee that the work from their traditional customers would eventually end up with them. It depended upon the preference of the particular graphic designers concerned.

All these factors combined to threaten the financial viability of GK and, for the first time ever, the company lost money. The loss was only small (£20,000), but it came as a major shock to a company which had grown used to making a reasonable, if not spectacular, profit. The result of this was that the Managing Director and the company's Printing Manager, along with other members of the owning family, formed a 'crisis committee' to review the future of the business.

Phase One: developing a strategy

It rapidly became clear to the committee that to do nothing was not an option; the result would be to go out of business. The two main options considered were whether to sell the business, or, in some way, to change it to secure a viable future. Without exception, the crisis committee preferred the second option, if only because it was clear that it would be very difficult to find a buyer for the company. No one was sure, however, what it was that they needed to do to change the fortunes of the business.

In desperation, almost, they approached a lecturer at the local polytechnic who was a friend of the Printing Manager. His suggestion was that one of his business studies students should undertake a project to examine the company's options. This took two months, during which the Managing Director and Printing Manager worked closely with the student.

The student's final report had a dramatic impact on the company. Its main findings were that:

- *The printing market was expanding rather than contracting. This was mainly due to companies recognising the need to promote themselves more and in a better way than in the past.*

- *The market expansion was mainly at the higher value-added end of the market, in the area of high-class, glossy promotional material.*

- *The newer print bureaux were not as strong competitors as the company had thought. Their product quality was both variable and, at best, no better than GK's. Furthermore, their costs appeared to be higher.*

- *GK's existing customer base would prefer to continue to do business with them, but perceived them as old-fashioned, lacking in key capabilities (mainly graphic design), slow, and not particularly flexible.*

- *GK's printing equipment was not capable of producing the higher value-added products that customers were more and more demanding.*

These findings were met with some astonishment and a great deal of relief by the crisis committee. Without exception they had steeled themselves for a report which would be doom-laden. Instead, they could see that a future did exist, and possibly a very profitable one. Some major changes would be required however. Before making any decisions, the Managing Director and Printing Manager insisted that the findings should be discussed with the workforce.

Employee relations were very good in the company and, while not being paternalistic, the tendency was to see the company almost as an extended family. The print workers, who made up the majority of the workforce, were all union members, and two of them were prominent activists in their local union branch. The workforce knew that a review was taking place; it would have been almost impossible to keep it from them, given the nature of the company, but in any case the management had been very open about it. Like the crisis committee, the workforce were relieved that the findings were more optimistic than many had believed possible. However, they wanted to know what the management intended to do to change the company in order to take advantage of the opportunities that appeared available.

The Managing Director was slightly taken aback by the workforce's apparent eagerness for change; he had expected some resistance, especially from the print workers. Instead, the reverse was the case – the two union activists were the strongest advocates of new equipment. As one later said: 'We knew what was happening elsewhere; skilled workers were being replaced by glorified typists. But we also knew that we needed new equipment. The deal we struck with management was that we would accept anything they bought, but we would be trained for it and we would operate it.'

Indeed, they went beyond this – they actually told the management what to buy and from whom.

On the basis of the report from the student, the management constructed a strategy for rejuvenating the company. The strategy had three main elements:

1 The appointment of a Marketing and Design Manager to develop the company's customer base and provide a graphic design capability.

2 Upgrading the company's image. The above appointment was part of this process, but it also involved remodelling the company's frontage and reception areas, redesigning its stationery and creating a company logo.

3 Progressively replacing old printing machines with newer, more capable equipment.

Though the company never formally created a 'vision' of its future, the Managing Director later said:

> After the student's report I began to see a picture in my own mind of what I would like the company to be. I wanted it to be a one-stop shop for all our customers' printing needs. In the past, if we could not do it ourselves, or if we were too busy, we turned people away. Not any more. If we could not do it, we sub-contracted, just like the graphic designers. But we would ensure that we could do the money business in-house (the high value-added business) and eventually only sub-contract out the cheap stuff.

Therefore, the company began its transformation by the appointment of a Marketing and Design Manager and upgrading its image. Initially, it did not buy any new equipment, but took the decision to sub-contract work they could not do until such time as the volume of work necessitated new investment. This allowed them to turn round the business without having to borrow large sums of money.

Nevertheless, within 12 months, such was the success of the strategy that the company began buying new equipment. After that, as the economy grew in the 1980s, the company's fortunes also grew. By the late 1980s, GK employed 40 staff (double its previous number) and had quadrupled its turnover to £4 million. In the process, it had managed to improve its profitability substantially.

In 1989, however, it grew concerned that the increased volume of business, made more complicated by both the need to design as well as print, and having to co-ordinate their sub-contracting activities, was having an adverse effect on customer service. The main problems were: controlling paperwork (especially orders and invoices), the company's costing system, and production scheduling. They undertook a review of these activities to see how they could be improved. Thus began the second phase of the transition of GK into a highly competitive printing company.

Phase Two: changing systems

Reasons for change

As mentioned above, market, product and operational changes meant that the company needed to provide a faster and better service to its customers. While much had been done to achieve this, in 1989 it was also realised that better business systems were required, especially in the area of costing, invoicing and production control.

Given that GK was only a small company, it was relatively easy for the Managing Director to bring together the six people who were responsible for these activities and, in effect, to state the problems and give them the authority to come up with their solution.

The people concerned agreed to meet for two hours each Friday afternoon to review the issues involved and come up with options. They were clear that they did not want to rule anything out, but set out instead to identify all the available alternatives, and choose the one that suited them and the company best.

After three weeks they had reached a consensus on the root cause of their problems: they were all being asked to do more and more without any additional resources. Not only did this mean that backlogs occurred, but also that the greater need to communicate across functions, which the company now required, was not taking place.

Given this analysis, their first inclination was to ask for more staff. However, they also looked at other options, the main one being to introduce better systems – ones which reduced duplication. This raised the additional question: manual or computer systems?

Eventually they agreed a number of key objectives against which any option had to be tested. These were that any new system should provide:

- *a faster and better response to customers' requests for quotations;*
- *speedier invoicing and improved debtor control;*
- *better record-keeping and a reduction in duplication;*
- *an increase in productivity of clerical staff;*
- *better control of production, resulting in reduced lead times, and quicker and more reliable service to customers;*
- *system integration.*

Having decided upon these criteria, the people involved then asked the Printing Manager if he would approach his contact at the local polytechnic for assistance. This he did, and once again the assistance came in the form of a student project. The student evaluated the company's existing operations and looked at alternatives. Her report stated that it was possible to improve the existing systems but that this would not allow them to achieve their objectives. Instead, she advocated introducing computer-based systems instead.

As they had witnessed the successful introduction of computerised printing equipment during recent years, staff were neither overawed nor complacent about computerising their systems. They discussed with the local polytechnic how best to approach an evaluation of the benefits of computer systems, and selection of a system.

The group then prepared a written report for the Managing Director which detailed their investigations, their initial objectives, and the advice they had received. Their recommendation was that the company should invite a number of computer companies to visit them to discuss their needs. A long discussion took place between the Managing Director and the group, which resulted eventually in their report being accepted. However, the Managing Director did add one proviso. This was that the group should be responsible for deciding whether to computerise, and, if so, what system to select and from whom it should be purchased. The Managing Director said he would sit in on any negotiations that took place with computer companies, but that he would not take the decision away from them; rather he would bolster their authority by his presence.

A number of computer companies were invited to discuss the company's requirements with them. In total, some 20 companies visited them. The upshot of these visits was that the company became convinced that its needs could best be met by purchasing a computerised business system which could perform the necessary work and integrate its existing manual systems. However, the cost of this was likely to be between £20,000 and £30,000, which – for a company of GK's size – was significant. The Printing Manager, and others, pointed out that such an amount spent on printing equipment would greatly extend their capabilities. Nevertheless, after much discussion, the decision was taken to go ahead with the purchase of a computerised business system (CBS).

Though it took a number of meetings to reach this decision, which was subject to much discussion throughout the company, the final decision was almost unanimous.

The reason for this was that the company was performing well on all fronts except in the areas covered by the proposed changes. Late and inadequate quotations, poor debtor control and erratic delivery performance were all causing the company problems. These were not as yet major problems, but could be expected to get worse as the company expanded.

Introduction and development of the CBS

Once the decision had been made, the original group was given the responsibility, as the Managing Director had earlier stated, for specifying and deciding which equipment to purchase. Its task was made difficult because, while it was clear that standard software packages were suitable for such tasks as sales ledgers, wages and invoicing, special software would need to be written to accommodate the company's production control needs. The members of the CBS steering group, as they jokingly referred to themselves, spent a number of months identifying and writing a specification of their exact requirements from a production control system. They then asked the computer companies to quote for a CBS on the basis of this specification. Of the original companies who had shown interest, however, only two were prepared to provide the bespoke software the company required. The company wished to ensure that both the hardware and software were supplied by the same vendor, not only to avoid any incompatibility problems, but also to have only one organisation responsible for any problem that might arise. Further discussions took place with the two companies, during which the software specification was further refined, and eventually a supplier was chosen. The entire process, from the Managing Director raising the issue, to actually placing the order, took over a year.

The computer for running the systems, and the standard packages, were delivered almost immediately, but it was another six months before the production control package was installed. This was because it had to be specially written. The company ensured that it closely monitored the writing of the software and that the final package met the specification. It then took some three months to bring the production control package on line. During this period, manual records were still kept in parallel to the computerised system. After this, it took a further three months before the total CBS package was up and running satisfactorily. Therefore, in total, it took two years from the inception to the completion of the project. Nevertheless, no one regretted the time spent. As the Managing Director said:

> **If you'd told me at the beginning it would take so long I'd have laughed at you. But now we've ended up with a system that gives us all we want – and more. It's a system that 'belongs' to the people who work it – it's not my system, it's theirs.**

Though the company only bought one workstation initially, it had specified that the CBS should be capable of networking. This was done with the intention that once the CBS had proved itself, further workstations would be acquired. Since then, three more workstations have been purchased and the company has also doubled the memory capacity of the system. In total, some £35,000 has been spent on the CBS.

As with other aspects of the CBS, the company was careful to ensure that adequate training was provided for those who would use the system. Once again, this was made easier because it was the users who had selected the system, so they knew what it could do and what training they required. This ranged from three days to a week, depending upon the users' requirement. The training was provided by the equipment supplier. Training took place in stages, allowing users to become familiar with one aspect of the system before being trained on another aspect of it. Training was provided for clerical staff who would use and maintain the system, and also for senior managers who needed to access it for information.

As might be imagined, staff appear to have taken to the CBS very well. Though initially there was an additional workload for them in terms of inputting information into the system, they now find that it is better and faster than the previous manual system. Their workload is no less than before, but they take satisfaction from being more effective by using 'their' system. Obviously, the system has had a knock-on effect elsewhere in the company, both in the collection and use of information. This adjustment appears to have been accomplished with little or no difficulty.

The benefits

The CBS has not transformed the fortunes of GK; no single system will do that for any company. It has made a significant contribution, however, in the areas it covers, to improving the service GK provides to its customers and meeting its own requirements.

The company believes that computerising its business systems has brought the following benefits:

- *better and more accurate records;*
- *quicker access to information;*
- *better control of resources;*
- *a speedier and more accurate response to quotation requests;*
- *higher productivity from clerical staff;*
- *reduced lead times;*
- *faster and more reliable deliveries;*
- *a greater integration of business functions;*
- *an improvement in staff morale and skills.*

Though this appears to be a case of successful technical change, it would be wrong to perceive it exclusively in this light. Certainly, that is not how those involved saw it. Rather they believed that the main benefit gained was the ability to work together more effectively. The CBS assisted this by automating some of the more routine elements of their work, thus allowing them to put their skills to better use. However, they are the ones who know what customers and the company require, not the CBS.

Whether their perception is true or not may not matter: the real issue is that they believed it to be so. This clearly had a substantial effect on their effectiveness, self-esteem and morale.

Reasons for success

To the outsider, at least, this appears to be an almost textbook case of how to manage change. However, the staff involved, while clearly pleased with their role, are also not uncritical of their performance. With hindsight, they say that they should have completed the process in a year rather than two years. They also believe that they should have included additional features in the CBS.

While these criticisms may be true, they are only so from the vantage point of having gone through the process of change and having gained confidence and experience from it. They also reflect a key reason for the success of the process: a willingness to be open and critical about themselves and their requirements, and a belief that they all needed to be convinced of what was required before proceeding.

Nor should the role played by the Managing Director be undervalued. In a company where – a few years earlier – change, of any sort, was very rare indeed, it takes considerable courage for a senior manager to delegate authority to users. Indeed, at one point he openly told the group, 'If you succeed, it's your success – not mine. If you fail, I carry the can – not you.' This created the climate of trust and responsibility which made those involved determined to succeed.

Nevertheless, it would be remiss not to draw attention to several other factors which contributed to successful change in this instance:

- *The company had a strategy for its future development (or at least a general view of what it wanted to become) and therefore was able to take an overview of all areas of its business in relation to future objectives.*

- *Because the company was strategy-driven, it was able to establish not only where problems lay in the company, but also whether the problems were high, low or medium priority. This meant that the company could establish that there was a need to improve business systems and that this was a priority.*

- *The company did not rush into making a decision about what exactly was the problem, what solution to adopt or what equipment to purchase.*

- *The company clearly documented its requirements, and identified where standard packages were sufficient and where bespoke software was required.*

- *It carefully selected a supplier in whom it had confidence and with whom it could work closely.*

- *It constructed a timetabled implementation plan with clear objectives for the introduction of the CBS.*

- *It ensured that the appropriate training was provided.*

Two further points should be stressed about the introduction of the CBS. First, the company was attempting to move from being an organisation where change was the exception, to one where it became the norm. In such a situation, it is impossible for change to be controlled exclusively by management or 'experts'. The sheer volume of work would overwhelm them. Without devolving the responsibility to those affected, change either would not take place or would be unsuccessful. Nor would it be possible for senior managers to concentrate on the longer-term strategic aspects of their business. Therefore, sustaining the changes in managerial behaviour which promote involvement and teamwork are essential to GK's prosperity.

Second, devolving responsibility in this way ensures that those who have to live with the change take ownership of the process, and are committed to it. It allows those involved to develop their skills and confidence. It also ensures that once the changes do take place, they become fully operational as rapidly as possible. It should have the additional advantage that it encourages those concerned to continue to search for improvements.

Unfortunately, as business increased, thanks to the changes at GK, there was a tendency to concentrate on output rather than development, and to revert back to old patterns of behaviour. This was particularly the case with the Managing Director, who felt that the priority was to meet customers' requirements rather than to involve other managers in decisions which had always been his responsibility. When an organisation is operating successfully, as GK appeared to be, it is difficult to argue that time should be spent improving what already, apparently, works well. Similarly, though teamworking had proved its usefulness in facilitating major decisions and changes, it was more difficult for managers, especially the Managing Director, to appreciate its effectiveness on a day-to-day basis.

Therefore, though major organisational changes had taken place at GK, changes in managerial behaviour were not sustained. By 1993, it was apparent that the pace of improvement was slowing down under the pressure of work. This situation continued until the beginning of 1994 when, once again, the company recognised that it faced serious problems.

Phase Three: changing attitudes and behaviour

Accelerating the pace of change

Unlike many companies, GK's business continued to grow throughout the early 1990s. Though its existing customers were being hit by the recession, it was winning new business which more than compensated for this. Nevertheless, in 1993 GK started to become aware that its customers, old and new, were becoming increasingly demanding with regard to price and delivery. In addition, there were signs that its competitors were beginning to win back some of the work they had lost to GK.

By the beginning of 1994 it was clear that GK was losing a significant amount of business. This was partly due to increased competition, but mainly it was because its customers, in seeking to cut their own costs, were reducing the size and frequency of their orders (though when orders were placed, they were often required far faster than previously). This presented a double threat to GK. First, the fall in overall volumes was having an adverse effect on turnover and profit. Second, the reduction in size of individual print runs was having an adverse effect on costs because, though the actual volume was smaller, the design, order processing and set-up costs remained constant. In effect, as volumes decreased, the cost of each printed item increased. In addition, there were worrying signs that some customers were using wordprocessing packages and colour printers to produce their own publicity material instead of going to a printer.

At a time when its customers were facing severe pressure to cut their costs, GK was faced with the dilemma of whether to increase its prices to offset rising costs (and risk customers going elsewhere or developing their own facilities), or to maintain or reduce prices and see its profits plunge. This was not a situation unique to GK; practically every company in the UK was experiencing a similar dilemma. However, this knowledge did not make it any less painful or any easier to resolve.

The knee-jerk reaction of many in the company was, 'If customers want smaller runs, the price goes up.' However, the Managing Director and the other managers in GK came reluctantly to accept that, while the logic was impeccable, the result could be disastrous. After much seemingly futile discussion, it was the Marketing and Design Manager who eventually came up with a suggestion which, though laughed at initially, later turned out to be the key to GK's survival. He pointed out that to maintain its existing volume of business, and perhaps even increase it, GK needed to improve on its already good level of service. In particular, it needed to cut costs in order to cut prices and improve the efficiency of its internal operations to cut delivery times. The initial reaction to these suggestions was, perhaps predictably, very negative. After all, if volumes decrease, unit costs must increase because set-up costs are constant; furthermore, an increase in the number of smaller print runs actually extends turnaround times for a similar reason – more set ups are required. The Marketing and Design Manager was attempting to turn the conventional wisdom regarding printing on its head. In addition, in some people's eyes, he was still a newcomer to GK and consequently was believed to lack an in-depth knowledge of the printing industry. Finally, GK had made significant strides in improving efficiency and cutting costs, and there was some doubt as to the scope for any real improvements in these areas.

A false start

Despite the initial adverse comments, the Managing Director began to wonder if it might be possible to reduce set-up times and costs. If it could, he reasoned, the company would be able to attract more business, prevent customers seeking in-house solutions, and undermine its competitors. He considered asking for outside assistance again, but instead asked the Marketing and Design Manager to put forward some suggestions for reducing costs and set-up times. This was for two reasons.

First, he wanted to give him a chance to prove himself to the rest of the team who, to an extent, thought he still had to learn the ropes. Second, the Managing Director wanted to demonstrate that they now had the managerial talent to dispense with outside assistance.

The Marketing and Design Manager quickly responded and within a fortnight presented his proposals to the Managing Director and other senior staff. He began by identifying what he saw as the main problems the company faced:

1 Though there had been a slight decline in the number of individual orders, the actual reduction in the volume of business was much greater because customers were ordering shorter print runs.

2 The result of this was that, while office staff, marketing, design, administration, etc., were as busy as ever, the print shop was short of work, and it was not unusual to see printers sitting reading the paper with nothing else to do.

3 Though the printers were underworked, however, this did not provide much scope for reducing delivery times, because most of GK's lead time was accounted for by non-printing activities – especially design, which could take anything up to two weeks.

Having laid out what he saw as the problem, the Marketing and Design Manager went on to offer a solution. He argued that the key to solving the company's problems lay in speeding up design time. He pointed out that there was always a backlog of design work ranging from one to two weeks. Given that everything, even repeat orders, went through design, total lead time could be anything from three to five weeks. While this was considerably better than in the 1980s, it was no longer acceptable as customers were cutting stock to a minimum. Many customers were asking to have their printing back within seven days, sometimes even sooner where promotional material was concerned. The solution, therefore, he argued, was to have more design staff. If one extra designer was employed and another design workstation purchased, the Marketing and Design Manager believed that design lead time could be reduced to two or three days.

The Managing Director and other managers, especially the Printing Manager, who had been arguing unsuccessfully for new equipment for some time, were taken aback by this proposal. The analysis, they believed, was correct but the solution, they felt, was an outrageous piece of opportunism. The case for more design staff had been raised and rejected in the recent past. The Marketing and Design Manager colleagues felt that he was blatantly using the company's current problems to empire-build. Not surprisingly, he vigorously denied this. Nevertheless, the meeting ended acrimoniously and no decision was taken.

The Managing Director was particularly infuriated, as he had genuinely been expecting an acceptable solution to emerge from the meeting. Instead, the friendly working atmosphere he valued, and which he felt he did much to promote, had been shattered. Nor did he see an easy way to bring his managers back together to seek a co-operative solution. He was also annoyed because he realised that he had made a mistake in asking only one person to put forward a view. Not only would a team have avoided favouring one area rather than another; it would not have even occured to anyone to make the accusation. However, having made the mistake, he was not sure how to remedy it. If a team were to be set up to examine the options that did not include the Marketing and Design Manager, he would rightly see it as a snub and probably attack any solution that was put forward. If he were to be included, it was likely that he would continue to push his proposal and the other managers would react badly. His inclination was to impose a solution and tell everyone to get on and implement it. Unfortunately, he did not have a solution to impose.

Towards a new way of working

After several weeks of indecision, during which tensions within the management team continued to rise, the Managing Director decided once again to seek outside assistance. He approached GK's contact at the local polytechnic and, at length and with some passion, explained the situation. However, rather than proffering help, as expected, the lecturer stated that the situation was outside his area of expertise. He explained that there seemed little point in offering a 'technically appropriate' solution, because relations were so bad in the company that, whatever it was, it would be met by hostility from some quarters. He pointed out that the success of earlier interventions was due to achieving unanimity about both the problem and solution; at present, this was unlikely. However, he did refer the Managing Director to a colleague at the polytechnic who was skilled in team-building. Though the Managing Director was sceptical, the lecturer pointed out that, working together, there was enough experience in GK to solve its current dilemma. Therefore, the issue was how to bring people together, rather than seeking outside solutions.

The Managing Director met with the team-builder, who impressed him not only with his general demeanour of professionalism but also with the impressive array of organisations he had worked with. The team-builder said that the process he used was straightforward.

1 All the relevant managers had to be involved.

2 He would meet each of them individually and then, as a group, would take them away from the company for two days to work on the problem.

3 Each member of the team would have to agree to operate in an open and constructive fashion during the two days. This meant not only responding positively to each other's ideas, but also being honest.

4 The team would agree to reach a commonly agreed solution by the end of the two days.

It was on this basis that the team-building exercise went ahead. Though the GK management later admitted that the first day had been decidedly uncomfortable, they also agreed that the two days had been a success. The proceedings began with the team-builder reporting on his findings from the individual interviews. Though he did not reveal who said what, in a small organisation such as GK, it was relatively easy for managers to make a good guess as to the source of particular comments. This was one of the reasons why they found the first day uncomfortable.

The team-builder's report was split into positive and negative findings. On the positive side, there was a strong commitment to making the company a success, and common agreement regarding priorities for change (primarily, cost reduction and increasing responsiveness to customers). On the negative side, there was considerable tension between the managers, especially the Printing Manager and the Marketing and Design Manager. Underlying this, however, was the style of the Managing Director.

Though on a number of occasions the Managing Director had used teams to make crucial decisions and had been prepared to consult widely, this was not his normal mode of operation. He tended to make decisions either by himself or in consultation with one other manager. He justified this on the grounds that most decisions were not related to overall policy but to particular areas of the business. If new printing equipment was to be purchased, then this concerned him and the Printing Manager. If the issue was customers, then the Marketing and Design Manager would be involved. Decisions concerning finance were, the Managing Director felt, mainly his responsibility. The counter-argument to this, identified and articulated by the team-builder, was that it inevitably created suspicion among managers excluded from decisions, and led to accusations of favouritism. All the managers, other than the Managing Director, favoured a more open and collective style of management.

The Managing Director was very upset and said so. He believed he had always acted to promote teamwork and good relations in the company. To be accused of the reverse came as a shock. He wanted, he said, to 'clear the air' there and then. The team-builder suggested, however, and agreement was eventually reached, that they should all reflect on what had been said, and return to the issue at the end of the second day. They then moved on to discuss the immediate problems facing GK: how to reverse the decline in turnover and profitability. With the delicate matter of the Managing Director's approach to decision-making out in the open but put to one side, everyone seemed happy to focus on these problems. For the rest of Day 1 and most of Day 2, they alternated between working in two groups and working as one team. The result was that they reached an agreement on the way forward which they all accepted.

The main areas of action were very straightforward:

1 GK should meet with its main customers to identify what their needs were and discuss how these could best be met. It was felt that not all of a customer's requirements were urgent, and that what was necessary was to identify those that were and agree that they would be dealt with in a speedy fashion.

2 The company's CBS – computerised business system – was much more

efficient than the previous manual system, but all orders, large or small, urgent and non-urgent, were dealt with in the same manner and at the same speed. The same applied to design: though the actual design time varied between orders, they were all scheduled and dealt with in the same fashion. This meant that they all tended to take between one and two weeks, depending on the design office's workload. It was also a similar story when it came to printing and dispatch: everything was in the same queue. It was agreed that the entire process from order intake to dispatch be examined, with the intention of either reducing it for all orders, or possibly shortening it for specific categories of orders.

These actions were to be carried out by two groups comprising managers and employees from the areas involved, who would report directly to the management team.

This then left the thorny issue of the Managing Director's role. Since the issue had been raised on the first day, he had spoken to the team-builder and his colleagues informally, and had come to recognise the strength of feeling on the issue, though he did not fully accept their interpretation of his actions. Nevertheless, he was prepared to amend his management style. He agreed that there would be regular management team meetings which would deal with all major decisions. He also agreed that he would not seek to impose a decision on the team unless the managers themselves could not reach agreement.

Six months later

The investigation of customer requirements and the order-to-dispatch process resulted in changes which brought significant improvements in the service GK could offer to its customers, and a reduction in lead times and costs.

The company now offers its customers a choice of lead times and prices: normal – a two-week delivery and a 5 per cent reduction on the standard prices; accelerated – a one-week delivery charged at standard prices; and urgent – a one working day delivery charged at 10 per cent above standard prices.

GK was able to achieve these improvements owing to three factors:

1 *Understanding what its customers wanted and were prepared to pay for.* In speaking to customers, GK also identified what its competitors were offering in terms of prices and deliveries.

2 *Eliminating time wastage and reducing lead times.* In examining the order-to-dispatch process, GK came to appreciate that there was a large amount of wasted time involved which could be eliminated with better co-operation between functions, especially design and printing, and a greater awareness of the need to reduce lead times. In examining the entire process in detail and involving everyone in this, some very glaring examples of wasted time emerged. For convenience, incoming orders were processed in batches. As a

result an order could sit for two days just waiting to be entered on the system. Similar delays were identified in dispatch, with completed orders sitting for one or two days waiting either for collection or for GK to make a delivery in that part of the city where the customer was located. As the dispatch clerk commented, 'No one told me it was a problem.' Once staff realised it *was* a problem, there was almost a competition to see who could come up with the best suggestion.

Most of this did not require additional expenditure, merely better communication and a willingness to help each other. Reducing set-up time on the printing presses did require some modest expenditure, but this led to reductions in set-up times of between 50 and 80 per cent. Some small expenditure was also required to modify the computer system to cope with the new three-tier delivery price system.

3 *Increasing the capacity of the design department.* The design office made a number of changes to the way it operated which speeded up its activities. Nevertheless, it was recognised that there was also a capacity shortage: it simply had more work than it could cope with. Much of the work was simple and did not need a fully-qualified designer and only about 50 per cent of a designer's time was actually spent on the computer. Therefore, it was decided to employ someone else to perform the more simple design tasks.

At first, GK was going to recruit a new member of staff for this post, but the printers, who had always wanted to be involved in design, suggested that they might do this. When the suggestion was discussed, a number of possibilities opened up, including that simple but urgent jobs be given straight to a printer who would undertake the entire design and printing process at one go. The actual mechanics of this were difficult to work out, and many practical obstacles were apparent, but GK nonetheless decided to undertake a trial with one printer in order to identify the difficulties and evaluate the benefits.

In addition to these changes, the management team, after some initial difficulties (such as identifying what constituted a major decision), found that working together and having all information out in the open reduced the tension, not only between individual managers but between the individual functions as well.

The outcome

After the first two phases of changes at GK, the company felt it could rightly take pride in how it had responded to the situation in which it had found itself. Rather than falling into a spiral of decline, as seemed possible, it reinvigorated itself. It introduced new equipment and, initially at least, developed a new sense of co-operation. However, its own success began to eat away at some of its gains. The pressures of day-to-day business began to take precedence over both improvement activities and co-operation. In particular, the Managing Director went back to taking decisions either without consulting anyone else or only in consultation with the 'appropriate' manager. In effect, though the company had maintained the operational changes, it had failed to maintain behaviourial changes, especially those associated with teamwork, co-operation and delegation. Therefore, the first two phases of the company's turnaround can be characterised by successful operational changes but less successful behaviourial changes.

The result of the failure to sustain behaviourial changes was that:

- *GK failed to adopt a continuous improvement approach.*

- *Poor co-ordination and co-operation led to inefficiencies in the processing and dispatch of work.*

- *Most importantly, an undercurrent of discontent and fighting for position arose among managers, which made it difficult to reach agreement about how the organisation should respond to its changed circumstances.*

For these reasons, the key action in the third phase of the transformation of GK was not any of the operational changes, but the changes in attitudes among managers and other staff regarding co-operation, and in particular, the Managing Director's belated conversion to team-based decision-making.

It was the new element of co-operation which allowed GK successfully to identify what to change and how to change it.

CONCLUSIONS

In Part Two, it was argued that while approaches to strategy and change needed to be matched to the constraints under which an organisation operated, these constraints were themselves amenable to change and in any case could conflict with each other. This means that the freedom of action or manoeuvre of managers is potentially very significant. In the three case studies we have examined in this chapter, we can see managerial choice in action.

In the Volvo study, we can see that managers made a determined and apparently successful attempt to break away from the industry standard approach to car assembly. However, in challenging and changing a powerful constraint on their freedom of manoeuvre, they were very much in tune with societal, environmental and, at least in some instances, their own orientations. Furthermore, there were parallel changes in the structure of the organisation towards decentralisation and flexibility, which supported and made more appropriate the emergent and open-ended approach to strategy used by Volvo.

The Rover study is another case where managers sought to break out of the constraints on their freedom of action. Recognising that they could no longer operate on a 'them and us' basis, Rover managers set about building a new relationship with its workforce. In order to turn them from the threat they were perceived to be in the early 1980s, to become the organisation's main competitive edge in the 1990s, managers initiated a programme of learning and development for staff. Given the traditional nature of its internal relationships, this constituted a major attempt to restructure the organisational constraints managers faced. Such a change, however, is clearly in line with the operation of leading car companies such as Honda, Nissan and Toyota. It is also in line with the changing and competitive nature of the environment in which the motor industry operates.

Therefore, to an extent, Rover, as with Volvo, could be seen as making an attempt to harmonise the constraints it faced. In Volvo's case, it attempted to bring internal arrangements into line with societal and environmental constraints (though in so doing they strongly contradicted industry constraints). In Rover's case, changes in internal constraints clearly assisted in bringing Rover into line with industry and environmental constraints (though not perhaps societal). In both cases, the approach to strategy adopted was emergent and open-ended. The same point can be made with regard to change. Though a role for planned change can be seen, in both Rover and Volvo the implementation of strategy also had elements of experimentation and open-endedness. In Volvo's case, each successive attempt at Job Design built on and developed past projects, but also tended itself to change and develop. Rover's experience was that, in trying to transform itself into a learning organisation, individual initiatives tended to evolve and take on a life of their own.

The case of GK Printers is somewhat different. It is much more difficult to perceive any distinct societal or industry constraints on the organisation. However, both environmental and organisational constraints were clearly apparent, and the changes which took place were to a greater or lesser extent aimed at both changing and harmonising these constraints. One reason for the internal changes in the company was to tie customers more closely to the company, and thus reduce the uncertainty present in the environment. As with Volvo and Rover, GK's strategy emerged rather than being preplanned, but it also seems to have been much more stop–go than either of the other companies. Furthermore, its approach to change appears to be more in line with the planned approach than the emergent.

Therefore, as far as managerial choice and strategy development and change management are concerned, the case studies provide some interesting and thought-provoking insights:

- *Managerial freedom is clearly constrained but this does not mean that managers cannot break out of or change these constraints. In so doing, however, the tendency appears to be to resolve or reduce conflict between constraints rather than necessarily to rewrite the managerial rule book completely.*

- *The process of strategy development and change management in these cases was mainly emergent and open-ended, though some instances of planned change were also evident. However, managerial conflict and politics also played a part in decision-making and, in the case of Rover, managerial changes preceded attempts to achieve organisational changes.*

- *Planned change as such appears to be less effective than emergent change in these instances, though a role for it can be seen in each of the companies. Some aspects of planned change are applicable, especially those relating to problem definition and implementation planning. However, where the two approaches diverge is that planned change programmes tend to have a finite duration and are an end in themselves. Emergent change, on the other hand, is not only open-ended, but the process of change can itself be seen to be a process of learning as well.*

Discussion points

1 To what extent can the process of change in each of the three companies be characterised as planned, emergent or a combination of both?

2 What were the key factors in each company which contributed (either positively or negatively) to the degree of success achieved by its change programmes?

3 Do the studies show evidence that involvement of those affected by change in its planning and execution is necessary for successful change?

4 How useful is the concept of organisational learning to the understanding of developments in each of the three case studies?

5 In terms of the short- and long-term fortunes of Volvo, Rover and GK Printers, which were more important: changes in attitudes and behaviour or changes in structure and technologies?

6 What evidence exists from any of the three companies to show that the various changes which took place were the result of strategy (either emergent or intent) as opposed to accidental or *ad hoc* reactions to particular occurrences?

7 To what degree can the managers in each case study be seen to be working within, as opposed to attempting to change, the constraints they faced?

8 To what extent and in what manner do any of the case studies give support to the notion of organisations as rational entities?

Chapter 9

Case studies in changing external relationships

Introduction

The previous two chapters have presented examples of strategies and initiatives which have resulted in new internal relationships within organisations through structural, operational and behavioural change. Over the past decade, however, more and more, companies have also sought to change their external relationships, by developing closer and more harmonious links with their suppliers and customers. As the case studies in this chapter will show, this is usually preceded or accompanied by internal changes within suppliers and/or customers as well. These changes are taking place due to a growing climate of opinion that customers and suppliers working co-operatively must be more beneficial than the more traditional adversarial purchasing relationships (Hines, 1994; Lamming, 1993). Though this move has been led by the automotive and electronics industries, the concept has spread into many other sectors as well (Partnership Sourcing Ltd, 1991).

There is little doubt that customer–supplier partnerships are becoming seen as the most beneficial and effective method of organising the purchase of goods and services (Burnes and Whittle, 1995; Morris and Imrie, 1992). A recent survey in the UK conducted by the University of Manchester Institute of Science and Technology and the management consultants AT Kearney Ltd found that over 90 per cent of respondents thought such an approach was relevant to them, and over 60 per cent were using or implementing partnership schemes with their suppliers and/or customers (AT Kearney Ltd, 1994). These results are broadly comparable with a survey in the same period by Partnership Sourcing Ltd (Tett, 1994). Nevertheless, as the UMIST–AT Kearney survey also showed, the benefits of this approach to purchasing are often difficult to quantify.

The partnership approach to customer–supplier relationships originated in Japan, and is especially prevalent in the Japanese motor and electronics industries (Bhote, 1989; Lloyd *et al*, 1994; Ishikawa, 1985). In attempting to understand the factors which underpinned the competitiveness of Japanese companies, attention in the West was first directed at their internal arrangements; but it quickly became apparent that this told only half of the story. Typically, bought-in parts and services account for over 70 per cent of the cost of a finished product. Therefore, it became apparent that to understand the advantages that Japanese companies had over their Western counterparts, in terms of costs, quality, time to market, etc., it was necessary to understand the unique relationship they had with their suppliers (Francks, 1992; Womack *et al*, 1990).

A number of European companies, notably Phillips with its Co-Makership initiative, tried to emulate the Japanese. However, it was only with the arrival of Japanese transplants, especially the building of the Nissan car plant in the mid-1980s, that interest in customer–supplier partnerships really took off in the UK, with the rest of Europe some way behind (Burnes and Whittle, 1995; NEDC, 1991 a and b; Lloyd *et al*, 1994).

Though there is no universally-agreed definition of customer–supplier partnerships, Partnership Sourcing Ltd (1991:2), the UK body established by government and industry to promote the concept, appear to have captured its essence by defining it as a situation:

> ... where customer and suppliers develop such a close and long-term relationship that the two work together as partners. It isn't philanthropy: the aim is to secure the best possible commercial advantage. The principle is that teamwork is better than combat. If the end-customer is to be best served, then the parties to a deal must work together – and both must win. Partnership sourcing works because both parties have an interest in each other's success. (*Partnership Sourcing Ltd, 1991:2*)

The move to more co-operative and stable relationships between customers and suppliers is not merely a case of adjustments at the organisational interface. Rather, to be successful, it requires more fundamental changes in both customers and suppliers. The three case studies in this chapter show how such partnerships work in practice and, in particular, illustrate how the concept leads not only to changes between organisations but also to attitudinal, behavioural and structural changes within them.

Each of the three studies relates to a different aspect of the partnership process. Case Study 8 deals with Vickers Defence Systems' attempt to promote closer relations with its suppliers. It describes why and how it developed these new working arrangements. The study shows that although Vickers was already moving to establish new relationships with its suppliers, the need for Vickers and its suppliers to work as a team to win a crucial government contract accelerated the process. Case Study 9 concerns one of the leading advocates of customer–supplier partnerships, the UK plant of the car company Nissan. It focuses upon Nissan's Supplier Development Team (SDT), which is one of its prime mechanisms for cementing partnerships and assisting suppliers to improve their performance. The study describes the purpose and operation of the SDT, and shows how Nissan has moved beyond exhortation to become directly involved in the process of change within its suppliers. Case Study 10 shows that the move to develop new relationships is not just driven by customers. In this instance a supplier, Speedy Stationers, took the first step. It recognised that, in its case, the partnership approach was not just a means of providing a better service to its customers; it could also be an effective mechanism for securing increased business. The case study recounts how Speedy Stationers came to this conclusion, the steps it took to convince one of its customers to enter into a partnership and to co-operate, and the resulting changes and benefits.

The chapter concludes by arguing that though much attention has been given to the creation of new internal relationships and structures as a mechanism for coping with environmental turbulence and uncertainty, changes in external relationships can also play an important role in this process. Therefore, partnerships can help organisations to restore, to an extent, a degree of stability and predictability to their lives.

The conclusion also points out that it is very difficult for organisations to quantify in advance the benefits of developing partnerships: Nissan, for example, believed it would have to wait some ten years before it began to see real benefits from its partnership activities. Therefore, the move to new customer–supplier relations is not driven by rational and quantitative decision-making. Rather, the move to partnership requires an act of faith based on an instinctive and philosophical belief that the old methods do not work and that 'the game requires new rules', rules which cannot be written in advance but emerge as the game unfolds.

Case study 8

VICKERS DEFENCE SYSTEMS – BUILDING A DEDICATED SUPPLIER BASE

Background

Vickers Defence Systems is part of the Defence and Aerospace Division of Vickers plc, a diverse UK-based engineering group with sales of around £800 million in 1990 and employing around 12,500 employees. The company is a world leader in the design and manufacture of armoured fighting vehicles, and manufactures the British Army's main battle tank, Challenger 2, as well as a wide range of other military vehicles. Vickers employs approximately 1,700 people at the Armstrong works in Newcastle-upon-Tyne and the Barnbow works in Leeds. The Leeds plant was owned by the UK government until 1986, when it decided to sell its tank-building activities to Vickers Defence Systems, thus making Vickers the UK's only manufacturer of battle tanks. Initially, both sites continued to manufacture tanks but, since the late 1980s, tank manufacture has been concentrated at the Leeds plant, while the Newcastle plant has specialised in the provision of armoured support vehicles. This was done in order to increase competitiveness. Vickers recognised that as the sole British tank builder, it would more than likely have to win future orders from the UK government in the face of stiff foreign competition.

Modern fighting vehicles, especially the Challenger 2, are sophisticated and highly complex weapons which have more in common with fighter aircraft than the tanks of World War One and World War Two. For this reason, the company now regards itself as a systems designer and integrator. As one senior manager put it: 'Twenty years ago we built tanks, now we integrate systems on to platforms.' Some three-quarters of the order value of Challenger 2 consists of bought-in materials and supplies. Vickers Defence Systems is, therefore, increasingly reliant upon the technological expertise of its suppliers, particularly those providing highly complex 'black box' systems, such as weapons control computers. In terms of manufacture, Vickers concentrates upon fabricating the hull and turret superstructures, internal and external metal work and final assembly. It follows that, though it can increase the efficiency of its own internal operations, one of the main ways Vickers can increase its competitiveness is through the improved performance of its suppliers.

Vickers Defence Systems operates in an unusual competitive environment. Vickers sells exclusively to governments, and its main, most reliable and sole UK customer has been the Ministry of Defence. In seeking to purchase a replacement for the Vickers-supplied Challenger 1 battle tank, however, the MoD, faced with only one UK supplier, began seriously to consider purchasing from one of Vickers' main foreign competitors – General Dynamics in the USA, Krauss Maffei in Germany or GIAT in France. Indeed, at one point, it looked as though the British army had made its mind up to purchase its next generation of battle tanks from the USA. In order to respond to this threat, which could have led to the closure of the Leeds plant, Vickers began to accelerate its programme of establishing longer-term and closer links with its suppliers. This was not just to enable it to become more competitive, but also to help it mount a public campaign to win the Challenger 2 order.

The Vickers supply chain

The Leeds plant's supply chain is dedicated to producing one product – the Challenger 2 battle tank. It relies on around 30 major suppliers for Challenger 2 and a larger number of smaller suppliers. Many of the major suppliers are responsible for critical systems on the tank, such as the engine, the gun and the sighting and firing systems. Taken together, these major UK suppliers account for around 60 per cent of the value of the Challenger 2 order, with smaller suppliers accounting for an additional 15 per cent.

Generally speaking, none of the suppliers are dependent upon Challenger 2 work for their survival, though the order as originally conceived (it was subsequently scaled down) represented approximately 10 per cent of turnover for the major UK suppliers (the effect on the turnover of minor suppliers was projected to be much smaller). The importance of the Challenger 2 order for many suppliers lay not in the direct order itself, but in the reputation-enhancing effect of being involved in such a technologically advanced high-profile project which might then help the suppliers to win orders from other customers. Despite the apparent mutual benefits to be gained from working together, the tendency in the past was for Vickers and its suppliers to operate on a confrontational rather than collaborative basis.

The overall philosophy at Vickers is exemplified by the motto 'keep it simple'. However, though this philosophy had led to the Leeds plant being housed in a new purpose-built factory which allowed its manufacturing operations to be streamlined, it had influenced purchasing much less. At the beginning of the 1990s, the Leeds plant was still heavily influenced by its public sector past, especially the requirement for price-based competitive tendering. The majority of its purchasing staff were still ex-public servants, who had spent their working lives operating under the mutually reinforcing assumptions that (a) competitive tendering was the only way to ensure value for money, and that (b) suppliers would take any and every opportunity to increase prices unless specifically prevented from doing so by a legally-binding purchase contract. Therefore, not only did the Leeds plant have an antagonistic approach towards its suppliers, but it also saw customer–supplier relations as something of a game in which if the suppliers 'won', then Vickers must by definition 'lose'.

The relationship between Vickers and its suppliers was and is also complicated by the peculiarities of the UK defence industry. It is generally accepted that the first bid for a government contract will never be successful and that, in attempting to whittle down the price, the Ministry of Defence may well require four or five rounds of bidding before a contract is finally awarded. This process usually also involves changes to the original technical specification and order quantities, which in turn can have an impact on price.

This approach to purchasing does not necessarily mean that the UK government pays less than it might otherwise have done. Rather, the tendency has been for companies to build a sufficient margin into their initial bid price in order to give them the flexibility to reduce it later. This clearly also has implications for suppliers. If the main contractors cut their prices in successive rounds of bidding, they expect their suppliers to do likewise. Consequently, like the main contractors, suppliers have also tended to build a margin of price flexibility into their initial quotations. In the past, this has made it very difficult for any of the parties involved to get a realistic cost for supplying defence equipment before the first round of bids has actually begun. It has also meant that the entire supply chain tends to be dominated by secrecy and gamesmanship.

Changing customer–supplier relations at Vickers

In the late 1980s, Vickers began to move away from its antagonistic mode of purchasing and to develop a new relationship with its suppliers. Vickers said it wanted to move towards a relationship which would be half way between the old relationship that existed in the defence industry and the partnership relations which exist in the car industry.

Apparently, the original idea for this approach came from the Aerospace industry which, like tank builders, needs to continue to offer major product support for many years after a sale takes place. Vickers, therefore, decided to reduce its supplier base, identify preferred suppliers and establish long-term supply agreements which would guarantee work to the supplier for up to ten years after a tank was delivered. With this objective in mind, the company sought to build a new approach to supplier management, though it did not define or attempt to publicise a new purchasing style and philosophy as such.

This was a major departure from past practice between Vickers and its suppliers. Previously, when the company received orders for battle tanks, it would initially place only half of the order with its suppliers. When the first half of the order was completed, it would then invite tenders for the supply of components for the second half of the order. This put the original suppliers in a very difficult position. They had put a lot of time and effort into developing the components for the tanks but, owing to contractual obligations, they had to turn over their designs and knowledge to Vickers, who would make the information available to all potential suppliers. Capitalising on the hard work of the original suppliers, it was not unusual for a different supplier to win the contract to supply the second half of the order. Not surprisingly, this caused considerable resentment among suppliers, and not just those who were unsuccessful. It also involved Vickers in the additional cost of re-tendering, and made suppliers reluctant to work with Vickers to reduce costs and improve product quality.

It might be assumed that the new approach would, therefore, be welcomed by suppliers. However, Vickers experienced some problems with bigger suppliers who were suspicious of the initiative and reluctant to change their ways. There was also a degree of scepticism within Vickers regarding the move to partnerships.

Nevertheless, Vickers did begin to reduce its supplier base and start identifying preferred suppliers. This was followed by an attempt to draft a new-style purchase agreement acceptable to suppliers. The intention was to be able to designate suppliers without a bidding process, and to conclude single-source long-term agreements with key suppliers which would give them a longer planning horizon and result in earlier and closer collaboration. The new purchase agreement also aimed to set a pricing structure which would encourage suppliers to initiate continuous improvement, with the benefits of such improvements shared on a 50:50 basis between themselves and Vickers.

One of the first steps Vickers took in developing its new approach to suppliers was to circulate the draft purchase agreement to its 70 most important suppliers. Though the response was slow, there were surprisingly few objections to the form of the contract and only minor queries regarding its actual wording. In the main, although they might have had suspicions regarding Vickers' motives, suppliers did seem to feel that putting their relationship with Vickers on a more stable footing was to be welcomed – provided they were one of the preferred suppliers.

The development of the new approach to purchasing progressed very slowly. However, this situation began to change quite rapidly when Vickers realised that the British army might not choose Challenger 2 as its next generation of battle tanks. In the past, the British army had always purchased its main battle tanks from a UK producer. Now that there was only one UK supplier, however, the Ministry of Defence's competitive tendering procedures, allied to European Union regulations regarding public sector purchasing, meant that it had to seek bids from outside the UK.

This galvanised Vickers' efforts to establish closer relations with its suppliers for two reasons:

● *The other main foreign bidders, especially the German and American companies, did not operate in the same fashion or on the same assumptions as UK defence contractors. Instead, they put in a competitive price for the tank contract at the beginning. In addition, because they worked closely with their suppliers, they started out with an accurate cost forecast for supplying the order.*

● *Vickers' Challenger 2 tank was still in the development stage, whereas its main competitor, an American company, already had a fully developed product which had proved itself in combat. Mainly for this reason, the British army appeared to favour the American tank. In order to counter this argument, Vickers needed to show that, in partnership with its suppliers, it had the capability rapidly to develop a tank that would outperform anything on offer from its competitors.*

If the British army had opted to purchase from abroad, the Challenger 2 project would have died, because foreign governments would be unlikely to purchase a tank from Vickers which had been rejected by the British government. This would probably have had the effect of ending Vickers', and thus the UK's, involvement in tank production, with considerable implications in terms of jobs and defence industry capabilities.

For these reasons, the decision regarding which tank to purchase became as much a political as a technical/cost decision. In a response to the threat of losing the order, Vickers recognised that it would need to mount a campaign on two fronts. First, it would have to convince the British army and the Ministry of Defence that Challenger 2 was both technically and economically better than the opposition. Second, it needed to gain public support for its case and in particular win over key politicians to lobby on its behalf. On both counts, it needed to work with and enlist the support of its suppliers in a way that it never had in the past. This meant developing a new relationship, one based on mutual support and co-operation.

New ways of working with suppliers

The need for Vickers and its suppliers to work together to win the Challenger 2 order forged a new sense of purpose and a trust between them. After a great deal of public and political concern and pressure, as well as considerable hard work in convincing the British army that the tank was a viable option, Vickers was awarded the contract in June 1991. The fact that it was successful in winning the order only added to this new sense of joint commitment between the company and its suppliers. The experience of competing for and winning the Challenger 2 order, and the team spirit it generated between Vickers and its suppliers, played a key role in winning over those (within both suppliers and Vickers) who doubted the wisdom of closer working relations. The way they all worked together, in the opinion of Vickers and its suppliers, played a crucial role in winning the order. While the battle to win the order had accelerated the development of a close working relationship between Vickers and its suppliers, however, it had slowed down the development of the mechanisms which Vickers saw as central to supporting its new approach to suppliers.

In particular, the Challenger 2 campaign delayed the development of the new purchase agreement. This was because both Vickers and its suppliers recognised that, until the order was won, there was little point in sorting out the fine detail of a contract which might never be put into operation. Nevertheless, Vickers did continue to examine the responses it received and began to discuss with individual suppliers how the new purchase agreement could be customised to meet their specific needs and concerns. The result was that, when the Challenger 2 order was awarded, Vickers was in a position to issue the new purchase agreement to suppliers which covered not only the contract for Challenger 2, but also future tank contracts.

The new agreement made the relationship between Vickers and its key suppliers transparent to both sides, with the intention of removing suspicion and generating trust. The company also held a number of supplier conferences, which helped to forge links between suppliers and which eventually led to the formation of a 'suppliers' club'. In order to show Vickers' full commitment, the Chief Executive of Vickers played a major role in these events. Vickers is now working much more closely with suppliers at all levels, including providing assistance to help them resolve internal production problems. In addition, suppliers are talking to and helping each other with their problems – something which would have been considered unthinkable in the past.

The new single-sourcing, long-term contract agreement which Vickers has now established with many of its suppliers is producing benefits. The company is finding that suppliers are informing them much earlier when problems arise, which means that Vickers can not only accommodate any disruptions better, but can also offer assistance to prevent disruption. In the past, there was a positive disincentive for suppliers to tell Vickers at an early stage of actual or potential problems, as Vickers might then seek another supplier for that particular component.

Selecting suppliers earlier has also allowed Vickers to start the design process at a much earlier stage and, thus, reduce design lead times. The intention is for suppliers to take more and more of the responsibility for designing as well as supplying components. The tendency in the past was for Vickers to do as much of the design work as it could: suppliers were expected to manufacture to a drawing supplied by Vickers. Now, for some components, the company supplies a specification rather than a drawing. In other cases, joint design takes place. There is also an increasing tendency to purchase 'black box' products, such as gun controls, where Vickers has no design responsibility at all. At present, however, there are still a large number of components designed in-house, and suppliers are simply instructed to follow the drawing exactly, though this tends to apply more to simpler parts and components. In order to facilitate this new process, each supplier now has two main contact points with Vickers – a purchasing contact and an engineering contact.

One of the benefits the company hoped to gain from its new approach to purchasing was a commitment by suppliers to continuous cost reduction. In the past, there was no incentive for suppliers to work to reduce costs once they had won the first half of an order, because the benefits of this could be passed on to a competitor who might then win the second half of the order from them. Now Vickers have developed an approach where suppliers feel secure that they will continue to supply that component, and are therefore prepared to work with Vickers to reduce costs and split the benefits that accrue from this.

Built into the new contract is a method for establishing future price increases. This method is called variation of price (VOP), and uses standard reference sources for price increases which allow suppliers to increase prices in line with these. However, these only cover some 85 per cent of any price increase, and therefore there is a built-in incentive for suppliers to undertake cost reduction activities in order to cover the other 15 per cent.

One of the main fears expressed by purchasing staff was that suppliers would have no incentive to meet agreed performance targets for delivery, quality, costs, etc., once they had got the contract. In order to prevent this, Vickers established a system that encourages suppliers to inform them or seek help early if performance problems arise. There is a penalty system that specifies that the supplier incurs no penalty in the first month of any interruptions to supplies; however, penalties become progressively steeper after this. This acts as a strong incentive to identify and resolve problems at an early date. The objective of this, and Vickers' approach to supplier relations in general, is to make the ground rules absolutely clear, but also to work closely and co-operatively to resolve any problems. One example of this new co-operation is that Vickers made available the service of one of its staff to help a supplier overcome some problems it had with computer software. The company is also working closely with its suppliers to improve their quality standards, and hopes eventually to eliminate the need for the inspection of incoming components.

The need to develop closer ties with its suppliers on a number of fronts (i.e. purchasing, design, quality, production) has led to major internal changes within Vickers, especially within the purchasing function. It was decided to split the existing purchasing organisation into two separate sections. One section (containing 80 per cent of purchasing staff) would be responsible for day-to-day purchasing. The other section, comprising two groups – commercial and development – would be responsible for the negotiation of high-value contracts and the development of long-term supply agreements. In order to achieve a consistent approach to suppliers and prevent functions within Vickers pulling suppliers in different directions, the company has had to examine and overhaul its own internal communications and co-ordination systems. One result of these changes is that there is better understanding between functions, especially purchasing and design, with the latter, apparently, having become more commercially aware.

Vickers intends that the group of suppliers it has established for Challenger 2 will be its first choice for any future tank projects, though it also monitors changing customer requirements and alternative sources of supply to ensure that its existing suppliers' performance and capabilities continue to be appropriate. The company hopes that, by making clear to suppliers what performance levels and capabilities are required for the future, and by providing them with a degree of security through long-term contracts, they will be more inclined than in the past to invest in new technologies, to develop new capabilities and update existing ones, and to adopt a continuous improvement mentality which will allow themselves and Vickers to stay ahead of the competition.

The outcome

The relationship between Vickers and its suppliers has changed considerably since 1986, when it took over the Leeds plant. Though it was already moving in this direction, it was the need by Vickers and its suppliers to win the Challenger 2 order which appears to have been decisive in bringing about the change. However, despite the new atmosphere of co-operation this has created, the company is far from complacent. It recognises that the history of mistrust in the defence industry between suppliers and customers cannot be easily overcome, and that hard-won gains can be lost by a single ill-conceived action. This is why senior managers feel that they still have 'a battle to fight' internally and with suppliers before the company's new purchasing philosophy is fully accepted.

In understanding its changed relationship with suppliers, it is important to appreciate why Vickers decided to embark on this new approach and the difficulties it encountered.

● *In buying the Leeds plant from the government, Vickers became the sole UK tank builder. It recognised that the UK government's increasing emphasis on value for money, and European Union regulations regarding opening up public sector purchasing, made it likely that it would face strong foreign competition for domestic orders. In examining ways of improving its competitiveness, Vickers believed that it needed to develop a more co-operative relationship with its suppliers.*

● *Past defence industry procurement procedures had created an atmosphere of conflict rather than co-operation between customers and suppliers in the industry and the relationship between Vickers and its suppliers was no exception. However, the need to work together to win the Challenger 2 order helped to overcome much of the mistrust that existed between Vickers and its suppliers.*

Therefore, there were both short- and long-term reasons why Vickers should move to a more co-operative relationship with its suppliers. There were also considerable barriers to be overcome in doing so, however. The main barriers were, and to an extent still are, as follows:

● *There was a history of mistrust in the industry, whereby co-operation and flexibility were often rewarded by loss of further work, rather than the opposite.*

● *Purchasing and other staff at the Leeds plant had been trained over many years to follow Ministry of Defence purchasing procedures – i.e. to obtain multiple quotations, and award the order to the supplier offering the lowest price (though the formal need to follow these procedures ended when the plant was sold by the government in 1986). The idea that purchasing staff should work co-operatively with suppliers, and that contracts need not be awarded on the basis of competitive tender, appeared both radical and threatening to many at the Leeds plant.*

Nevertheless, there was one overriding reason for change: survival. If the Leeds plant had not won the order for Challenger 2, it would have gone out of business. Therefore, though the company was already moving towards closer ties with its suppliers, it was this threat to its survival which finally spurred it (and its suppliers) to move from antagonism to partnership. In doing so, the company and its suppliers were rewarded by winning the order for the British Army's new battle tank.

Case study 9

Nissan motor manufacturing (UK) ltd – the supplier development team approach

Background

When Nissan established its British operation in the mid-1980s, it recognised that European – especially UK – component suppliers fell far short of Japanese standards of quality, reliability and cost. Measuring suppliers' capabilities on a scale of 0 to 100, Nissan rated Japanese suppliers at 100, suppliers in mainland Europe were rated at 80 and UK suppliers were rated at 65–70. Nissan was required by the European Union to produce cars which contained, by value, 80 per cent local content. Therefore, it needed to improve the capabilities of its European suppliers, if it was to maintain the quality and cost standards achieved by its plants in Japan.

Though Ford had put considerable effort into improving the quality standards of suppliers in the UK and other European countries, Nissan believed that it also needed to offer direct assistance to suppliers if major improvements were to be achieved. As one means of helping suppliers to improve their capability, Nissan decided in 1987 to form a Supplier Development Team (SDT). The aim of the SDT was and is to help suppliers to develop their business to the stage where they can meet Nissan's present and future performance requirements. A similar function had been in operation for 15 years in Japan, and this was considered to be a suitable model for its UK operation.

Initially, two engineers were sent to Japan for a nine-week training course. This training included extensive practice in undertaking improvement activities within Nissan's Japanese suppliers. On their return, based on the techniques learnt in Japan, the engineers developed a 'ten-day improvement activity' for use with UK suppliers. Their aim was to establish an approach which, while achieving immediate productivity and quality improvements, would convince UK suppliers to adopt the Japanese approach to manufacturing. Consequently, though Nissan was concerned that the outcome of any improvement activity should be positive, its ultimate objective was for suppliers to recognise the value and benefits of adopting the Japanese approach, and to continue with it once the SDT had left.

The SDT approach was officially launched in the UK in November 1988, and involved a group of 12 medium-sized suppliers. From these small beginnings, the size of the SDT has grown, and it has become an established and important part of Nissan's operations. It has worked with a considerable number of Nissan's suppliers, and has established a reputation among them for its expertise and commitment. Though it originally concentrated on shopfloor improvement projects, which still form the core of its work, it also provides a broader range of assistance, such as cost reduction initiatives, joint product development, supervisory training and strategic planning programmes. In essence, it offers a consultancy service to Nissan's suppliers which is, normally, free of charge.

The role of the SDT, therefore, is to help suppliers develop and improve their overall capability and performance. It seeks to improve productivity, reduce costs and maintain quality-assured production among suppliers. Though the SDT is a dedicated and high-profile resource which is available to help suppliers, it is only one part of Nissan's overall commitment to developing its suppliers. Although other areas of Nissan also provide specialist assistance to suppliers, it is the SDT which is charged with assessing the overall requirements and capabilities of suppliers and, where possible, helping them to become capable of meeting Nissan's needs.

Though the assistance given by the team to suppliers is in effect free consultancy with no obvious or short-term benefit to Nissan, this is not totally philanthropic. Nissan tends to see supplier development as essentially a long-term process, with payback times of the order of ten years or more. However, it believes that, by assisting them to develop improved working practices and engendering a continuous improvement mentality, it will enable suppliers to achieve world-class performance standards. This in turn, Nissan believes, will help it to produce world-beating cars.

The SDT in action

The SDT approach is to work co-operatively with suppliers to help them identify areas for improvement, and then to assist them to develop and monitor improvement plans. In particular, the SDT will train supplier personnel in quality and production improvement methods, and support supplier initiatives to improve production and reduce defects. The idea of free consultancy by an organisation such as Nissan sounds attractive, but suppliers can also perceive such an offer as either 'big brotherish' or patronising. Nissan's relations with its suppliers were and are very positive; but, given the history of antagonism between customers and suppliers in the UK car industry – which still persists to some degree (Lamming, 1994) – it tends to tread warily and prepare the ground carefully before offering assistance.

Initial approach

Before undertaking the first improvement activity in a supplier, the SDT makes a presentation to the senior managers of the company concerned. This is because it regards senior management commitment and understanding as an essential pre-condition for success. Unless this commitment is gained, SDT cannot and does not proceed further. Though the SDT approach is now well established with and valued by suppliers, in the initial stages, some suppliers were sceptical and resistant to such an approach. Nevertheless, most suppliers respond more favourably to the initial presentation.

The SDT's standard presentation begins by describing what continuous improve-ment (*kaizen*) is and the benefits it brings. The SDT then outlines a typical improvement activity, including the various tools and techniques used. The team stresses that most improvement activities can be carried out at little or no cost, provided that the employees working in the area concerned are involved in planning and making the necessary changes.

If, after the presentation, senior managers are willing to proceed, the SDT briefs other staff and undertakes a factory assessment.

The factory assessment

The length of time devoted to a factory assessment varies, but typically it takes a day. Assessments are not compulsory, but most suppliers welcome an independent review of their operations, especially by a world-class company such as Nissan. The factory assessment does not form part of Nissan's formal supplier assessment procedure and, therefore, is less threatening than might otherwise be the case.

Factories are assessed under ten headings:

- *Company policy*
- *Quality performance and procedures*
- *Delivery control methods and performance*
- *Productivity*
- *Equipment maintenance procedures*
- *Stock control*
- *Production process development*
- *Housekeeping (how tidy and orderly the factory is)*
- *Health and safety*
- *Employee morale.*

Each heading is scored out of five and the scores recorded on a factory assessment summary sheet. The assessment is then discussed with and explained to the supplier's management. From the assessment, the supplier and SDT can begin to identify areas of concern and possible targets for improvement. SDT then proceeds to suggest how it might be of assistance and, if this offer is accepted, agrees an improvement project with the supplier.

Improvement activities

Though the ten-day improvement activity offered by the SDT is based on the tools, techniques and experience of Nissan in Japan, it has been tailored to meet the specific needs of its European suppliers (who are mainly based in the UK). Improvement activities usually include some or all of the following:

- *reducing assembly time and improving methods;*
- *reducing overhead costs – including reducing inventory and improving equipment availability;*

● *reducing work-in-process;*

● *preventing defects;*

● *improving productivity by reducing throughput times and introducing just-in-time scheduling.*

As mentioned, most improvement activities are usually achieved at little or no cost to the supplier; but, the supplier does need to commit time and personnel to the activity. The improvement process revolves around a multifunctional team composed of the supplier's own staff, who are assisted by the SDT. The supplier's team includes operators and supervisors from the production area concerned as well as maintenance, process engineering, quality and sometimes administrative staff. The team is led by someone from the supplier. The SDT stresses that the most important members of the team are the operators working on the process which is to be improved. Not only does this prevent change simply being imposed on those who will be directly affected by it, with all the scope for resentment and mistrust that this can cause, but it also ensures that the valuable knowledge that operators have of the process is utilised. Perhaps more importantly, it provides operators with the skills and motivation to continue to improve the process even after SDT has ceased to be involved. An independent study (Lloyd *et al*, 1994) found that this approach led to greater commitment to the activity, and improved morale in the areas concerned. It also found that improvement activities helped to break down functional barriers, and assisted the development of greater co-operation and team spirit.

Once the process or activity which is to be improved has been agreed, targets for the improvement are then established (e.g. reductions in lead time, improvements in quality). The supplier prepares the ground for the activity by briefing staff and making any necessary resources available, such as a dedicated meeting room. If the improvement activity is likely to cause a disruption to production, a stock of components may be built up before the activity commences to compensate for this.

Day One of the ten-day improvement activity is devoted to providing training for the supplier's team. If it is the first time the supplier has been involved in such an activity, the SDT will take the lead in this. If the supplier has previous experience of SDT improvement activities, however, then a member of its staff is expected to take the lead. SDT sees its prime purpose as ensuring that: everyone understands the concept of *kaizen*; the procedures for the ten-day activity are clear; and the team becomes familiar with the tools and techniques necessary for its task. In this latter respect, the most frequently used tools and techniques are flow charts, work flow diagrams, pareto charts, cause and effect (fish bone) diagrams, brainstorming and critical path analysis. Where necessary, these are reinforced and supplemented as the ten-day improvement activity develops.

On *Day Two* of the improvement activity, the team splits into smaller groups to analyse and discuss the process to be improved. The groups use a combination of hard data, such as scrap rates, equipment down time and stock levels, and more subjective opinions, such as comments about layout, ease of use and the provision of information, to identify causes of waste and possible counter-measures. The SDT encourages the use of stop watches and even video cameras to assist the supplier's team to analyse the process in question, though these can sometimes be viewed with suspicion by operators.

Once the individual groups have completed their deliberations, they reconvene as a team. The team usually make a flow diagram of the entire process in order that everyone can appreciate what is involved and agree the changes which will bring the best benefits. The data that has been collected by the groups is analysed by the entire team. To make this easier, it is ordered and analysed under a number of standard headings:

Quality	Are quality problems due to material, process, design or training deficiencies?
Technology	Is the equipment appropriate, well-maintained, and used correctly?
Ease of operation	Can work be made easier through ergonomic improvements such as by eliminating bending, or through modifications to the equipment?
Layout	Does the layout of the process result in time delays or excessive work-in-process?

For each of the above categories, the team proceeds to identify concerns, causes and counter-measures. Most suppliers' teams find this a demanding approach. In the space of two days, not only do they have to learn new tools and techniques, but they also have to deploy these in a rigorous and constructive fashion. Nevertheless, by the end of the second day, teams have normally identified what the problems are, what is causing them and the measures necessary to correct them. Sometimes, the outcome is a recognition that existing equipment is inadequate for its task, but it is more usually the case that the team comes up with a list of low cost/no cost changes which they can implement themselves. In some cases, other members of the supplier's staff may be called in to discuss the feasibility of some of the ideas generated. In the main, however, the suppliers' teams are usually capable of making their own judgments.

Days Three to Eight of the improvement activity are spent implementing the agreed improvements. Though the SDT does come back on Day Six to observe progress and can be contacted for assistance at anytime, the responsibility for this phase of the programme lies firmly with the supplier's personnel. The changes they make may be small and simple, or may involve the rearrangement of complete areas of a factory. Where feasible, the team makes the changes in conjunction with personnel in the area concerned. The changed process is then tested, reanalysed and, if necessary, fine-tuned. To minimise disruption, any major changes in layout tend to take place during the weekend which falls in the middle of the improvement activity.

For *Days Nine and Ten* of the improvement activity, the SDT returns to help the team review what they have learnt and achieved, and to ensure that all changes are fully documented. They also discuss outstanding issues and concerns, and potential future improvement projects. The final task is to prepare and deliver a presentation to the company's senior managers describing the changes achieved and the benefits gained. Not only does this give staff the opportunity to show senior managers what they have achieved (and receive well-earned praise), but it also helps those unused to public speaking to develop their skills in this area.

The SDT has come to be considered as a valuable resource by Nissan's suppliers, and there is always a queue for its services. From the suppliers' perspective, this is understandable. Improvement activities usually meet or exceed their targets. Productivity increases of between 20 and 40 per cent are quite common, as are similar improvements in quality and reductions in work-in-process. From Nissan's point of view, it is not the individual improvement projects *per se* which are important, but the ability of suppliers to carry on making improvements once the SDT presence is removed. For many, this is the case, and individual improvement projects act as a catalyst to the development of continuous improvement both on and off the shopfloor. Nevertheless, this does not always occur, and some suppliers do appear to find difficulty sustaining and spreading the SDT philosophy. However, though the main focus of the SDT's work is improvement projects with suppliers, it is also involved in a wide range of other educational, training, advisory and development work aimed at enhancing the capabilities of Nissan's suppliers.

Training for supplier personnel

Over the years, through its work with suppliers, the SDT has identified particular forms of training which it considers crucial for supplier development.

- *An improvement manager course. This is designed for suppliers' staff who, following the SDT lead, are given responsibility for running improvement activities. The course covers all the techniques used during improvement activities. As well as classroom instruction, all course members take part in an improvement activity either in the Nissan plant or with one of its local suppliers.*
- *A trouble-shooting course. This teaches the principles and techniques of problem-solving.*
- *A supervisor development course. SDT members assist in running a development course for Nissan's own supervisors. In the past, the SDT had arranged for suppliers' personnel also to take part in these courses. However, such was the demand from suppliers that the SDT now organises a supervisor development course specifically for suppliers.*

Strategy development activities

In addition to the SDT activities, Nissan is involved in a wide range of activities with its suppliers, ranging from cost reduction exercises to joint product development programmes. Most of these focus on one particular aspect of a supplier's business, usually manufacturing-related. In the early 1990s, however, Nissan began to be increasingly aware that the success of these individual activities in generating a long-term and sustainable improvement in performance depended upon the ability of suppliers to take a strategic approach to their business. In cases where significant progress had been made, it was noticeable that Nissan's efforts formed part of, and were incorporated within, the supplier's own proactive and long-term business plans. In companies where progress was slow and often not sustained, Nissan's efforts did not link in to any overall plan, and remained isolated and fragmented pockets of activity.

Nissan recognised that while most suppliers had a strategic plan, in some cases these tended to be short-term, reactive or unambitious. In such instances, these were no more than paper plans which no one appeared to be committed to implementing. The SDT felt that without a workable strategy, no matter how much assistance Nissan gave, suppliers would make little overall progress, though there might be considerable improvements in isolated aspects of their business.

Nissan's response to this was to develop a strategic planning package which it could offer to appropriate suppliers. Though the SDT was responsible for sponsoring and promoting the package, it did not feel it should also deliver it itself. This was for two reasons. First, neither the SDT by itself, nor Nissan in total, had or could make available the time, resources and expertise necessary to provide such assistance. Second, for such an approach to be successful, it required the full co-operation of suppliers, and a willingness to open up all aspects of their business. Given that suppliers usually deal with a number of car manufacturers, this would involve revealing confidential information about Nissan's competitors, not to mention the suppliers' own future intentions. For obvious reasons, it was not considered either reasonable or possible to ask suppliers to reveal this information.

In order to overcome these obstacles, Nissan entered into a partnership with the National Economic Development Office (NEDO) and the University of Manchester Institute of Science and Technology (UMIST) to produce and provide a strategy development package to its suppliers. The package was developed and piloted jointly by the SDT, NEDO and UMIST. Once it became fully operational, however, the SDT restricted its role to identifying suitable suppliers and promoting the package. The actual delivery of the programme was the responsibility of NEDO and UMIST, though SDT still maintains a quality assurance role.

Unlike many other SDT activities, suppliers have to pay for this service. Nevertheless, it appears to have been well-received by suppliers who, often having had a poor experience of using external bodies for such activities in the past, welcome a strategy development package sponsored by a major customer and delivered by two such reputable bodies. For Nissan, it ensures that an appropriate supplier, who it feels has a particular need in this area, can use a service which Nissan has confidence in without compromising commercial confidentiality.

The strategy development programme was launched by Nissan in 1992 and, although NEDO's involvement ended shortly afterwards, NEDO's role is now provided by an independent consultancy service.

The outcome

Since it first embarked on the supplier development route, Nissan has moved from trying to sell the concept to a few suppliers to a position where suppliers are queuing up for the services of its Supplier Development Team. At the same time, the SDT has expanded its role from undertaking improvement activities within suppliers, which still accounts for the majority of its time, to offering a range of training courses and even to providing assistance with strategic planning. Given the traditional distrust between suppliers and customers in the car industry, for the former to welcome such levels of 'interference' in their internal affairs is remarkable, and provides clear evidence of partnerships in action.

It is nevertheless important to set Nissan's SDT activities in context. Today, the UK car industry is, arguably, the healthiest in Europe (Flynn *et al*, 1995); but when Nissan announced its intention to establish a car assembly plant in the UK, the domestic industry was in crisis. All the (then) UK-based producers were experiencing financial difficulties, imports were at an all-time high, and component suppliers genuinely feared for their future. Therefore, the prospect of one of the mighty Japanese car companies establishing a new plant in the UK was seen not just as a much-needed vote of confidence in Britain's future as an industrial nation, but also as a major opportunity by component suppliers. In addition, Nissan let it be known that it wanted to establish the same sort of long-term, mutually beneficial partnerships with British suppliers as it enjoyed with its Japanese ones. Though many were unsure of what this meant, the prospect of working with a car company whose fortunes were waxing rather than waning was clearly very attractive.

Unlike other producers in the UK at the time, Nissan did not establish a tender list and ask for quotations. It identified the suppliers it wanted, rigorously assessed their capabilities, established cost, quality and delivery targets with them, and awarded them contracts for the lifetime of the car for which they were supplying components. It also declared that it expected suppliers to stay with Nissan for the next car it built and the one after, performance and technological factors permitting. In addition, as a customer it was seen to be reliable, predictable and trustworthy – it kept its word.

Accordingly, when Nissan arrived in the UK it met with considerable goodwill and co-operation, which tended to grow rather than diminish as suppliers came to appreciate its approach to purchasing. There was also a great deal of prestige attached to being associated with Nissan, and this applied to its suppliers as much as anyone else. The fact that Nissan was also a good customer who changed the rules of customer–supplier relationships, from an antagonistic one based on a win–lose equation to a partnership one based on win–win, was almost a bonus.

It was in this context that Nissan launched its Supplier Development Team. Car industry customers seeking to improve suppliers was not new – Ford had been doing it for some years with its quality assurance programmes. The difference was that, while Ford unilaterally imposed requirements on suppliers, Nissan took a voluntary and co-operative approach and did not seek to penalise those who did not take part. Nissan's aim was, and still is, to transfer to its European suppliers practices and techniques that had proved successful in Japan. The SDT activities should therefore be seen not as an end in themselves, but rather as a catalyst to stimulate the search for continuous improvement.

Despite some early suspicion, there is little doubt that Nissan's Supplier Development Team has proved an effective force for change, not just in terms of the internal arrangements of Nissan's suppliers, but also with regard to customer–supplier relations (Lloyd et al, 1994). This change in relationships has been reinforced by the arrival of Toyota and Honda, adding to the latter's continuing influence on Rover.

Regardless of the context in which the SDT was launched and still operates, the approach it adopts when working with suppliers is also extremely important. The key elements of this approach are as follows:

- *The team operates as part of Nissan's partnership approach to purchasing.*
- *Suppliers are at liberty to choose whether or not to invite the SDT into their plant.*
- *SDT begins by explaining to senior managers in suppliers that its objective is to help them to develop a continuous improvement philosophy.*
- *It seeks to train and guide a supplier's personnel to undertake change projects for themselves, rather than doing the work for them.*
- *The SDT insists that operators and supervisors in the area where change is to take place are involved.*
- *The SDT's own members are extremely well-trained and proficient and, consequently, are able to win the confidence of the people with whom they work.*
- *It seeks to ensure that those who carry out the improvement get the credit and praise for it, rather than seeking to take the credit itself.*
- *Above all, the SDT members see themselves as ambassadors for Nissan and for Nissan's approach to partnership. Therefore, they seek to promote trust and co-operation between themselves and suppliers' personnel.*

It would be misleading to give the impression that Nissan was in anyway 'soft' on suppliers. Nissan may have given its 'partners' new rights, but they have also acquired new responsibilities. In return for openness and trust on its part, it expects the same from suppliers, who are expected to open up every aspect of their business to inspection and scrutiny. As Ian Gibson, Nissan's Managing Director stated:

> **Co-operative supply relationships are not an easy option, as many imagine, but considerably harder to implement than traditional buyer–seller relationships'. (*quoted in Burnes and Whittle, 1995:10*)**

However, the success of Nissan's approach is demonstrated by the fact that since it initiated the move towards partnerships, not only have most other UK-based car companies followed suit, but also a considerable number of companies in other industries.

Case study 10

....

SPEEDY STATIONERS LTD AND UTL (TURBINES) LTD – SUPPLIER-DRIVEN CHANGE[*]

Background

In the vast majority of cases, it is customers who take the initiative to change relationships rather than suppliers. This is for quite obvious reasons to do with power (it is the customer who has the money and who decides what to purchase and from whom) and experience (there are very few examples of how suppliers can influence customers). However, unlike the Vickers and Nissan studies, where it was the customers who were attempting to bring about significant changes in their suppliers, this case study deals with organisational change driven by a supplier.

The case examines the development of a partnership between Speedy Stationers Ltd and UTL (Turbines) Ltd, whereby the former took responsibility for the provision and in-company management of all UTL's stationery requirements.

Speedy Stationers was founded in 1953, and in 1994 had a turnover of roughly £50 million. Originally the firm acted just as a wholesaler selling to distributors and retailers. In the mid-1980s, almost by accident (an acquaintance of the Managing Director happened to be appointed to the same position in UTL), it began dealing directly with a small number of large industrial companies. Typically, these companies' total stationery bill was over £200,000 per year. However, because Speedy did not deal with printed stationery, letterheads, etc., it rarely did more than more £50,000 worth of business with any of these customers. Nevertheless, the Managing Director, whose pet project this was, had high hopes for direct selling.

Influenced partly by the possibility of selling directly to large companies, Speedy embarked on an expansion programme in the late 1980s which doubled its number of distribution centres from three to six. This geographical spreading of risk allowed

---

[*]This case study is based on original research by Dr Steve New of the Manchester School of Management at UMIST. The names, locations and some details have been changed to preserve anonymity.

the company to weather the recession of the early 1990s without any significant loss of business – though its profit margins were squeezed. Nevertheless, by 1993, senior managers came to recognise that the possibilities of continued expansion through the establishment of more distribution centres was limited, as well as expensive. Furthermore, selling stationery directly to end users, while potentially attractive, had failed to live up to its initial promise. This was partly because there was a limited number of companies whose stationery bills made it worthwhile dealing with them directly, and partly due to the fact that even the ones they did deal with tended to flit around pursuing, in some cases, extremely small savings. A continuing bone of contention was also the amount of the Managing Director's time taken up with servicing the direct customers. Orders had originally been won on the basis of his contacts, and he felt that they could only be maintained on this basis.

A strategy emerges

It was in 1993, after much heated debate, that senior managers took the decision to set up the direct sales business as a distinct entity within Speedy. It was given its own manager, and a small team of staff was assembled to run the operation. The intention was to allow the rest of the company to focus on its core business, the provision of stationery to distributors and retailers, while giving the direct sales operation one last chance to prove itself. Though this was something of a 'sink or swim' approach, Speedy was not abandoning direct sales to fate. As a concession to the Managing Director's strong commitment to direct sales, the person given responsibility for its development was a board member who, it was felt, would eventually succeed the present Managing Director.

Before informing its customers of this change, the Direct Sales Division (to give it its official title) set about establishing its strategy. Though this was mainly the work of the Director for Direct Sales, he was careful to involve all his staff and to ensure the continued support of the Managing Director. The strategy that emerged had three objectives:

- *to offer a complete stationery service to its existing customers, including printed letterheads, forms, etc.;*
- *to develop partnerships with its customers whereby the Direct Sales Division would supply and manage their stationery stock;*
- *to triple turnover in three years while maintaining its profit margin;*

The thinking behind this strategy stemmed from four characteristics of its present business:

1 The turnover of the direct business was £750,000 (out of Speedy's total turnover of £50 million) from 15 customers. The profit margin on this business was 7.5 per cent (as opposed to 5 per cent on Speedy's main business).

2 Direct customers were mainly located near its headquarters in Birmingham and therefore could easily be serviced by one group of staff. A geographical expansion would be proportionately more costly owing to distance.

3 At present, Speedy only accounted for some 20–25 per cent of direct customers' stationery requirements, because it did not provide printed stationery. Once this was on offer, doubling or tripling business with each customer seemed quite possible.

4 In the early 1990s, the concept of partnerships between suppliers and customers began to take off. Already, the wholesale business was discussing managing the inventory for a number of medium-sized distributors, so it did not seem totally unfeasible to offer a similar service to direct customers – especially if they were likely to be supplying the majority of their stationery needs in any case.

In developing the strategy, it was agreed that the first two priorities were to establish a partnership with a printer, and to identify the first customer to approach regarding partnering. The first part of this was relatively easy: they approached the printer who had dealt with all Speedy's own printing requirements over the past 20 years, and with whom they had a very close relationship already. The printer readily agreed to the arrangement – apart from anything else, it did not entail any major cost for them, but did promise additional lucrative business.

Identifying a customer for partnership was more problematic, but eventually they decided to approach UTL (Turbines) Ltd. Not only had UTL been Speedy's first direct customer (thanks to the relationship between the two Managing Directors) but it was well known that it wanted to develop partnerships with its suppliers. Therefore, it was decided to make an approach to them.

UTL (Turbines) Ltd

In 1992, UTL spent some £200,000 per annum on stationery, but this was small compared to the £30 million it spent on buying components for its turbines. It had a very traditional, distrusting and arms-length approach to purchasing, which it applied to all its purchases. It had at least five suppliers for each commodity and, with some exceptions, it purchased purely on price. Not surprisingly, it had over 1,500 suppliers, and the main contact most of these had with UTL was in response to written requests for quotations. Owing to the friendly relations at senior level, Speedy was one of the few suppliers who ever met purchasing staff.

The company is part of a large multinational group, and serves markets worldwide. UTL (Turbines), as its name implies, is the division responsible for the design and manufacture of turbines which are supplied to a wide range of industrial users.

Like many manufacturing operations in the UK, the plant had experienced severe reductions in the number of people employed. From over 1,500 in 1987, the number working at the factory by 1994 had shrunk to about 900. In recent years, purchasing activities had undergone significant reorganisation. In 1992, two different aspects of the business – export and domestic turbines – merged their operations. Purchasing was one of the first functional groups to combine, and a new manager was brought into the company to take charge of the combined department.

As noted above, the company had a very traditional purchasing orientation. With the creation of the new purchasing function, however, a number of important changes were introduced to encourage staff to take a wider view of their role. In particular, the new manager wanted to focus attention on the total cost of doing business with a particular supplier, rather than just favouring those who submitted the lowest tender. The manager recognised that he needed to change staff attitudes towards suppliers, and indeed the Purchasing Department's view of its role in general. As a starting point, several innovations were introduced, including a series of lunchtime seminars which the manager saw as a vehicle for both team-building and idea generation. The seminar programme consisted of outside speakers (including suppliers), presentations from staff in the department who had been on training courses, and videos.

When vacancies in the department arose, these were generally filled from outside the company, with appointments favouring youth and enthusiasm over age and experience. The new manager was keen that the importance of the group should be recognised in the organisation, and was keen to develop a team with a clear professional focus. He believed that the traditional perceptions of purchasing as merely a bureaucratic support activity had to be challenged.

As might be imagined, most of the Purchasing Department's attention was focused on suppliers of production components. This did not change under the new manager; indeed, as far as he was concerned, the less he had to do with non-production suppliers the better. It was this that gave Speedy Stationers its opportunity for building a partnership with UTL.

Speedy takes the initiative

By 1993, the reorganisation and reorientation of the Purchasing Department was well under way. In particular, the seminar series, which at first attracted some adverse comment within the company, was proving a key vehicle for introducing new ideas and generating fresh thinking. When the Director for Direct Sales at Speedy heard about the seminar programme, he offered to come and talk about its new approach to working with customers. The Purchasing Manager was at first resistant, as were many of his staff, because this was not the area on which he wished to focus attention. Nevertheless, he finally agreed when the Speedy Director told him that the title of his presentation would be 'Contract Out Stationery Management and Reduce Costs by 10 Per Cent'.

Under the existing system, ordering stationery was a slow, complicated process. When individual departments required stationery, a requisition would be raised which was then translated by the Purchasing Department into a purchase order. On arrival, items would be inspected – which, for stationery, meant that the content of each delivery would be counted and checked against the delivery note and original order. The items would then be booked into the stores, from which they could be withdrawn to departmental stores after more paperwork. As there were many stationery suppliers, problems with shortages were sometimes difficult to resolve. Each supplier would send invoices, which needed to be checked against orders and delivery notes. In addition, there was a particular problem with printed stationery: it was not unusual for the wording which the originating department thought it had specified to be incorrect when the stationery finally arrived with them. However, tracing where the fault lay could be a tortuous process. It was also the case that departments ordered, and kept, far more stationery than they needed in order to avoid shortages. It was clear to the Direct Sales Division at Speedy, if not to UTL's own purchasing staff, that inefficiencies were rife, and that a 10 per cent reduction in costs should be achievable.

Speedy's proposal for managing all UTL's stationery needs was to establish two or three stationery bunkers in each department, close to the point of use (one for general stationery – e.g. photocopying paper; one for specialist items – e.g. printed forms; and one for consumables – e.g. pens and pencils, printer ribbons, etc.). These bunkers were to be clearly labelled; the average requirement for each type of stationery would be calculated and two weeks' worth of inventory was to be held in each. Speedy staff would visit weekly and top up the bunkers to the agreed level. Each delivery would be signed for by a designated manager for that area and, at the end of each month, all the supplies would be consolidated onto a single invoice. None of the incoming stationery would go through goods inwards or inspection, and there would be no need to raise individual orders. Indeed, the only work required of the Purchasing Department would be to pay the monthly invoice.

Though the Director for Direct Sales presented a very well-argued case, he met with some incredulity, not to mention hostility. Some staff thought the plan simply would not work. Others felt that UTL would be swindled. Yet another group feared for their jobs if this type of approach spread from stationery to other purchased items. Nevertheless, the prospect of getting rid of stationery purchasing, plus all the complaints it generated, and thus releasing staff for what he considered more important activities, proved too tempting for the Purchasing Manager. The estimated 10 per cent saving, and informal encouragement from his Managing Director, also assisted the decision. In addition, Speedy pointed out that, for the first time, UTL would have accurate and regular figures for stationery consumption broken down by area and type of stationery.

Towards the end of 1993, Speedy and UTL signed a two-year contract covering the provision of all stationery requirements from the beginning of 1994. Though the contract included certain specific details (especially regarding auditing the new system), it was acknowledged that most of the mechanics of the arrangements would only emerge as the system was implemented.

Implementing the new system

Under the new system, UTL was divided into 20 separate stationery zones, each with three stationery bunkers. The initial target was to set up this system for two of these zones from the beginning of 1994, with the remainder in place by March 1994. Speedy promised a maximum three-hour response time to resolve problems.

The new system entails significant reductions in the bureaucracy of supplying stationery, but also challenges many traditional approaches to buyer–supplier relationships, especially in relation to trust. First, in the absence of direct checks, UTL has to have complete confidence in the quality of the products supplied by Speedy and the reliability of its operation. Second, UTL has to trust that Speedy is actually delivering what it is invoicing for. Finally, UTL has to be sure that a single-source supplier will not exploit its position and introduce opportunistic price rises.

Managers from different functions within UTL needed to be reassured that the system was going to work, and that Speedy was capable of providing the new style of service. Presentations were held at which reservations could be expressed, and the new approach explained. However, it was not only managers within UTL who had some concerns; so did some of the workforce. To set up the new system, Speedy had up to five staff carrying out the initial analysis and making the arrangements for the new stocking locations. It became clear that UTL employees were suspicious and wary of what was going on. A major source of this unease was a fear that a system for delivering items direct to departments and zones would threaten the jobs of those in the goods inward, the incoming inspection and stores activities.

To help overcome these doubts, representatives from all areas concerned, including trade unions, were included in the series of presentations organised jointly by Speedy and UTL. Many of the questions raised related to the logic of the planned arrangement from UTL's point of view, and the potential vulnerability of being dependent on a single source. Other objections reflected the more immediate fear about the loss of jobs. Despite his earlier reservations, UTL's Purchasing Manager became the main champion for the Speedy initiative. In essence, he pointed to the need for all UTL employees and resources to focus on improving the competitiveness of their core business, rather than 'messing about trying to find an envelope'. This, together with a promise that no one's job was threatened by the initiative, seemed to overcome most of the reservations.

Despite winning staff over to the new arrangements, the practicalities still had to be worked out. One of the major obstacles in implementing the new delivery system was the amount of stationery already held at UTL. The problem was not just the inventory held centrally and in each department's own store, but also the large quantities of stationery 'hidden' in various locations around the factory. These had arisen because staff, especially those working on the shopfloor, frequently took more from the stores than they actually needed in order to avoid 'shortages'.

As part of the implementation programme Speedy staff scoured UTL for these 'private' stationery cupboards. The office of one supervisor on the night shift became known as 'WH Smith' because of the large collection of stationery, much of it years out of date, which was held there. He had been unable to draw stationery from the stores at night, and so had assembled his own supply. In some cases, the unofficial inventory amounted to a year's worth of a particular item.

UTL had estimated that they held about two months' worth of stationery overall. In order to integrate this with the new system, Speedy began sorting this by type into agreed quantities. It transpired, however, when all the existing stationery had been accounted for, that in fact existing stocks were nearer four months' worth of inventory. This meant that for the first few months of the relationship, Speedy delivered relatively little of its own material, and so had little for which to invoice.

Like many aspects of the new stationery management system, this factor was not covered by the written contract; episodes like this were, and are, dealt with on the basis of mutual understanding and trust.

The outcome

By the end of 1994, the new system was fully up and running. Despite a number of hiccups, the change appears to have been much smoother than anyone really imagined possible. Furthermore, both parties feel that they have obtained major benefits from the change. The benefits to Speedy are as follows:

- *It has increased its business with UTL from approximately £50,000 per year to over £200,000, and has actually improved its profit margin to 8.5 per cent.*

- *It has proved that the new arrangements can work, and has three other customers keen to develop similar arrangements.*

For UTL, the benefits have also been significant:

- *It has made a 20 per cent saving on its annual stationery bill – twice as much as anticipated, even taking account of using up old stock.*

- *Consumption of stationery has declined significantly in some areas, partly thanks to better stock control, and partly owing to a decline in 'home usage' – as one manager put it.*

- *The number of complaints relating to stationery has dwindled almost to zero.*

However, UTL managers feel there is a more important, if less quantifiable, benefit, which is that managers at UTL (not just in Purchasing) have seen the possibilities for new ways of conducting and organising business. In particular, managers now have a more favourable view of the prospects for achieving change in the company. As one manager commented:

> **We've had our eyes opened. No one suspected some of our people would so easily accept such radical changes, especially ones driven by a supplier. The improvements**

we've made in handling stationery are really secondary to the confidence it's given us in our ability to manage change and make improvements.

One clear sign of this new confidence is that UTL is seriously examining how it can develop similar links with other suppliers and its own customers.

The Speedy–UTL story has important implications for customer–supplier relations in particular, and change management in general:

- *While it has been recognised since the 1960s that customers and suppliers can impact on each other's internal operations, the general view has been that this occurs in an unintended and unplanned fashion. What this case study shows is that customers and suppliers can link together consciously to change the nature of the environment in which they operate to their mutual benefit.*

- *The study also shows the serendipitous and unplanned nature of much of business life. Speedy only moved into the direct sale of stationery because of a friendship between its Managing Director and UTL's. It was only by chance that Speedy's decision to extend its operations into printed stationery and to develop partnerships occurred at a time when UTL was receptive to such an approach. A year earlier, and the approach would undoubtedly have been rejected; a year later, and UTL might have moved away from the idea, or might have been busy developing partnerships with production suppliers.*

- *The manner in which suspicion and resistance were overcome is also worth noting. From the start, Speedy approached the project in an open and frank manner – it raised the suggestion of a partnership in an open seminar attended by all purchasing staff, and open to all other UTL managers. UTL for its part chose to hide nothing from its workforce; both parties took account of worries and suspicions, and did their utmost to resolve these before embarking on change. Furthermore, UTL gave an assurance that the changed arrangements would not lead to any job losses.*

- *Finally, a major point is that both parties were prepared to set aside the distrust which permeates so many business relationships, and attempt to establish a partnership based on trust. Nevertheless, the trust was based on adequate checks and a belief, subsequently proved correct, that such an approach was mutually beneficial.*

Conclusions

....

The three case studies in this chapter amply demonstrate the manner in which companies are changing not just their internal relationships, but also their external ones. Though the move towards closer relationships between customers and suppliers clearly makes for a more stable and harmonious atmosphere in which to conduct business, these are almost side effects and not the main reason for the change. Increasingly, companies have come to recognise the need to make major improvements in their performance but, as anything up to 70, 80 or even 90 per cent of the value of their products comprises bought-in goods and services, this cannot be achieved solely on the basis of internal performance improvements. Rather, what is required is that their suppliers also improve their business. As Ford found out in the car industry, seeking to impose improvements has its limitations. Suppliers have to be keen to improve and willing to work with customers. The argument for adopting a partnership approach to purchasing in the UK, and other Western countries, is that this is one of the cornerstones of Japan's success and, therefore, must be beneficial (Womack *et al*, 1990).

What we have seen in this chapter is three aspects of this type of relationship. Case Study 8, Vickers Defence Systems, showed how companies can begin moving away from antagonistic relationships. It demonstrated that, despite the good intentions of senior managers, it is not always easy to convince the rest of the organisation to renounce the habits of a lifetime. Vickers were moving slowly down the route of partnership, but were experiencing some internal and external resistance and mistrust. It was only when a crisis occurred, the potentially fatal threat to the Challenger 2 order, that Vickers found that it could effectively challenge old beliefs and methods of working, both among its own staff and in its suppliers, and so accelerate the pace of change. Even then, progress was not preplanned or fully envisioned in advance, but the steps taken to pursue partnership emerged in an *ad hoc* and open-ended fashion.

Case Study 9, Nissan's Supplier Development Team, showed a more advanced form of the partnership approach. Nissan, with a long history of working closely with its suppliers in Japan, was intent on doing the same in the UK. It recognised the need to transfer knowledge and practices from Japan to its new suppliers, if they were to meet Nissan's exacting performance standards. A key method of achieving this in Japan is the supplier development approach; so Nissan established a Supplier Development Team, along Japanese lines. However, the Team adapted its approach to meet local needs. In Japan, improvement activities tend to average two days; in the UK, the duration tends to be ten days. This reflects the different starting points of UK companies. However, as the SDT worked with suppliers to change their internal working arrangements, it recognised a need to offer further assistance. In the first instance, this took the form of training for suppliers' staff. As time progressed, however, Nissan came more and more to appreciate the strategic weakness of some of its suppliers, and began to offer assistance in this area as well. Though the strategic planning package emphasised vision-building and strategic intent, the SDT adopts a much more planned and preprogrammed approach. Each activity has clear objectives and timescales, and is highly focused.

Taking Nissan's activities with its suppliers as a whole, it can be seen that, though Nissan had a clear picture both of how it wished to work with suppliers, and of the end result in terms of improved performance by suppliers, the actual details emerged over time, as was the case with Vickers. Nevertheless, this emerging strategy was based less on trial and error than on a well thought-out and planned approach. New developments, especially the strategic planning package, were the object of much discussion and planning, and were piloted before being fully launched. The Nissan approach, therefore, while being emergent, was neither *ad hoc* nor trial and error, but the product of a great deal of thought and planning.

The last case study, Speedy Stationers, offers a new twist on the development of closer customer–supplier relationships. Normally, it is the customer who takes the lead in promoting changes in purchasing behaviour. This is for the obvious reason that the customer is usually the one with the power in the relationship (they can generally choose where to purchase and on what terms). In this instance, however, Speedy took the initiative and approached its customer with a suggestion for change. This was for basic commercial reasons – it needed to win additional business and saw partnerships as being the prime vehicle. It believed that the partnership approach would not only be commercially beneficial but would also give Speedy a competitive edge over its rivals. Speedy was fortunate in that it was able to approach a customer responsive to this type of initiative. The process of building the relationship led to many changes, both in Speedy and particularly in its customer. Much information only came to light as the new arrangements were developed and implemented, and it was only by actually putting the new approach into practice that sceptics could come to appreciate its benefits. For both Speedy and its customer, this new approach was something of a leap into the unknown which appeared to succeed, though only time will tell to what extent.

In reviewing these three case studies, what is remarkable is the extent to which organisations have moved from changing their own internal operations and relationships, in order to improve their performance, to a situation where they recognise the need, and are able to develop approaches, for achieving change in their suppliers and customers. In undertaking such changes, three points stand out from the case studies.

The first is that these companies are changing the rules of the game; they are challenging the prevailing orthodoxy in the UK and the rest of Europe with regard to commercial relationships between customers and suppliers.

The second point is that, although this type of action is based on others' successful experiences, it nevertheless requires a considerable act of faith by the parties concerned. It is not possible in advance to spell out either the exact form of the new relationships or the specific measurable benefits they might bring. However, dissatisfaction with traditional relationships, and the potential for commercial advantage, have spurred the case study companies described in this chapter to take such decisions. As can be seen, the move towards partnerships is nevertheless more an act of faith than the product of rational analysis and the pursuit of quantified and clear commercial objectives.

The last point to note relates to one of the major benefits or consequences of partnerships. One reason why companies are seeking to develop new ways of working is to help them to cope with the competitive pressures and uncertainty of the modern world. Partnerships appear not only to allow companies to strengthen their competitive position, but also to reduce a major source of environmental uncertainty, i.e. they make the actions of customers and suppliers more predictable and transparent. This goes against those, such as Tom Peters, who argue for increasing chaos rather than reducing it. It also shows that one of the major constraints or contingencies organisations face, environmental uncertainty, can be manipulated in such a way that the ability to plan for the future, in terms of product development and production, is increased. As the Contingency theorists, described in Chapter 2, argued over three decades ago, the external environment does affect the internal workings of an organisation, but an organisation's internal arrangements can also affect the environment. Therefore, if a turbulent environment leads to changed internal relationships, then given that organisations are open systems, we can expect these to be mirrored in changed external relationships. Therefore, although internal changes are often seen as mechanisms for coping with environmental uncertainty, the move by suppliers and customers to develop closer links can go one step further, actually reducing uncertainty.

Discussion points

1 To what extent do the case studies support any of the four perspectives on strategy discussed in Chapter 5?

2 To what extent do the case studies support the suggestion made in Chapter 5 that organisations can manipulate constraints and contingencies?

3 In the discussion on change management in Chapter 6, two main approaches to change were identified – planned and emergent. Do the case studies support either of these?

4 Do the case studies show any evidence of attempts to manipulate contingencies and constraints in order to align them with the managers' own world view or best interests?

5 Do the tools and techniques used to bring about change in the case studies show any common features in their approach to structural, technological or organisational change?

6 What are the five key factors in each study which most influenced the outcome achieved?

7 In what manner do the actions of the case study companies support or undermine the Classical view of organisations as rational entities?

PART 4

MANAGING
CHOICE

Chapter 10

Managing choice – managing change

Introduction

In the previous three parts of this book, we have examined the theory and practice of how organisations develop and change. From the Industrial Revolution to the present day, we can see that the history of organisations is one of change and upheaval. In the light of this, the idea that organisations have ever operated in a stable state or a predictable environment, other than for relatively brief periods, is difficult to sustain. Whether because of economic fluctuations, the development of new products and processes, social change or war, organisations and entire indust-ries tend to face recurrent bouts of upheaval. Some, such as the UK car industry, emerge leaner and fitter from this process but others, such as the UK coal industry, shrink to a shadow of their former selves and appear doomed to be relegated to the role of bit player on the industrial stage.

Nevertheless, many writers do argue that organisations and society at large are in a period of rapid and unprecedented change: a period where old certainties no longer hold good, and new ones have yet to emerge. An alternative view is that the pace and uncertainty of change varies from company to company, industry to industry and even country to country. As a consequence, at any one point in time, some organis-ations will be experiencing extreme turbulence while others appear to operate in a relatively stable environment. However, whether either of these views offers a suitable explanation of the stability–turbulence question is perhaps irrelevant. The pertinent issue is how organisations can cope with both the environment in which they operate and the constraints, challenges and threats they face. In undertaking this task, one thing is perfectly clear: the amount and diversity of information and advice on offer is certainly greater than ever before.

No longer are business analysis and advice confined to a few specialist publishers and journals, or locked up in business school libraries. Books, magazines and videos on 'how to' management can be found in airports and railway stations as well as almost any bookshop. Newspapers, radio and television also play their part in popularising the latest panacea or giving a platform to practitioners and theorists. In addition, the ubiquitous management consultant can always be relied upon to offer the latest approach, at a price. Therefore, managers cannot claim to lack advice or offers of assistance. The problem, as this book has shown, is that no two approaches appear to be exactly the same and in some cases they almost entirely contradict each other. Almost in despair, many managers must ask themselves the simple question: if the experts can't agree, what hope is there for me?

This question illustrates the powerlessness some managers feel when faced with issues which, quite wrongly, appear to have become the territory of the specialist. Though there are managers who adopt an almost fatalistic attitude to their situation, believing that events are beyond their control, others, fortunately, adopt a more positive stance. However, even these managers often give the impression that their job is to implement the particular approach to strategy and change which the specialists recommend, or which other more successful organisations have adopted. This book has sought to argue that this is not only an incorrect, but a potentially dangerous notion.

Though most 'experts' would claim some sort of universal applicability for their favoured approach or theory, the reality is that such approaches are developed in particular circumstances, at particular times and often with particular types of organisations in mind. It follows that a key role for organisations and their managers is to understand the approaches on offer, identify their own circumstances and needs, and choose the approach which best suits them. By doing this, in effect, as this book has attempted to argue, managers can cease to be prisoners of circumstances and experts, and begin to make their own choices about the future operation and direction of their organisations.

This chapter draws together the previous three Parts of this book and proposes a new model for understanding and implementing organisational change: one which not only incorporates the planned and emergent approaches to change, but also indicates how managers can restore their freedom of choice. The chapter begins by reviewing Chapters 5 and 6 and identifying a number of key common points, especially with regard to managerial choice. These are then used to examine the case studies presented in Chapters 7, 8 and 9. It is then argued that the case studies show that in practice, as well as theory, managers can and do influence and change the constraints they operate under. A choice management–change management model is then presented, which comprises three core organisation processes: the choice process, the trajectory process and the change process. The chapter concludes by arguing that though organisations may choose to restructure their internal operations and practices in order to align them with the external circumstances they face, they can also choose to change or modify external and internal conditions and constraints in order to avoid extensive internal upheaval and/or to bring the constraints into line with their preferred modus operandi. Whatever choices are made, it is the role of managers consciously to explore and identify all the available options, however improbable they seem, rather than assuming that they have no, or only limited, choice in the matter.

Lessons from theory and practice

Chapters 5 and 6 began to develop a new model of managerial choice and change management. The case studies which followed, showed how ten organisations dealt with these issues. The case studies will now be compared with the findings from Chapters 5 and 6. First, the two chapters will be reviewed and key issues identified; these issues will then be used to examine the case studies. The intention is to begin to combine theory and practice in order to develop a Choice Management–Change Management model for understanding and implementing organisational change.

Issues from Chapters 5 and 6

Chapter 5 examined the origins and development of approaches to strategy. It showed that strategy was originally conceived of as a rational, quantitative process concerned with an organisation's external environment, especially products and markets. The key role for managers was to identify trends, establish future objectives or targets, and then implement them. In the 1980s and 1990s, the dominant approaches to strategy tend to be more complex, and acknowledge the importance of the internal as well the external environment. Furthermore, more recent approaches tend to view rationality and quantification as less important than intuition and creativity; and to see the role of managers as both wider and more nebulous. Managers are seen as primarily responsible for creating a vision or strategic direction for their organisations, which they then pursue through day-to-day decisions concerning such matters as resource allocation and product/market development. From this standpoint, an organisation's strategy is not set in advance, but emerges as decisions are taken. These newer perspectives, therefore, draw no distinction between strategy development and implementation – an organisation's decisions are informed by its visions or intent, but the nature and details of the strategy they pursue emerge from the decisions they take. Despite the apparent plausibility of the newer approaches to strategy and change, more rational and quantitative approaches have not been replaced. Rather, as Chapters 5 and 6 show, the situation is that a number of more or less competing perspectives on strategy and change are available.

In Chapter 5, it was argued that none of the competing perspectives on strategy were necessarily true or false. Instead, they tended to be appropriate to given situations. The main elements determining their appropriateness were: national characteristics, the business environment, industry-specific factors, and the internal characteristics of the organisation in question. However, rather than arguing that the role of managers was to choose the appropriate approach to strategy for their organisation's circumstances, the chapter concluded by arguing that managers could choose to amend these circumstances to fit in with their preferred approach to strategy.

Chapter 6 moved from examining strategy to reviewing change management. It began by looking at three of the main theories which underpin approaches to change management. These concerned the behaviour and importance of individuals, groups and systems within organisations. The chapter then moved on to examine what has been the dominant approach to change management – planned change. This tends to concentrate on individuals and groups, but has less to say about the overall organisation and its environment, though it does acknowledge the importance of sub-systems. This approach regards change very much as a planned and conscious process of moving parts of organisations from one fixed state to another. It is an approach that seeks to change individual and group perspectives and behaviour through participation.

The alternative, and newer, approach to change management reviewed in Chapter 6 was the emergent approach. This approach rejects the concept of a planned change process with a definite and fixed outcome. Instead, it conceives of organisations as operating in a continuous state of flux and turbulence. Under these conditions, the role of managers is to develop a climate in which everyone in the organisation has a responsibility for identifying the need for and implementing change. The objective is not to achieve a fixed outcome but continually to align and realign the organisation with the changing needs of an unpredictable environment.

Chapter 6 concluded that, though the nature of the environment in which their organisations operated placed constraints on managers' freedom of choice, managers could influence or alter these constraints – in line with the arguments developed in Chapter 5 – to make them better suited to their and their organisations' own preferences and needs.

To summarise, the evidence and arguments from these two chapters are as follows:

- *There are a number of valid and well-supported approaches to strategy development and change management available to organisations.*

- *The dominant view is that managers have to adopt the approach which appears to fit in with the constraints, especially environmental ones, they face.*

- *An alternative perspective, however, is that it is possible for managers to influence these constraints, in effect to change the rules of the game, to make them more appropriate to the particular approach to strategy and change management which suits them and their organisations.*

In order to examine the validity of this last point, the ten case studies from Part Three will be reviewed to see to what extent the experience of real life organisations support or contradict this view. In particular, drawing on Chapter 5 and 6, for each case study the following key issues will be explored:

1 *Strategy.* How was the organisation's strategy developed?
2 *Constraints.* What were the constraints the organisation faced, and did the strategy seek to work within or influence these?

3 *Managers.* What role did managers play in strategy development and change management?

4 *Change management.* How were change projects managed and who was involved?

5 *Planned or emergent change.* To what extent were strategies and/or change projects fully planned in advance and to what extent can they be seen as emergent and open-ended?

6 *Objectives.* Was the focus of strategy development and/or change projects to alter individual and group behaviour or to change systems and subsystems?

Reviewing the case studies – Chapters 7, 8 and 9

In examining the ten case studies against the above six issues, it should be borne in mind that Case Studies 1 to 4 (Chapter 7) deal specifically with strategy development, and Case Studies 5 to 10 (Chapters 8 and 9) concentrate on change management projects. Nevertheless, all the case studies, to a lesser or greater extent, contain elements of strategy development and all contain elements of change management. With that proviso in mind, we can now move to a brief examination of the individual case studies. Each case will be reviewed under the six headings above.

Case Study 1: Oticon

1 *Strategy.* The company's strategy was developed and driven by one person (the new Chief Executive). He created a vision of a service-based organisation and pursued it by, in effect, razing the existing organisation to the ground and starting again.

2 *Constraints.* Though there is no clear evidence that existing constraints influenced the strategy, the new flexible structure which emerged was certainly compatible with Danish norms or expectations regarding job design. As far as industry norms were concerned, Oticon was at a disadvantage in that competition was based on the technical sophistication of products, and its capability in this respect was falling behind that of other companies. To counter this disadvantage, Oticon chose to rewrite the rules of competition in the industry by moving the focus from technology to service. The business environment in which Oticon operated had been and still remained very turbulent. Indeed, by attempting to change the basis of competition in the industry, Oticon can be seen as adding to rather than reducing uncertainty. In terms of organisation characteristics, the Chief Executive was again attempting to rewrite the rule book. The existing structure was demolished, its culture was challenged and the style of management changed drastically.

3 *Managers.* The strategy was developed by the Chief Executive, and though

he explained it to other managers, it is clear that he neither expected nor wanted them to modify it. Their role was to support him and to help sell the idea, rather than necessarily to be part of the process of its development and implementation.

4 *Change management.* The approach taken was to prepare the ground carefully but then to change overnight. This part of the approach was, in effect, to use Kanter *et al*'s (1992) phrase, a 'bold stroke' rather than a 'long march' approach. Employees left the company and its old systems and practices on a Friday night, and on Monday walked into a completely different organisation. However, what followed was months of chaos as everyone tried to work out what they were doing and how they should do it.

5 *Planned or emergent change.* We can see evidence of both. The Chief Executive had a vision of the organisation's future, but the actual details and nature of the change process emerged as the company struggled to implement it. Furthermore, change was open-ended and, given the nature of the new organisation, it is not clear if it will ever settle down into a fixed state. Once again, to use Kanter *et al*'s (1992) analogy, it was a 'bold stroke' followed by a 'long march'.

6 *Objectives.* The aim was no less than a total transformation of the organisation in all its aspects, and to move from being a traditionally structured technology-driven organisation to a learning organisation focused on service delivery.

Case Study 2: Flair Engineering

1 *Strategy.* The strategy was driven by the vision of Flair's Managing Director who, though supported by his fellow directors, appeared to make things happen by the force of his personality. His aim was to transform the company from a small seller of capacity to a leading designer and supplier of components to the motor industry.

2 *Constraints.* Flair faced and overcame a number of major obstacles. The financial needs and objectives of the company, as well as the way it wished to organise itself, stood in sharp contrast to existing financial and industrial practices in the UK. The company used a number of methods to overcome this including, eventually, becoming part of a German combine. Though philosophically moving in the same direction as the rest of the UK motor component industry, it tended to be in advance of it and, therefore, in the absence of a domestic model, tended to draw on Japanese experience. Throughout the last 15 years, Flair has been operating in an uncertain and, to an extent, hostile business environment. Internally, Flair has changed its structure, culture and management style. Also, the more extensive the changes became, the more it had to overcome sectional interests in order to achieve success.

3 *Managers.* Though the Managing Director and his colleagues drove the strategy and early changes, as time progressed more and more of the work was devolved to line managers, especially the cell managers and the staff in the cells themselves. At various times, the company was also assisted by their customers and by outside consultants.

4 *Change management.* Identifying and managing larger change projects is still the prerogative of senior managers. More and more change projects, however, particularly small-scale improvements, are devolved to line managers and their teams.

5 *Planned or emergent change.* The development of the company's strategy has emerged over the years and has tended to be open-ended. Nevertheless, many of the projects, such as new product introduction, by nature have to have specific objectives and a fixed timetable; although this does not mean they were not the object of attempts at continuous improvement. Furthermore, such improvement activities themselves, as the Nissan study in Chapter 9 showed, tended to have specific objectives and timescales. Therefore, change can be characterised as comprising emergent and open-ended elements which include more focused and finite projects.

6 *Objectives.* Though the vision became clarified as the company developed and grew successful, the overall objectives tended to be global rather than specific, with particular emphasis on transforming the organisation into something comparable to its Japanese counterparts. Although Flair did not explicitly set out to change its culture, this did happen.

Case Study 3: Process Control Inc

1 *Strategy.* The strategy to transform PCI into a world-class manufacturing company was originally driven by an interim Chief Executive. Despite his strong personality, he failed to win the support of the majority of his management team; when he was recalled, the strategy ground to a halt. When the company was later threatened with closure, however, the strategy was resurrected by the management team who, this time, saw its potential and based the company's case for survival upon it.

2 *Constraints.* The vision, and particularly the personality, of the interim Chief Executive appeared to run counter to UK norms, although the vision seemed to be consistent with practices elsewhere in the international electronics industry. There was nothing in the business environment which constrained the vision. However, the organisation's internal characteristics – structure, culture and management style – were at odds with it. This seems to have been a major reason why most managers, and many staff, were suspicious of and opposed it.

3 *Managers.* The vision and strategy were originally driven by the interim Chief Executive. However, his management team were given the main

responsibility for developing the elements of the strategic plan and convincing their own staff to support it. Although the intention was to involve other staff, this did not materialise. Efforts by one manager to pursue the strategy once the interim Chief Executive had departed were hampered by lack of support from his colleagues, and the perception that he was jockeying for position. With the second coming of the strategy, even if the managers had wanted to involve others, they were prevented from doing so – or so they felt – by the need to keep the threatened closure a secret.

4 *Change Management.* The original vision for the company was created by the management team with the aid of an Organisation Development specialist. Subsequent attempts to maintain a team approach to developing and implementing the strategy carried echoes of this. The individual members of the management team took responsibility for the changes in their areas. In some cases, change projects were planned in detail in advance with specific objectives and deadlines. This was especially the case with those projects involving changes to the PCB assembly areas. However, change projects in other areas appear to have had less clear objectives and more open-ended timescales.

5 *Planned or emergent change.* The strategy itself was clearly emergent. Nevertheless, the changes occasioned by the strategy appeared to be a mixture of planned and emergent.

6 *Objectives.* The original vision for the company seemed unclear to many managers. Even those elements of the strategy which were clear did not, originally at least, gain the support of the majority of managers. In the end, the key objective became survival and this alone seemed to galvanise the management team into action. Though there was a shift in the attitudes and beliefs of managers, this clearly did not amount to an organisation-wide culture change.

Case Study 4: Midshires College of Midwifery and Nursing

1 *Strategy.* The most striking feature of the case study was the lack of either a vision or a strategy for creating the new college.

2 *Constraints.* The business environment in which the college operated had become markedly less certain and more complex. This clearly had an adverse impact on the ability of the Project Leader to manage change in the directive–mechanical fashion he preferred. The other constraints which seem to have had a significant effect in this case related to the characteristics of the organisation itself and of those bodies which controlled its destiny. Of particular relevance was the combination of managerial style and organisational politics, neither of which was openly addressed, adapted or changed. The transactional orientation of the Project Leader, coupled with the lack of support from his colleges and the manoeuvring for advantage of

some members of the Steering Committee, held back progress considerably.

3 *Managers.* Initially the Project Leader attempted to involve the other managers by allocating to them responsibility for particular aspects of the amalgamation process. When this failed to produce results, he, in effect, pushed them to one side and took most of the decisions himself. When this also failed to show progress, he too was, to an extent, side-lined and decisions were imposed from above.

4 *Change management.* Initially the Project Leader adopted a very mechanistic approach to change, pursued through a number of planning groups. When he realised that this approach was not working, he switched to the use of more directive means, but the success of this approach was also limited.

5 *Planned or emergent change.* Despite obvious attempts to plan, this was a situation where, for much of the time, change failed to take place at all. The progress that was eventually made emerged out of the confusion in which the organisation found itself.

6 *Objectives.* Though the ultimate objective of the change process was clear – to create one entity from the five separate colleges – many of the issues which surrounded this remained unclear and unresolved. Though the Project Leader addressed the structural issues concerned, he seemed incapable of acknowledging or coping with the more behavioural/attitudinal issues involved.

Case Study 5: Volvo

1 *Strategy.* Volvo's strategy for Job Design was to reorganise its plants to eliminate the moving assembly line, and replace it with group-based assembly. The strategy originated from a need to reduce labour turnover and absenteeism. Even when these were no longer an issue, however, the company continued to pursue the move away from assembly-line working.

2 *Constraints.* Though national public opinion favoured a move away from the assembly line, it was and remains the car industry's established mode of operation. Therefore, Volvo was clearly aiming to change industry constraints while aligning itself with national ones. From the perspective of the business environment, Volvo's move to 'humanise' car assembly appeared to bring them much valuable publicity. In the early years, however, internal constraints (both attitudinal and technical) acted to limit the radicalness of the initiative.

3 *Managers.* All the change projects involving Job Design were driven by senior managers. However, trade union representatives and outside experts in Job Design were also involved at the planning stage.

4 *Change management.* Each project was planned in great detail in advance. This involved not only managers, but also trade union representatives and

outside experts. Once in operation, however, the actual arrangements were modified in order, so it was claimed, to meet business needs and operational difficulties. In most cases these modifications appear to have reduced the ability of workers to set their own pace and to expand their range of activities.

5 *Planned or emergent change.* Though Volvo's strategy for Job Design was driven by a clear intent, it was implemented on different sites and in different ways over a considerable period of time. In terms of the individual Job Design projects, the Volvo case shows that even where changes are planned in detail in advance, the final outcome emerges through a process of iteration and modification once the new practices are put into operation.

6 *Objectives.* The objectives were twofold. The first was financial – to reduce absenteeism and labour turnover. The second was social – to humanise the assembly of cars. These were pursued through a combination of structural and behavioural change. However, when social objectives clashed with financial ones, it was financial objectives which took precedence.

Case Study 6: Rover Group

1 *Strategy.* Rover's vision and strategy – to rebuild itself as a world-class car company – have emerged and taken shape over a long period of time. In the early 1980s, strategy was driven by a few senior managers and was aimed at restoring managerial authority. Now responsibility for strategy is spread across a wider group of managers, and focuses on creating a learning organisation through behavioural and cultural change, and by building involvement and commitment at all levels.

2 *Constraints.* In the late 1970s, it appeared that Rover faced insurmountable obstacles to its survival. External forces seemed lined up against it, and internally the company appeared to be at war with itself. Since then, partly through its links with Honda and partly owing to changes in managerial personnel, Rover has recreated itself as a modern and efficient car company. It has either coped with or changed the constraints it faced, especially market perceptions and labour force attitudes. Rover has not tried to change the rules of the game in the motor industry, though its attempt to become a learning organisation is aimed at developing its own distinctive competencies in order to compete more effectively than its rivals. What it has done, however, is to align its internal operations and external image with the needs of the environment and industry in which it operates.

3 *Managers.* The changes at Rover have been led by successive waves of senior managers – each wave, seemingly, prepared to become more radical and ambitious than its predecessors. As its strategy has developed, more managers have been involved in developing and implementing it. One of Rover's current objectives is for all of its employees to take responsibility for initiating and implementing change.

4 *Change management.* The development of Rover as a learning organisation is open-ended, and driven by a vision, rather than by a list of concrete objectives to be achieved in a prescribed timescale. Nevertheless, there are also change projects which are preplanned and do have clear objectives and fixed timetables.

5 *Planned or emergent change.* At Rover, it appears that larger projects, particularly ones aimed at behavioural/culture change, tended towards an open-ended and emergent nature. However, there are other change projects, generally technical or production-related, which adopt a more planned approach.

6 *Objectives.* There have been successive waves of change at Rover aimed at transforming the company in all its aspects. An important emphasis in recent years has been on changing the attitudes of individuals, promoting teamwork and eradicating the 'them and us' mentality which used to permeate the company. Taken together, these initiatives appear to have led to a culture change at Rover.

Case Study 7: GK Printers

1 *Strategy.* GK's strategy tended to emerge in response to potential crises rather than being proactively led by its management. The company's intent was to reinvent itself as a modern, service-orientated company by aligning its internal arrangements with the changing needs of its environment and customers. Originally, this was pursued mainly through technological change. However, later the emphasis shifted to behavioural change, especially by managers.

2 *Constraints.* External considerations, such as the national climate, business environment and industry-specific factors did not appear to constrain the freedom of action of GK's managers. Indeed, the turbulence and increased competition in the external environment seemed to assist GK with its internal changes. GK's main constraints were internal and related to existing attitudes, technology and practices. Increasingly, however, as the need arose to develop a more collective leadership, it was the directive style of the managing director which was seen as a key constraint on progress.

3 *Managers.* The company's managers took responsibility for strategy development, but devolved responsibility for some change projects to staff in the areas affected.

4 *Change management.* A mixture of approaches to managing change projects can be seen at GK. In all instances, managers took responsibility for identifying the need for change, and in some instances actually directed it. In the case of the computerised business system, the company left selection and implementation to the staff concerned.

5 *Planned or emergent change.* A mixture of both approaches can be seen at GK. The company tried to adopt a planned approach, especially when introducing new technology, but new developments or improvements to existing arrangements tended to be reactive and emergent rather than proactive and planned.

6 *Objectives.* The original aim was to change its technology and image in order to improve its competitiveness. As events unfolded, however, it became clear that the key to competing effectively was to change people's attitudes, especially at management level, and to create a greater commitment to teamwork and collective decision-making.

Case Study 8: Vickers Defence Systems

1 *Strategy.* Though Vickers declared its intention to work more closely with its suppliers, the company did not appear to have a clear view of what this meant. Instead, the actual form of its new approach to suppliers emerged as events unfolded. It was the takeover of the Leeds plant which first made Vickers consider working more cooperatively with its suppliers. This led the company to begin developing new mechanisms to allow closer working; these moved slowly, however, until the threat to the Challenger 2 order, which accelerated the process of change.

2 *Constraints.* The constraints Vickers faced were twofold: first, the UK government's attitude and practices with regard to the defence procurement, which had created a history of antagonism and mistrust throughout the industry; and second, its own internal practices, especially the attitude of its own staff towards suppliers. Vickers' purchasing strategy was aimed at influencing both of these.

3 *Managers.* Both in initiating the move towards closer relationships with suppliers, and in accelerating this process later, senior managers played a leading role.

4 *Change management.* The implementation of changes to structures and practices tended to be left to staff in the areas concerned, especially purchasing. However, the degree of urgency with which the changes were pursued tended to reflect the signals sent by senior managers and, especially, the importance that everyone attached to winning the Challenger 2 order.

5 *Planned or emergent change.* Though there were some initial plans for changing customer–supplier practices (e.g. the development of a new form of purchase agreement), both the overall shape of the changes and individual initiatives tended to emerge from events rather than being preplanned.

6 *Objectives.* The company's initial aim was to develop new mechanisms to allow it to work more cooperatively with suppliers. As the process of change developed, the scope of the supplier strategy became wider, and Vickers'

original objective became subsumed in an attempt to achieve an wholesale change in attitudes and structures between itself and its suppliers.

Case Study 9: Nissan

1 *Strategy.* Based on its experience in Japan, Nissan had a clear picture of how it wished to work with suppliers and the results it wished to achieve. One of the main initiatives it took in this respect was to establish a Supplier Development Team (SDT) to educate suppliers in the practices and approaches used successfully in Japan. However, the actual tools and mechanisms used in developing suppliers emerged in response to Nissan's developing perception of suppliers' needs.

2 *Constraints.* Though the UK's overall practices and industrial culture did not fit in with the Nissan approach, this seems to have had little effect on Nissan's own plant or its approach to suppliers. It was helped, to an extent, by the stagnant business environment which made suppliers eager for new business, especially from internationally competitive firms such as Nissan. The main constraint it faced was the past history of antagonistic customer–supplier relations which existed in the UK and European motor industries. Though this was an industry characteristic, it was manifested in the behaviour, attitudes, structures and practices of individual supplier companies. In the light of this, Nissan faced a choice: should it work within existing arrangements or should it try to change them? For what appeared to be sound business reasons, Nissan chose to adopt the same partnership approach to its UK/European suppliers as it used in Japan – in effect, it chose to change the rules of the game.

3 *Managers.* Once the original objectives for the SDT had been set by senior managers at Nissan, the Supplier Development Team was expected to develop its own plan of action, though it had to convince colleagues and superiors that its plans constituted the most effective use of resources. As far as the improvement activities were concerned, the role of suppliers' senior management was to give approval, or not, to SDT involvement. However, after an improvement activity had demonstrated the potential of such an approach, managers were then expected to initiate and sustain their own programme of improvement activities.

4. *Change management.* The SDT initiative was originally created by senior managers. Once in operation, however, it was the SDT's responsibility to continue to develop it. Individual improvement activities were mainly driven by suppliers' own personnel, who decided upon and implemented changes.

5 *Planned or emergent change.* Though Nissan started out with a clear picture of how it wished to work with its suppliers and the results it expected, the actual details and mechanisms for achieving these emerged over time. The improvement activities, on the other hand, were planned in advance and

highly focused. Areas of improvement were identified, analysed and improvement targets set. These activities were all carried out within the framework of a highly structured programme. In many respects – such as short timespan, the educational role of the SDT, and staff involvement – the improvement activities carry the hallmark of the planned approach to change.

6 *Objectives.* Nissan's objectives covered a number of different levels. Its overall objective was to develop a co-operative relationship with its suppliers. In terms of individual suppliers, Nissan wished to see major changes in their whole approach to manufacturing and promote a teamwork mentality. The catalyst for achieving this was the SDT's ten-day improvement activity. By achieving a beneficial change to a small part of a company, Nissan believed it could show the potential of the Japanese approach to manufacturing. Linking all this together was Nissan's belief that it needed to change attitudes, perceptions and behaviour in its suppliers. Though not explicitly aimed at changing culture, Nissan's approach did stress the need for teamwork and an end to 'them and us' attitudes in its suppliers.

Case Study 10: Speedy Stationers

1 *Strategy.* The development of Speedy's vision or strategy tended to be driven by force of events or opportunism rather than necessarily being preplanned. Each time a major opportunity or concern arose, Speedy examined its options and chose the one which appeared to be more favourable to the development of its business.

2 *Constraints.* The degree to which external or internal factors affected Speedy's strategy is unclear. Certainly, the company did not appear to have faced great restrictions on its freedom of manoeuvre. Nor, except in one case, did it appear to have sought to change or influence the constraints it faced. The exception is its attempt to develop a partnership approach to customers. In this instance it was attempting to change industry practice. Though this met with support internally, it had to overcome a large degree of scepticism in the customer concerned.

3 *Managers.* It was Speedy's Managing Director who originally developed its partnership strategy. He later, and not necessarily willingly, handed responsibility for its continuing development to another director of the company. He established his own plans which he then had to convince his colleagues, and Speedy's customers, to accept.

4 *Change management.* The actual implementation of the partnership approach required not only the involvement of Speedy's own staff, but also co-operation from its customer's (UTL) managers and staff at all levels.

5 *Planned or emergent change.* The development of the strategy itself, and the

partnership with UTL, was an open-ended process in which the form and content of the strategy emerged on a day-to-day basis.

6 *Objectives.* The aim of Speedy's strategy was to develop a new type of business relationship with its customers. Implementing this led to changes in both Speedy and UTL – the first customer with whom it attempted this. Though some of these changes were structural, most changes concerned the attitudes and behaviour of individuals and groups; however, there was too little evidence to be able to judge whether or not these would lead to cultural change.

Summary: theory and practice

One should be wary of drawing any firm conclusions about either theory or practice from such a small number of case studies. However, the case studies presented in Part Three are rich in detail, mainly cover an extended time period, and do raise some important issues which it would be unwise to ignore.

Strategy

Though in some cases this was driven by a clear vision, more often it was triggered by perceived opportunities, problems or crises. The actual form of each organisation's strategy emerged from attempts to pursue visions or respond to events.

Constraints

The case studies reveal that external and internal constraints do affect the degree of choice managers have or perceive themselves to have. However, the studies also show that managers can take action either to align their organisation more closely with external demands, or to influence or change the constraints they face to suit their personal preferences and/or the organisation's existing arrangements.

Managers

In all the instances examined, managers played a central role in initiating or developing visions and strategies. Managers also played a leading role in implementing strategies or attempting to create the conditions for their implementation. In some cases they also led change projects.

Managing change

A variety of approaches to change management can be seen in the case studies. These range from instances where all the major decisions were taken by one manager, to others where staff in the areas concerned led and planned change projects. The general tendency was for both employees and managers to be involved in planning and implementing smaller more short-term projects, while larger and more long-term projects, especially those concerned with attitudinal or behavioural change, were very much driven by managers.

Planned or emergent change

Once again, the picture is mixed. Longer-term and larger projects were usually open-ended, with diffuse objectives, and involving large numbers of people; whereas smaller, better-defined projects were inclined to be more tightly controlled and planned. However, perhaps the main distinction was between those projects aiming to change attitudes and behaviour, which by their nature needed to be more flexible, and those concentrating on structural or technical change, especially at the operational level, which tended to have clearer objectives and required more fixed timescales.

Objectives

A variety of objectives could be discerned, ranging from localised structural change to organisation-wide cultural change. In all the organisations, however, either at the outset or over time, changes to the behaviour and attitudes of individuals and groups came to be considered as more important than either technical or structural adjustments.

We can see, therefore, that, depending on the circumstances or constraints, strategy development and change management can take many forms. In the case study examples, we can see deliberate and conscious attempts to shape strategy as well as more unconscious and accidental approaches. We can also see cases where an organisation's strategy or change programme, by design or accident, resulted in the reshaping or realignment of the constraints the organisation faced. In terms of change management, there were cases where the process of change and the process of strategy development were the same. However, there were also cases where change was planned and followed on from a particular strategy.

The case studies, therefore, illustrate the arguments regarding managerial choice, strategy and change developed in Chapters 5 and 6. They also show that where decisions are taken in an open manner, when those concerned are genuinely listened to and involved, and where serious attempts are made to identify and resolve reservations and resistance, there is less likelihood that political behaviour, individual interests or bias will be able to subvert the process.

Having examined and compared the theory and practice of strategy development and change management, we are now in a position to present a new Choice–Change model of strategy development and change management, one which incorporates both planned and emergent approaches. Before doing so, however, there are two outstanding and interrelated issues which need to be clarified. These concern rapid and wholesale organisational transformation, and employee involvement. Dunphy and Stace (1993) argued that planned change could not incorporate large-scale change undertaken in a directive or coercive fashion. Nor, by definition, can the emergent approach apparently incorporate this type of change.

This would seem to call for a new perspective on organisational change which is neither planned nor emergent. However, the Oticon study in Chapter 6 appears to offer a different explanation. This was a case of rapid organisational transformation carried out in a directive rather than a participative fashion. It was also both planned and emergent rather than being neither. A great deal of planning went into the rapid structural change at Oticon, but this was followed by a period of emergent change where staff had to develop and adjust to new ways of working with, and behaving towards, each other. Therefore, Dunphy and Stace's (1993) argument that rapid change invalidates the planned approach, and by implication the emergent approach, may be based on a failure to appreciate that such changes do have to be well planned, but they are then followed by a period of adjustment and consolidation in which staff have to establish what is expected from them and how to achieve this.

Though this planned–emergent argument appears to explain part of the issues raised by Dunphy and Stace, it still leaves the question of how such fundamental changes can be achieved without the full co-operation and involvement of the people concerned. Current wisdom, as described in Chapter 6, regards involvement as the key to successful change. Schmuck and Miles (1971), however, argued that involvement is not necessary in all situations. Instead they argue that the level of involvement required is dependent on the impact of the change on the people concerned.

Huse (1980) developed this distinction further. Building on earlier work by Harrison (1970), Huse categorised change interventions along a continuum based on the 'depth' of intervention, ranging from the 'shallow level' to the 'deepest level'. The greater the depth of the intervention, Huse argues, the more it becomes concerned with the psychological make-up and personality of the individual, and the greater the need for the full involvement of individuals if they are to accept the changes.

The argument, therefore, is that it is necessary to link levels of involvement to the types of change involved. The key is that the greater the effect on the individual, especially in terms of psychological constructs and values, the deeper the level of involvement required if successful behaviour change is to be achieved. This appears to explain why, in some cases, involvement can be dispensed with or minimised, while in other cases it is vital. It does not, explain, however, why major changes at Oticon were successful without a great deal of involvement, nor indeed why PCI was not successful despite a high level of involvement.

In seeking to understand and explain such apparent contradictions, Burnes and James (1995) draw on the theory of Cognitive Dissonance. This theory states that people try to be consistent in both their attitudes and behaviour. When they sense an inconsistency either between two or more attitudes or between their attitudes and behaviour, people experience dissonance; that is, they feel frustrated and uncomfortable – sometimes extremely so – with the situation (Jones, 1990). Therefore, individuals will seek a stable state where there is minimum dissonance. This latter point is important. It is unlikely that dissonance can ever be totally avoided, but where the elements creating the dissonance are relatively unimportant, the pressure to correct them will be low. Where the issues involved are perceived by the individual to be significant, however, the presence of such dissonance will motivate the person concerned to try to reduce the dissonance and achieve consonance, by changing either their attitudes or behaviour to bring them into line (Robbins, 1986; Smith *et al*, 1982). This may involve a process of cognitive restructuring, which is unlikely to be free from difficulties for the individual concerned (Mahoney, 1974). However, as Festinger (1957), one of the originators of the concept, pointed out, in addition to trying to reduce the dissonance, people will actively avoid situations and information which would be likely to increase the dissonance. Since the emergence of the theory of cognitive dissonance in the 1950s, it has been developed and refined (*see* Cooper and Fazio, 1984; Fazio *et al*, 1977; Jones, 1990).

Applying principles of Cognitive Dissonance to organisation change, it can be seen that, if an organisation embarks on a change project which is decisively out of step with the attitudes of those concerned, it will meet resistance unless those concerned change their attitudes. On the other hand, where the level of dissonance occasioned by proposed changes is low, attitudinal adjustments will be minor and potential resistance negligible. Therefore, the level and type of involvement should be geared to the level of dissonance to which any proposed changes may give rise.

Up to this point, Cognitive Dissonance supports the work of Schmuck and Miles (1971) and Huse (1980). If we apply the theory to situations, such as Oticon's, however, where old certainties have proved inadequate and the very survival of the organisation is at stake, a different picture emerges. The crisis (or potential crisis) raises the level of dissonance in the organisation as it becomes apparent that existing practices are no longer viable and change is required. Not only does this make individuals and groups more receptive to radical change, but in addition, change can be one of the main ways of reducing dissonance. Therefore, the dissonance is occasioned not by the change, but by the condition of the organisation before the change. This perspective also helps to explain the cases of PCI and Vickers, where initially managers and others were resistant to changes or were only prepared to move slowly. In such situations, the absence of a sense of deep crisis prevented existing certainties being successfully challenged. Later, in both companies, when more severe threats arose, these old certainties were challenged, and those involved became more prepared to accept and promote radical solutions that had previously been rejected.

Therefore, what we can say of the issue of involvement is that, in most cases, it is necessary to convince staff of the need to challenge their existing beliefs and behaviours. However, this questioning of beliefs and behaviours can also arise in situations of crisis without the need for elaborate involvement techniques, because those concerned can see that, unless major or radical changes are made, the organisation may cease to survive.

Having resolved the apparent inability of the planned and emergent approaches to incorporate rapid and directive change, we can now move on to suggest a new model for strategy development and change management.

CHOICE MANAGEMENT–CHANGE MANAGEMENT: TOWARDS A NEW MODEL

From the above, we can see that, while organisational change can be a complex, ambiguous and open-ended phenomenon, it can also be relatively straightforward with understandable and limited objectives. This in itself is not a new or radical finding – anyone who works in or studies organisations will have noted that change comes in a wide variety of shapes and sizes. It was argued in Chapter 5 and 6, however, that, in order to cope with the wide variety of types of change, there is a need for a corresponding variety of approaches to strategy development and change management.

This point, the need to match types of change with appropriate approaches to managing change, is not prominent in the literature on organisational change and behaviour. Despite the widespread influence of Contingency Theory, there are still many writers and practitioners who are committed to a 'one best way' approach to strategy and change. The call by Dunphy and Stace (1993) for a situational or contextual approach to these issues has been taken up by few others. Though there are writers on strategy, such as Mintzberg (1994) and Whittington (1993), who identify the various approaches to strategy, they tend, eventually, to opt for one as the preferred approach. This is even more pronounced in the change literature where there is a clear distinction between those who support the planned approach (such as Cummings and Huse, 1989, and French and Bell, 1984) and those who adhere to the emergent approach (such as Dawson, 1994, and Wilson, 1992).

Many of those arguing for their own favoured approach to strategy and change do so, either explicitly or implicitly, on the basis of their perception of the nature of the environment in which organisations operate. Those arguing for a planned approach to strategy and/or change appear to assume that the environment is relatively stable and predictable. Those who take a more emergent approach to both seem to operate on the assumption that the environment is turbulent and unpredictable.

Furthermore, most writers seem to assume that the principal role of managers and the ultimate objective of strategy and change is to align or realign an organisation with its environment. In Chapters 5 and 6, and the subsequent case study chapters, we have sought to reject this argument and adopt a different stance. Rather than accepting the view that managers are prisoners of the circumstances in which their organisations operate or find themselves, it was argued that managers can and do exercise a considerable degree of choice. It was further argued, however, that the scope and nature of the choices managers face and make are constrained by a range of external factors (national characteristics, the business environment and industry norms) and internal organisational characteristics (especially structure, culture, politics and managerial style). This argument goes much further than many by challenging the assumption that managers are in some way the passive agents of forces beyond their control, but it still leaves them as prisoners of circumstances –

although the prison in this case is much roomier than many of the writers we have discussed would acknowledge.

However, the final arguments in Chapters 5 and 6 challenged even this definition of managerial choice. It was suggested that the constraints on choice are themselves amenable to managerial actions – in effect, organisations can influence or change the constraints under which they operate. This possibility was first suggested when examining Contingency theory in Chapter 2; it was further developed in Chapters 4, 5 and 6; and in Chapters 7, 8 and 9, it has been shown to be more than a possibility. The case studies reveal that, though organisations do try to align and realign themselves with their environment, they also attempt to influence and restructure the environment and other constraints in their favour. Sometimes, by accident or design, this results in a reconfiguration of the accepted rules on which the industry in which they operate competes; while in other instances, it prevents organisations being forced to undertake more radical internal upheavals.

In the case of Oticon (Chapter 7), it can be seen that the company deliberately set out to change the basis on which it competed. Lacking the technological strength of its competitors, which was the accepted cornerstone of competition in its industry, it proposed to offer a superior level of service instead. By changing the rules of the game in its industry, Oticon hoped to steal a march on its competitors. In the case of Nissan, to accept the antagonistic relationship with suppliers that was the norm in the UK motor industry might have necessitated radical alterations to the culture and practices it wished to promote in its new UK car plant. To avoid this, Nissan sought to build a new type of relationship with UK/European suppliers, one which would increase the element of predictability and stability in its environment and fit in with its own preferred way of working. Though Vickers' attempts to develop closer links with suppliers also increased the stability and predictability of its environment, its main objective was to reduce its cost base and speed up product development. Failure to achieve this might have compelled Vickers to consider a more radical overhaul of its own internal structures and practices. It could also be maintained that, in addition, Vickers was trying to align itself more closely with the way its foreign competitors operated.

The implications of managerial choice for the nature and focus of change management are, as the above shows, significant. Change management need not be seen as a mechanism for achieving a specified and predicted outcome (the planned approach). Nor need it be conceived of as a continuing process of aligning and realigning the organisation with its environment (the emergent approach). Instead, by linking managerial choice to the management of change, organisations can open up a much wider spectrum of options. These range from focusing on achieving radical internal change to align an organisation with its external constraints, doing the same in an attempt to restructure such constraints, to influencing or changing external constraints in order to avoid internal upheavals.

From this perspective, as the Choice Management–Change Management model in Fig. 10.1 shows, organisational change can be viewed as the product of three interdependent organisational processes:

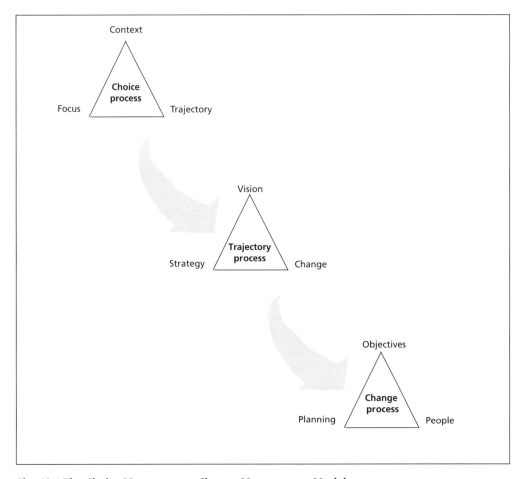

Fig. 10.1 The Choice Management–Change Management Model

- *The choice process – which is concerned with the nature, scope and focus of organisational decision-making.*

- *The trajectory process – which relates to an organisation's past and future direction and is seen as the outcome of its vision, purpose and future objectives.*

- *The change process – which covers approaches to, mechanisms for achieving, and outcomes of change.*

These processes are interdependent because, as Fig. 10.1 shows, the change process is itself an integral part of the trajectory process and this, in turn, is a vital part of the choice process. Within each of these processes there is a group of elements, or forces, which interact, clash and influence each other in subtle and complex ways. It is this interaction of elements or forces which prevents decision-making and change management from being a rational-mechanical process, and ensures that they are based on subjective and imperfect judgment.

Each of these three processes will now be described, not only to show their complexity and interdependence, but also to provide a guide to putting the Choice Management–Change Management model into practice. For this latter reason, the description of the change process, in particular, will dwell on the steps necessary to accomplish change successfully.

The choice process

The choice process comprises three elements:

- *Organisational context*
- *Focus of choice*
- *Organisational trajectory*

Organisational context

One of the standard prescriptions for successful organisations is that they should know their own strengths and weaknesses, their customers' needs and the nature of the environment in which they operate. As the case studies show, however, many organisations appear only to begin collecting this sort of information when they are in trouble. How can organisations hope to understand and appreciate the options open to them, however, unless they develop mechanisms for collecting and analysing information on their performance and general situation?

No one would suggest that assembling information on past, present and future performance is easy or that understanding the nature of the constraints faced by an organisation is simple. However, there are relatively well established methods for benchmarking an organisation's performance against a range of internal and external comparators (Camp, 1989). The main internal and external organisational constraints are also reasonably well documented. As discussed in Chapter 5, these comprise national characteristics, industry/sector norms, the business environment, and organisational characteristics such as structure, culture, politics and management style.

Gathering this sort of information, as well as discussing it and agreeing how to interpret it, will require the participation of a wide range of people and functions. Not only should this provide a robust basis for decision-making, it can also develop a sense of teamwork, co-operation and mutual understanding among those concerned. Also, by working in this fashion, organisations can promote openness and reduce, though probably not eliminate, political behaviour and conflict. Nevertheless, some organisations will find that owing to the context in which they operate, teamwork, co-operation and openness are very difficult to achieve without first changing those factors which hinder or prevent these. Perhaps the prime consideration in this respect is the prevalent style of management. Managers are really the only group who initiate change and will rarely (as a group) voluntarily adopt changes which adversely affect them. It follows that, faced with a mismatch between their organisation and its environment, some managers will seek to achieve re-alignment by influencing the environment rather than pursuing an internal upheaval which may involve changes in management style and personnel.

Focus of choice

At any one point in time, organisations appear to focus their attention on only a narrow range of short-, medium-, and long-term issues. Some of these will relate to the organisation's performance, while others may be more concerned with building or developing particular competencies or technologies. In some cases, the issues may be of passing interest only, while in other cases they may be fundamental to the organisation's survival. Certainly, in most instances, organisations will in one way or another focus on aligning themselves with or even influencing or changing the constraints under which they operate.

How an organisation decides upon which issues to focus, and whether this is done in a concerted fashion (as at Flair and Rover), or in a way which allows many different groups and individuals to pursue their own agenda (as at Midshires College), is a fundamental factor in any organisation's decision-making process. Certainly, the received wisdom is that a concerted and co-ordinated approach, which focuses upon a small number of issues at any one time, is more effective than a fragmented one (Kay, 1993; Senge, 1993).

Organisational trajectory

An organisation's trajectory or direction is shaped by its past actions, and future objectives and strategies. As such it provides a guide or framework within which to judge the acceptability, relevance or urgency of issues, concerns and proposed actions. The trajectory process encompasses the determination of and interplay between an organisation's vision, strategies and its approach to change.

In some respects, the concept of trajectory comprises both an organisation's 'memory' of past events and its intent in terms of future ones. For some organisations, the trajectory will be clean and unambiguous. In others, the interpretation of past events and proposals for future actions will be the subject of dispute and uncertainty.

It will also be the case that some organisations will consciously attempt to plot their trajectory in minute detail, whilst others may adopt a more global and distant set of objectives. Many organisations may find that their trajectory emerges from a set of apparently unrelated actions.

Indeed, as the case studies show it is the interplay between past actions and future intent coupled to the wide variety of approaches to these which makes decision-making so complex.

Each of the three elements of the choice process is complex in itself, but they also interact with each other in an intricate and unpredictable fashion. An organisation's trajectory can influence both the focus of its decision-making, and the context within which the organisation operates. Likewise, the context provides a framework within which the trajectory is developed. Similarly, the focus of choice will influence which aspect of the organisation's context its trajectory will be directed towards, not only in the short term but also in the medium and long term.

Given the complex and multifaceted nature of decision-making, it is not, perhaps, surprising that writers have drawn attention to the tendency for managers to 'muddle through' rather than attempt an exhaustive and exhausting examination of all the available options (Lindblom, 1968). Nor is it surprising that some managers prefer 'fire-fighting' to tackling fundamental issues (Burnes, 1991) – at least the objective is immediate and clear, and a favourable outcome can be achieved (though it is usually short-lived). Appreciating the complexity of decision-making also casts the Japanese ringi system (discussed in Chapter 3) in a favourable light. Only by an exhaustive analysis of the issue concerned and the options available is the most appropriate decision likely to be arrived at. However, the ringi system is usually aided by and carried out within the framework of a strong corporate vision and clear strategies for its pursuit.

By framing decisions within such a framework, Japanese companies ensure that they do not have to explore all the available possibilities when taking decisions – merely those that are in harmony with their vision/strategy/intent. In this way, the entire choice process is simplified and made more achievable. Japanese companies have shown themselves to be masters of developing visions and strategies which not only make them successful but also, and not incidentally, reduce the uncertainty in the environment, alter the basis of competition in their favour, and narrow the focus of decision-making (Hamel and Prahalad, 1989). The result is that though the choice process remains complex, not only does it have a greater degree of consistency between the elements and people involved, but it is also more focused in the range of issues and decisions required.

What can be seen, therefore, is that while the choice process is uncertain, complex and time-consuming, there are approaches which do reduce these factors and can make the process more transparent and effective. In order to understand further how this can be achieved, we shall now examine the trajectory process.

The trajectory process

Like the choice process, the trajectory process comprises three elements:

- *Vision*
- *Strategy*
- *Change*

Vision

As described in Chapter 5, the use of scenario-building and 'visioning' techniques has become increasingly popular in recent years. The ten case studies in Part Three showed that not all companies have visions, and not all visions find favour with the managers and employees who have to implement them. However, the concept of organisations driving themselves forward by creating an ambitious vision (or intent or scenario) of where they wish to be in the long term has become increasingly influential over the last decade (Cummings and Huse, 1989; Johnson and Scholes, 1993; Senge, 1993). The argument, in brief, for this approach is that previous attempts to plan the future have either fallen foul of the difficulty of accurately translating past trends into future projections, or have not been ambitious enough because they have allowed future plans to be constrained by present resources (Hamel and Prahalad, 1989). The process of developing an organisation's vision attempts to overcome this by encouraging senior managers to think freely, without considering present resource constraints, about where they would like to take the organisation in the long term.

This can produce very ambitious objectives, such as Honda's declaration in the 1960s (when it was barely more than a motorcycle producer little known outside Japan) that it wanted 'to become the second Ford'. The creation of visions is an iterative process whereby an initial vision is created, and the gap between this and the present circumstances is identified. The organisation then considers its strategic options to bridge the gap, and in so doing refines the vision itself. This refining process serves partly to ensure that the vision is discussed widely within the organisation, and to gain employees' commitment to its objectives, thus using the vision as a motivating and guiding force for the organisation.

The organisational vision can best be described as a beacon shining from a faraway hillside at night that guides travellers to their destination. Travellers can usually only see a few feet ahead but are prevented from getting lost by the beacon. Occasionally the traveller will have to make a detour, or sometimes even reverse course, but this is done in the certain knowledge that they still know where it is that they are travelling to. The concept of the beacon is a useful analogy, in that it highlights one of the main differences between vision-building and other forms of long-range planning. Normally it is only the leadership of an organisation that has a clear view of where the organisation is going in the long term. The vision, however, like the beacon, should shine clearly for everyone in the organisation to see, so that they can all know where they are heading.

Cummings and Huse (1989) developed guidelines to help organisations construct visions. They argue that there are four aspects to constructing a vision:

1 *Mission*. This states the organisation's major strategic purpose or reason for existing. It can indicate such factors as products, markets and core competencies.

2 *Valued outcomes*. Visions about desired futures often include specific performance and human outcomes the organisation would like to achieve. These can include types of behaviour and levels of skill as well as more traditional outcomes such as turnover and profit. These valued outcomes can serve as goals for the change process and standards for assessing progress.

3 *Valued conditions*. This element of creating a vision involves specifying what the organisation should look like to achieve the valued outcomes. These

valued conditions help to define a desired future state towards which change activity should move. Valued conditions can include issues relating to structure, culture, openness and managerial style as well as external issues such as relations with customers and suppliers.

4 *Mid-point goals.* Mission and vision statements are often quite general and usually need to be fleshed out by identifying more concrete mid-point goals. These represent desirable organisational conditions but lie between the current state and the desired future state. Mid-point goals are clearer and more detailed than desired future states, and thus, they provide more concrete and manageable steps and benchmarks for change.

By constructing a vision in this manner, the organisation not only has a picture of what it wishes to become but also some concrete targets to aim for. In the case of Nissan (Chapter 9), its vision of what it wanted from suppliers and how it preferred to work with them was clear. The actual details had to be worked out as Nissan developed its supplier base. It recognised the need for supplier development; later, it saw that training would also be required; and then it moved on to offer strategy development packages. The point is that visions (and components of visions such as Nissan's vision for its suppliers) identify the intent, and mid-point goals are then needed to help identify a way forward. These goals will have to be renewed periodically and revisited in the light of their achievement or non-achievement, but this is always within the context of the vision. However, the possibility always exists for the process of implementation to cast new lights on the vision itself and cause this to be rethought. Visions are implemented and brought to life through the development of strategy.

Strategy

In the context of a vision, strategy can be defined as a coherent or consistent stream of actions which an organisation takes to move towards its vision. This stream of actions can be centrally planned and driven, they can be delegated and distributed throughout the organisation, and they can be either conscious actions in pursuit of the vision, or unconscious or emergent ones resulting from past patterns of decisions or resource allocations or current responses to problems and opportunities. In reality, organisations tend to pursue a mixture of these. Therefore, there can be a central strategy, sub-strategies and, influenced by the vision and circumstances, a general awareness of the need to act or respond in a particular way.

Such strategies would usually cover marketing, product development, manufacturing, personnel, finance, and – increasingly – information technology, and quality. The characteristics of conscious strategies are that they generally look five years or more ahead, but only contain firm and detailed plans for the next 12 to 18 months (this is because changing circumstances usually prevent most companies being firm about their intentions for any longer than this). These strategies are put together in one strategic plan which is, usually, formally reviewed annually, but is frequently reviewed informally and when major and unexpected events occur. Because the strategies are not ends in themselves, but means to an end (the vision), they are by necessity both flexible and pragmatic. They will be constructed and pursued only to the extent that they facilitate the pursuit of the vision.

One way of viewing strategy is to see it as a series of links in a chain which stretches from the present to the indeterminate future where the vision lies. Each link in the chain represents particular strategies or groups of decisions that organisations pursue to move themselves forward, in the light of both their eventual target and the prevailing circumstances of the time. The links (strategies) are continually having to be forged and reforged (to use Mintzberg's (1987) term, 'crafted') over time. Strategy contains, therefore, both planned and emergent elements – the exact balance being determined by the circumstances of the particular organisation in question rather than any intrinsic merit of either the planned or emergent approach.

One final point: it follows from this that organisations do not need to be able to see all the links in the strategic chain: merely those which will guide them over the next few years. Nor do they need to dictate centrally or identify what should be done and when. Instead, they need to establish both a climate of understanding and a general willingness to pursue certain courses of action, as the opportunity arises or circumstances necessitate.

Change

Just as organisation's trajectory is both an important element of the choice process and a process in its own right, the same applies to change. The change process will be discussed below, but in the context of the trajectory process it is necessary to note that, though visions and strategies can be crucial in shaping the life of organisations, it is only when some facet of the organisation is changed or changes that visions and strategies advance from being mere possibilities to become reality. This is also a two-way street. On the one hand, visions and strategies shape and direct change. They indicate what needs to change and where. They also create the conditions and climate within which change takes place. On the other hand, because visions and strategies only become reality through the actions of the organisation, it is these changes, these actions which shape visions and strategies.

In summary, we can see that the trajectory process, whilst playing a key role in shaping choice, is also itself a complex process comprising vision, strategy and change. Though it is difficult to conceive of any organisations that do not possess some elements of all three, the degree to which they are held in common or are consistent with each other or are part of a conscious effort clearly varies. This relates partly to the circumstances of the organisation. Under conditions of stability and predictability, even without prompting from senior managers, it is much easier for people to develop a common view of how an organisation should operate, what its future should be and what changes need to be made. In rapidly changing circumstances, however, where certainties and fixed points of reference are few and far between, a common understanding is unlikely to arise automatically. Where it does exist, in such situations, it is likely to be outmoded and inappropriate. This is why organisations more and more are trying consciously to use visions to create a common cause. They want to reduce uncertainty and create a broad understanding of what needs doing, and how. For many organisations, the merit of this approach is not only that it makes change easier, but that it also allows staff to judge for themselves what changes need making and what approach to adopt. In order to explore this further, we can now examine the change process itself.

The change process

Once again, as with the other two processes, the change process comprises three interlinked elements:

- *Objectives and outcomes*
- *Planning the change*
- *People*

Objectives and outcomes

It was noted in Chapter 6 that a high proportion of change efforts end in failure. Burnes and Weekes (1989) found that, in many cases, change projects failed because their original objectives or the desired outcomes were poorly thought-out and inconsistent. In addition, it was suggested in Chapter 4 that organisational change, because it affects the distribution of power and resources, is an inherently political process driven by sectional interests rather than organisational needs.

Though it is difficult to envisage a situation where political interests are not present, Burnes (1988) suggested an approach to assessing the need for and type of change which attempts to make the process of establishing objectives and outcomes more rigorous and open. Openness and rigour not only make it harder to disguise political considerations, they also allow assumptions regarding the merits (or lack of them) of particular options to be tested. Burnes' approach has four phases:

- *the trigger*
- *the remit*
- *the assessment team*
- *the assessment*

The trigger Organisations should only investigate change (other than minor projects which can be easily accommodated) for one of the following reasons:

- *The company's vision/strategy highlights the need for change or improved performance.*
- *Current performance or operation indicates that severe problems or concerns exist.*

● *Suggestions or opportunities arise (either from the area concerned or elsewhere) which potentially offer significant benefits to the organisation.*

If one or more of the above arises, then this should trigger the organisation to assess the case for change, which leads to the next phase.

The remit This should state clearly the reasons for the assessment, its objectives and timescale, and who should be involved and consulted. The remit should stress the need to focus as much on the social aspects as the technical considerations involved. In addition, it must make clear that those who will carry out the assessment must look at all options rather than merely considering one or two alternatives. Organisations need to be clear who draws up such remits and who has the final say on the assessment team's recommendations. As was shown by Burnes and Weekes (1989), this responsibility is often unclear. In traditional organisations, this responsibility would lie with senior managers. In many of today's organisations, the responsibility for such activities is devolved. However, there is usually a requirement to inform senior managers of change, and certain types of major change remain the responsibility of senior managers. Furthermore, where change affects other areas, co-ordination between areas will be essential. The important point is that there must be clarity and agreement about who has the responsibility and authority to initiate change before an assessment begins.

The assessment team In most cases, this should be a multidisciplinary team consisting of representatives from the area affected (both managers and staff), specialist staff (finance, technical and personnel), and, where appropriate, an outside consultant or change facilitator. It may also require the involvement of senior managers.

The assessment The first task of the assessment team is to review and if necessary clarify or amend its remit. Only then can it begin the assessment, which should comprise the following four steps:

● *Clarification of the problem or opportunity. This is achieved by gathering information, especially from those involved. In some situations it might be found that the problem or opportunity is redefined, or does not exist, or can be dealt with easily by those most closely concerned. If so, this is reported back and probably no further action needs to be taken. However, if the clarification reveals that a significant problem or opportunity does exist, then the remaining steps need to be completed.*

● *Investigation of alternative solutions. A wide-ranging examination should take place to establish the range of possible solutions. This should be tested against an agreed list of criteria covering costs and benefits, in order to eliminate those solutions which are clearly inapplicable and to highlight those which appear to offer the greatest benefit. This then leads on to the next step.*

● *Feedback. The definition of the problem or opportunity and the range of possible solutions should be discussed with interested or affected parties, to obtain their views and to establish the criteria for selecting the preferred solution or solutions.*

● **Recommendations and decision.** *The team should present their recommendations in a form which clearly defines the problem/opportunity, identifies the range of solutions, establishes the criteria for selection and makes recommendations. These recommendations should include not only the type of change, but also the mechanics and timescale for making such changes and the resource implications, as well as performance targets for the new operation.*

   This then leaves those responsible for decision-making in a position to assess, modify, defer or reject the assessment team's recommendations in the light of the strategic objectives of the organisation. If the decision is to proceed with the proposed changes, then it becomes necessary to begin planning the implementation process.

Planning the change

Whether the need for change arises from an organisation's strategy or emerges in some other way, once it has been established that it should take place and what form it should take, it is then necessary to plan how this will be achieved and then to implement the plan. This process comprises six interrelated activities:

1 *Establishing a change management team.* This must include some, if not all, of those responsible for the original assessment of the need for change, including the assistance of an outside consultant or change facilitator. However, it will usually also have a greater user input, especially at the implementation stage. Sometimes, for large change projects, a sub-group comprising primarily those affected by the changes, both managers and others, is established to handle the day-to-day implementation issues.

2 *Management structures.* Because organisational transition tends to be ambiguous and to need direction, special structures, for example in order to establish appropriate reporting relationships to senior management, may need to be created to support and guide the change management team. These management structures should include people who have the power to mobilise resources to promote change.

3 *Activity planning.* This involves constructing a schedule for the change programme, citing specific activities and events that must occur if the transition is to be successful. Activity planning should clearly identify and integrate discrete change tasks, and should link these tasks to the organisation's change goals and priorities. Activity planning should also gain top management approval, should be cost-effective, and should remain adaptable as feedback is received during the change process. It must

therefore determine the final and intermediate objectives, and where possible these must be tied to a specific timetable in order to avoid uncertainty amongst those who have to carry out the changes.

4 *Commitment planning.* This activity involves identifying key people and groups whose commitment and support is needed for change to occur, and deciding how to gain their support. It can be seen in the case of PCI that the interim Chief Executive failed to appreciate how difficult this is. The Nissan SDT, on the other hand, establishes the support of senior management before beginning and then goes on to win the support of others, in particular by involving them in selecting and planning change.

5 *Audits and post-audits.* It is important to monitor progress and to see to what extent objectives are being met. This allows plans to be modified in the light of experience. The more uncertain and unclear the change process, the greater the need for periodic review. After change or when a particular milestone has been passed, a post-audit should be carried out to establish (a) that the objectives have really been met, and (b) to ascertain what lessons can be learned for future projects.

6 *Training.* This is a key part of any change project and takes a number of forms. The obvious one is in relation to new skills that might be necessary. As the Nissan approach to suppliers shows, however, training can have a number of other purposes. It may aim to give staff the skills to undertake the change themselves. It may be the intention to leave them with the ability to pursue continuous improvement, once the change has been substantially achieved, or it may be intended to make them aware of the need for change and to win them over. One aspect of this might be team-building sessions. Furthermore, there is a need to give general awareness training to those in the organisation who might be indirectly affected. To ensure that the various types of training are targeted at the right people or groups, a training programme – starting before implementation and continuing after completion – should be established, showing who needs training, the form of the training and when it will take place.

Though planning change is in some ways a 'technical' issue, it is also about involving and motivating the people concerned and those whose support is necessary.

People

As mentioned earlier, organisational change takes many forms. It can be of a structural or technical form which requires little of individuals in terms of behavioural or attitudinal change. On the other hand, as the case studies have shown, increasingly it requires individuals and groups to reconsider radically their attitudes towards how work is performed, and how they behave towards both their colleagues internally and their counterparts externally. Whatever form it takes, however, there are three people-related activities that need to be undertaken:

- creating a willingness to change;
- involving people; and
- sustaining the momentum.

Creating a willingness to change. Even where change is purely of a technical or structural form, there has to be a willingness among those concerned to change, to want to be involved. There are organisations who have put, and are continuing to put, a great deal of effort into creating a climate where change is accepted as the norm (as described in Chapter 7, Oticon is an example of this). However, perhaps most organisations are still at the stage where they have to convince staff of the need for change.

For many people, organisational change involves moving from the known to the unknown, with the possibility of loss as well as gain. Companies therefore need to create a readiness for change among their employees, and adopt an approach which is aware of the possibility and causes of resistance, and deals with these at an early stage. In order to achieve this, there are four steps an organisation can take:

- *Make people aware of the pressures for change.* The organisation should inform employees on a regular basis of its plans for the future, the competitive/market pressures it faces, customer requirements and the performance of its key competitors. Obviously, promoting the vision and explaining the strategic plan are vital components in this. Through this approach, members of the organisation come to appreciate that change is not only inevitable, but is being undertaken to safeguard rather than threaten their future.

- *Give regular feedback on the performance of individual processes and areas of activity within the organisation.* This allows a company to draw attention to any discrepancy between actual performance and desired present and future performance. It allows those concerned to begin to think about how this situation can be improved, and prepares them for the need for change. In looking at the case study companies, it is noticeable that there was a greater readiness to change in those organisations where management was open about its objectives and the company's or function's current performance than in those organisations where information was guarded. This can clearly be seen by comparing the approach of Nissan's Supplier Development Team with that of the management of Midshires College. In the former, the SDT's openness appeared to encourage change, while in the latter, secrecy and uncertainty had the opposite effect.

- *Publicise successful change.* In order to create a positive attitude towards change, companies should publicise the projects which are seen as models of how to undertake change, and the positive effects it can have for employees. This does not mean that mistakes should be hidden or poor outcomes ignored; these should be examined, explained and lessons learned. However, staff should be encouraged to expect and set credible and positive outcomes for change programmes. Once again, the experience of the case study companies illustrates this point. In Rover, there has now been over a decade of successful change, which has produced a positive attitude among employees and managers alike. In PCI, on the other hand, before the threat of closure, its recent history had been one of problems in introducing new products, frequent managerial comings and goings, and a stop–start approach to developing and implementing strategy. Obviously, this situation led to the demoralisation of both managers and employees.

● *Understand people's fears and concerns.* One of the major mistakes made by the interim Chief Executive at PCI was his failure to recognise the real and legitimate fears of his managerial colleagues. Their fears may or may not have been groundless, but the fact that the Chief Executive failed to recognise their existence and take appropriate action was a major reason why his vision was put into abeyance when he left. Organisations need to recognise that change does create uncertainty and that individuals and groups may resist, or may not fully co-operate with it, if they fear the consequences. Furthermore, resistance should be seen as a signal that there is something wrong with the change process rather than with those who are resisting. From this perspective, resistance can be viewed as positive: it reminds the organisation that it has not considered all the consequences of its actions, and forces it to review its plans. It follows that those championing change need to pay special attention to the potential for resistance, both in terms of the adverse consequences it can bring and the underlying problems it may indicate.

Involve People. Though some change projects can be short-lived and easily achieved, many are not. Achieving a successful change can be and usually is a long and complex task. There will be difficult obstacles to overcome, not all of which can be anticipated in advance. To overcome these, and to develop the momentum necessary to ensure the project is successful, the commitment and support of all concerned are required, especially those who are most closely affected. In effect, these people are required to take ownership of the process so that it is 'their' project and 'their' success. This is unlikely to be achieved unless they can be involved in its planning and execution. This type of involvement has two main facets:

● *Communication.* One way of avoiding the uncertainty that change can promote is to establish a regular and effective communications process. The purpose of this should be to inform those who will be affected by the change process from the early stages what is happening, how it might or definitely will affect them, and to give them reports on the progress being made. It is important to give both the context for proposed changes, as well as the details and consequences.

Communication should be a regular rather than a one-off exercise. In some cases, such as GK Printers where all those affected were involved, this ceases to be an issue. However, GK's size makes it an exception. In most cases, it is impractical to give everyone this level of involvement; therefore, as at Flair and Rover, it is important to communicate proposals from the outset. This involves not only providing information, but also listening to the response and taking it seriously. This has a number of benefits. The change management team will very quickly pick up any worries and concerns and can respond to these; they will also be made aware of aspects which have been overlooked that need to be taken into consideration; and assumptions which have been made will be tested and sometimes challenged.

- *Getting people involved.* Communication does help to overcome fears and does encourage those concerned to assist rather than resist change. However, one of the most vital initiatives an organisation can take with staff is not to treat them as objects of, or obstacles to, change, but to involve them in it and make them responsible for it. Though not everyone can be involved in all aspects of planning and execution, it may be possible to ensure that all those most closely affected are involved in some, if not all, aspects. Where possible, responsibility for aspects of the change project should be given to those who will be directly affected by the result.

Sustaining the momentum. Even in the best run organisations, it sometimes happens that initial enthusiasm for change wanes, and in the face of the normal day-to-day pressures to meet customer needs, progress becomes slower and can grind to a halt. In organisations which are less well run, the momentum may not even be present in the beginning. In such situations, people will return to the methods and types of behaviour with which they are familiar. Given that momentum does not arise of itself nor continue without encouragement, organisations need to consider how to build and sustain it. The points already made above regarding planning and implementation, and especially involvement, are clearly part of this. In addition, however, organisations should:

- *Provide resources for change.* To achieve any change will normally require additional resources, both financial and human. In cases where staff are required to keep up the same level of output during the transition phase, it may require considerable additional resources to achieve this. It is important that these extra resources are budgeted for and allocated as necessary, whether for the provision of training, senior management time or whatever. Nothing is guaranteed to be more demoralising than having to make changes without the necessary resources or support.

- *Give support to the change agents.* An enormous responsibility falls upon the change management team. They have not only to plan and oversee the change project, but also to motivate others and deal with difficulties, sometimes very personal problems. Just as they have to support others, however, so too must they receive support themselves. Otherwise they may be the ones who become demoralised and will no longer be in a position to motivate others.

- *Develop new competencies and skills.* Change frequently demands new knowledge, skills and competencies. Increasingly, managers are having to learn new leadership styles, staff are having to learn to work as teams, and all are expected to be innovators and improvers. This requires more than just training and retraining. It may also include on-the-job counselling and coaching. Therefore, organisations need to consider what is required, who requires it and – the difficult part – how to deliver it in a way which encourages rather than threatens staff.

- *Reinforce desired behaviour.* In organisations, people generally do those things which bring rewards or avoid criticism. Consequently, one of the most effective ways of sustaining momentum for change is to reinforce the kinds of behaviour required to make it successful. Sometimes this may be monetary – linking increased pay or bonuses to particular types of activity or progress. Sometimes it may be symbolic – such as Oticon's tearing down of walls and elimination of personal desks. Sometimes it may be through recognition, whereby senior managers openly single out individuals or groups for particular praise. Such activities are particularly important during the early stages of change, when achieving an identifiable and openly recognised success helps participants develop a positive attitude about the change project.

The actual change process therefore, is a complex blend of objective-setting, planning and people. None of these are technical exercises. Establishing objectives involves testing assumptions and challenging preconceived ideas. It also involves gathering both fact and opinion, and making judgments about which is the most important. Similarly, planning change involves an impressive array of challenges and activities, some of which are amenable to straightforward techniques of analysis and decision, many of which are not. The final element, though, is the most complex: people. People are not just important because they are often the 'object' of change, but also because they are the ones who have to carry it out. In a real sense, they are the glue which holds it together. They can influence the choice of objectives and the way change is planned. In turn, objectives and planning can also affect their willingness to accept or become involved in change.

One final point: even after a change project has been 'completed', the story does not end there. As the Japanese have shown, even when change has resulted in a stable state being achieved, there always remains scope for improvement. As is clear from the case studies, however, many change projects are open-ended. Change will continue to take place. Therefore, both in planning a project and evaluating its outcomes, it is necessary to identify the open-endedness of it, and the degree to which the final outcome will require a continuous improvement approach or a continuing change approach.

CONCLUSIONS

....

This chapter has sought to merge the theory and practice of strategy development and change management as presented in Chapters 5 to 9. In doing so, it has also drawn on many of the arguments and insights into the behaviour, operation and rationality of organisations presented in Chapters 1 to 4. Based on Chapters 1 to 9, the underlying themes of this chapter have been:

- *Organisations are not rational entities but highly complex social systems that operate under a range of external and internal constraints.*

- *Managers, far from being the prisoners of these constraints and the passive appliers of other people's theories, can and do have a great deal of choice over the decisions they make and the constraints they face.*

This chapter began by reviewing the theories of strategy development and change management discussed in Chapters 5 and 6. This showed that, while there are a number of well supported but contradictory theories and approaches to these subjects, there seems to be a general assumption that the main role of managers is to align their organisations to the constraints they face. An alternative proposition was then advanced, positing that instead of being prisoners of these constraints, managers could shape them to meet their own and their organisation's preferences and needs.

Following the review of Chapters 5 and 6, and in the light of the conclusions reached, the ten case studies presented in Chapters 7 to 9 were then also reviewed. This review showed that:

- *While managers do seek to align their organisations with the external constraints they face, they can also influence and restructure these as well.*

- *Depending on the circumstances and the objectives being pursued, organisations tend to use a combination of planned and emergent approaches to strategy development and change management. Therefore, instead of conflicting, these two approaches, as argued in Chapter 6, tend to lie at either end of a spectrum of possible methods for developing strategy and managing change.*

- *Radical and rapid organisational transformation could be incorporated within the planned–emergent spectrum and, also, any lack of employee involvement in such situations did not necessarily constitute a rebuff to either approach.*

The chapter then went on to present a new model for understanding and managing organisational change, the Choice Management–Change Management model, which comprised three interrelated organisational processes: the choice process, the trajectory process and the change process (*see* Fig. 10.1). It was argued that not only did this model incorporate both the planned and emergent approaches to strategy and change but it also demonstrated how managers could attempt to change their organisation's circumstances to fit them to the approach which best suited them and their organisation.

It was asserted that the Choice Management–Change Management model covers the full scope of the various approaches to strategy and change, ranging from the planned to the emergent, and that it could also accommodate the use of more directive approaches. However, one of the fundamental differences between this model and many other approaches to strategy and change is that it recognises that managers are active players rather than passive spectators in the development of their own organisations. The model is based on the assumption that not only can managers choose to align their organisation with the external conditions and constraints it faces, but they can also do the reverse and align these external conditions and constraints to their preferred way of structuring and running their organisation.

Whether they choose to attempt to influence, alter or align their organisation to the circumstances it faces will depend on a range of issues, not least their own views about whether they or the organisation are better suited by a stable, planned situation or whether more turbulent/emergent conditions are preferable. As Fig. 10.2 shows, the planned approach is more likely to be applicable to situations where the environment is relatively stable, change is small scale and localised, and is of a technical or structural nature. The emergent approach is, more appropriate on the other hand, where the environment is turbulent and the objective is organisation-

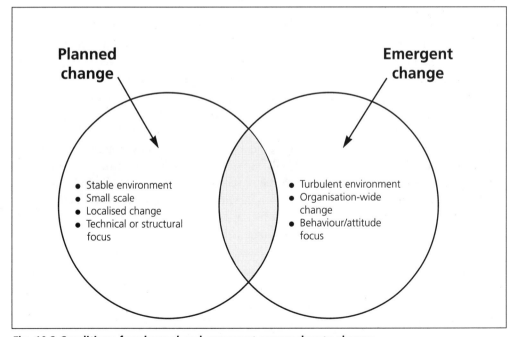

Fig. 10.2 Conditions for planned and emergent approaches to change

wide behavioural and/or attitudinal change. Therefore, if the situation does not suit the organisation's chosen modus operandi, it is the factors and constraints in Fig. 10.2 that become the objective of change.

Though the Choice Management–Change Management model appears to offer significant theoretical avenues for understanding how organisations and managers operate, it also offers considerable practical benefits as well. In Chapter 3, we examined the Culture–Excellence perspective on organisations. The proponents of this view, especially Tom Peters, argue that organisations have no choice but to change radically if they are to survive. The Culture–Excellence theory is based on a particular view of the environment and other constraints organisations face. Assuming that this view is accurate, the Choice Management–Change Management model shows that organisations need not radically restructure themselves, but could seek to influence the constraints they face to bring them more in line with their existing organisational arrangements. Even if, in the long term, organisations did have to structure themselves along the lines advocated by Peters, Kanter and Handy, they could still seek to influence the conditions under which they operated to achieve this over a longer time scale than might otherwise be assumed. Indeed, as Chapter 3 revealed, this is just the approach the Japanese take. Japan's leading organisations have transformed themselves over the past 30 years. However, this has been achieved by slow and gradual transformation rather than by rapid shock tactics. Japanese companies have achieved this gradual transformation by a combination of long-term vision allied to the ability to influence and restructure the constraints under which they operate, especially, as argued by Hamel and Prahalad (1989), their ability to change the rules of competition in their particular industries. In so doing, they provide much support for Kanter *et al*'s (1992) view that a 'long march' is more effective than a 'bold stroke' for building competitive organisations.

Therefore, the Choice Management–Change Management model, potentially at least, resolves the dispute between proponents of planned and emergent approaches to strategy development and change. In doing so, however, it does raise fundamental questions about what managers do and what they can do in terms of running and shaping their organisations. Many writers, especially from the Culture–Excellence perspective, have made a case for visionary leadership being the key to an organisation's success. Certainly, the transactional, steady-as-she-goes type of manager is very much out of favour (Senge, 1993). However, the case for transforming managers, as well as organisations, tends to be based on a biased view of what managers need to do and, often, only a shallow understanding of what they actually do. In order to come to grips with the nature of managerial work and the extent to which the Choice Management–Change Management model requires a fundamental rethink of how managers operate, the concluding chapter of this book will examine the role of managers.

Chapter 11

MANAGEMENT, CHANGE AND CHOICE

INTRODUCTION

The challenges facing organisations and those who manage them seem to increase by the day. The globalisation of world trade may open up new markets and create new opportunities, but it also brings with it new competitors and new uncertainties. The same holds true for scientific advance. The beneficial effects of computers are there for all to see, though their full implications and potential have yet to be realised. However, advances such as genetic engineering are much more controversial and unpredictable. In any case, the final outcome of many of the developments we see around us will be determined by political and ethical considerations rather than economic or organisational ones.

Nevertheless, regardless of the potential benefits or disbenefits of particular developments, the overall message is clear – the environment in which organisations operate will continue to change and managers will continue to have to find ways of ensuring that their organisation and its environment, and the other constraints under which it operates, are, as far as possible, kept aligned. As argued in Chapter 10, this does not necessarily mean that each and every organisation has to change rapidly and radically, though many will. Instead, managers can seek to influence the constraints under which their organisation operates to make them more favourable to their preferred way of working. Over time, however, the likelihood is that both the organisation and its environment will change.

As the case studies in Part Three have shown, and as most people's everyday experiences confirm, change is neither easy nor necessarily always successful. Regardless of this, however, organisations either by design or default do change, and managers do play a crucial role in determining whether the outcome is success or failure. Managers are the ones who have the responsibility for ensuring that options are identified, choices made and action taken. In concluding this book, therefore, it is only right that we look at how well or not managers are equipped for this task.

The chapter begins by reviewing the literature on what managers are supposed to do and what they really do. This shows that, despite what leading thinkers such as Fayol and Weber believed and advocated, most managers are driven by expediency and operate in a responsive mode. The chapter then moves on to discuss the importance and nature of leadership in organisations. In particular, it seeks to identify the characteristics and contexts which make for effective leadership. Arising from this, the leadership role played by managers in the case studies is examined. This is followed by an examination of the education and development of managers. The chapter and the book conclude by arguing that managers have an important responsibility to identify and exercise choice, when faced with situations which require change. Though choice can be determined on a very narrow basis of short-term financial return, increasingly managers will have to take into account wider organisational and societal factors. Especially important in this respect is that managers should be prepared to question trends and advice which seem designed to increase organisational and societal instability and fragmentation, as the interests of society in general and their own organisations in particular may be better served by seeking stability.

THE MANAGER'S ROLE
....

It has never been easy to define the role of managers, though this has not prevented a great number of attempts over the years (*see* for example Barnard, 1938; Carlson, 1951; Brewer and Tomlinson, 1964; Horne and Lupton, 1965; Mintzberg, 1973 and 1975; Silverman and Jones, 1976; Stewart, 1976; Kotter, 1982; Constable and McCormick, 1987; Handy *et al*, 1987). As Hales (1986) found when he reviewed many of these studies, the information available presents managers, and others, with a confusing and conflicting picture of what managers should do and how they should do it.

Definitions of the role of managers have ranged from attempts to list basic tasks:

> **[The manager] plans, organises, directs and controls, on proprietors' or own behalf, an industrial, commercial or other undertaking, establishment or organisation, and co-ordinates the work of departmental managers or other immediate subordinates. (*quoted in Dakin and Hamilton, 1990:32*)**

to more ambitious attempts to define the essence of the manager's role:

> **[The manager has the] task of creating a true whole that is larger than the sum of its parts, a productive entity that turns out more than the sum of the resources put into it. (*Drucker 1985:53*)**

Drucker (1985) also likened the manager to the conductor of a symphony orchestra. As conductor, the manager is the one through whose effort, vision and leadership the various instrumental parts, that are so much noise by themselves, become the living whole of music. In this instance, the manager is also the composer as well as the conductor.

Handy (1986), on the other hand, likened the manager to a doctor: the manager is the first recipient of problems. The manager's role is, therefore, to identify the symptoms in any situation; to diagnose the disease or cause of the trouble; to decide how it might be dealt with, through a strategy for health; and to start the treatment.

Such analogies are useful in that they create a concrete picture of the manager's role, but they can also be misleading. Conducting is an art form; is management an art form? Or, as Handy's analogy implies, is it a science in the same way that medicine is a science? As Part One of this book showed, the clash between those who see management as a rational, science-based process, and those who believe it to be more intuitive and less rational, is not new.

Duncan (1975) tried to resolve this conflict by taking a holistic view of the job of the manager. He identifies three distinct levels of management activity: *philosophical* (goal formation); *scientific* (goal accomplishment and evaluation); and *art* (implementation of decisions). At the philosophical level in forming goals, the manager – Duncan argues – is mainly concerned with the effects of the actions and reactions of other individuals and groups within the wider economic and social context within which the organisation is set. At this level, managers and their associates formulate clear and precise strategies that will encompass all envisaged effects that can result from the set goals, not only on the various pressure groups within its internal and external environment, but also on competitors and regulatory agencies. It is also at this level that the ethics of managerial behaviour, values and priorities of the organisation are formulated and established. At the scientific level, management develops plans, methods and techniques for achieving set goals, and establishes procedures for monitoring and evaluating progress.

The 'art' level is concerned with the implementation of decisions; this is the level at which tactical and administrative decisions are made to deploy the organisation's resources and attain the optimum degree of operational efficiency. This level is an 'art' because, according to Duncan, there appears to be a particular talent necessary to persuade others that management-generated goals and decisions should be accepted.

While not necessarily agreeing with his definitions, especially in terms of strategy formulation, Duncan's three-level approach is extremely useful in that it shows, as Mullins (1989) argued, that management is both a science and an art. By its very nature, management is forced to deal with both rational, science-based activities, such as the design and operation of manufacturing systems, and less rational, more intuitive activities, especially those concerning managing and motivating people. The extent to which a manager is involved in any of these activities, however, will depend on the kind of organisation the manager works for, the type of job the manager has, and crucially the manager's level in the organisation's hierarchy (Hales, 1986). Position in the hierarchy, formally at least, is likely to exert the greatest influence on the role given to and expected of a manager. The three main hierarchical levels are:

- *Top management: which is the policy-making group responsible for the overall direction of the company.*
- *Middle management: which is responsible for the execution and interpretation of policies throughout the organisation and for the successful operation of assigned divisions or departments.*
- *First level or supervisory management: which is directly responsible to the middle management group for ensuring the execution of policies by their subordinates. They are also responsible for the attainment of objectives by the units they control, through practices and procedures approved and issued by top or middle management.*

Superficially, at least, these three categories appear to mirror Duncan's three levels. On a closer examination, however, it becomes more difficult to match them because each category can encompass all three levels. This can be seen more clearly by examining what it is that managers actually do, as opposed to what academics say they should do.

There have been a number of important studies conducted to determine how managers spend their time (*see* for example Brewer and Tomlinson, 1964; Child and Ellis, 1973; Kotter, 1982). Perhaps the best known and replicated work in this area is by Mintzberg (1973, 1975). Synthesising his results and the previous research on the role of managers, he concluded that:

- *Although much managerial work is unprogrammed, all managers do have regular, ordinary duties to perform.*
- *Rather than being systematic, reflective thinkers and planners, managers simply respond to the pressures or demands of their jobs.*
- *Managerial activities are characterised by brevity, variety and discontinuity.*
- *Managers' jobs are remarkably similar and their work can be described in terms of three very important roles: interpersonal, informational and decision-making.*

Interpersonal roles

One of the most time-consuming and important aspects of most managerial jobs is to work with, direct and represent people. The three key functions in this respect are as follows:

- *Figurehead – as the formal representative of the organisation.*
- *Liaison – forming connections with other organisations.*
- *Leader – in relation to members of a group within the organisation.*

Informational roles

Those in managerial positions have unique opportunities to obtain and disseminate information. The three key functions involved are given below:

● *Monitor – as monitors, managers seek, receive and store information which can be used to the advantage of the company.*

● *Disseminator – the manager must broadcast this useful information to the organisation.*

● *Spokesperson – on behalf of the organisation, the manager communicates information to other relevant groups and bodies, both internal and external.*

Decision-making roles

One of the main parts of any manager's job is to take decisions. In this respect, there are four key functions involved:

● *Entrepreneur – looking for ways to improve the operation of the organisation or for new product/market opportunities.*

● *Disturbance-Handler – handling crises effectively.*

● *Resource Allocator – responsible for constructing budgets and allocating resources.*

● *Negotiator – according to Mintzberg, managers spend a great deal of their time as negotiators, because only they have the necessary information and the authority to carry out this role.*

Mintzberg (1975) argued that the lack of uniformity in managerial jobs can be accounted for by hierarchical and functional differentiation. He contended that Chief Executive Officers (CEOs), for example, focus considerable attention on external roles, such as liaison, spokesperson and figurehead, which link the organisation to its environment. At lower levels, work is more focused, more short-term in outlook, and the characteristics of brevity and fragmentation are more pronounced. As a result of this, the external managerial roles are less important, and real-time internal roles (disturbance-handler and negotiator) concerned with daily operating problems and maintaining the work flow become relatively more important. Furthermore, he argued that interpersonal roles are more important to sales managers, that staff managers give more attention to informational roles and production managers focus on decisional roles. Mintzberg's observations have been supported by a number of other studies (Kotter, 1982; Silverman and Jones, 1976; Stewart, 1976).

Hales (1986: 102), in reviewing the research on the manager's role, concluded that:

Much of what managers do is, of necessity, an unreflective response to circumstances. The manager is less a slow and methodical decision maker, more a 'doer' who has to react rapidly to problems as they arise, 'think on his feet', take decisions in situ and develop a preference for concrete activities. This shows in the pace of managerial work and the short time span of most activities ...

Therefore, in examining the role of managers, it can be seen that there is a discrepancy between what the literature says managers should do and what the managers actually do. Indeed, as Mintzberg (1975:49) pointed out, this discrepancy even extends to managers' own observations on their role:

> If you ask a manager what he does, he will most likely tell you he plans, organizes, co-ordinates and controls. Then watch what he does. Don't be surprised if you can't relate what you see to those four words.

Nevertheless, regardless of the difficulty in identifying what managers do or how they should do it, there is a strong tradition in the literature on organisations that it is managers' leadership ability, especially in situations of change and crisis, which is a crucial attribute (Yukl, 1994). As the following shows, however, leadership is a nebulous concept.

MANAGEMENT AND LEADERSHIP

It has been a long-held belief that the major factor which distinguishes successful organisations from their less successful counterparts is the presence of dynamic and effective leadership (Yukl, 1994). Though the literature suggests that an organisation's strategy is not always driven by senior managers (*see* Chapter 5), it is certainly the case that they are held responsible for success or failure. They are the people who are formally charged with taking decisions, directing others and creating a framework of rules, systems and expectations within which the organisation operates.

Given the importance of leadership, therefore, it is surprising to find that it is such an elusive concept. Even in the 1950s, when there had been much less research on the subject than now, Bennis (1959:259) commented:

> Always it seems that the concept of leadership eludes us or turns up in another form to taunt us again with its slipperiness and complexity. So we have invented a proliferation of terms to deal with it ... and still the concept is not sufficiently defined.

In the 1990s, when there is a proliferation of articles and books on the subject, the topic is still more fragmented than ever. However, it is possible to separate leadership theorists into three main groups:

- *those who focus on the personal characteristics and process of leadership;*
- *those who concentrate on the leader–follower situation;*
- *those who attempt to relate leadership styles to the overall organisation context and climate.*

The characteristics and process of leadership

Early investigations into leadership tended to concentrate on such factors as personal qualities (intelligence, age, experience), or personality traits (extroversion, dominance). Consequently, regardless of the task or situation, if a person did not possess the appropriate personal attributes, then he or she was deemed unlikely to be a good leader. However, the numerous studies of leadership failed to reveal any consistent pattern of traits or characteristics related to leadership (Gibb, 1969).

In an effort to breathe new life into this approach, attempts were made to view leadership as a process, and the focus moved to examining the interaction between leaders and followers, and how leaders influence individuals and groups to pursue the achievement of a given goal. This view, that leadership behaviour rather than attributes may predict leadership success more effectively, has been advanced in a variety of approaches. Fleishman (1953 and 1969) identified two separate classes of behaviour as important in determining effective leadership:

1 *Consideration* – the quality of the interpersonal relationship between the leader and their subordinates; and

2 *Initiating structure* – the degree to which leaders are the centre of decision-making and action as opposed to taking a more facilitative role.

In the 1950s and 1960s, this approach gave rise to a number of 'universal theories' of effective leader behaviour – which is to say, researchers began to argue for a 'one best way' approach to leadership (*see* for example Argyris, 1964; Likert, 1967; McGregor, 1960). These theories postulated that the same style of leadership is optimal in all situations (Yukl, 1994).

Perhaps the best known and most influential of these 'universal theories' is Blake and Mouton's (1969) Managerial Grid. Their grid has two critical dimensions: *concern for people* – similar to *consideration*; and *concern for production* – similar to *initiating structure*. By examining how these two dimensions interact, in both their strong and weak states, Blake and Mouton identified four different styles of management:

- *Team management. This arises from a high concern for people and high concern for production. The objectives are to achieve high levels of both performance and job satisfaction by gaining subordinates' willing commitment to achieving their assigned tasks.*

- *Country club management. This occurs when concern for production is low but concern for people is high. The main concern of this approach is to achieve the harmony and well-being of the group in question by satisfying people's social and relationship needs.*

- *Task management. This can be defined as a high concern for production but a low concern for people. The objective is to achieve high productivity by planning, organising and directing work in such a way that human considerations are kept to a minimum.*

● *Impoverished management. This ensues from a low concern for both production and people. This form of managerial behaviour centres on exacting the minimum effort from subordinates in order to achieve the required result.*

Though Blake and Mouton (1969) identify these four forms of management, for them the most effective is team management where leaders are both task- and people-orientated – the so-called 'high–high' leader. However, despite the wide number of studies seeking to test and elaborate this concept, the evidence in support of it, or for any of the universal theories, is limited (Evans, 1970; Larson *et al*, 1976; Yukl, 1994). Because of the difficulty of relating leadership traits and behaviours with effectiveness, many writers have turned to looking at the situations in which leaders are perceived to be effective.

The leader–follower situation approach

In response to the inability of researchers to make a convincing case for a 'one best way' approach to leadership, attention began to focus on identifying the situations in which leaders were effective. Kerr *et al* (1974) took the two forms of leadership behaviour identified by Fleishman (1969) – consideration and initiating structure – and applied these to a framework which included three situational variables or contingencies:

1 *Subordinate considerations* – such as the subordinates' experience and abilities, and their expectations of the leader.
2 *Superior considerations* – in particular, the amount of influence subordinates have over the behaviour of their superiors.
3 *Task considerations* – including factors such as time urgency, amount of physical danger, permissible error rate, presence of external stress, degree of autonomy and scope, importance and meaningfulness of work, and degree of ambiguity.

Kerr *et al* (1974) argued that the effectiveness of the two forms of leadership behaviour (consideration and initiating structure) in promoting high levels of performance from subordinates is moderated by the three situational variables. For example, if the task to be performed is characterised by time pressure, subordinates will be more amenable to a higher level of initiating structure (i.e. direction by superiors) and there will be a stronger relationship between job satisfaction, perform-ance and initiating structure. Alternatively, when a task is seen as intrinsically very satisfying to a subordinate, a leadership style with high consideration will not significantly increase satisfaction or performance. Support for the central premises of Kerr *et al*'s (1974) model has been limited. Research by Schriesheim and Murphy (1976) produced mixed results. There was evidence that high levels of initiating structure did increase performance in high-pressure situations and reduce it under low levels of pressure. However, different levels of pressure did not appear to impact on subordinates' satisfaction with their superiors. Nor, where tasks were viewed as having higher clarity, were either consideration- or initiating structure-based styles significantly related to satisfaction.

The most influential situational theory of leadership has been Fiedler's (1967) Least Preferred Co-worker (LPC) model. This postulates that leadership traits or behaviour and effectiveness are moderated by the situation in which they are deployed. The measure used to define the personal behaviour of the individual leader was built around a scale of bi-polar adjectives (e.g. pleasant–unpleasant, distant–close, efficient–inefficient) which purports to measure whether a person is 'task' or 'relationship' orientated. Fiedler argued that effectiveness is related to the level of influence the leader exercises over his or her subordinates. This influence is determined or strongly influenced by:

1 *The leader–follower relationship* – friendliness and loyalty from subordinates increases the leader's influence over them.

2 *Task structure* – the greater the degree of standardisation, detailed instructions and objective measures of performance, the more favourable the situation for the leader.

3 *The leader's formal position and power* – the more discretion and authority the leader has regarding the reward and punishment of subordinates, the more influence he or she will be able to exert.

Fiedler argued that the situation in which leaders are most effective is where leader-follower relations are good, the task is well-defined and highly structured, and the leader has a high level of formal authority. Despite – or perhaps because of – being the most widely utilised situational theory of leadership, it is also the most widely criticised. The main criticisms are that it lacks empirical support, that it fails to explain how particular leadership behaviour affects subordinates' performance, and that the measures used by Fiedler are arbitrary and lack any explicit rationale (Ashour, 1973; Vecchio, 1983; Shiflett, 1973). Fiedler's model has also been subjected to the same type of criticism as other contingency/situational approaches (*see* Chapter 2). In particular, critics maintain that it ignores a manager's ability to change or influence contingencies. In this respect, a number of writers have pointed out that Fiedler treats structure, an important component of his model, as a given, whereas in many instances, determining and changing organisation and job structures is a major component of a manager's role (O'Brien and Kabanoff, 1981).

The contextual approach to leadership

One of the weaknesses of the leadership literature is, as the above demonstrates, that it tends to concentrate on the traits of individual managers and their relations with subordinates. The assumption, both explicit and implicit, is that effectiveness is an attribute of the individual manager, moderated by the leader–subordinate situation; a good manager in one organisation will be a good manager in all organisations. Yet, as Burnes (1991) and Hales (1986) have argued, a manager's effectiveness may be determined as much by the nature of the organisation in which he or she operates as by the qualities of the individual manager.

It is out of and in response to such observations that the contextual approach to leadership developed. This approach is a variant of the situational approach to leadership; however, instead of concentrating on leadership behaviour it focuses on leadership style, and instead of the narrow leader–follower situation, it focuses on the overall organisation context and climate. In addition, it is the only one of the three approaches to leadership which incorporates change as a variable. The requirement for managers to adapt their style and approach to the circumstances of the organisation in which they operate has been commented on by a number of writers (Burnes and James, 1995; Burns, 1978; Beatty and Lee, 1992; Gibbons, 1992). Primarily, these writers identify two basic organisation states or contexts – convergent and divergent, and two matching leadership styles – transactional and transformational.

A *convergent* state occurs when an organisation is operating under stable conditions; where there are established and accepted goals and a predictable external and internal environment. The most appropriate style of management in such a situation, it is contended, is *transactional*. Transactional managers concentrate on optimising the performance of the organisation through incremental changes within the confines of existing policy, structures and practices – basically, they seek to work within and maintain the status quo.

A *divergent* state occurs when environmental changes challenge the efficiency and appropriateness of an organisation's established goals, structures and ways of working. The most appropriate style of leadership in this situation, it is argued, is *transformational*. Transformational leaders are seen as being opposed to the status quo; they aim to change their followers' behaviour and beliefs and unite them behind a new vision of the organisation's future.

The compatibility between organisational state and leadership style is seen as essential for successful leadership. Where the organisation is required to face new challenges and develop new ways of adapting to these for the sake of survival, then a purely transactional approach would be counter-productive – the phrase 'fiddling while Rome burns' springs to mind. However, transformational leadership is just as likely to be counter-productive during periods where maintenance of the current operational systems would be most appropriate.

As can be seen, the contextual approach does not seek to invalidate either the characteristics or situational approaches, rather it tries to incorporate them within and link them to the wider organisational context. It explicitly recognises that a manager's personal characteristics are an important component of leadership style, and consequently, effectiveness. In addition, it acknowledges the crucial importance of the relationship between leader and led (Burns, 1978). In particular, as Gibbons (1992:5) remarked:

... organizational survival and success are dependent on the ability of leader–follower relations to resolve the problems of internal integration and external adaptation.

Kanter (1989) developed a similar leadership style categorisation. She argued that archetypal images of managers tend to derive from two basic models: the 'corpocrat' (i.e. the transactional manager) and the 'cowboy' (i.e. the transformational manager). The former is the corporate bureaucrat, the conservative resource-preserver who lives by, and controls the organisation through, established and detailed rules. The latter, the 'cowboy', is a maverick who challenges the established order, who wants to seize every opportunity, question every rule and who motivates and controls through personal loyalty. However, instead of arguing that there is a need to relate these two approaches to their appropriate organisational setting, Kanter (1989: 361) argues that, in future, organisations will require managers who combine the best of both the corpocrat and cowboy:

> **Without the bold impulses of the take-action entrepreneurs and their constant questioning of the rules, we would miss one of the most potent sources of business revitalization and development. But without the discipline and coordination of conventional management, we could find waste instead of growth, unnecessary risk instead of revitalization.**

In effect, Kanter is attempting to turn the leadership debate full circle and make the case for a universal – one best way – approach to leadership. Her argument, as mentioned in Chapter 2, is basically that all organisations operate in the same turbulent context, face the same challenges and, consequently, require the same style of management.

Just as a review of the role of managers produced a confusing and conflicting picture, so too appears to be the case when we look at the three approaches to leadership. Nevertheless, the argument for considering context and style together does, partly at least, fit in with the arguments developed in the previous parts of this book; namely that there is a need to match the approach to change to the context of the organisation. However, this argument was developed to include the possibility that managers could reverse this process and match the organisation's context to their preferred style of working.

Though the style-context approach to leadership is as open to criticism as any of the other approaches – especially a lack of empirical support (see Yukl, 1994) – it does offer a useful categorisation for analysing the behaviour of the managers in the ten case studies in Part Three. By establishing whether their approach was tranactional or transformational and the context convergent or divergent, it becomes possible to judge not only the appropriateness of their behaviour in the situation in which they were operating, but also the usefulness of the contextual approach to leadership.

Leadership in action

If we examine the case studies in Part Three, we find that managers and the context within which they operated varied enormously. Merely analysing what managers did in each situation, interesting though it would undoubtedly prove, is to produce more heat than light. Using the transactional–transformational and convergent–divergent categorisation identified above, however, allows a clearer picture to develop. Taking the case studies in order:

Oticon. There is little doubt that the company's Chief Executive exhibited transformational qualities and that it was operating in a divergent environment. However, it should be noted that, for the first two years of his appointment, the Chief Executive operated within the same industrial and organisational mould as his predecessors. It was only then that he recognised the limitations of continuing to attempt to improve an organisation which was out of step with its environment and competitors. His response was to change the internal organisation of the company, not to align it with the external environment, but in an attempt to change that as well, by changing the rules of the game in his industry.

Flair. At one level this is a similar story to Oticon – a company in decline appoints a new Managing Director who transforms its fortunes. Certainly there is little doubt that the company operated in a divergent environment, and that the Managing Director was in the transformational mould. It could be assumed, however, because he was promoted, that the Managing Director had operated successfully as a transactional manager before seeing the need to change. The process of transformation was slow and emergent; he was not seeking to realign the company with its environment, but instead, he wanted to build a new company in a new environment.

PCI. This company and its various managers went through a number of stages. Undoubtedly, the interim Chief Executive was a transformational leader; however, despite difficult internal problems, it was not originally clear that PCI was operating in a divergent environment. The next phase saw the company being managed by apparently transactional managers and operating under the same internal and external conditions. It was only with the threat to close the company that the divergence between its internal practices and structures and external requirements of the market became clear. It was at this point that the transactional Chief Executive and his team began to exhibit transformational characteristics.

Midshires College. This was very much a case of an organisation in a divergent state being managed by a transactional manager. The result of this mismatch was that the organisation failed to change and the Project Leader became increasingly ineffective.

Volvo. Once again, this was a case where neither the state of the organisation nor the type of leadership was clear, possibly because the organisation is so large. The changes in Job Design were clearly, for the industry at least, transformational. However, this does not appear to have been matched by extensive changes in other structures and practices at Volvo. Nor does it seem to be the case that Volvo was out of step with its markets and environment – divergent. Furthermore, despite the Chief

Executive's conversion to Job Design, it is unclear how far other managers shared his transformational leanings.

Rover. This was a company that was in a state of almost terminal divergence in the late 1970s. Through a series of major initiatives, the early phases of which could be classed as transactional, the organisation was, and still is being, transformed. However, it was noticeable that successive waves of new senior managers were brought into the company, each one of which appeared to be more transformational than the last.

GK Printers. Certainly the company can be characterised as one which was out of step with its environment. Though initial changes appeared to be transformational, it was only later, when the organisation came to tackle internal relationships and managerial behaviour, that a more genuinely transformational approach to the company began to emerge.

Vickers. Though this was a case where the company's environment had changed, the extent of the divergence could be accommodated by managers seeking to transform its relations with its suppliers rather than via a wholesale change to its internal practices. Therefore, Vickers can be classed as a situation where there was partial divergence; at first managers tried to accommodate this by a mainly transactional approach, but the approach became increasingly transformational.

Nissan. This is an instance of a company which, starting from a clean sheet, tried to develop a relationship with its suppliers which broke with past UK traditions. However, Nissan was attempting to transform its suppliers not because Nissan was out of step with its environment, but because they were. Therefore, while Nissan operated in a convergent state, because its suppliers did not, it had to adopt a transformational approach towards managing them.

Speedy Stationers. In this case, the company was trying to develop a new business area which could not be approached or managed in the same way as its existing business. However, it eventually chose to isolate the new business from its existing activities. This allowed it to pursue a transformational approach to the new business, while allowing its existing business to operate and be managed as before. It also enabled it to limit the transformation of external relationships to the new business customers.

Therefore, the case studies show a very diverse range of approaches, situations and outcomes. They also show the limitations of attempting to apply simple definitions to complex situations. The categorisation of leadership types and organisational states are useful in situations where a clear and relatively unambiguous picture of events is possible, such as in the case of Oticon and Midshires College. However, in many of the cases – PCI, Volvo, GK Printers, Nissan – the picture is less clear.

Elements of divergence exist, but these appear to be limited to certain areas of their environment or change over time. Because of this, managers can be required to exhibit both transactional and transformational qualities either at the same time or in turn. In addition, the case studies also show instances where managers attempt to alter their environment to limit the need for internal changes and to bring it into line with their preferred style of a management.

Though the evidence from the case studies fits in with the general literature on managers' activities, which sees them as fragmented, lacking in consistency and reactive, it does appear to contradict leadership theory, which tends to value consistency of approach. The picture which emerges from the case studies is one where effective managers are required to possess and utilise a wide range of skills and attributes depending upon the situation and context. Effective managers must be capable, often at the same time, of being both transactional and transformational, given that the environmental pressures and other constraints do not appear to affect all parts of an organisation in the same manner nor at the same time. In particular, as Thompson (1967) remarked in relation to Contingency theory (*see* Chapter 2), organisations do seem adept at sealing off their productive cores from environmental uncertainty while allowing other functions to be more directly affected. The result is that managers can be required to adopt distinct approaches towards managing different parts of the same organisation. This 'Jekyll and Hyde' approach to management raises important questions about how managers can be prepared and developed to cope with situations where they might have to maintain some parts of their organisation on a transactional basis, while rebuilding other parts in a transformational style while, at the same time, attempting to influence constraints either to prevent, reduce, or even promote the need for transformational change. In order to address this question, the next part of this chapter will discuss managerial learning and adaptation.

MANAGERIAL LEARNING AND ADAPTATION
....

The case studies, as was the case with the literature on management and leadership, give some support for the notion that different situations require different approaches from managers. They also show that managers are, sometimes at least, required to exhibit transactional and transformational approaches to different parts of their organisations at the same time. This is also consistent with the argument in Chapter 10 that managers can and do adopt both the planned and emergent approaches to strategy and change management simultaneously. The case studies also show that managers, not necessarily by conscious design, create situations in which the context in which their organisations operate is changed to suit their preferred or existing approach to both management and change. As argued in Chapter 10, the latter – changing the situational context – is very important; yet in terms of leadership roles and managerial expectations, the main finding from the case studies is the apparent ability of effective managers not only to adapt their style to the particular situation, but also to adopt transactional and transformational approaches at the same time.

In part at least, this runs counter to some of the literature on managerial learning discussed in Chapter 6. Miller (1993:119) argued that as they gain experience, managers 'form quite definite opinions of what works and why'. This view was supported by earlier work from Nystrom and Starbuck (1984) who maintained that managers interpret the world through their own perceptions and expectations, which are built up over time. Yet as mentioned, managers do seem capable, under certain conditions – especially the imminence or arrival of a crisis – of restructuring their mental models of how the world is and how they should respond. In Chapter 10, the concept of cognitive dissonance was used to explain why it was that employees could, in crisis situations, support radical change without involvement. However, this does not help explain how some managers, in situations necessitating organisational change, can shift their mental model from a transactional to a transformational one or, indeed, are capable of adopting both at the same time.

The work of Mintzberg (1976) offers some clues as to how managers do or might accomplish this mental juggling act. In studying brain functions and successful managers, he concluded that effective and proficient managers are 'whole thinkers' – they use both the left and the right hemispheres of their brain. That is, they can combine a rational–analytical approach to management with creativity and lateral thinking. Mintzberg argued, however, that, in general, Western managers tend to think on the left side of their brain – they tend to adopt a rational-analytical approach. Interestingly, this is compatible not only with a transactional approach to management, but also with the planned approach to strategy and change.

In contrast, Nonaka (1991) argued that one of the great strengths of Japanese companies is that, while Western managers place great emphasis on scientific and quantifiable knowledge, Japanese managers believe that creating new knowledge depends more on tapping the tacit and often subjective insights and intuitions of employees. He maintains that traditional Western management sees organisations as information processing machines with the only useful knowledge being formal, scientific and rational. He contends that such a perspective limits the creation of new knowledge which, in turn, makes it difficult for organisations to respond to changing and new situations. He argues that new knowledge always begins with the individual. One of the main foundations of the success of Japanese companies is, he argued, managers' ability to gather and combine the insights and intuitions of individual employees and use them for the benefit of the entire organisation. The tendency of Japanese managers to use softer, more creative approaches and to involve staff in decision-making was also noted in Chapter 5 when discussing approaches to strategy.

The case studies and the success of many Western firms, particularly those concerned with creative processes (such as software development) and the performing arts (such as film-making), show that it is not inevitable that Western managers should operate solely in a rational–analytical mode. However, Hofstede's (1980 and

1990) work on national cultures does reveal a predisposition in Western societies towards this way of working. Furthermore, as Miller (1993), points out, a manager's view of the world and what works is shaped by his or her previous work experience. If this has been in organisations that have operated on traditional Western principles, which are structured in a Classical way and give credence only to formal and scientific knowledge, then they undoubtedly will tend to operate on the left side of the brain. However, this does not mean that such managers cannot develop or access the right side of their brain. In addition to experience, managers can broaden their outlook and develop the creative, inductive and questioning side of their personalities through more formal learning situations. The drawback is that, as a number of studies revealed in the 1980s, the UK is particularly poor at providing this type of formal and structured education for managers (Constable and McCormick, 1987). Nevertheless, in recent years there has been a growing interest in management education, or management development as it is often referred to (Sissons and Storey, 1988; Storey, 1989 and 1990).

Management development has been defined in a number of ways:

... a conscious and systematic decision-action process to control the development of managerial resources in the organisation for the achievement of organisational goals and strategies. (*Ashton* et al, *1975:5*)

... that function which from deep understanding of business goals and organisational requirements, undertakes: (a) to forecast needs, skill mixes and profiles for many positions and levels; (b) to design and recommend the professional, career and personal development programmes necessary to ensure competence; (c) to move from the concept of 'management' to the concept of 'managing'. (*Beckhard, 1985:22*)

... an attempt to improve managerial effectiveness through a planned and deliberate learning process. (*quoted in Mumford, 1987:29*)

The above help to define management development, but they do not indicate what the objectives of such programmes are. To an extent this is understandable, given that individual organisations will initiate such programmes for different reasons. Nevertheless, more and more companies are recognising the benefits that management development can bring to organisational change and renewal (Lippitt, 1982; Marsh, 1986; Morgan, 1988; Pearson, 1987; Storey, 1989).

If management development programmes are to be successful in developing effective managers and improving the performance of organisations, then it is self-evident not only that they will vary from company to company, but also that they will need to vary from individual to individual. This makes it important to determine the training needs of individual managers accurately, in order to ensure that it is these that determine the nature of the management development programme, rather than vice versa. Unfortunately, there is plenty of evidence that this is not the case, and that management development programmes are often standard packages which everyone is sent on, regardless of how appropriate they are in relation to the needs of the individual and the objectives of the organisation that employs them (Mangham Working Party, 1987; Sissons, 1989; Storey, 1989; Thornberry, 1987).

Though there are many reasons why such programmes are inappropriate, ranging from cost to sheer laziness, the main problems appear to be twofold. First, many organisations do not know sufficiently well what their future needs will be and tend to wish to develop managers within their existing patterns and expectations. Therefore, traditional organisations will tend to continue to produce transactional managers, regardless of the presence or not of formal training and education programmes. The second reason relates to the difficulty in assessing the needs of individual managers, and shaping these into a tailor-made programme of development and training. While it is relatively easy to identify a manager's training requirements in terms of technical skills (such as accountancy, engineering, etc.), the difficulty comes in trying to identify the skills and mental attitudes necessary to be an effective manager. This chapter has already shown that it is difficult to define the role of a manager and that, in any case, this will vary from organisation to organisation and is likely to change over time.

In order to overcome this second problem, some organisations are moving away from standard packages of off-the-job training, which some see as an expensive waste of time (Newstrom, 1985; Wilkinson and Orth, 1986), to more individually tailored and job-related programmes. These type of personalised programmes have a number of common characteristics:

- *The use of assessment and assessment centres to identify potential managers and the developmental needs of existing managers (Long, 1986).*

- *Regular coaching by a more senior manager, a mentor, to allow the manager to talk over problems and issues and learn from the experience of the senior manager (Willbur, 1987).*

- *Self-development appears to have come to the fore as a reaction to disappointing results from formal training courses. The purpose of self-development is to allow managers to identify and develop a programme to meet their own needs. Obviously, managers are more likely to feel that such a programme is better suited to their needs; they may consequently be more committed to it and may get more out of it than a standard programme (Burgoyne and Germaine, 1984).*

As with all general developments, this move away from formal, off-the-job training programmes to more personalised and on-the-job programmes needs to be viewed critically. Drawbacks have been identified, particularly the need to avoid isolation if self-development is too heavily relied upon (Stuart, 1986). Furthermore, as Storey (1989) pointed out in a major review of the management development literature, drawing a distinction between on-the-job and off-the-job training may miss the main issue, which is the requirement to assess development and training needs of individual managers accurately and to develop programmes which allow managers to develop a much more critical and intuitive approach to their situation.

In this respect the work of a number of writers on single-loop learning and double-loop learning is useful (Argyris and Schon, 1978; Bateson, 1972). Single-loop learning is the process whereby individuals respond to changes in the internal and external environment by detecting errors, and modify strategies within the existing norms and practices of the organisation. Bateson (1972) argues that these 'learning episodes' function to preserve a form of stability and constancy in the organisation.

The drawback of this type of learning, according to Argyris and Schon (1978) and Bateson (1972) is that it merely preserves the status quo – it does not allow assumptions to be challenged and tested, but tends to promote transactional learning. Bateson believes that the most effective form of learning is double-loop or second order learning, which draws a distinction between the process of learning, and the process of learning to learn. The latter means that managers must reflect more widely, rather than simply seeking to solve a problem. They must inquire into the context of learning or the failure to learn – why isn't this working? – and question the appropriateness of their actions. In this way, self-questioning and experience enable managers to assess the wider context within which they operate, to question and challenge the status quo, to look at opportunities and threats from a different perspective and by so doing begin to change their mental models of the world (Garratt, 1987).

Argyris (1991) believed that one of the main barriers to developing double-loop learning is that, within the narrow confines of single-loop learning, many managers do operate effectively, even though, looking at the wider picture, their organisation may be in trouble. This is akin to Peters and Waterman's (1982) concept of 'irrational rationality' – managers applying the 'right' solution even when the situation means that it is no longer appropriate. Argyris believes that, if managers could experience failure or recognise the inappropriateness of their approaches, it would have a positive effect in leading managers to question their assumptions and practices, and develop their ability to be critical. Senge (1993) argued that the most important factor in developing such a questioning approach and achieving organisational success is the ability to comprehend in a critical fashion the overall organisational context. The case studies in Part Three support this argument. In some of the companies, the combination of a form of crisis, which threatened the organisation's future, coupled with a search for alternative solutions, played a positive role in moving some managers from single-loop to double-loop learning.

From the foregoing examination of managerial learning and adaptation, three factors can be discerned as important in allowing managers successfully to align organisations, contexts and style of leadership:

1 *Managers' past experience*, and whether this has reinforced their beliefs or, instead, led them to question their appropriateness.

2 *The managers' learning style*: are they adapters – single-loop learners – or challengers – double-loop learners?

3 *Do managers perceive the whole picture?* Can they see the organisation in its

context? Particularly, do they perceive the choices for change in the organisation itself, its context, and their approach to leadership, strategy and change?

SUMMARY AND CONCLUSIONS

In reading some of the literature on strategy and change, one might be forgiven for asking whether managers and what they do matter at all. If strategy is emergent, often unrelated to conscious decisions, what real role exists for managers? Alternatively, if, as the evolutionary perspective on strategy would have it, luck plays a greater part in success than conscious action, does the quality of the manager matter? The answer, of course, is yes. As the case studies show, this is for both negative and positive reasons.

On the negative side, managers can act to hold back organisations, to prevent change and to create a climate of blame and in-fighting. On the positive side, managers can identify opportunities for progress, can ensure the organisation and its environment remain in harmony. They can create the conditions for growth and prosperity. Effective managers are, therefore, for very positive reasons, important to an organisation. However, they do not operate in isolation or have a totally free rein.

The chief executives of Oticon and PCI both wanted to transform their organisations. One gained the support of his colleagues and employees and succeeded, the other did not and failed. This is not to say that successful organisations are based solely on dominant or charismatic leaders. There may be leaders, such as Lee Iacocca when he ran Chrysler, Pehr Gyllenhammar before his untimely departure from Volvo, Lord Hanson at Hanson Trust, Tiny Rowland in his days at Lonrho or Rupert Murdoch at News International, who through sheer force of personality dominated and transformed organisations. Nevertheless, these are a minority; such people often outstay their organisational welcome and their departures can be acrimonious and/or followed by the need for major restructuring.

Most managers, even of very large corporations, have to rely far less on their personality than on their business knowledge, skills and experience. They are also called upon to perform a wide range of duties and activities. Though the theories and approaches to strategy and change appear to paint managers as either directing change or facilitating it, and the leadership literature tends to dwell on whether they are transactional or transformational managers, the reality is that they are often required to be all of these things, depending on the circumstances. In bringing about organisational change, there will be occasions when managers will need to devolve responsibility to subordinates; sometimes, though, they will need to participate and support change projects, and, in other instances, they will have to lead the process themselves. Although the approach adopted will depend to a certain extent upon the size and importance of the change project, the timescale involved and the state of the organisation, in the final analysis it will rely on managerial judgment to make the appropriate choice. Changing organisations is a complex process fraught with more opportunities for failure than success. If managers are to accomplish and keep accomplishing this task, as this book has argued, they have to be aware of the choices and approaches available and be willing themselves to change their beliefs and attitudes.

Despite views expressed to the contrary, there can never be any general recipes or formulas for organisational success. The vast variety of organisations, each with its own differing constraints and pressures, make that impossible. What there is, however, is a large body of theories and associated advice which organisations can draw upon to assist them. As this book has shown, there is no such thing as an uncontested theory – all have their drawbacks. In particular, most tend to be situation-specific, even if they do not acknowledge this. Managers and organisations need to treat theories with a degree of scepticism. They also need to realise, however, that if they can identify the main theories for running and changing organisations, and they do understand the context in which they operate, they are in a position to identify choices and make changes.

Sometimes managers may choose to change their organisations radically and quickly; sometimes they may choose to influence the context. In other cases, change may take place more slowly and over a long period, as both organisation and context are shaped and changed. The key factor in all this is to make conscious decisions rather than rely on untested assumptions. This will require managers to question and challenge their own assumptions. It will also require them to gather and be open to a wide variety of information – the experience of Japanese companies is that this should be an organisation-wide and continuous process, rather than one limited to a few like-minded individuals at one point in time.

Even where choices are identified, managers should not assume that exercising choice is easy or that the results will be beneficial for all concerned, including themselves. For this reason, managers have a responsibility in making and implementing choices to consider the implications in the widest context. In the West, especially the UK and USA, there is a tendency to think mainly in terms of short-term profitability, and ignore the long-term and social consequences of actions. We can see this in the context of the Classical school, whose concentration on narrow issues of control and efficiency leads to the creation of jobs which are both physically strenuous and mind-numbingly boring. However, the adverse consequences of organisation theory are not limited to the Classical school; in many ways, the policies and approaches advocated by the Culture–Excellence school could be considered even worse. Though both Handy (1989) and, to a lesser extent, Kanter (1989) are concerned about the impact of fragmented organisations and insecure jobs on society at large and family life in particular, neither appears to believe that these can be avoided.

Yet the consequences of this approach in creating instability and unpredictability in the job market are disastrous. For example according to Hutton (1995), that the UK is now more socially divided than at any time since the Second World War, with some 60 per cent of the population either marginalised or living in very insecure circumstances. The situation is even worse in the USA where, increasingly, the better-off are retreating into walled compounds patrolled by armed guards. If this seems a somewhat apocalyptic vision, then bear in mind that the latest guru from the USA, William Bridges, is advocating the jobless organisation. He believes that there should no longer be any permanent jobs, not even for managers. Instead, he wants to see the labour force form one enormous pool of labour waiting for temporary employment – the just-in-time workforce to complement the just-in-time organis-ation (Golzen, 1995). In support of his view that jobless organisations are the future, he points out that General Motors is no longer the largest employer in the USA; instead, it is the temporary employment agency, Manpower.

The fragmentation and insecurity of the labour market is less pronounced in some countries. This is especially the case in those nations which, historically, have seen the objectives of individual organisations as subservient to national interests. Despite recent economic problems associated with reunification, Germany still has an enviable record of attempting to prevent job losses and job insecurity, as do the Scandinavian states and Japan. France, on the other hand, who would once have been included in this group, has experienced high levels of unemployment throughout the 1980s, in an attempt to maintain Franc–Mark parity.

This, of course, emphasises that national governments as well as individual organisations have a major contribution to make when considering the wider con-text and implications of managers' decisions. In the West, especially the UK, there has been an increasing move to deregulation, privatisation and the introduction of market forces into the operation of government. Whatever the merits of these policies in terms of efficiency, and they are debatable (Flynn, 1993), no one can doubt that they have acted to increase instability both in the economy at large and in government bodies such as the National Health Service. As the case study of Midshires College showed, there are now high levels of unpredictability in what was a very stable system. Whether it leads eventually to better patient care or not is obviously an issue, but so is the effect on the social fabric. Post-1945, all Western governments used their public sectors both to provide services and as a means of creating employment and maintaining economic and social stability. These latter functions have now been abandoned in many countries, and the resulting insecurity is evident for all to see.

The point of mentioning this is not merely to show concern, but to argue that it need not be the case. The Culture–Excellence concept is only one of many app-roaches to running organisations. All have their down side, but not all result in job cuts and labour market instability. One alternative is for managers to choose to adopt approaches which reduce instability in their environment, rather than to implement policies which increase the use of short-term contracts, part-time and casual working. If followed widely, this would have two effects. First, the result of many organisations seeking stability would be to reduce the overall level of turbulence in the environment. This is because organisations and their environment are not separate entities, but part of the same system. If organisations become more stable, so too does the environment. Similarly, if – as argued by Tom Peters –

organisations adopt internal chaos to cope with external chaos, this merely acts to increase the overall turbulence in the system – in effect, a vicious spiral of increasing chaos is created. The second consequence of organisations seeking stability is that it increases the stability in society – jobs and communities become more stable.

Therefore, as a final note: organisations face many challenges and choices. Some organisations will find that their room for manoeuvre is very limited. Others may find that there is considerable scope for discretion. It is the role of managers to ensure that all available options and choices are identified, and that the choices made take account of both the short- and long-term interests of all their stakeholders – whether these be shareholders, employees, the managers themselves or the community at large. The worst managers may not be those who make poor choices; it may be those who fail to recognise that any choice exists at all.

BIBLIOGRAPHY

Abegglen, J (1958). *The Japanese Factory*. Free Press: Glencoe, Ill., USA.

Abegglen, J and Stalk, G (1984). *Kaisha, the Japanese Corporation*. Basic Books: New York, USA.

Abell, DF (1977). *Using PIMS and Portfolio Analysis in Strategic Market Planning: A Comparative Analysis*. Intercollegiate Case Clearing House, Harvard Business School: Boston, Mass., USA.

Abell, P (1975). 'Organisations as technically constrained bargaining and influence systems'. In Abell, P (ed): *Organisations as Bargaining and Influence Systems*. Heinemann: London.

Abodaher, D (1986). *Iacocca*. Star: London.

Ackroyd, S, Burrell, G, Hughes, M and Whitaker, A (1988). 'The Japanisation of British Industry.' *Industrial Relations Journal*, 19(1), 11–23.

Aguren, S, Bredbacka, C, Hansson, R, Ihregren, K and Karlsson, KG (1984). *Volvo/Kalmar Revisited: Ten Years of Experience*. The Development Council: Stockholm, Sweden.

Allaire, Y and Firsirotu, ME (1989). 'Coping with Strategic Uncertainty.' *Sloan Management Review*, 30(3), 7–16.

Allaire, Y, and Firsirotu, ME (1984). 'Theories of organizational culture'. *Organization Studies*, 5(3), 193–226.

Allen, FR and Kraft, C (1982). *The Organizational Unconscious. How to Create the Corporate Culture You Want and Need*. Prentice-Hall: Englewood Cliffs, New Jersey, USA.

Allen, RW, Madison, DL, Porter, LW, Renwick, PA and Mayes, BT (1979). 'Organizational Politics: Tactics and Characteristics of its Actors.' *California Management Review*, 22, 77–83.

Anderson, C and Paine, F (1978). 'PIMS: a re-examination'. *Academy of Management Review*, 3 (3), 602–612.

Andrews, KR (1980). *The Concept of Corporate Strategy*. Irwin: Homewood, Ill., USA.

Ansoff, HI (1965). *Corporate Strategy*. McGraw-Hill: New York, USA.

Ansoff, HI (1987). *Corporate Strategy (revised version)*. McGraw Hill: New York, USA.

Argenti, J (1974). *Systematic Corporate Planning*. Nelson: London.

Argyris, C (1964). *Integrating the Individual and the Organization*. John Wiley: New York, USA.

Argyris, C (1970). *Intervention Theory and Method*. Addison-Wesley: Reading, Mass., USA.

Argyris, C (1973). Peter Blau. In Salaman, G and Thompson, K (eds): *People and Organizations*. Longman: London.

Argyris, C (1977). 'Double-Loop Learning in Organizations.' *Harvard Business Review*, Sept–Oct, 115–25.

Argyris, C (1991). 'Teaching Smart People How to Learn.' *Harvard Business Review*, May–Jun, 99–109.

Argyris, C and Schon, D (1978). *Organizational Learning*. Addison Wesley: Reading, Mass., USA.

Ashforth, BE and Fried, Y (1988). 'The Mindlessness of Organizational Behaviours.' *Human Relations*, 41(4), 305–29.

Ashour, AS (1973). 'The Contingency Model of Leadership Effectiveness: An Evaluation.' *Organizational Behavior and Human Performance*, 9, 339–55.

Ashton, D, Easterby-Smith, M and Irvine, C (1975). *Management Development: Theory and Practice*. MCB: Bradford.

Ashton, TS (1948). *The Industrial Revolution 1760–1830*. Oxford University Press: Oxford.

Ashworth, W (1987). *A Short History of the International Economy since 1850*. Longman: London.

AT Kearney Ltd (1992). *Total Quality: Time to Take Off the Rose-Tinted Spectacles*. IFS: Kempston.

AT Kearney Ltd (1994). *Partnership or Powerplay?* AT Kearney: London.

Auer, P and Riegler, C (1990). *Post-Taylorism: The Enterprise as a Place of Learning Organizational Change - A Comprehensive Study on Work Organization Changes and its Context at Volvo*. The Swedish Work Environment Fund: Stockholm, Sweden.

Babbage, C (1835). *On the Economy of Machinery and Manufacture*. Knight: London.

Bachman, JG, Bowers, DG and Marcus, PM (1968). 'Bases of Supervisory Power: A Comparative Study in Five Organizational Settings.' In Tannenbaum, AS (ed): *Control in Organizations*. McGraw-Hill: New York, USA.

Barnard, C (1938). *The Functions of the Executive*. Harvard University Press: Cambridge, Mass., USA.

Barratt, ES (1990). 'Human Resource Management: Organisational Culture.' *Management Update*, 2(1), 21–32.

Barrie, C (1995). 'Saatchi Loses Accounts to New Agency.' *The Guardian*, Feb 16, 15.

Bateson, G (1972). *Steps to an Ecology of the Mind*. Ballantine: New York, USA.

Batten, JD and Swab, JL (1965). 'How to Crack Down on Company Politics.' *Personnel*, 42, 8–20.

Beach, SD (1980). *Personnel*. Macmillan: London.

Beatty, CA and Lee, GL (1992). 'Leadership Among Middle Managers – An Exploration in the Context of Technological Change.' *Human Relations*, 45(9), 957–89.

Beckhard, R (1985). 'Whither management development?' *Journal of Management Development*, 4(2).

Beer, M, Eisenstat, RA and Spector, B (1993). 'Why Change Programmes Don't Produce Change.' In Mabey, C and Mayon-White, B (eds): *Managing Change* (2nd edn). The Open University/Paul Chapman Publishing: London.

Bell, RM (1973). *The behaviour of labour, technical change, and the competitive weakness of British manufacturing*. Technical Change Centre: London.

Benjamin, G and Mabey, C (1993). 'Facilitating Radical Change.' In Mabey, C and Mayon-White, B (eds): *Managing Change* (2nd edn). The Open University/Paul Chapman Publishing: London.

Bennett, R (1983). 'Management Research.' *Management Development Series* 20: Geneva.

Bennis, WG (1959). 'Leadership theory and administrative behaviour.' *Administrative Science Quarterly*, 4, 259–301.

Bennis, WG (1966). 'The coming death of bureaucracy.' *Think*, Nov–Dec, 30–5.

Bernstein, L (1968). *Management Development*. Business Books: London.

Bessant, J (1983). 'Management and manufacturing innovation: the case of information technology.' In Winch, G (ed): *Information Technology in Manufacturing Processes*. Rossendale: London.

Bessant, J, and Haywood, B (1985). *The introduction of flexible manufacturing systems as an example of computer integrated manufacture*. Brighton Polytechnic: Brighton.

Bhote, KR (1989). *Strategic Supply Management*. American Management Association: New York, USA.

Bigge, LM (1982). *Learning Theories for Teachers*. Gower: Aldershot.

Blackler, F and Brown, C (1984). 'Alternative models to guide the design and introduction of new information technologies into work organisations.' *Journal of Occupational Psychology*, 59(4), 287–314.

Blackler, FHM and Brown, CA (1978). *Job Redesign and Management Control: Studies in British Leyland and Volvo.* Saxon House: Farnborough.

Blake, RR and Mouton, JS (1969). *Building a Dynamic Corporation Through Grid Organisation Development.* Addison-Wesley: Reading, Mass., USA.

Blake, RR and Mouton, JS (1976). *Organizational Change by Design.* Scientific Methods: Austin, Texas, USA.

Blau, PM (1970). 'The formal theory of differentiation in organizations.' *American Sociological Review*, 35, 201–18.

Blau, RM, and Schoenherr, RA (1971). *The Structure of Organizations.* Basic Books: New York, USA.

Borchardt (1973). In Cipolla, C (ed): The *Fontana Economic History of Europe Vol.4.* Fontana: London.

Bowers, DG, Franklin, JL and Pecorella, P (1975). 'Matching problems, precursors and interventions in OD: a systematic approach.' *Journal of Applied Behavioural Science*, 11, 391–410.

Bowles, M (1989). 'Myth, Meaning and Work Organisation' *Organization Studies*, 10 (3), 405-23.

Bowman, C and Asch, D (1985). *Strategic Map.* Macmillan: London.

Bracker, J (1980). 'The historical development of the strategic management concept.' *Academy of Management Review*, 5(2), 219–24.

Bratton, J (1992). *Japanization at Work: Managerial Studies for the 1990s.* Macmillan: London.

Brewer, E and Tomlinson, JWC (1964). 'The manager's working day.' *Journal of Industrial Economics*, 12, 191–7.

Brown, DH and Jopling, D (1994). 'Some Experiences of Outsourcing: A Systemic Analysis of Strategic and Organisational Issues.' *Paper Presented to the British Academy of Management Annual Conference, University of Lancaster*, Sept.

Bruland, K (1989). In Mathias, P and Davis, JA (eds): *The First Industrial Revolutions.* Blackwell: Cambridge.

Buchanan, D and Boddy, D (1992a). *Take the Lead: Interpersonal Skills for Change Agents.* Prentice-Hall: London.

Buchanan, D and Boddy, D (1992b). *The Expertise of the Change Agent.* Prentice-Hall: London.

Buchanan, DA (1984). 'The impact of technical implications and managerial aspirations on the organization and control of the labour process.' *Paper presented to the second Annual Conference on the Control and Organisation of the Labour Process.* UMIST/Aston, 28–30 March.

Buckley, PJ and Mirza, H (1985). 'The Wit and Wisdom of Japanese Management.' *Management International Review*, 25, 16–32.

Buckley, W (1968). *Modern Systems and Research for the Behavioral Scientist.* Aldine Publishing: Chicago, USA.

Bullock, RJ, and Batten, D (1985). 'It's just a phase we're going through: a review and synthesis of OD phase analysis.' *Group and Organization Studies*, 10, December, 383–412.

Burawoy, M (1979). *Manufacturing Consent: Changes in the Labour Process under Monopoly Capital.* University of Chicago Press: Chicago, USA.

Burgoyne, J and Germaine, C (1984). 'Self development and career planning: an exercise in mutual benefit.' *Personnel Management*, 16(4), Apr, 21–3.

Burke, W (1980). *Organisation Development*. Little, Brown and Co: Toronto, Canada.

Burnes, B (1988). *Strategy for Success: Case Studies in Advanced Manufacturing Technologies*. EITB: Watford.

Burnes, B (1989). *New Technology in Context*. Gower: Aldershot.

Burnes, B (1991). 'Managerial competence and new technology: don't shoot the piano player – he's doing his best.' *Behaviour and Information Technology*, 10(2), 91–109.

Burnes, B and James, H (1995). 'Culture, Cognitive Dissonance and the Management of Change.' *International Journal of Operations and Production Management*, 15(8).

Burnes, B and Salauroo, M (1995). 'The Impact of the NHS Internal Market on the Merger of Colleges of Midwifery and Nursing.' *Journal of Management in Medicine*, 9(2).

Burnes, B and Salauroo, M (1995). 'The Impact of the NHS Internal Market on the Merger of Colleges of Midwifery and Nursing: Not Just a Case of Putting the Cart Before the Horse.' *Journal of Management in Medicine*, 9(2), 14–29.

Burnes, B and Weekes, B (1989). *AMT: A Strategy for Success?* NEDO: London.

Burnes, B and Whittle, P (1995). 'Supplier Development: Getting Started.' *Logistics Focus*, Feb, 10–14.

Burns, JM (1978). *Leadership*. Harper and Row: New York, USA.

Burns, T and Stalker, GM (1961). *The Management of Innovation*. Tavistock: London.

Burton, F, Yamin, M and Young, S (eds) (Forthcoming). *Europe in Transition*. MacMillan: London.

Butler, VG (1985). *Organisation and Management*. Prentice-Hall: London.

Byars, LL (1984). *Strategic Management: Planning and Implementation*. Harper and Row: London.

Camp, RC (1989). *Benchmarking*. ASQC Quality Press: Milwaukee, Wisc., USA.

Carew, A (1987). *Labour Under the Marshall Plan: The Politics of Productivity and the Market*. Manchester University Press: Manchester.

Carlson, S (1951). *Executive Behaviour*. Strombergs: Stockholm.

Carnall, CA (1990). *Managing Change in Organizations*. Prentice-Hall: London.

Carr, C, Tomkins, C and Bayliss, B (1991). 'Strategic Controllership – a Case Study Approach.' *Management Accounting Research*, 2, 89–107.

Carr, P and Donaldson, L (1993). 'Managing Healthily: How an NHS Region is Managing Change.' *Personnel Management*, Oct, 48–51.

Carroll, DT (1983). 'A Disappointing Search for Excellence.' *Harvard Business Review*, Nov–Dec, 78–88.

Chandler, AD (1962). *Strategy and Structure: Chapters in the History of American Industrial Enterprise*. MIT: Cambridge, Mass., USA.

Chapman, SD and Chassagne, S (1981). *European Textile Printers in the Eighteenth Century. A Study of Peel and Oberkampf*. Heinemann: London.

Child, J (1972). 'Organizational structure, environment and performance: the role of strategic choice.' *Sociology*, 6(1), 1–22.

Child, J (1984). *Organization*. Harper and Row: Cambridge.

Child, J and Smith, C (1987). 'The Context and Process of Organisational Transformation – Cadbury Limited in its Sector.' *Journal of Management Studies*, 24(6), 565–93.

Child, J, and Ellis, T (1973). 'Predictors of variation in managerial roles.' *Human Relations*, 26(2), 227–50.

Cipolla, C (ed) (1973). *The Fontana Economic History of Europe Vol.4*. Fontana: London.

Clark, P (1972). *Action Research and Organisational Change*. Harper and Row: London.

Clark, RC (1979). *The Japanese Company*. New Haven, Conn., USA.

Clarke, L (1994). *The Essence of Change*. Prentice-Hall: London.

Clegg, CW (1984). 'The derivation of Job Design.' *Journal of Occupational Behaviour*, 5, 131–46.

Coghlan, D (1993). 'In Defence of Process Consultation.' In Mabey, C and Mayon-White, B (eds): *Managing Change* (2nd edn). The Open University/Paul Chapman Publishing: London.

Cohen, MD, March, JG and Olsen, JP (1972). 'A Garbage Can Model of Organizational Choice.' *Administrative Science Quarterly*, 17, 1–25.

Cole, RE (1979). *Work, Mobility and Participation: a Comparative Study of Japanese and American Industry*. University of California Press: Los Angeles, USA.

Constable, J and McCormick, R (1987). *The Making of British Managers*. British Institute of Management/Confederation of British Industry: London.

Coombs, R and Hull, R (1994). 'The Best or the Worst of Both Worlds: BPR, Cost Reduction, and the Strategic Management of IT.' *Paper Presented to the OASIG Seminar on Organisation Change Through IT and BPR: Beyond the Hype*, Sept, London.

Cooper, J and Fazio, RH (1984). 'A new look at dissonance theory.' In Berkowitz, L (ed): *Advances in Experimental Social Psychology*, 17, 229–67. Academic Press: New York, USA.

Copley, FB (1923). *Frederick Winslow Taylor: Father of Scientific Management, Vol. 2*. Harper and Row: New York, USA.

Coulson-Thomas, C and Coe, T (1991). *The Flat Organization*. British Institute of Management: London.

Cowe, R (1995). 'Compete Carefully.' *The Guardian*, Mar 25, 40.

Crosby, PB (1979). 'Quality is Free.' McGraw-Hill: New York.

Crozier, M (1964) *The Bureaucratic Phenomenon*. Tavistock: London.

Cruise O'Brien, R and Voss, C (1992). *In Search of Quality. Working Paper*, London Business School: London.

Cummings, TG and Huse, EF (1989). *Organization Development and Change*. West: St Paul, Minn., USA.

Cuthbert, N (1970). 'Readings from Henri Fayol, General and Industrial Management.' In Tillett, A, Kempner, T and Willis, G (eds): *Management Thinkers*. Pelican: Harmondsworth.

Dakin, SR and Hamilton, RT (1990). 'How "general" are your general managers?' *Management Decision*, 28(2), 32–7.

Dale, BG and Cooper, CL (1992). *TQM and Human Resources: An Executive Guide*. Blackwell: Oxford.

Dale, PN (1986). *The Myth of Japanese Uniqueness*. Croom Helm: London.

Dastmalchian, A (1984). 'Environmental dependencies and company structure in Britain.' *Organization Studies*, 5(3), 222–41.

Davis, E and Star, J (1993). 'The World's Best Performing Companies.' *Business Strategy Review*, 4(2), 1–16.

Davis, JA (1989). In Mathias, P and Davis, JA (eds): *The First Industrial Revolutions*. Blackwell: Cambridge.

Davis, LE (1979). 'Job Design: Historical Overview.' In Davis, LE and Taylor, JC (eds): *Design of Work*. Goodyear: Santa Monica, Calif., USA.

Davis, LE and Canter, RR (1955). 'Job Design.' *Journal of Industrial Engineering*, 6(1), 3.

Davis, LE, Canter, RR and Hoffman, J (1955). 'Current Job Design Criteria.' *Journal of Industrial Engineering*, 6(2), 5–11.

Davis, R (1928). *The Principles of Factory Organization and Management*. Harper and Row: New York, USA.

Dawkins, W (1993). 'Costly Burden of Tradition.' *Financial Times*, Dec 1, 10.

Dawkins, W (1994). 'Loosening of the Corporate Web.' *Financial Times*, Nov 30, 15.

Dawson, P (1994). *Organizational Change: A Processual Approach*. Paul Chapman Publishing: London.

Deal, T and Kennedy, A (1983). 'Culture: A New Look Through Old Lenses.' *Journal of Applied Behavioural Science*, 19 (4), 497–507.

Dess, GG and Davis, PS (1984). 'Porter's (1980) generic strategies as determinants of strategic group membership and original performance.' *Academy of Management Journal*, 27(3), 467–88.

Dobson, P (1988). 'Changing Culture.' *Employment Gazette*, December, 647-50.

Dolvik, JE and Stokland, D (1992). 'Norway: The "Norwegian Model" in Transition.' In Ferner, A and Hyman, R (eds): *Industrial Relations in the New Europe*. Blackwell: Oxford.

Done, K (1994). 'Up to Strength Once Again: Volvo.' *Financial Times*, Dec 2.

Donovan, P (1995). 'Saatchis in Row Over Share Deal.' *The Guardian*, Feb 15, 22.

Drory, A and Romm, T (1988). 'Politics in the Organization and its Perception within the Organization.' *Organization Studies*, 9(2), 165–79.

Drucker, PF (1974). *Management: Tasks, Responsibilities, Practices*. Harper and Row: London.

Drucker, PF (1985). *Innovation and Entrepreneurship*. Pan: London.

Duncan, WJ (1975). 'Organisations as political coalitions: a behavioral view of the goal function process.' *Journal of Behavioral Economics*, 5, Summer, 25–44.

Dunham, AL (1955). *The Industrial Revolution in France*. Exposition Press: New York, USA.

Dunphy, D and Stace, D (1993). 'The Strategic Management of Corporate Change.' *Human Relations*, 46(8), 905–18.

Dunphy, DD and Stace, DA (1988). 'Transformational and coercive strategies for planned organizational change: beyond the OD model.' *Organization Studies*, 9(3), 317–34.

Economist Intelligence Unit (1992). *Making Quality Work – Lessons from Europe's Leading Companies*. Economist Intelligence Unit: London.

Edwardes, M (1983). *Back from the Brink*. Collins: London.

Egan, G (1994). 'Cultivate Your Culture.' *Management Today*, Apr, 39–42.

Eldridge, JET, and Crombie, AD (1974). *A Sociology of Organizations*. George Allen and Unwin: London.

Elliot, K and Lawrence, P (1985). *Introducing Management*. Penguin: Harmondsworth.

Etzioni, A (1975). *A Comparative Analysis of Complex Organizations*. Free Press: New York, USA.

Evans, MG (1970). 'The Effects of Supervisory Behaviour on the Path-Goal Relationship.' *Organizational Behavior and Human Performance*, 5, 277–98.

Ezzamel, M, Green, C, Lilley, S and Willmott, H (1994). *Change Management: Appendix 1 - A Review and Analysis of Recent Changes in UK Management Practices*. The Financial Services Research Centre, UMIST: Manchester.

Farrell, D and Petersen, JC (1983). 'Patterns of Political Behaviour in Organizations.' *The Academy of Management Review*, 7, 403–12.

Fawn, J and Cox, B (1985). *Corporate Planning in Practice*. Strategic Planning Society: London.

Fayol, H (1949). *General and Industrial Management* (trans). Pitman: London.

Fazio, RH, Zanna, MP and Cooper, J (1977). 'Dissonance and self-perception: an integrative view of each theory's proper domain of application.' *Journal of Experimental Social Psychology*, 13, 464–79.

Ferguson, CH (1988). 'From the People who brought you Voodoo Economics.' *Harvard Business Review*, May–Jun, 55–62.

Ferner, A and Hyman, R (eds) (1992). *Industrial relations in the New Europe*. Blackwell: Oxford.

Festinger, L (1957). *The Theory of Cognitive Dissonance*. Stanford University Press: Stanford, Calif., USA.

Fielder, FE (1967). *A Theory of Leadership Effectiveness*. McGraw-Hill: New York, USA.

Filby, I and Willmott, H (1988). 'Ideologies and Contradictions in a Public Relations Department.' *Organization Studies*, 9 (3), 335-51.

Fitton, R and Wadsworth, A (1958). *The Strutts and the Arkwrights 1758–1830*. Manchester University Press: Manchester.

Fleishman, EA (1953). 'The Description of Supervisory Behaviour.' *Personnel Psychology*, 37, 1–6.

Fleishman, EA (1969). *Manual for the Leadership Opinion Questionnaire*. Science Research Associates: USA.

Flynn, J, Dawley, H, Templeman, J and Bernier, L (1995). 'Suddenly British Carmaking is Burning Rubber.' *Business Week*, Apr 3, 21.

Flynn, N (1993). *Public Sector Management*. Harvester Wheatsheaf: London.

Fohlen, C (1973). 'France 1700–1914.' In Cipolla, C (ed): *The Fontana Economic History of Europe Vol.4*. Fontana: London.

Ford, TM (1981). 'Strategic planning – myth or reality? A chief executive's view.' *Long Range Planning*, 14, Dec, 9–11.

Fortune (1990). 'Global 500: The World's Biggest Industrial Corporations.' *Fortune*, July 30.

Fox, JM (1975). 'Strategic planning: a case study.' *Managerial Planning*, 23, May/Jun, 32–38.

Francks, P (1992). *Japanese Economic Development: Theory and Practice*. Routledge: London.

Freeman, C (1988). 'The factory of the future: the productivity paradox, Japanese just-in-time and information technology.' *ESRC PICT Policy Research Paper 3*.

French, WL and Bell, CH (1984). *Organization Development*. Prentice-Hall: Englewood Cliffs, NJ, USA.

Friedman, G (1961). *The Anatomy of Work*. Heinemann: London.

Frost, PJ and Hayes, DC (1979). 'An Exploration in Two Cultures of a Model of Political Behaviour in Organizations.' In Allen, RW and Porter, LW (eds): *Organizational Influence Processes*. Scott, Foresman and Co: Glenview, Ill., USA.

Fruin, WM (1992). *The Japanese Enterprise System*. OUP: Oxford.

Fullerton, H and Price, C (1991). 'Culture Change in the NHS.' *Personnel Management*, March, 50–3.

Gandz, J and Murray, VV (1980). 'The Experience of Workplace Politics.' *Academy of Management Journal*, 23, 237–51.

Garratt, B (1987). *The Learning Organization*. Fontana: London.

Garvin, DA (1993). Building a Learning Organization. *Harvard Business Review*, Jul/Aug, 78-91.

Gibb CA (1969). 'Leadership.' In Lindzey, G and Aronson, E (eds): *Handbook of Social Psychology*, 4 (2nd Edn). Addison-Wesley: Reading, Mass., USA.

Gibbons, PT (1992). 'Impacts of Organisational Evolution on Leadership Roles and Behaviors.' *Human Relations*, 45(1) 1–18.

Gibson, JL, Ivancevich, JM and Donnelly, JH (1988). *Organizations: Behaviour-Structure-Processes*. Business Publications: Plano, Texas, USA.

Gilbreth, FB and Gilbreth, LM (1914). *Applied Motion Study*. Sturgis and Walton: New York, USA.

Glueck, WF (1978). *Business Policy and Strategic Management*. McGraw-Hill: New York, USA.

Golzen, G (1995). 'Jobbing Guru.' *Human Resources*, 16, Jan/Feb, 42–8.

Gordon, G (1985). 'The relationship of corporate culture to industry sector and corporate performance. In Kilmann, R, Saxton, M and Serpa, R (eds): *Gaining Control of the Corporate Culture*. Jossey-Bass: San Francisco, USA.

Grant, A (1983). *Against the Clock*. Pluto: London.

Grant, GM (1991a). *Contemporary Strategy Analysis*. Blackwell: Oxford.

Grant, GM (1991b). 'The Resource-Based Theory of Competitive Advantage: Implications for Strategy Formulation.' *California Management Review*, 33(3), 114–22.

Guest, RH (1957). 'Job Enlargement–Revolution in Job Design.' *Personnel Administration*, 20, 9–16.

Gyllenhammar, PG (1977). *People at Work*. Addison-Wesley: Reading, Mass., USA.

Habakkuk, HJ and Postan, M (eds) (1965). *The Cambridge Economic History of Europe, Vol.VI*. Cambridge University Press: Cambridge.

Hackman, JR and Lawler, EE (1971). 'Employee Relations and Job Characteristics.' *Journal of Applied Psychology*, 55, 259–286

Hackman, JR and Oldham, GR (1980). *Work Redesign*. Addison-Wesley: Reading, Mass., USA.

Hales, CP (1986). 'What do managers do?: a critical review of the evidence.' *Journal of Management Studies*, 22(1), 88–115.

Hall, DT and Nougaim, KE (1968). 'An examination of Maslow's need hierarchy in an organizational setting.' *Organizational Behaviour and Performance*, 3, Feb, 12–35.

Hamel, G, and Prahalad, CK (1989). *Strategic intent*. Harvard Business Review, May-Jun, 63–76.

Handy, C (1986). *Understanding Organizations*. Penguin: Harmondsworth.

Handy, C (1989). *The Age of Unreason*. Arrow: London.

Handy, C (1994). *The Empty Raincoat*. Hutchinson: London.

Handy, C, Gow, I, Gordon, C, Randlesome, C and Moloney, M (1987). *The Making of a Manager*. NEDO: London.

Hannam, R (1993). *Kaizen for Europe*. IFS: Kempston.

Hannan, MT and Freeman, J (1988). *Organizational Ecology*. Harvard University Press: Cambridge Mass., USA.

Hanson, P (1993). 'Made in Britain – The True State of Manufacturing Industry.' *Paper presented at the Institution of Mechanical Engineers' Conference on Performance Measurement and Benchmarking*, Birmingham, Jun.

Harrigan, RK (1980). *Strategy for Declining Businesses*. Lexington Books: Lexington, Mass., USA.

Harris, PR (1985). *Management in Transition*. Jossey-Bass: San Francisco, Calif., USA.

Harrison, R (1970). 'Choosing the depth of an organisational intervention.' *Journal of Applied Behavioural Science*, 6, 181–202.

Hassard, J and Sharifi, S (1989). Corporate culture and strategic change. *Journal of General Management*, 15(2), 4–19.

Hatvany, N and Pucik, V (1981). 'An Integrated Management System: Lessons from the Japanese Experience.' *Academy of Management Review*, 6, 469–80.

Hax, CA and Majluf, NS (1982). 'Competitive cost dynamics.' *Interfaces*, 12, Oct, 50–61.

Hax, CA and Nicholson, SM (1983). 'The use of the growth share matrix in strategic planning.' *Interfaces*, 13, Feb, 46–60.

Heller, F (1970). 'Group feed-back analysis as a change agent.' *Human Relations*, 23(4), 319–33.

Hendry, C (1979). 'Contingency Theory in practice, I.' *Personnel Review*, 8(4), 39–44.

Hendry, C (1980). 'Contingency Theory in practice, II.' *Personnel Review*, 9(1), 5–11.

Herzberg, F (1968). 'One More Time: How Do You Motivate Employees?' *Harvard Business Review*, 46, 53–62.

Herzberg, F, Mausner, B and Snyderman, B (1959). *The Motivation to Work*. Wiley: New York, USA.

Hickson, DJ and Butler, RJ (1982). 'Power and decision-making in the organisational coalition.' *Research report presented to the Social Science Research Council.*

Hickson, DJ, Pugh, DS and Pheysey, DC (1969). 'Operations technology and organisation structure: an empirical reappraisal.' *Administrative Science Quarterly*, 14, 378–97.

Hines, P (1994). *Creating World Class Suppliers: Unlocking Mutual Competitive Advantage.* Pitman: London.

HM Treasury (1992). 'Public Expenditure Analyses to 1994–95:' *Statistical Supplement to the 1991 Autumn Statement. CM192.* HM Treasury: London.

HMSO (1989). *Working for Patients*, Cm 555. HMSO: London.

Hobsbawm, EJ (1968). *Industry and Empire*. Pelican: Harmondsworth.

Hofer, CH and Schendel, DE (1978). *Strategy Formulation: Analytical Concepts.* West: St Paul, Minn., USA.

Hofstede, G (1980). 'Culture's Consequences: International Differences in Work-Related Values.' Sage: London.

Hofstede, G (1990). 'The Cultural Relativity of Organizational Practices and Theories.' In DC Wilson and RH Rosenfeld (eds): *Managing Organizations: Text, Readings and Cases.* McGraw-Hill: London.

Kempner, T (1970). 'Frederick Taylor and Scientific Management.' In A Tillett, T Kempner and G Wills (eds): Management Thinkers. Pelican: Harmondsworth.

Holden, N and Burgess, M (1994). *Japanese-Led Companies.* McGraw-Hill: London.

Horne, JH and Lupton, T (1965). 'The work activities of "middle managers" – an exploratory study.' *Journal of Management Studies*, 2(1), 14–33.

Hoskin, K (1990). 'Using history to understand theory: a re-consideration of the historical genesis of "strategy".' *Paper prepared for the EIASM Workshop on Strategy, Accounting and Control, Venice.*

Howarth, C (1988). 'Report of the Joint Design of Technology, Organisation and People Growth Conference – Venice.' pp 12–14. Oct. *Information Services News and Abstracts*, 95 Nov/Dec, Work Research Unit: London.

Hughes, M (1995). 'Halifax and Leeds Clear the Courts.' *The Guardian*, Mar 29, 15.

Hunter, JE (1989). *The Emergence of Modern Japan.* Longman: London.

Huse, EF (1980). *Organization Development and Change.* West: St Paul, Minn., USA.

Hussey, DE (1978). 'Portfolio analysis: practical experience with the Directional Policy Matrix.' *Long Range Planning*, 11, Aug, 2–8.

Hutton, W (1995). *The State We're In.* Cape: London.

Inagami, T (1988). *Japanese Workplace Industrial Relations.* Japan Institute of Labour: Tokyo.

Institute of Management (1995). *Finding the Time – A Survey of Managers' Attitudes to Using and Managing Time.* Institute of Management: London.

Ishikawa, K (1985). *What is Total Quality Control? The Japanese Way.* Prentice Hall: Englewood Cliffs, NJ, USA.

Ishizuna, Y (1990). 'The Transformation of Nissan – The Reform of Corporate Culture.' *Long Range Planning*, 23(3), 9–15.

Ivancevich, J (1970). 'An Analysis of Control, Bases of Control, and Satisfaction in an Organizational Setting.' *Academy of Management Journal*, Dec, 427–32.

Johnson, G (1993). 'Processes of Managing Strategic Change.' In Mabey, C and Mayon-

White, B (eds): *Managing Change* (2nd edn). The Open University/Paul Chapman Publishing: London.

Johnson, G and Scholes, K (1993). *Exploring Corporate Strategy*. Prentice Hall: London.

Jones, EE (1990). *Interpersonal Perception*. Freeman: New York, USA.

Jorberg, L (1973). 'The Nordic Countries 1850–1914.' In Cipolla, C (ed): *The Fontana Economic History of Europe Vol.4*. Fontana: London.

Kahn, H and Weiner, A (1978). *The Year 2000*. Macmillan: London.

Kamata, S (1982). *Japan in the Passing Lane*. Pantheon: New York, USA.

Kanter, RM (1989). *When Giants Learn to Dance: Mastering the Challenges of Strategy, Management, and Careers in the 1990s*. Unwin: London.

Kanter, RM, Stein, BA and Jick, TD (1992). *The Challenge of Organizational Change*. Free Press: New York, USA.

Karlsson, LE (1973). *Experiences in Employee Participation in Sweden: 1969–1972*. Mimeograph, Cornell University: New York, USA.

Kay, J (1993). *Foundations of Corporate Success*. OUP: Oxford.

Kearney, AT (1989). *Computer Integrated Manufacturing: Competitive Advantage or Technological Dead End?* Kearney: London.

Kearney, AT (1992). *Total Quality: Time to Take Off the Rose-Tinted Spectacles*. IFS: Kempston.

Kelly, JE (1982a). 'Economic and Structural Analysis of Job Design.' In Kelly, JE and Clegg, CW (eds): *Autonomy and Control at the Workplace*. Croom Helm: London.

Kelly, JE (1982b). *Scientific Management, Job Redesign and Work Performance*. Academic Press: London.

Kemp, T (1979). *Industrialization in Nineteenth Century Europe*. Longman: London.

Kempner, T (1970). 'Frederick Taylor and Scientific Management.' In A Tillett, T Kempner and G Wills (eds): *Management Thinkers*. Pelican: Harmondsworth.

Kerr, C and Fisher, L (1957). 'Plant Sociology: The Elite and the Aborigines.' In Komarovsky, M (ed): *Common Frontiers of the Social Sciences*. Greenwood: Westport, Conn., USA.

Kerr, S, Schriesheim, CA, Murphy, CJ and Stogdill, RM (1974). 'Towards a Contingency Theory of Leadership Based Upon the Consideration and Initiating Structure Literature.' *Organizational Behavior and Human Performance*, 12, 62–82.

Keshavan, K and Rakesh, KS (1979). 'Generating future scenarios – their use in strategic planning.' *Long Range Planning*, 12, Jun, 57–61.

Keys, JB and Miller, KR (1984). 'The Japanese Management Theory Jungle.' *Academy of Management Review*, 9, 342–53.

Kidd, P and Karwowski, W (eds) (1994). *Advances in Agile Manufacture*. IOS: Amsterdam.

Kipnis, D, Schmidt, SM and Wilkinson, I (1980). 'Intraorganizational Influence Tactics: Explorations in Getting One's Way.' *Journal of Applied Psychology*, Aug, 440–52.

Kipnis, D, Schmidt, SM, Swaffin-Smith, C and Wilkinson, I (1984). 'Patterns of Managerial Influence: Shotgun Managers, Tacticians, and Bystanders.' *Organizational Dynamics*, Winter, 58–67.

Kjellberg, A (1992). 'Sweden: Can the Model Survive.' In Ferner, A and Hyman, R (eds): *Industrial Relations in the New Europe*. Blackwell: Oxford.

Kotler, P (1978). 'Harvesting strategies for weak products.' *Business Horizons*, 21(4), Aug, 15–22.

Kotter, JP (1982). *The General Managers*. Free Press: New York, USA.

Kriede, P, Medick, H and Schlumbohm, J (1981). *Industrialization Before Industrialization*. Cambridge University Press: Cambridge.

Kuhn, TS (1962). *The Structure of Scientific Revolutions*. University of Chicago Press: Chicago, USA.

Lamming, R (1993). *Beyond Partnership: Strategies for Innovation and Lean Supply*. Prentice-Hall: Hemel Hempstead.

Lamming, R (1994). *A Review of the Relationships Between Vehicle Manufacturers and Suppliers*. DTI/SMMT: London.

Landes, DS (1969). *The Unbound Prometheus*. Cambridge University Press: Cambridge.

Landsberger, HA (1958). *Hawthorne Revisited: 'Management and the Worker'. Its Critics and Developments in Human Relations in Industry*. Cornell University Press: New York, USA.

Lanford, HW (1972). *Technological Forecasting Methodologies: A Synthesis*. American Management Association: New York, USA.

Larson, LL, Hunt, JG and Osborne, RN (1976). 'The Great Hi-Hi Leader Behavior Myth: A Lesson from Occam's Razor.' *Academy of Management Journal*, 19, 628–41.

Lawler, EE (1985). 'Challenging Traditional Research Assumptions.' In Lawler, EE and Associates: *Doing Research That is Useful for Theory and Practice*. Jossey-Bass: San Francisco, USA.

Lawler, EE and Suttle, JL (1972). 'A causal correlation of the need hierarchy concept in an organizational setting.' *Organization Behaviour and Human Performance*, 7, Apr, 265–87.

Lawrence, PR and Lorsch, JW (1967). *Organization and Environment*. Harvard Business School: Boston, USA.

Lawrence, RP (1973). 'How to deal with resistance to change.' In Dalton, W, Lawrence, RP and Grenier, E (eds): *Organisational Change and Development*. Dorsey: Homewood, Ill., USA.

Lee, J (1978). 'Labour in German Industrialization.' In Mathias, P and Postan, M (eds): *Cambridge Economic History of Europe, Vol. VII*. Cambridge University Press: Cambridge.

Leemhuis, JP (1990). 'Using scenario development strategies at Shell.' In Taylor, B and Harrison, J (eds): *The Manager's Casebook of Business Strategy*. Butterworth–Heinemann: Oxford.

Leifer, R and Huber, GP (1977). 'Relations amongst perceived environmental uncertainty, organisation structure and boundary-spanning behaviour.' *Administrative Science Quarterly*, 22, 235–47.

Leontiades, M (1986). *Managing the Unmanageable*. Addison–Wesley: Reading, Mass., USA.

Levine, AL (1967). *Industrial Retardation in Britain 1880–1914*. Basic Books: New York, USA.

Lewin, K (1958). 'Group decisions and social change.' In Swanson, GE, Newcomb, TM and Hartley, EL (eds): *Readings in Social Psychology*. Holt, Rhinehart and Winston: New York, USA.

Likert, R (1961). *New Patterns of Management*. McGraw Hill: New York, USA.

Likert, R (1967). *The Human Organization: Its Management and Values*. McGraw-Hill: New York, USA.

Lincoln, JR and Kalleberg, AL (1985). 'Work Organisation and Workforce Commitment: a Study of Plants and Employees in the US and Japan.' *American Sociological Review*, 50, 738–60.

Lindblom, CE (1968). *The Policy-Making Process*. Prentice Hall: Englewood Cliffs, NJ, USA.

Linneman, RE and Klein, HE (1979). 'The use of multiple scenarios by US industrial companies.' *Long Range Planning*, 12, Feb, 83–90.

Lippitt, G (1982). 'Management development as the key to organisational renewal.' *Journal of Management Development*, 1(2).

Lippitt, R, Watson, J and Westley, B (1958). *The Dynamics of Planned Change*. Harcourt, Brace and World: New York, USA.

Litschert, R and Nicholson, E (1974). 'Corporate long range planning groups – some different approaches.' *Long Range Planning*, 7, Aug, 62–66.

Little, R (1984). 'Conglomerates are doing better than you think.' *Fortune*, 28 May, 60.

Littler, CR (1978). 'Understanding Taylorism.' *British Journal of Sociology*, 29(2), 185–202.

Lloyd, AR, Dale, BG and Burnes, B (1994). 'A Study of Nissan Motor Manufacturing (UK) Supplier Development Team Activities.' *Proceedings of the Institute of Mechanical Engineers, 208, Part D: Journal of Automobile Engineering*, 63–8.

Locke, EW (1982). 'The ideas of Frederick W Taylor.' *Academy of Management Review*, 7(1), 14–24.

Long, P (1986). *Performance Appraisal Revisited*. IPM: London.

Lorsch, JW (1970). 'Introduction to the structural design of organizations.' In Dalton, GW, Lawrence, PR and Lorsch, JW (eds): *Organization Structure and Design*. Irwin-Dorsey: London.

Lovell, R (1980). *Adult Learning*. Croom Helm: London.

Luthans, F, McCaul, HS and Dodd, NG (1985). 'Organizational Commitment: a Comparison of American, Japanese and Korean Employees.' *Academy of Management Journal*, 28, 213–19.

Mabey, C and Mayon-White, B (1993). *Managing Change* (2nd edn). The Open University/Paul Chapman Publishing: London.

Mahoney, MJ (1974). *Cognition and Behavior Modification*. Ballinger: Cambridge, Mass., USA.

Malaska, P, Malmivirta, M, Meristo, T and Hansen, SO (1984). 'Scenarios in Europe – who uses them and why?' *Long Range Planning*, 17, Oct, 45–9.

Mangham Working Party (1987). *The Mangham Working Party Report: A Survey of the In-house Activities of Ten Major Companies*. British Institute of Management/Confederation of British Industry: London.

Mansfield, R (1984). 'Formal and informal structures.' In Gruneberg, M and Wall, T (eds): *Social Psychology and Organizational Behaviour*. Wiley: Chichester.

Mantoux, P (1964). *The Industrial Revolution in the Eighteenth Century*. Cape: London.

Marczewski, J (1963). 'The Take-Off Hypothesis and French Experience.' In Rostow, WW: *The Economics of Take-Off into Sustained Growth*. Macmillan: London.

Marglin, SA (1976). 'What do bosses do?' In Gorz, A (ed): *The Division of Labour: the Labour Process and Class Struggle in Modern Capitalism*. Harvester: Brighton.

Marsh, N (1986). 'Management development and strategic management change. *Journal of Management Development*, 5(1).

Marsh, RM and Mannari, H (1976). *Modernization and the Japanese Factory*. Princeton University Press: Princeton, NJ, USA.

Maslow, AH (1943). 'A theory of human motivation.' *Psychology Review*, 50, 370–96.

Massie, JL (1965). 'Management Theory.' In March, JG (ed): *Handbook of Organizations*. Rand McNally: Chicago, USA.

Mathias, P (1969). *The First Industrial Nation*. Methuen: London.

Mathias, P and Davis, JA (eds) (1989). *The First Industrial Revolutions*. Blackwell: Cambridge.

Mayes, BT and Allen, RW (1977). 'Towards a Definition of Organizational Politics.' *Academy of Management Review*, Oct, 672–78.

Mayo, E (1933). *The Human Problems of Industrial Civilization*. Macmillan: New York, USA.

Mayon-White, B (1993). 'Problem-Solving in Small Groups: Team Members as Agents of Change.' In Mabey, C and Mayon-White, B (eds): *Managing Change* (2nd edn). The Open University/Paul Chapman Publishing: London.

McCalman, J and Paton, RA (1992). *Change Management: A Guide to Effective Implementation*. Paul Chapman Publishing: London.

McGregor, D (1960). *The Human Side of Enterprise*. McGraw-Hill: New York, USA.

McIvor, G (1995). *'Returned Volvo Rises from the Ashes.'* The Guardian Jun 24, 37.

McKenna, S (1988). '"Japanisation" and Recent Developments in Britain.' *Employee Relations*, 10 (4).

McKracken, JK (1986). 'Exploitation of FMS technology to achieve strategic objectives.' *Paper to the 5th International Conference on Flexible Manufacturing Systems*. Stratford-Upon-Avon.

McLennan, R (1989). *Managing Organizational Change*. Prentice-Hall: Englewood Cliffs, New Jersey, USA.

McMillan, J (1985). *The Japanese Industrial System*. De Gruyter: Berlin.

McNamee, BP (1985). *Tools and Techniques of Strategic Management*. Pergamon: Oxford.

McNulty, CAR (1977). 'Scenario development for corporate planning.' *Futures*, 9(2), 128–38.

Meek, VL (1988). 'Organizational culture: origins and weaknesses.' *Organization Studies*, 9(4), 453–73.

Meyer, MW and Zucker, LG (1989). *Permanently Failing Organizations*. Sage: Beverly Hills, Cal., USA.

Miewald, RD (1970). 'The greatly exaggerated death of bureaucracy.' *California Management Review*, Winter, 65–9.

Miles, RE and Snow, CC (1978). *Organisational Strategy, Structure and Process*. McGraw-Hill: New York, USA.

Miles, RE and Snow, CC (1978). *Organizational Strategy, Structure and Process*. McGraw-Hill: New York, USA.

Mill, J (1994). 'No Pain, No Gain.' *Computing*, Feb 3, 26–7.

Miller, D and Friesen, PH (1984). *Organizations: A Quantum View*. Prentice Hall, Englewood Cliffs, NJ, USA.

Miller, E (1967). *Systems of Organisation*. Tavistock: London.

Milward, A and Saul, SB (1973). *The Economic Development of Continental Europe 1780–1870*. George Allen & Unwin: London.

Minett, S (1992). *Power, Politics and Participation in the Firm*. Ashgate: Brookfield, Vt., USA.

Mintzberg, H (1973). *The Nature of Managerial Work*. Harper and Row: New York, USA.

Mintzberg, H (1975). 'The manager's job: folklore and fact.' *Harvard Business Review*, 53(4), 49–61.

Mintzberg, H (1976). 'Planning on the Left Side and Managing on the Right.' *Harvard Business Review*, Jul/Aug, 49–58.

Mintzberg, H (1979). *The Structure of Organizations*. Prentice-Hall: Englewood Cliffs, NJ, USA.

Mintzberg, H (1983). *Power in and Around Organizations*. Prentice-Hall: Englewood Cliffs, NJ, USA.

Mintzberg, H (1987). 'Crafting Strategy.' *Harvard Business Review*, 19(2), 66–75.

Mintzberg, H (1994). *The Rise and Fall of Strategic Planning*. Prentice Hall: London.

Mintzberg, H and Quinn, JB (1991). *The Strategy Process: Concepts, Contexts, and Cases*. Prentice-Hall: London.

Mintzberg, H, Quinn, JB and James, RM (1988). *The Strategy Process: Concepts, Contexts and Cases*. Prentice Hall: London.

Mirvis, PH (1990). 'Organization Development: Part 2 – A Revolutionary Perspective.' *Research in Organizational Change and Development*, 4, 1–66.

Mitroff, II and Mason, RO (1981). *Challenging Strategic Planning Assumptions*. Wiley: New York, USA.

Moore, JI (1992). *Writers on Strategy and Strategic Management*. Penguin: Harmondsworth.

Morgan, G (1986). *Images of Organizations*. Sage: Beverly Hills, Calif., USA.

Morgan, G (1988). *Riding the Waves of Change*. Jossey-Bass: San Francisco, USA.

Morieux, YUH and Sutherland, E (1988). 'The Interaction Between the Use of Information Technology and Organization Change.' *Behaviour and Information Technology*, 7(2), 205–13.

Morris, J and Imrie, R (1992). *Transforming Buyer–Supplier Relationships*. Macmillan: Basingstoke.

Mullins, L (1989). *Management and Organisational Behaviour*. Pitman: London.

Mullins, LJ (1993). *Management and Organisational Behaviour* (3rd edn). Pitman: London.

Mumford, A (1987). 'Myths and reality in developing directors.' *Personnel Management*, 19(2), Feb, 29–33.

Mumford, E (1979). 'The design of work: new approaches and new needs.' In Rijnsdorp, JE (ed): *Case Studies in Automation Related to the Humanisation of Work*. Pergamon: Oxford.

Murray, F (1989). 'The Organizational Politics of Information Technology: Studies from the UK Financial Services Industry.' *Technology Analysis & Strategic Management*, 1(30), 285–97.

Myers, CS (1934). *An account of the work carried out at the National Institute of Industrial Psychology during the years 1921–34*. NIIP: London.

Nadler, DA (1993). 'Concepts for the Management of Strategic Change.' In Mabey, C and Mayon-White, B (eds): *Managing Change* (2nd edn). The Open University/Paul Chapman Publishing: London.

Naoi, A and Schooler, C (1985). 'Occupational Conditions and Psychological Functioning in Japan.' *American Journal of Sociology*, 90, 729–52.

Naylor, TH (1979). *Simulation Models in Corporate Measuring*. Draeger: New York, USA.

Naylor, TH (1981). 'Strategic planning models.' *Managerial Planning*, 30, Jul/Aug, 3–11.

NEDC (1991a). *The Experience of Nissan Suppliers: Lessons for the United Kingdom Engineering Industry*. NEDC: London.

NEDC (1991b). *Winning Together: Collaborative Sourcing in Practice*. NEDC: London.

Nelson, RR and Winter, SG (1982). *An Evolutionary Theory of Economic Change*. Harvard University Press: Cambridge, Mass., USA.

New, C (1989). 'The challenge of transformation.' In Burnes, B and Weekes, B (eds): *AMT: A Strategy for Success?* NEDO: London.

Newstrom, J (1985). 'Modern management: does it deliver?' *Journal of Management Development*, 4(1).

Nonaka, I (1988). 'Creating Organizational Order out of Chaos: Self-Renewal in Japanese Firms.' *Harvard Business Review*, Nov–Dec, 96–104.

Nonaka, I (1991). 'The Knowledge-Creating Company.' *Harvard Business Review*, Nov/Dec, 96–104.

Nord, W (1985). 'Can organizational culture be managed? a synthesis.' In Kilmann, R, Saxton, M and Serpa, R (eds): *Gaining Control of Corporate Culture*. Jossey-Bass: San Francisco, USA.

Norrie, J (1993). *Winning By Continuous Improvement: Facilitators' Guide*. Norrie: Northampton.

Norse, D (1979). 'Scenario analysis in interfutures.' *Futures*, 11(5), 412–22.

Nystrom, PC and Starbuck, WH (1984). 'To Avoid Crises, Unlearn.' *Organizational Dynamics*, 12 (4), 53–65.

O'Brien, GE and Kabanoff, B (1981). 'The Effects of Leadership Style and Group Structure upon Small Group Productivity: A Test of Discrepancy Theory of Leader Effectiveness.' *Australian Journal of Psychology*, 33(2), 157–8.

O'Reilly, C (1989). 'Corporations, Culture and Commitment.' *California Management Review*, 31(4), 9–24.

Odaka, K (1975). *Towards Industrial Democracy: Management and Workers in Modern Japan*. Harvard University Press: Cambridge, Mass, USA.

Ohmae, K (1986). *The Mind of the Strategist*. Penguin: Harmondsworth.

Ohmae, K (1990). Untitled article in *Special Report 1202, The Management Briefing, The Economist*, London.

Osborne, D and Gaebler, T (1992). *Reinventing Government: How the Entrepreneurial Spirit is Transforming the Public Sector*. Addison-Wesley: Reading, Mass., USA.

Pang, K and Oliver, N (1988). 'Personnel Strategy in Eleven Japanese Manufacturing Companies.' *Personnel Review*, 17(3).

Parsons, T (1947). 'Introduction.' In Weber, M (ed): *The Theory of Social and Economic Organization*. Free Press: Glencoe, Ill., USA.

Partnership Sourcing Ltd (1991). *Partnership Sourcing*. Partnership Sourcing Ltd: London.

Pascale, RT (1993). 'The Benefit of a Clash of Opinions.' *Personnel Management*, Oct, 38–41.

Pascale, RT, and Athos, AG (1982). *The Art of Japanese Management*. Penguin: Harmondsworth.

Patel, P and Younger, M (1978). 'A frame of reference for strategy development.' *Long Range Planning*, 11, Apr, 6–12.

Pavlov, IP (1927). *Conditioned Reflexes (trans)*. Oxford University Press: London.

Pearson, AE (1987). 'Muscle-build the Organization.' *Harvard Business Review*, 65(4), 49–55.

Pearson, B (1977). 'How to manage turnarounds.' *Management Today*, Apr, 75.

Pelling, H (1960). *American Labor*. Chicago University Press: Chicago, USA.

Perez, C (1983). 'Structural change and the assimilation of new technologies in the economic and social systems.' *Futures*, 15, 357–75.

Perrow, C (1967). 'A framework for the comparative analysis of organizations.' *American Sociological Review*, 32, 194–208.

Perrow, C (1970). *Organizational Analysis: a Sociological View*. Tavistock: London.

Perrow, C (1983). 'The organizational context of human factors engineering.' *Administrative Science Quarterly*, 28, 521–541.

Peters, T (1993). *Liberation Management*. Pan: London.

Peters, TJ (1989). *Thriving on Chaos*. Pan: London.

Peters, TJ and Waterman, R H (1982). *In Search of Excellence: Lessons from America's Best-Run Companies*. Harper and Row: London.

Pettigrew, A (1973). *The Politics of Decision-Making*. Tavistock: London.

Pettigrew, A (1985). *The Awakening Giant: Continuity and Change at ICI*. Blackwell: Oxford.

Pettigrew, A (1987). 'Context and Action in the Transformation of the Firm.' *Journal of Management Sciences*, 24(6), 649–70.

Pettigrew, A and Whipp, R (1993). 'Understanding the Environment.' In Mabey, C and Mayon-White, B (eds): *Managing Change* (2nd edn). The Open University/Paul Chapman Publishing: London.

Pettigrew, AM (1980). 'The politics of organisational change.' In Anderson, NB (ed): *The Human Side of Information Processing*. North Holland: Amsterdam, Netherlands.

Pfeffer, J (1978). *Organizational Design*. AHM Publishing: Arlington Heights, Ill., USA.

Pfeffer, J (1981). *Power in Organizations*. Pitman: Cambridge, Mass., USA.

Pfeffer, J (1992). *Managing with Power: Politics and Influence in Organizations*. Harvard Business School Press: Boston, Ma., USA.

Pollard, S (1965). *The Genesis of Modern Management*. Pelican: Harmondsworth.

Pollard, S (1981). *Peaceful Conquest: The Industrialization of Europe, 1760–1970*. Oxford University Press: Oxford.

Pontusson, J (1990). 'The Politics of New Technology and Job Redesign: A Comparison of Volvo and British Leyland.' *Economic and Industrial Democracy*, 11, 311–36.

Porter, LW (1976). 'Organizations as Political Animals.' *Presidential Address, Division of Industrial Organizational Psychology, 84th Annual Meeting of the American Psychological Association*, Washington, DC.

Porter, LW, Allen, RW and Angle, HL (1983). 'The Politics of Upward Influence in Organizations.' In Allen, RW and Porter, LW (eds): *Organizational Influence Processes*. Scott, Foresman and Co: Glenview, Ill., USA.

Porter, M (1980). *Competitive Strategy*. Free Press: New York, USA.

Prigogine, I and Stengers, I (1984). *Order out of Chaos: Man's New Dialogue with Nature*. Bantam Books: New York, USA.

Pugh, D (1993). 'Understanding and Managing Organizational Change.' In Mabey, C and Mayon-White, B (eds): *Managing Change* (2nd edn). The Open University/Paul Chapman Publishing: London.

Pugh, DS (ed) (1984). *Organization Theory*. Penguin: Harmondsworth.

Pugh, DS and Hickson, DJ (1976). *Organizational Structure in its Context: The Aston Programme 1*. Saxon House: Farnborough.

Pugh, DS, Hickson, D J, Hinings, CR and Turner, C (1969a). 'The context of organization structures.' *Administrative Science Quarterly*, 14, 91–114.

Pugh, DS, Hickson, DJ and Hinings, CR (1969b). 'An empirical taxonomy of structures of work organisation.' *Administrative Science Quarterly*, 14, 115–26.

Quinn, JB (1980). 'Managing strategic change.' *Sloan Management Review*, 21(4), 3–20.

Quinn, JB (1993). 'Managing Strategic Change.' In Mabey, C and Mayon-White, B (eds): *Managing Change* (2nd edn). The Open University/Paul Chapman Publishing: London.

Rafferty, K (1995). 'Tokyo and Mitsubishi Banks to Merge to Create World's Largest Bank.' *The Guardian*, Mar 25, 15.

Robbins, SP (1986). *Organizational Behavior: Concepts, Controversies, and Applications*. Prentice-Hall: Englewood Cliffs, NJ, USA.

Robbins, SP (1987). *Organization Theory: Structure, Design, and Applications*. Prentice-Hall: Englewood Cliffs, NJ, USA.

Roethlisberger, F and Dickson, WJ (1938). *Management and the Worker*. Wiley: New York, USA.

Roll, E (1930). 'An early experiment in industrial organisation: Boulton and Watt, 1775–1805.' Reprinted in Berg, M (ed) (1979): *Technology and Toil in Nineteenth Century Britain*. CSE Books: London.

Rose, M (1988). *Industrial Behaviour*. Penguin: Harmondsworth.

Rothwell, S (1994). 'Human Resources Management.' *Manager Update*, 5(3), Spring, 22–35.

Rubin, I (1967). 'Increasing self-acceptance: a means of reducing prejudice.' *Journal of Personality and Social Psychology*, 5, 233–38.

Sakai, K (1992). 'The Feudal World of Japanese Manufacturing.' In Kanter, RM, Stein, BA and Jick, TD: *The Challenge of Organizational Change*. Free Press: New York.

Salaman, G (1979). *Work Organisations*. Longman: London.

Sathe, V (1983). 'Some Action Implications of Corporate Culture: A Manager's Guide to Action.' *Organizational Dynamics, Autumn*, 4–23.

Schein, EH (1969). *Process Consultation*. Addison-Wesley: Reading, Mass., USA.

Schein, EH (1985). *Organizational Culture and Leadership: A Dynamic View*. Jossey-Bass: San Francisco, USA.

Schilit, WK and Locke, EA (1982). 'A Study of Upward Influence in Organizations.' *Administrative Science Quarterly*, Jun, 304–16.

Schmuck, R and Miles, M (1971). *Organizational Development in Schools*. National Press: Palo Alto, Calif., USA.

Schonberger, RJ(1982). *Japanese Manufacturing Techniques*. Free Press: New York, USA.

Schriesheim, CA and Murphy, CJ (1976). 'Relationships Between Leader Behavior and Subordinate Satisfaction and Performance: A Test of Some Situational Moderators.' *Journal of Applied Psychology*, 61, 634–41.

Schwartz, H and Davis, S (1981). 'Matching corporate culture and business strategy.' *Organizational Dynamics*, 10, 30–48.

Scott, WR (1987). *Organizations: Rational, Natural and Open Systems*. Prentice-Hall: Englewood Cliffs, NJ, USA.

Selznick, P (1948). 'Foundations of the theory of organization.' *American Sociological Review*, 13, 25–35.

Senge, PM (1993). *The Fifth Discipline*. Century Business: London.

Sheahan, J (1969). *An Introduction to the French Economy*. Merill: Columbus, Ohio.

Sheridan, K (1993). *Governing the Japanese Economy*. Polity Press: Oxford.

Shiflett, SC (1973). 'The Contingency Model of Leadership Effectiveness: Some Implications of Its Statistical and Methodological Properties.' *Behavioral Science*, 18(6), 429–40.

Short, JE and Venkatraman, N (1992). 'Beyond Business Process Redesign: Redefining Baxter's Business Network.' *Sloan Management Review*, Fall, 7–21.

Silverman, D (1970). *The Theory of Organizations*. Heinemann: London.

Silverman, D and Jones, J (1976). *Organizational Work*. Macmillan: London.

Simon, HA (1957). *Administrative Behaviour: A Study of Decision-making Processes in Administrative Organizations*. Macmillan: New York, USA.

Sissons, K (ed) (1989). *Personnel Management in Britain*. Blackwell: Oxford.

Sissons, K and Storey, J (1988). 'Developing effective managers: a review of the issues and an agenda for research.' *Personnel Review*, 17(4), 3–8.

Skinner, BF (1974). *About Behaviourism*. Cape: London.

Sloan, AP (1986). *My Years with General Motors*. Penguin: Harmondsworth.

Smith, A (1776). *The Wealth of Nations, Volume 1*. Methuen (1950 edition): London.

Smith, J (1987). 'Elton Mayo and the hidden Hawthorne.' *Work, Employment and Society*, 1(1), 107–120.

Smith, JG (1985). *Business Strategy*. Blackwell: Oxford.

Smith, M, Beck, J, Cooper, CL, Cox, C, Ottaway, D and Talbot, R (1982). *Introducing Organizational Behaviour*. Macmillan: London.

Smith, PB and Misumi, J (1989). 'Japanese Management – A Sun Rising in the West.' In Cooper, CL and Robertson, I (eds): *The International Review of Industrial and Organizational Psychology*. Wiley: London.

Smith, S and Tranfield, D (1987). 'The implementation and exploitation of advanced manufacturing technology – an outline methodology.' *Change Management Research Unit, Research Paper No 2*, Sheffield Business School.

Smithers, R (1995). 'Power Chiefs Pay Themselves £72m in Share Options.' *The Guardian*, Feb 13, 20.

Snow, C, Miles, R and Coleman, H (1993). 'Managing 21st Century Network Organizations.' In Mabey, C and Mayon-White, B (eds): *Managing Change* (2nd edn). The Open University/Paul Chapman Publishing: London.

Stacey, R (1990). *Dynamic Strategic Management for the 1990s*. Kogan Page: London.

Stacey, R (1993). *Strategic Management and Organisational Dynamics*. Pitman: London.

Stalk, G, Evans, P and Shulman, LE (1992). 'Competing on Capabilities – The New Rules of Corporate Strategy.' *Harvard Business Review*, Mar–Apr, 57–69.

Steiner, GA (1969). Top Management Planning. Macmillan: London.

Stewart, R (1976). *Contrasts in Management*. McGraw-Hill: London.

Storey, J (1989). 'Management development: a literature review and implications for future research – Part 1: conceptualisations and practices. *Personnel Review*, 18(6), 3–19.

Storey, J (1990). 'Management development: a literature review and implications for future research – Part 2: profiles and context.' *Personnel Review*, 19(1), 3–11.

Stuart, R (1986). 'Social learning.' *Management Decision*, 24(6), 32–5.

Student, J (1968). 'Supervisory Influence and Work-Group Performance.' *Journal of Applied Psychology*, Jun, 188–94.

Taguchi, G (1986). *Introduction to Quality Engineering*. Asian Production Organization: Dearborn, Michigan, USA.

Taylor, FW (1911a). *Shop Management*. Harper (1947 edition): New York, USA.

Taylor, FW (1911b). *The Principles of Scientific Management*. Harper (1947 edition): New York, USA.

Terry, PT (1976). 'The Contingency Theory and the development of organisations.' *Paper presented to the British Sociological Association*.

Tett, G (1994). 'Partnerships in Business Grow.' *Financial Times*, Jun 28, 12.

Thickett, M (1970). 'Gilbreth and the measurement of work.' In Tillett, A, Kempner, T and Willis, G (eds): *Management Thinkers*. Pelican: Harmondsworth.

Thomas, AB (1993). *Controversies in Management*. Routledge: London.

Thompkins, JM (1990). 'Politics – The Illegitimate Discipline.' *Management Decision*, 28(4), 23–8.

Thompson, AA Jnr and Strickland, AJ (1983). *Strategy Formulation and Implementation*. Business Publications Inc: Ill., USA.

Thompson, J (1967). *Organizations in Action*. McGraw-Hill: New York, USA.

Thornberry, NE (1987). 'Training the engineer as project manager.' *Training and Development Journal*, 41(10).

Tillett, A (1970). 'Industry and Management.' In Tillett, A, Kempner, T and Willis, G (eds): *Management Thinkers*. Pelican: Harmondsworth.

Toffler, A (1970). *Future Shock*. Random House: New York, USA.

Trist, EL, Higgin, GW, Murray, H and Pollock, AB (1963). *Organisational Choice*. Tavistock: London.

Turnbull, P (1986). 'The Japanisation of Production and Industrial Relations at Lucas Electrical.' *Industrial Relations Journal*, 17(3), 193–206.

Turner, B (1971). *Exploring the Industrial Subculture*. Macmillan: London.

Turner, I (1990). 'Strategy and Organisation.' *Manager Update*, 1(3), 1–10.

Tushman, M and Virany, B (1986). 'Changing characteristics of executive teams in an emerging industry.' *Journal of Business Venturing*, 37–49.

Udy, SH Jnr (1959). '"Bureaucracy" and "Rationality" in Weber's Organization Theory.' *American Sociological Review*, 24 (Dec), 791–95.

Urabe, K (1986). 'Innovation and the Japanese Management System.' *Keynote address, First International Symposium on Management, Japan Society for the Study of Business Administration*, Kobe University, 11–49.

Ure, A (1835). *The Philosophy of Manufactures*. Frank Cass (1967 edition): London.

Ure, A (1836). *The Cotton Manufacture of Great Britain Volume 1*. Johnson (1970 edition): London.

Uttal, B (1983). 'The corporate culture vultures.' *Fortune*, Oct 17, 66–72.

Van Maanen, J and Kunda, G (1989). 'Real Feelings: Emotional Expression and Organisational Culture.' In B Staw and L Cummings (eds): *Research in Organizational Behaviour*, 11, 43–103.

Vecchio, RP (1983). 'Assessing the Validity of Fielder's Contingency Model of Leadership Effectiveness: A Closer Look at Strube and Garcia.' *Psychological Bulletin*, 93, 404–408.

Voss, CA (1985). *Success and failure in advanced manufacturing technology*. Warwick University Working Paper.

Wall, TD, Burnes, B, Clegg, CW and Kemp, NJ. 'New Technology, Old Jobs.' *Work and People*, 10(2), 15–21.

Warner, M (1984). 'New technology, work organisation and industrial relations.' *Omega*, 12(3), 203–210.

Warr, P (ed) (1987). *Psychology at Work*. Penguin: Harmondsworth.

Wastell, DG, White, P and Kawalek, P (1994). 'A Methodology for Business Process Redesign: Experience and Issues.' *Journal of Strategic Information Systems*, 3(1), 23–40.

Watson, G (1994). 'The Flexible Workforce and Patterns of Working Hours in the UK.' *Employment Gazette*, Jul, 239–47.

Watson, T (1982). 'Group Ideologies and Organisational Change.' *Journal of Management Studies*, 19(3), 259–77.

Watson, TJ (1986). *Management Organisation and Employment Strategy: New Directions in Theory and Practice*. Routledge and Kegan Paul: London.

Weber, M (1928). *General Economic History*. George Allen and Unwin: London.

Weber, M (1946). *From Max Weber: Essays in Sociology (trans)*. Oxford University Press: London.

Weber, M (1947). *The Theory of Social and Economic Organization (trans)*. Free Press: Glencoe, Ill., USA.

Weick, KE (1979). *The Social Psychology of Organising*. Addison-Wesley: Reading, Mass, USA.

West, P (1995). *Learning Organisations* (Unpublished Report). UMIST: Manchester.

Wheatley, M (1992). *The Future of Middle Management*. British Institute of Management: London.

Wheelen, TL and Hunger, DJ (1989). *Strategic Management and Business Policy*. Addison-Wesley: Reading, Mass., USA.

White, RE (1986). 'Generic business strategies: organisational context and performance.' *Strategic Management Journal*, May/Jun, 217–31.

Whitehill, AM (1991). *Japanese Management: Tradition and Transition*. Routledge: London.

Whittington, R (1993). *What is Strategy and Does it Matter?* Routledge: London.

Whyte, J and Witcher, B (1992). *The Adoption of Total Quality Management in Northern England*. Durham University Business School: Durham.

Whyte, WH (1960). *The Organization of Man*. Penguin: Harmondsworth.

Wickens, P (1987). *The Road To Nissan*. Macmillan: London.

Wilkinson, A (1991). 'TQM and HRM.' *Working Paper*, Manchester School of Management, UMIST.

Wilkinson, HE, and Orth, DC (1986). 'Soft skill training in management development.' *Training and Development Journal*, 40(3).

Willbur, J (1987). 'Does mentoring breed success?' *Training and Development Journal*, 41(11).

Willcocks, SG (1994). 'Organizational Analysis: A Health Service Commentary.' *Leadership & Organization Development Journal*, 15(1), 29–32.

Williams, K, Haslam, C and Williams, J (1991). 'Management Accounting: the Western Problematic Against the Japanese Application.' *9th Annual Conference of the Labour Process, UMIST*, Manchester.

Williamson, O (1991). 'Strategizing, Economizing and Economic Organization.' *Strategic Management Journal*, 12, 75–94.

Wilson, DC (1992). *A Strategy of Change*. Routledge: London.

Witcher, B (1993). *The Adoption of Total Quality Management in Scotland*. Durham University Business School: Durham.

Womack, JP; Jones, DT; and Roos, D (1990). *The Machine That Changed the World*. Rawson Associates: New York, USA.

Wood, S (1979). 'A reappraisal of the contingency approach to organization.' *Journal of Management Studies*, 16, 334–54.

Wood, S (1991). 'Japanisation and/or Toyotaism?' *Work, Employment and Society*, 5(4), 567–600.

Woodward, J (1965). *Industrial Organization: Theory and Practice*. Oxford University Press: London.

Woodward, J (1970). *Industrial Organization: Behaviour and Control*. Oxford University Press: London.

Yukl, G (1994). *Leadership in Organizations* (3rd edn). Prentice-Hall: Englewood Cliffs, N J, USA.

Zairi, M, Letza, S and Oakland, J (1994). 'Does TQM Impact on Bottom Line Results?' *TQM Magazine*, 6(1), 38–43.

Zaleznik, A (1970). 'Power and Politics in Organisational Life.' *Harvard Business Review*, May-Jun, 47–60.

Zentner, RD (1982). 'Scenarios, past, present and future.' *Long Range Planning*, 15, Jun, 12–20.

Zinn, H (1980). *A People's History of the United States*. Longman: London.

Zwerman, WL (1970). *New Perspectives in Organization Theory*. Greenwood: Westport, USA.

Index